NAOKI URASAWA'S

MONSTER

volume 1

Naoki Urasawa's
Monster
Volume 1

VIZ Signature Edition

. STORY AND ART BY NAOKI URASAWA

English Adaptation/Agnes Yoshida
Translation/Satch Watanabe
Touch-up Art & Lettering/Steve Dutro
Design/Izumi Evers & Courtney Utt
Editor/Andy Nakatani

Managing Editor/Annette Roman
Director of Production/Noboru Watanabe
Vice President of Publishing/Alvin Lu
Sr. Director of Acquisitions/Rika Inouye
Vice President of Sales & Marketing/Liza Coppola
Publisher/Hyoe Narita

Printed in the U.S.A.

Published by VIZ Media, LLC
P.O. Box 77010
San Francisco, CA 94107

VIZ Signature Edition
10 9 8 7 6 5 4 3 2 1
First printing, February 2006

www.viz.com
store.viz.com

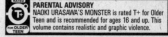

PARENTAL ADVISORY
NAOKI URASAWA'S MONSTER is rated T+ for Older
Teen and is recommended for ages 16 and up. This
volume contains realistic and graphic violence.

Naoki Urasawa's
Monster
Volume 1
Herr Dr. Tenma

Story and Art by Naoki Urasawa

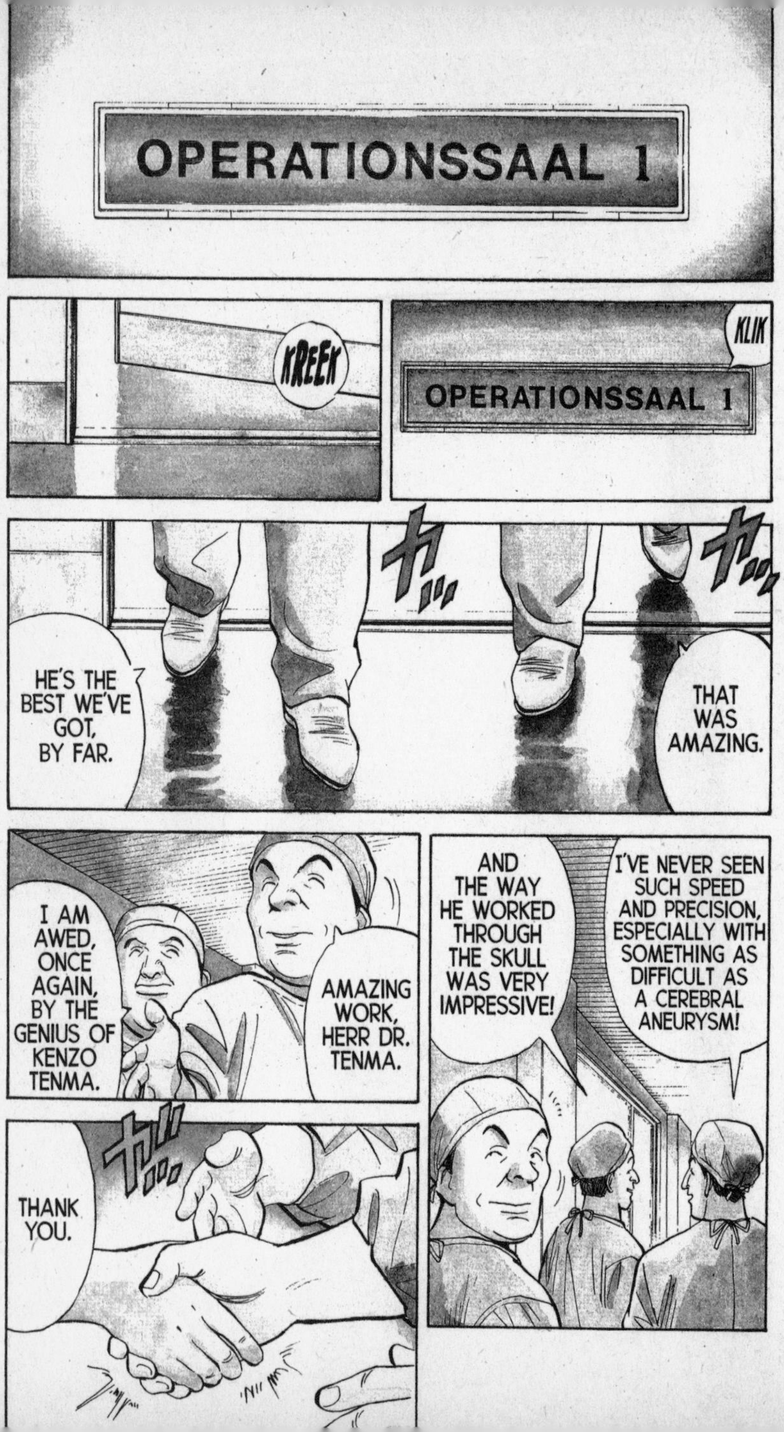
OPERATIONSSAAL 1
KLIK
OPERATIONSSAAL 1
KREEK
THAT WAS AMAZING.
HE'S THE BEST WE'VE GOT, BY FAR.
I'VE NEVER SEEN SUCH SPEED AND PRECISION, ESPECIALLY WITH SOMETHING AS DIFFICULT AS A CEREBRAL ANEURYSM!
AND THE WAY HE WORKED THROUGH THE SKULL WAS VERY IMPRESSIVE!
AMAZING WORK, HERR DR. TENMA.
I AM AWED, ONCE AGAIN, BY THE GENIUS OF KENZO TENMA.
THANK YOU.

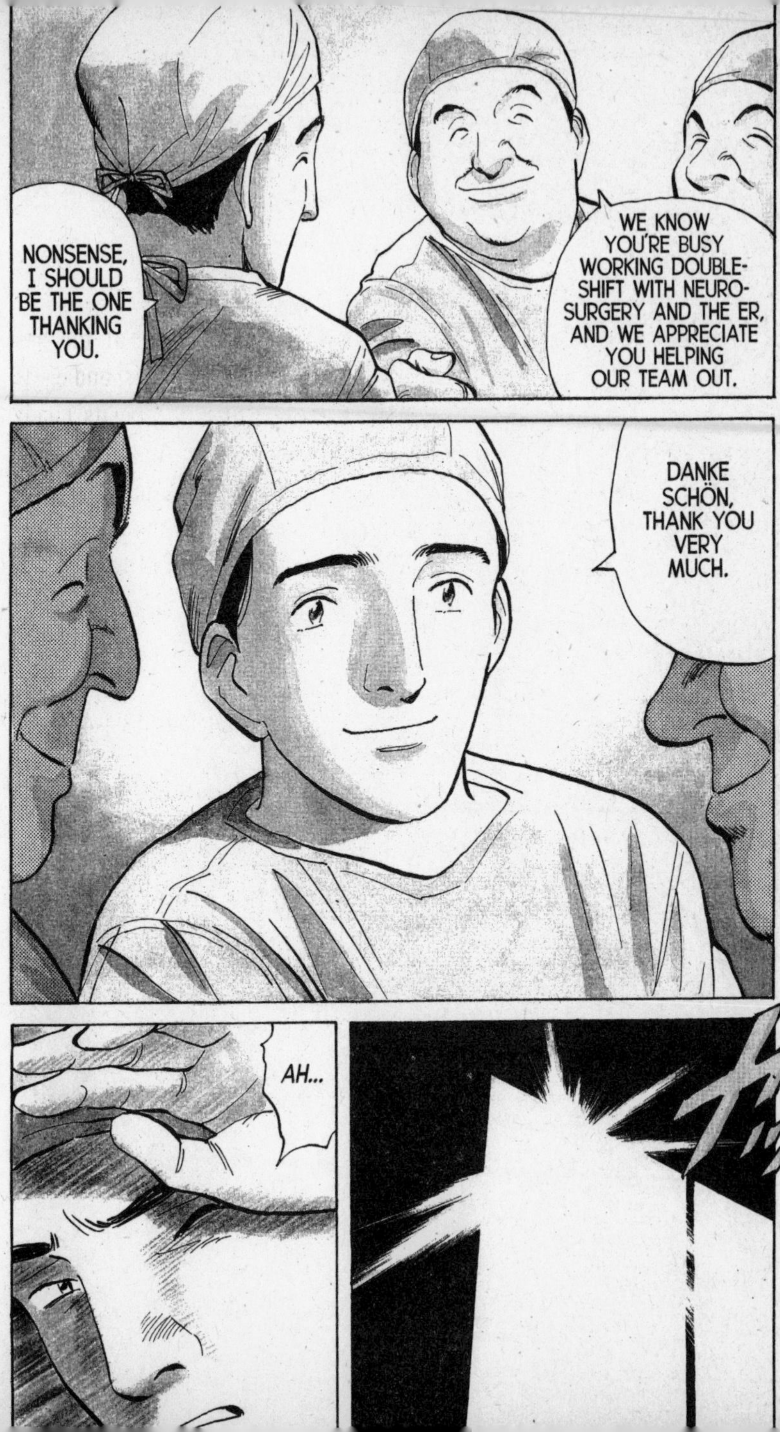
WE KNOW YOU'RE BUSY WORKING DOUBLE-SHIFT WITH NEURO-SURGERY AND THE ER, AND WE APPRECIATE YOU HELPING OUR TEAM OUT.
NONSENSE, I SHOULD BE THE ONE THANKING YOU.
DANKE SCHÖN, THANK YOU VERY MUCH.
AH...

And I saw a beast rising out of the sea having ten horns and seven heads; and on its horns were ten diadems, and on its heads were blasphemous names… And the dragon gave it his power and his throne and great authority… They worshipped the dragon, for he had given his authority to the beast, and they worshipped the beast, saying, 'who is like the beast, and who can fight against it?'

Revelations 13:1-4 NRSV

Chapter 1
Herr
Dr. Tenma

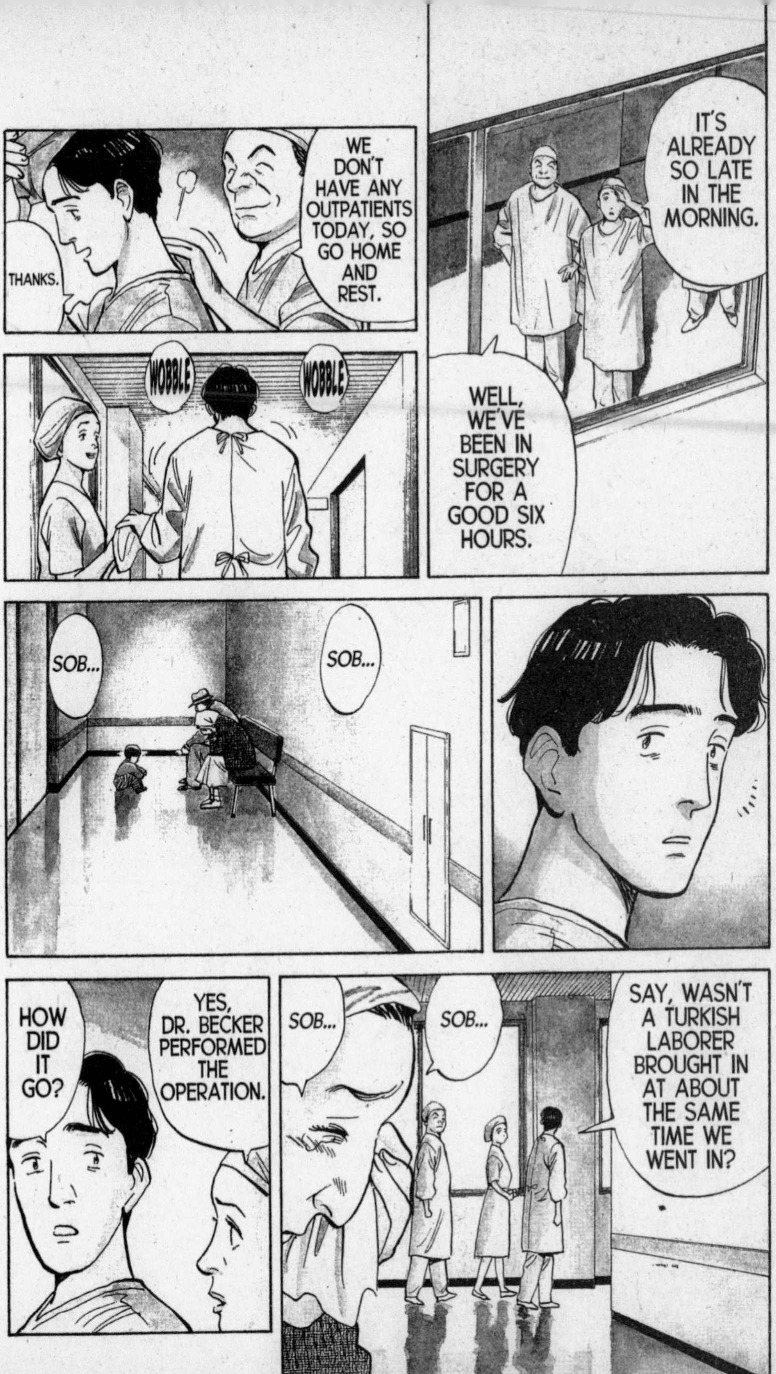
IT'S ALREADY SO LATE IN THE MORNING.
WELL, WE'VE BEEN IN SURGERY FOR A GOOD SIX HOURS.
WE DON'T HAVE ANY OUTPATIENTS TODAY, SO GO HOME AND REST.
THANKS.
WOBBLE
WOBBLE
SOB...
SOB...
SAY, WASN'T A TURKISH LABORER BROUGHT IN AT ABOUT THE SAME TIME WE WENT IN?
SOB...
SOB...
YES, DR. BECKER PERFORMED THE OPERATION.
HOW DID IT GO?

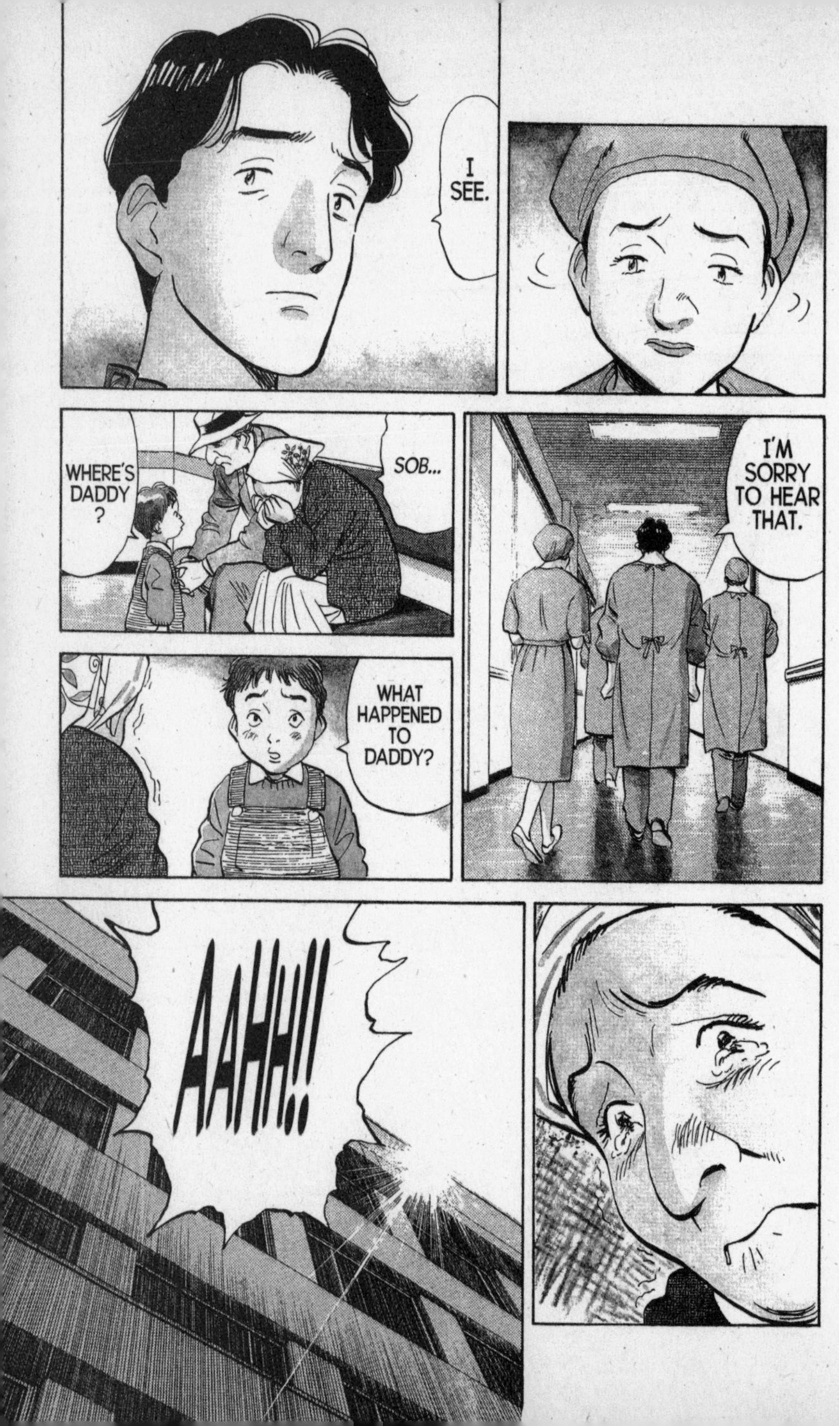
I SEE.
I'M SORRY TO HEAR THAT.
SOB...
WHERE'S DADDY ?
WHAT HAPPENED TO DADDY?
AAHH!!

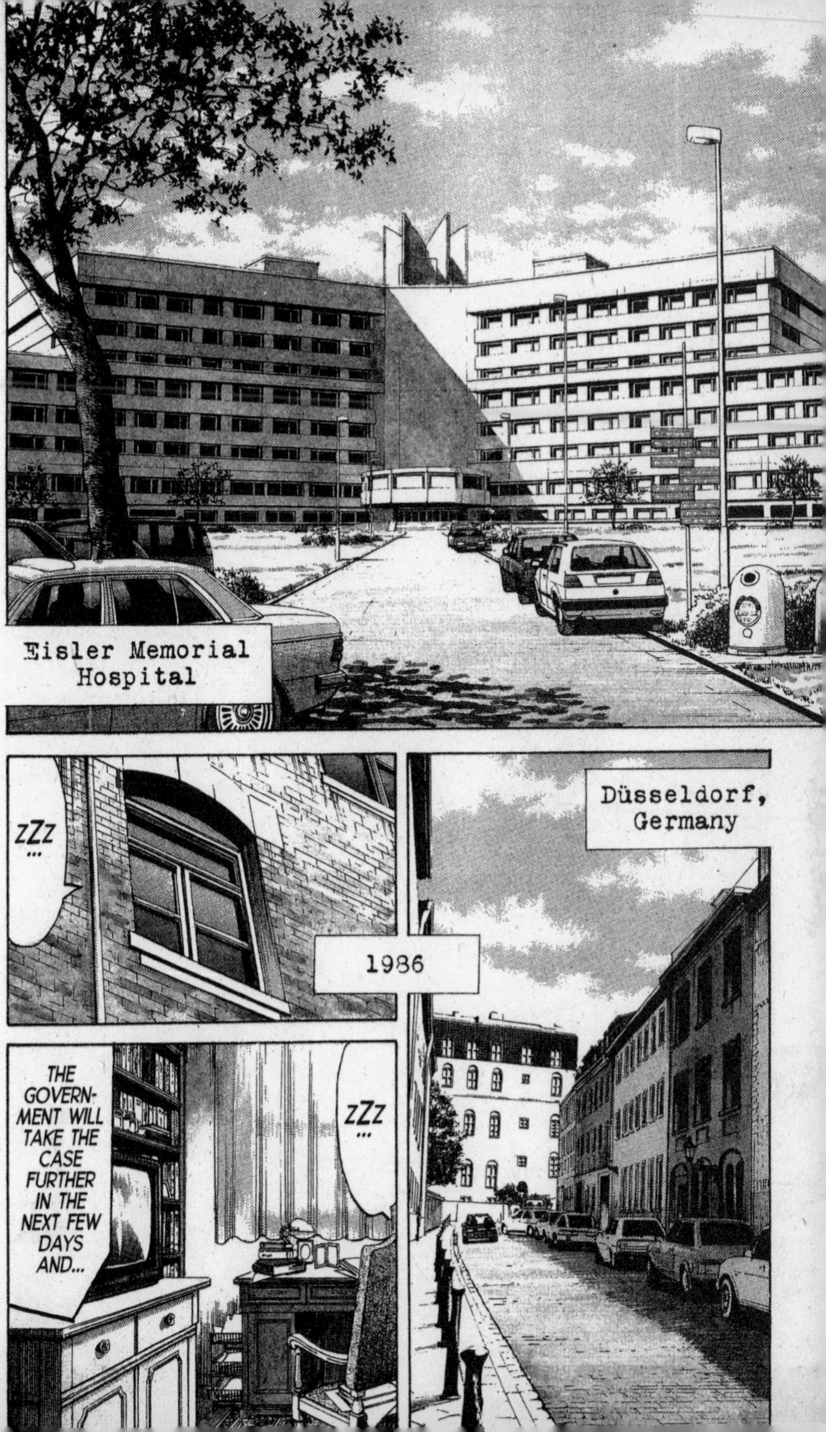
Eisler Memorial Hospital
Düsseldorf, Germany
1986
zZz...
zZz...
THE GOVERNMENT WILL TAKE THE CASE FURTHER IN THE NEXT FEW DAYS AND...

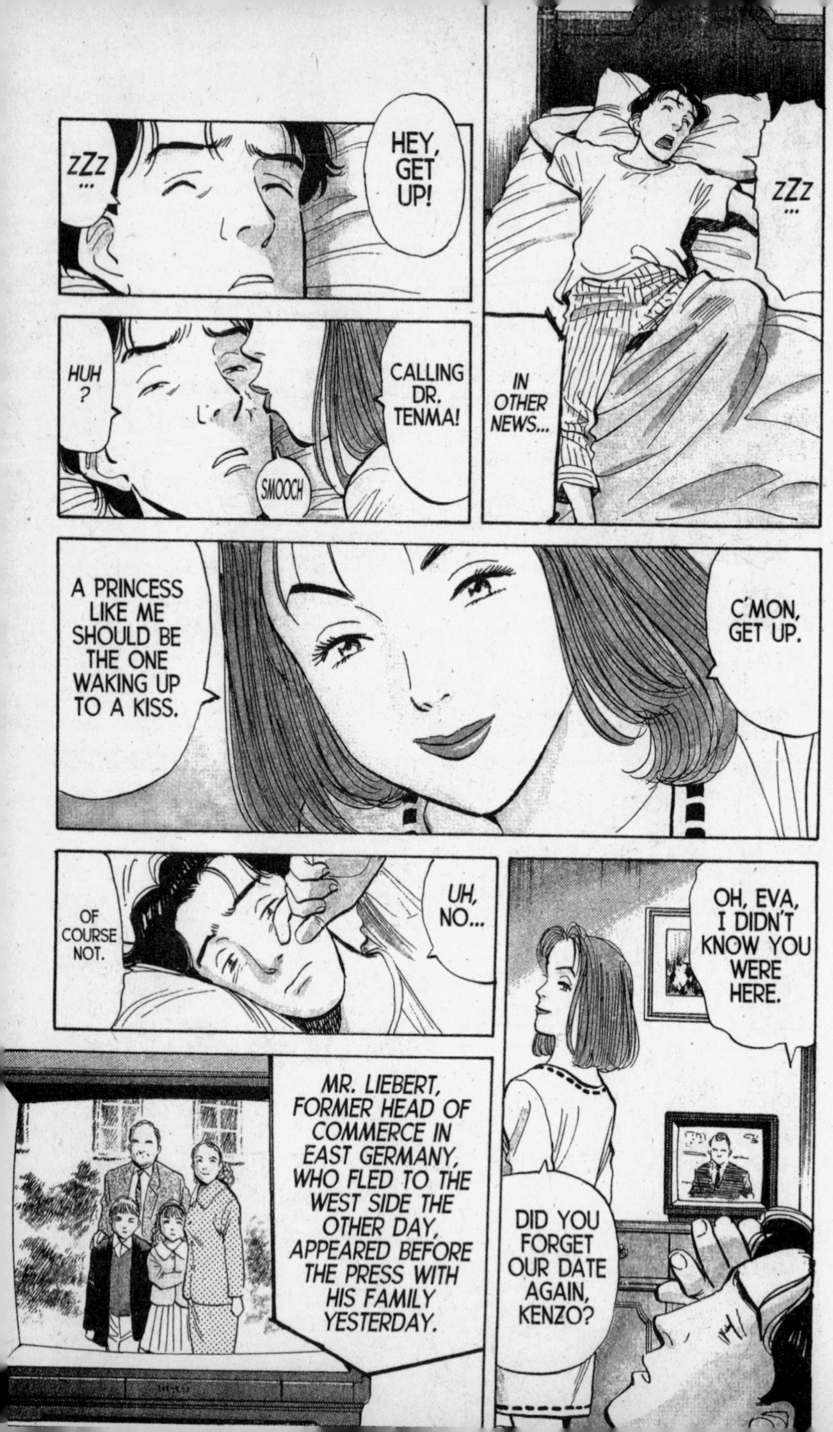
zZz...
IN OTHER NEWS...
HEY, GET UP!
zZz...
CALLING DR. TENMA!
SMOOCH
HUH?
C'MON, GET UP.
A PRINCESS LIKE ME SHOULD BE THE ONE WAKING UP TO A KISS.
OH, EVA, I DIDN'T KNOW YOU WERE HERE.
DID YOU FORGET OUR DATE AGAIN, KENZO?
UH, NO...
OF COURSE NOT.
MR. LIEBERT, FORMER HEAD OF COMMERCE IN EAST GERMANY, WHO FLED TO THE WEST SIDE THE OTHER DAY, APPEARED BEFORE THE PRESS WITH HIS FAMILY YESTERDAY.

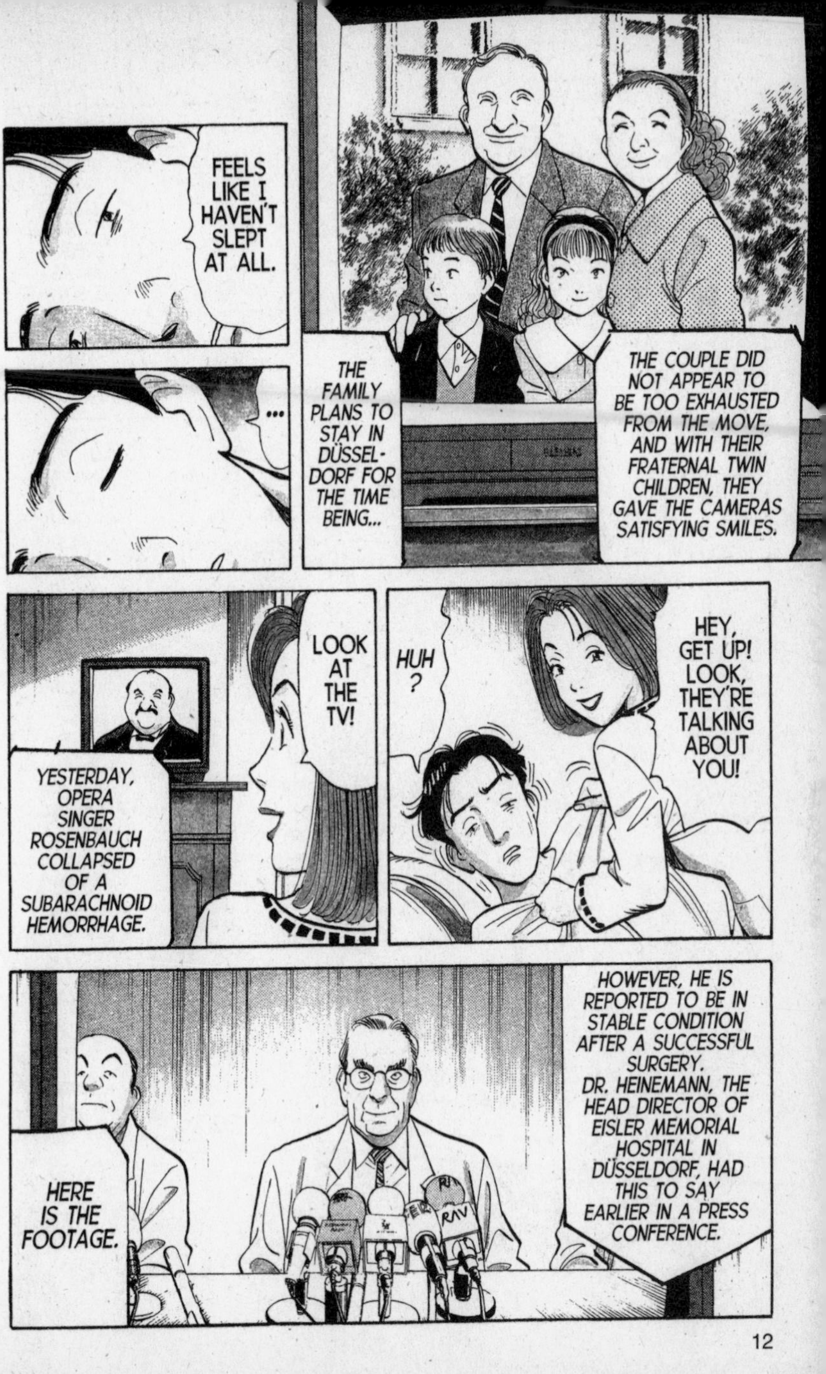
THE COUPLE DID NOT APPEAR TO BE TOO EXHAUSTED FROM THE MOVE, AND WITH THEIR FRATERNAL TWIN CHILDREN, THEY GAVE THE CAMERAS SATISFYING SMILES.
THE FAMILY PLANS TO STAY IN DÜSSEL-DORF FOR THE TIME BEING...
FEELS LIKE I HAVEN'T SLEPT AT ALL.
...
HEY, GET UP! LOOK, THEY'RE TALKING ABOUT YOU!
HUH?
LOOK AT THE TV!
YESTERDAY, OPERA SINGER ROSENBAUCH COLLAPSED OF A SUBARACHNOID HEMORRHAGE.
HOWEVER, HE IS REPORTED TO BE IN STABLE CONDITION AFTER A SUCCESSFUL SURGERY. DR. HEINEMANN, THE HEAD DIRECTOR OF EISLER MEMORIAL HOSPITAL IN DÜSSELDORF, HAD THIS TO SAY EARLIER IN A PRESS CONFERENCE.
HERE IS THE FOOTAGE.

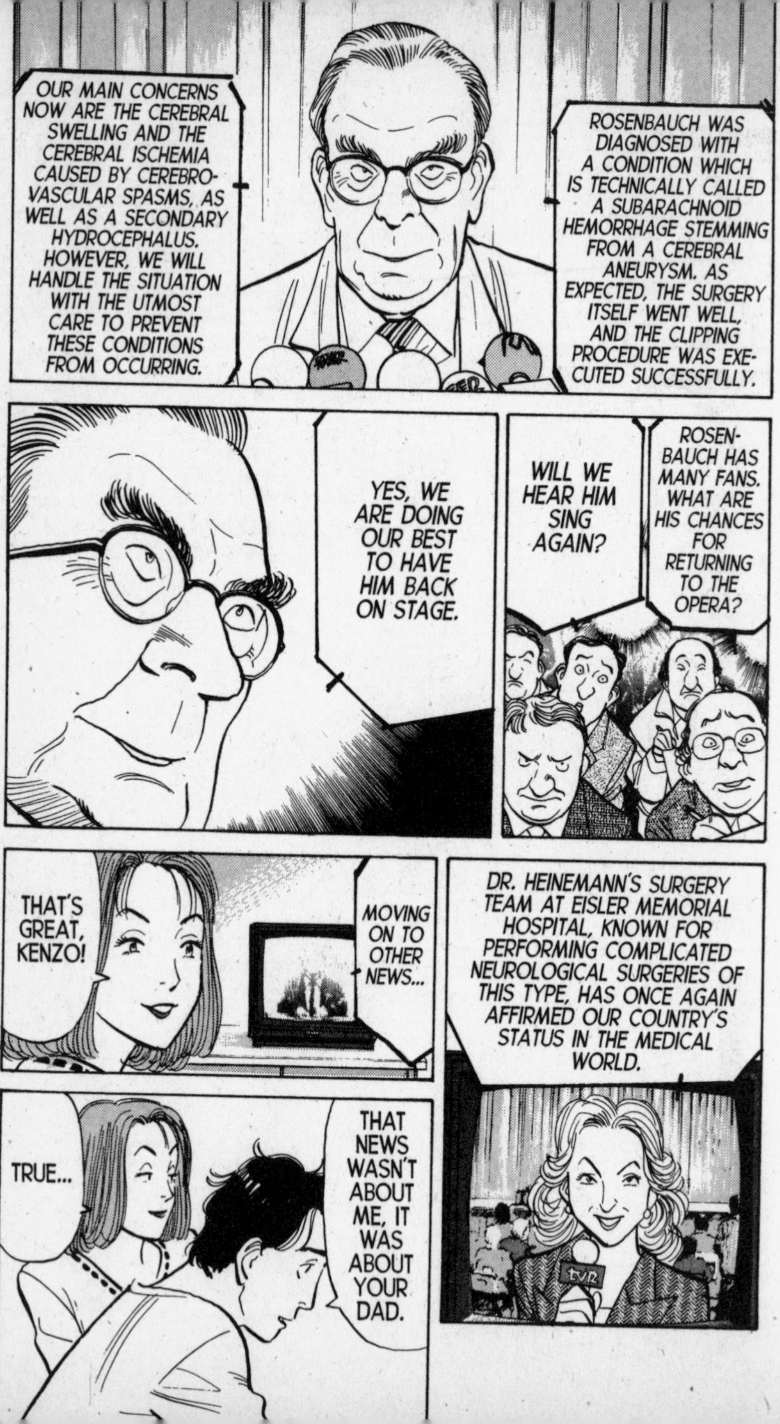

ROSENBAUCH WAS DIAGNOSED WITH A CONDITION WHICH IS TECHNICALLY CALLED A SUBARACHNOID HEMORRHAGE STEMMING FROM A CEREBRAL ANEURYSM. AS EXPECTED, THE SURGERY ITSELF WENT WELL, AND THE CLIPPING PROCEDURE WAS EXECUTED SUCCESSFULLY.
OUR MAIN CONCERNS NOW ARE THE CEREBRAL SWELLING AND THE CEREBRAL ISCHEMIA CAUSED BY CEREBROVASCULAR SPASMS, AS WELL AS A SECONDARY HYDROCEPHALUS. HOWEVER, WE WILL HANDLE THE SITUATION WITH THE UTMOST CARE TO PREVENT THESE CONDITIONS FROM OCCURRING.
ROSENBAUCH HAS MANY FANS. WHAT ARE HIS CHANCES FOR RETURNING TO THE OPERA?
WILL WE HEAR HIM SING AGAIN?
YES, WE ARE DOING OUR BEST TO HAVE HIM BACK ON STAGE.
DR. HEINEMANN'S SURGERY TEAM AT EISLER MEMORIAL HOSPITAL, KNOWN FOR PERFORMING COMPLICATED NEUROLOGICAL SURGERIES OF THIS TYPE, HAS ONCE AGAIN AFFIRMED OUR COUNTRY'S STATUS IN THE MEDICAL WORLD.
TVR
MOVING ON TO OTHER NEWS...
THAT'S GREAT, KENZO!
THAT NEWS WASN'T ABOUT ME, IT WAS ABOUT YOUR DAD.
TRUE...

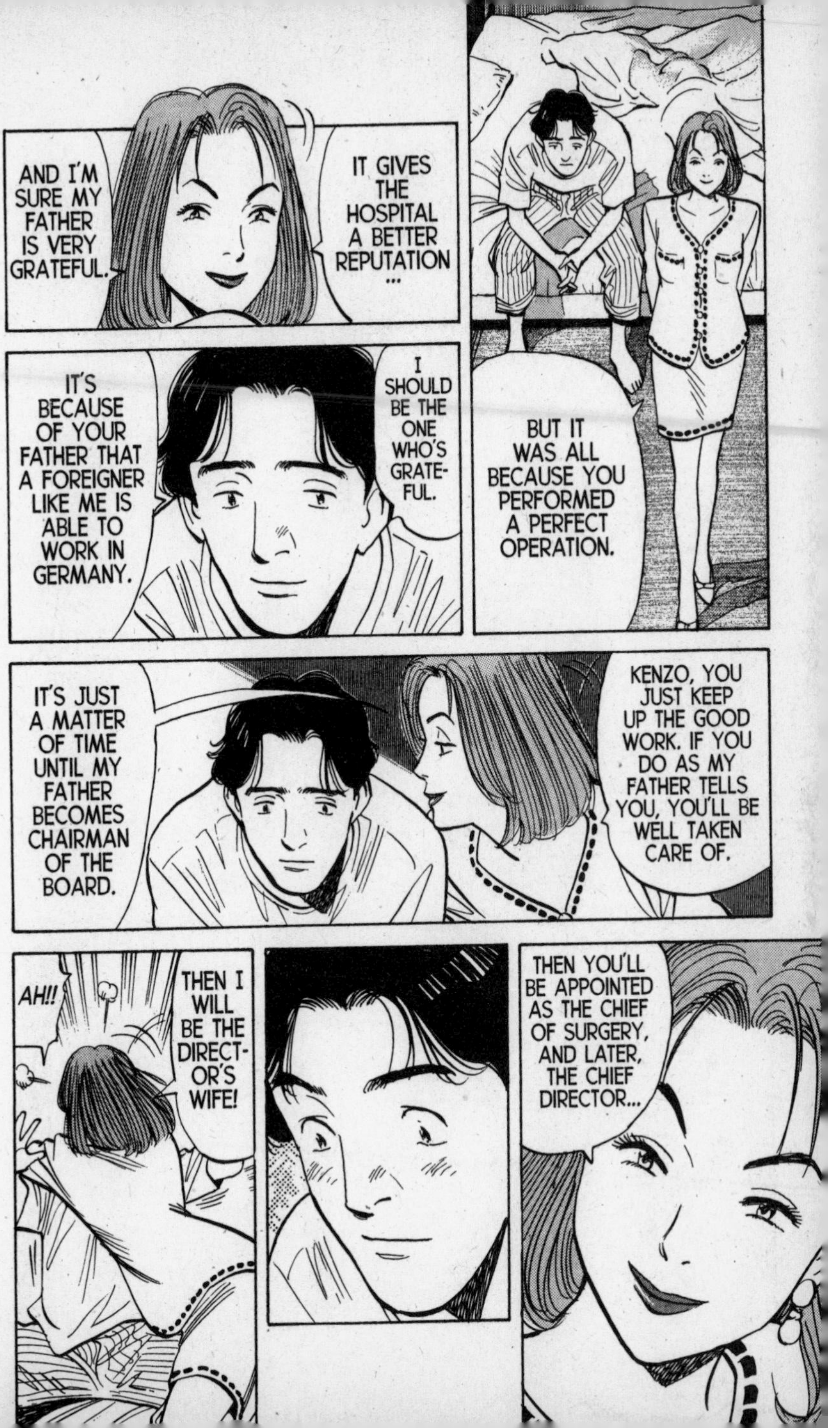
BUT IT WAS ALL BECAUSE YOU PERFORMED A PERFECT OPERATION.
IT GIVES THE HOSPITAL A BETTER REPUTATION ...
AND I'M SURE MY FATHER IS VERY GRATEFUL.
I SHOULD BE THE ONE WHO'S GRATE-FUL.
IT'S BECAUSE OF YOUR FATHER THAT A FOREIGNER LIKE ME IS ABLE TO WORK IN GERMANY.
KENZO, YOU JUST KEEP UP THE GOOD WORK. IF YOU DO AS MY FATHER TELLS YOU, YOU'LL BE WELL TAKEN CARE OF.
IT'S JUST A MATTER OF TIME UNTIL MY FATHER BECOMES CHAIRMAN OF THE BOARD.
THEN YOU'LL BE APPOINTED AS THE CHIEF OF SURGERY, AND LATER, THE CHIEF DIRECTOR...
THEN I WILL BE THE DIRECT-OR'S WIFE!
AH!!

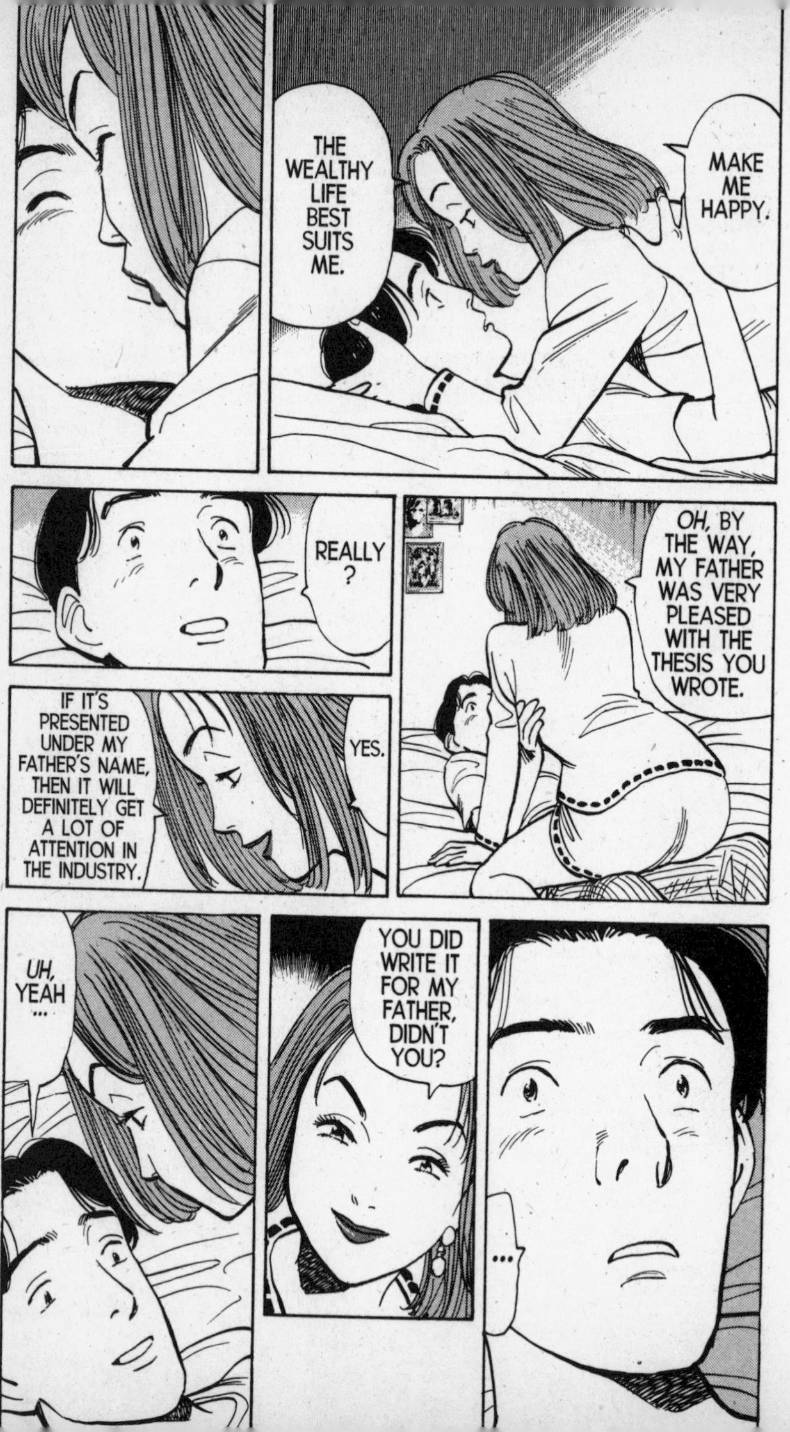
MAKE ME HAPPY.
THE WEALTHY LIFE BEST SUITS ME.
OH, BY THE WAY, MY FATHER WAS VERY PLEASED WITH THE THESIS YOU WROTE.
REALLY?
YES.
IF IT'S PRESENTED UNDER MY FATHER'S NAME, THEN IT WILL DEFINITELY GET A LOT OF ATTENTION IN THE INDUSTRY.
...
YOU DID WRITE IT FOR MY FATHER, DIDN'T YOU?
UH, YEAH ...

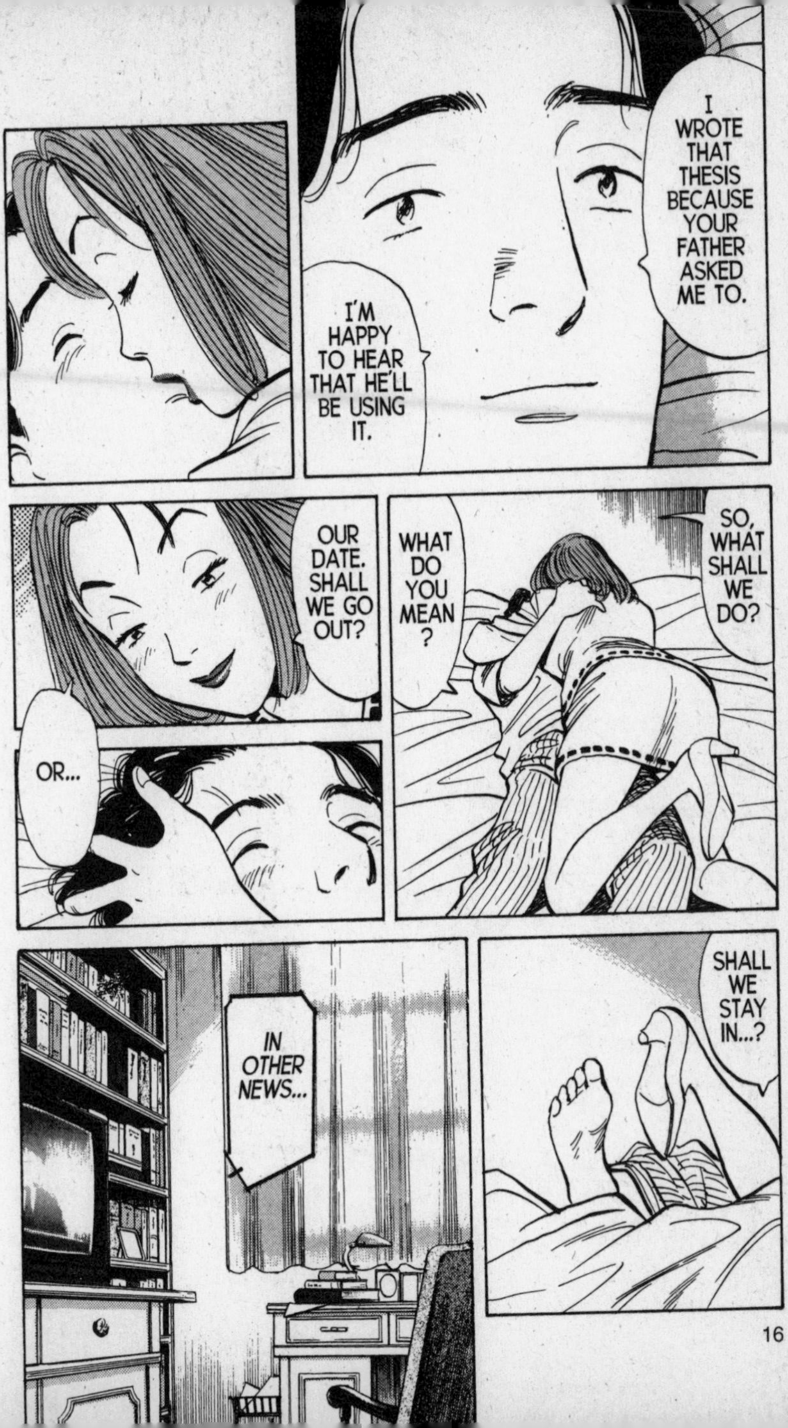
I WROTE THAT THESIS BECAUSE YOUR FATHER ASKED ME TO.
I'M HAPPY TO HEAR THAT HE'LL BE USING IT.
SO, WHAT SHALL WE DO?
WHAT DO YOU MEAN?
OUR DATE. SHALL WE GO OUT?
OR...
SHALL WE STAY IN...?
IN OTHER NEWS...

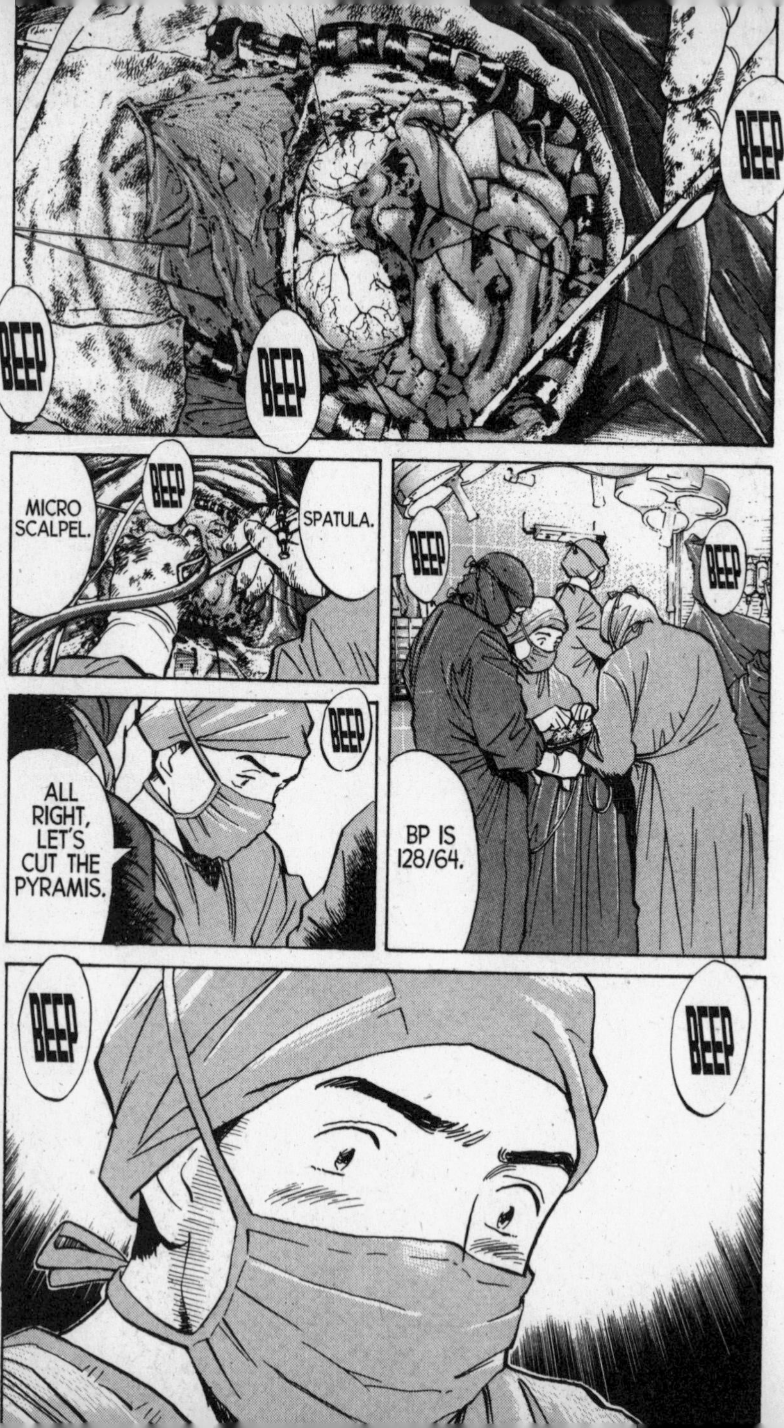

BEEP
BEEP
BEEP
BEEP
BEEP
BP IS 128/64.
SPATULA.
BEEP
MICRO SCALPEL.
BEEP
ALL RIGHT, LET'S CUT THE PYRAMIS.
BEEP
BEEP

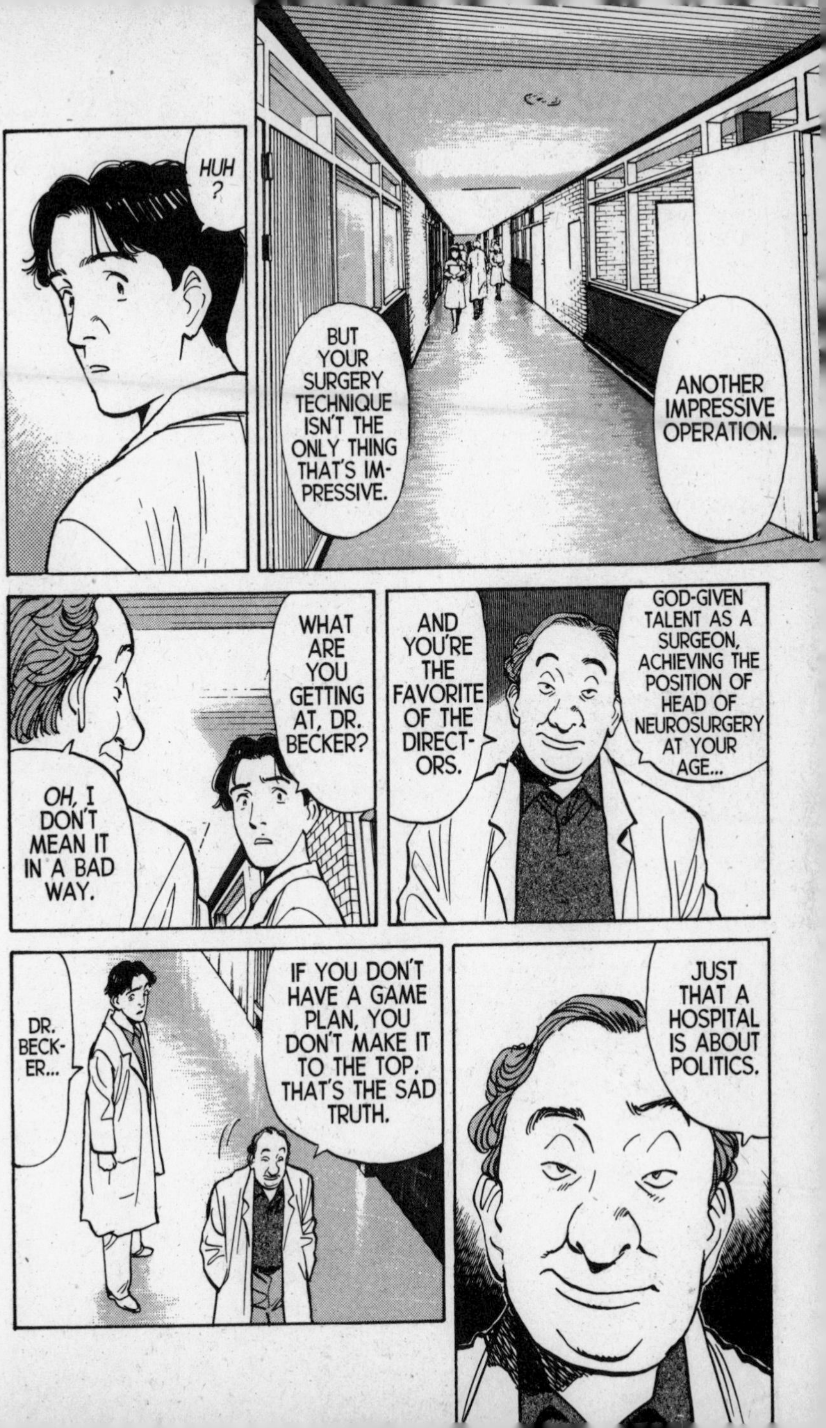
ANOTHER IMPRESSIVE OPERATION.
BUT YOUR SURGERY TECHNIQUE ISN'T THE ONLY THING THAT'S IMPRESSIVE.
HUH?
GOD-GIVEN TALENT AS A SURGEON, ACHIEVING THE POSITION OF HEAD OF NEUROSURGERY AT YOUR AGE...
AND YOU'RE THE FAVORITE OF THE DIRECTORS.
WHAT ARE YOU GETTING AT, DR. BECKER?
OH, I DON'T MEAN IT IN A BAD WAY.
JUST THAT A HOSPITAL IS ABOUT POLITICS.
IF YOU DON'T HAVE A GAME PLAN, YOU DON'T MAKE IT TO THE TOP. THAT'S THE SAD TRUTH.
DR. BECKER...

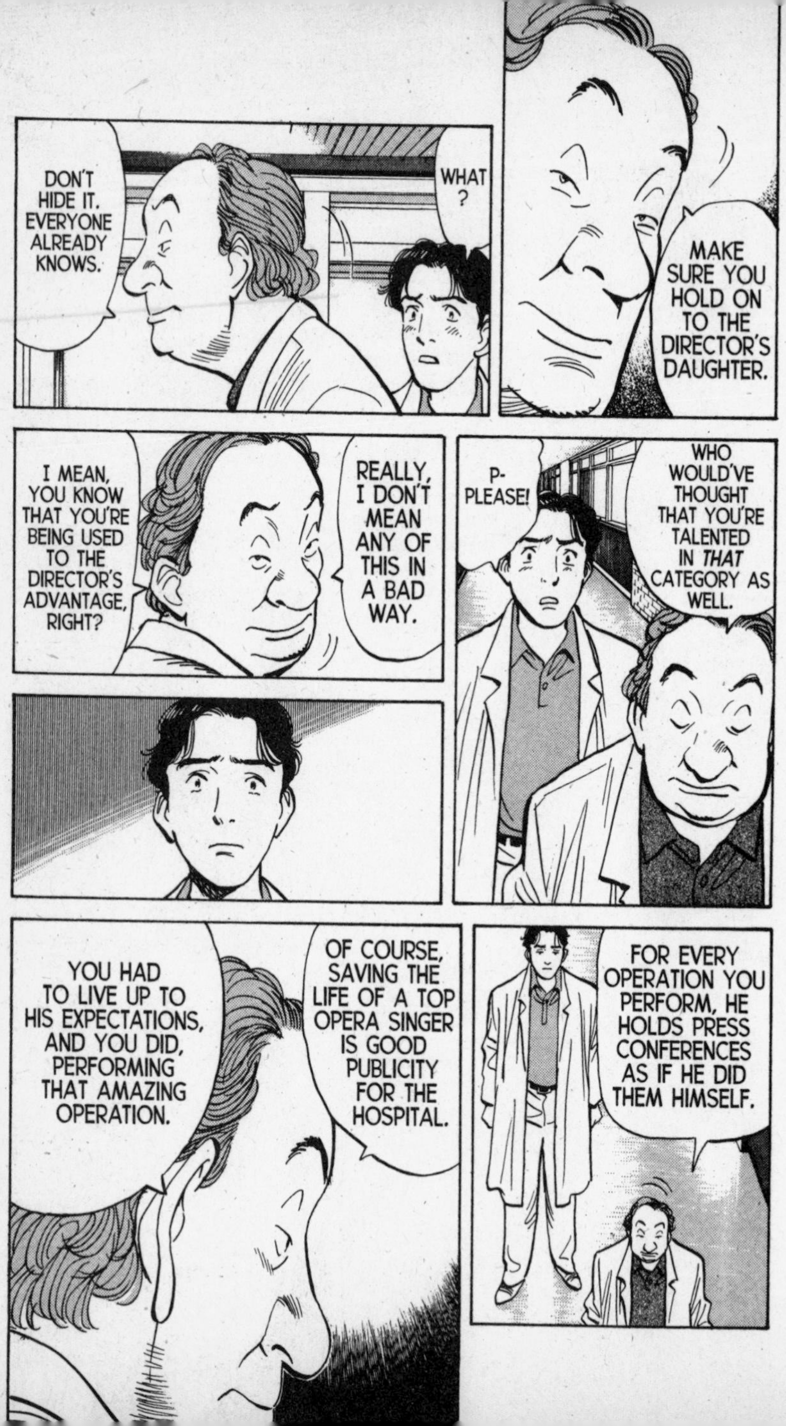

MAKE SURE YOU HOLD ON TO THE DIRECTOR'S DAUGHTER.
WHAT ?
DON'T HIDE IT. EVERYONE ALREADY KNOWS.
WHO WOULD'VE THOUGHT THAT YOU'RE TALENTED IN *THAT* CATEGORY AS WELL.
P-PLEASE!
REALLY, I DON'T MEAN ANY OF THIS IN A BAD WAY.
I MEAN, YOU KNOW THAT YOU'RE BEING USED TO THE DIRECTOR'S ADVANTAGE, RIGHT?
FOR EVERY OPERATION YOU PERFORM, HE HOLDS PRESS CONFERENCES AS IF HE DID THEM HIMSELF.
OF COURSE, SAVING THE LIFE OF A TOP OPERA SINGER IS GOOD PUBLICITY FOR THE HOSPITAL.
YOU HAD TO LIVE UP TO HIS EXPECTATIONS, AND YOU DID, PERFORMING THAT AMAZING OPERATION.

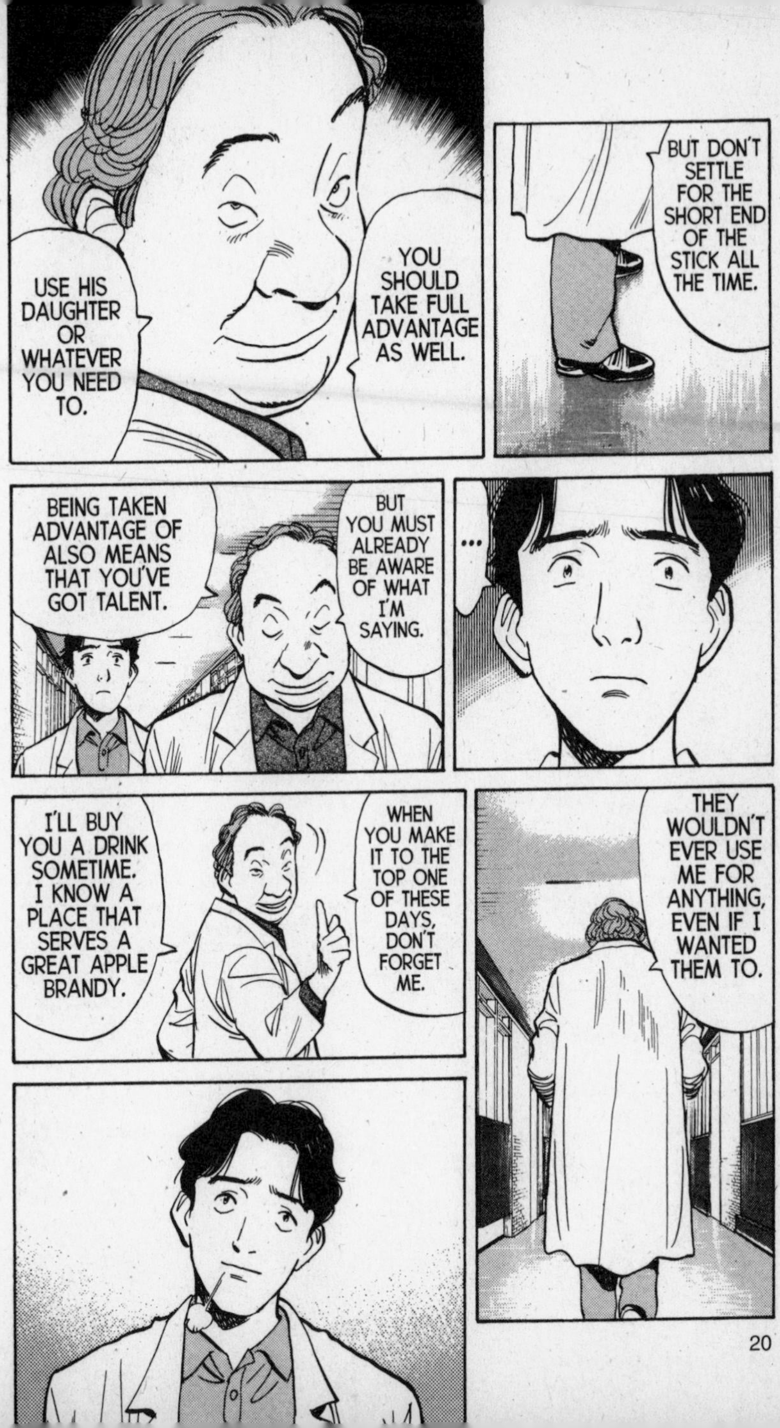
BUT DON'T SETTLE FOR THE SHORT END OF THE STICK ALL THE TIME.
YOU SHOULD TAKE FULL ADVANTAGE AS WELL.
USE HIS DAUGHTER OR WHATEVER YOU NEED TO.
...
BUT YOU MUST ALREADY BE AWARE OF WHAT I'M SAYING.
BEING TAKEN ADVANTAGE OF ALSO MEANS THAT YOU'VE GOT TALENT.
THEY WOULDN'T EVER USE ME FOR ANYTHING, EVEN IF I WANTED THEM TO.
WHEN YOU MAKE IT TO THE TOP ONE OF THESE DAYS, DON'T FORGET ME.
I'LL BUY YOU A DRINK SOMETIME. I KNOW A PLACE THAT SERVES A GREAT APPLE BRANDY.

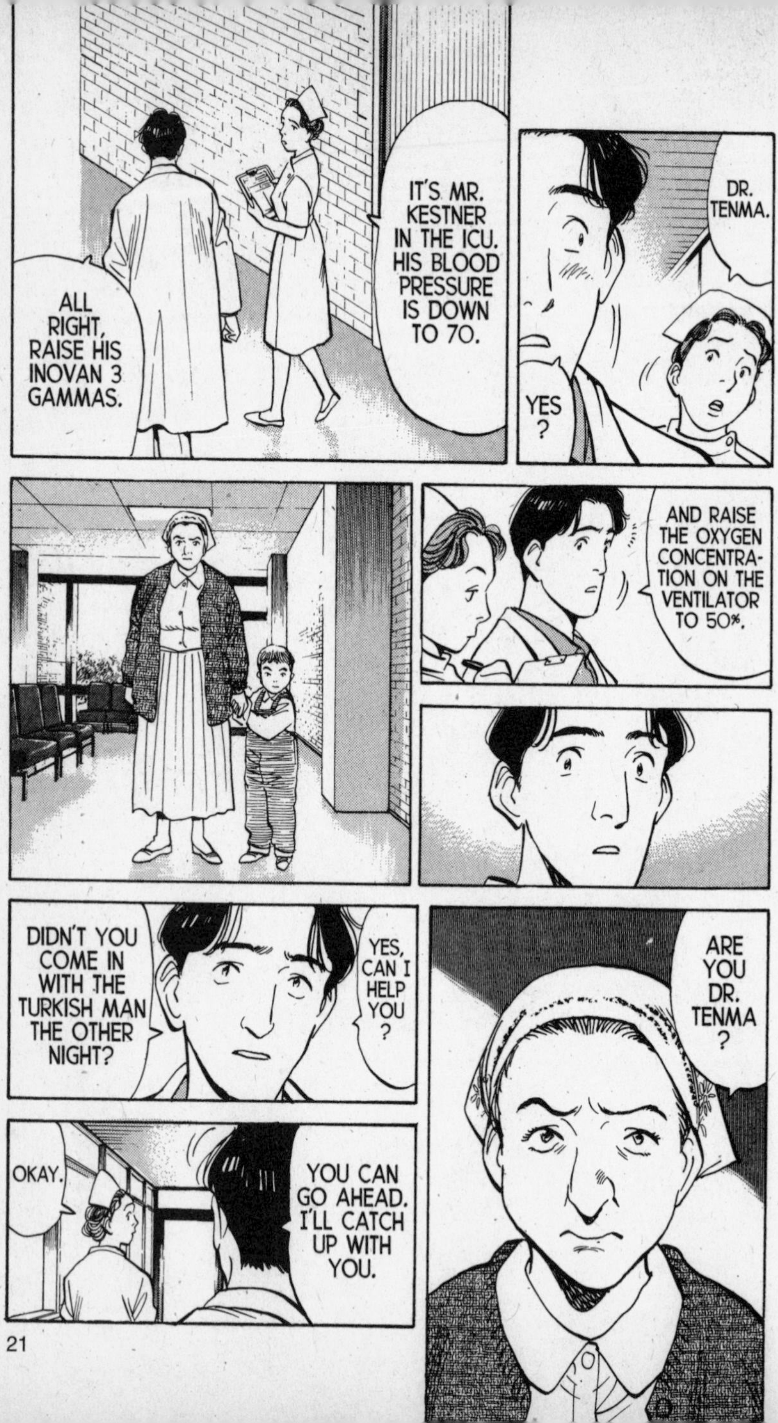
DR. TENMA.
YES?
IT'S MR. KESTNER IN THE ICU. HIS BLOOD PRESSURE IS DOWN TO 70.
ALL RIGHT, RAISE HIS INOVAN 3 GAMMAS.
AND RAISE THE OXYGEN CONCENTRA-TION ON THE VENTILATOR TO 50%.
ARE YOU DR. TENMA?
YES, CAN I HELP YOU?
DIDN'T YOU COME IN WITH THE TURKISH MAN THE OTHER NIGHT?
YOU CAN GO AHEAD. I'LL CATCH UP WITH YOU.
OKAY.

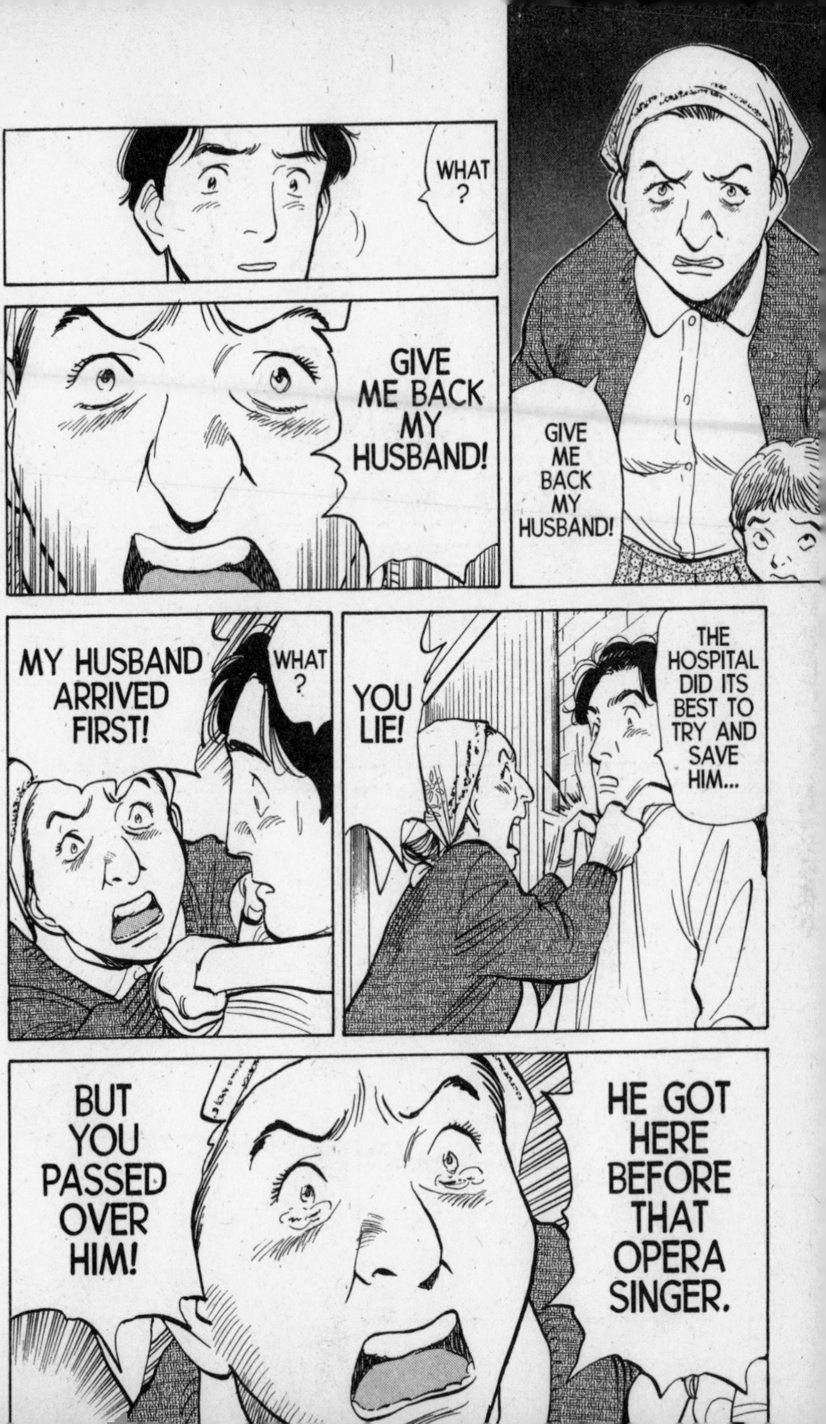
GIVE ME BACK MY HUSBAND!
WHAT?
GIVE ME BACK MY HUSBAND!
THE HOSPITAL DID ITS BEST TO TRY AND SAVE HIM...
YOU LIE!
WHAT?
MY HUSBAND ARRIVED FIRST!
HE GOT HERE BEFORE THAT OPERA SINGER.
BUT YOU PASSED OVER HIM!

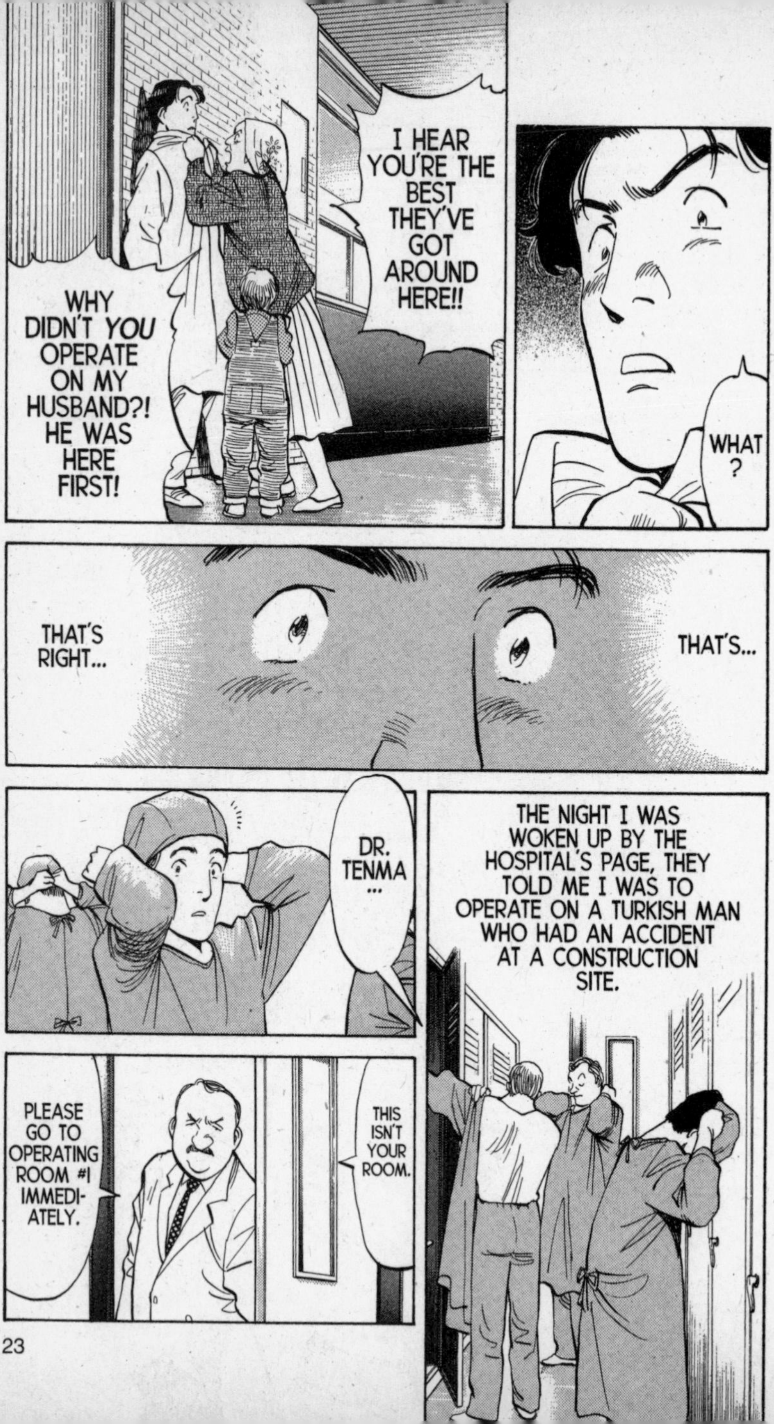
WHAT?
I HEAR YOU'RE THE BEST THEY'VE GOT AROUND HERE!!
WHY DIDN'T *YOU* OPERATE ON MY HUSBAND?! HE WAS HERE FIRST!
THAT'S...
THAT'S RIGHT...
THE NIGHT I WAS WOKEN UP BY THE HOSPITAL'S PAGE, THEY TOLD ME I WAS TO OPERATE ON A TURKISH MAN WHO HAD AN ACCIDENT AT A CONSTRUCTION SITE.
DR. TENMA...
THIS ISN'T YOUR ROOM.
PLEASE GO TO OPERATING ROOM #1 IMMEDIATELY.

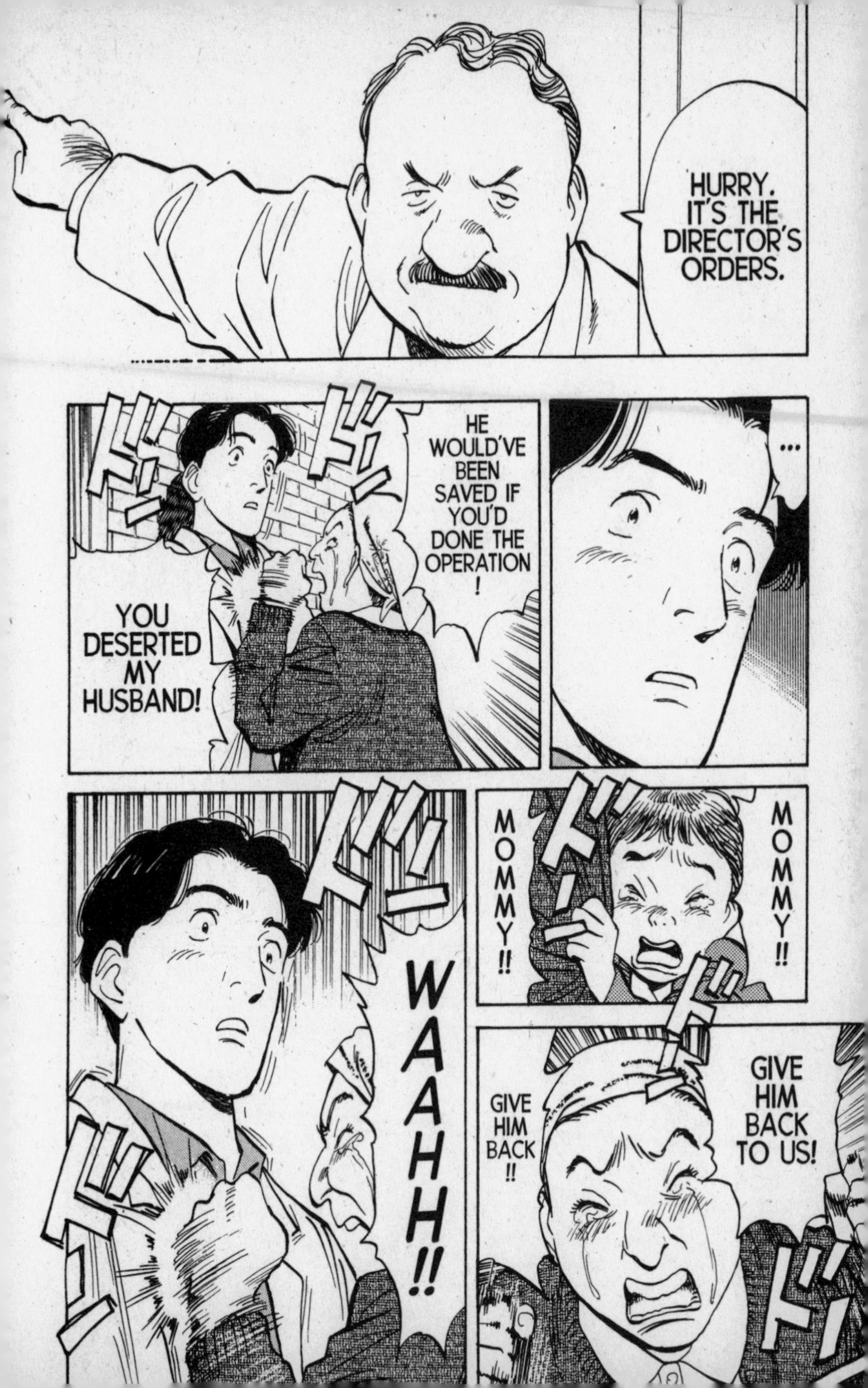
HURRY. IT'S THE DIRECTOR'S ORDERS.
...
HE WOULD'VE BEEN SAVED IF YOU'D DONE THE OPERATION!
YOU DESERTED MY HUSBAND!
MOMMY!!
MOMMY!!
GIVE HIM BACK TO US!
GIVE HIM BACK!!
WAAHH!!

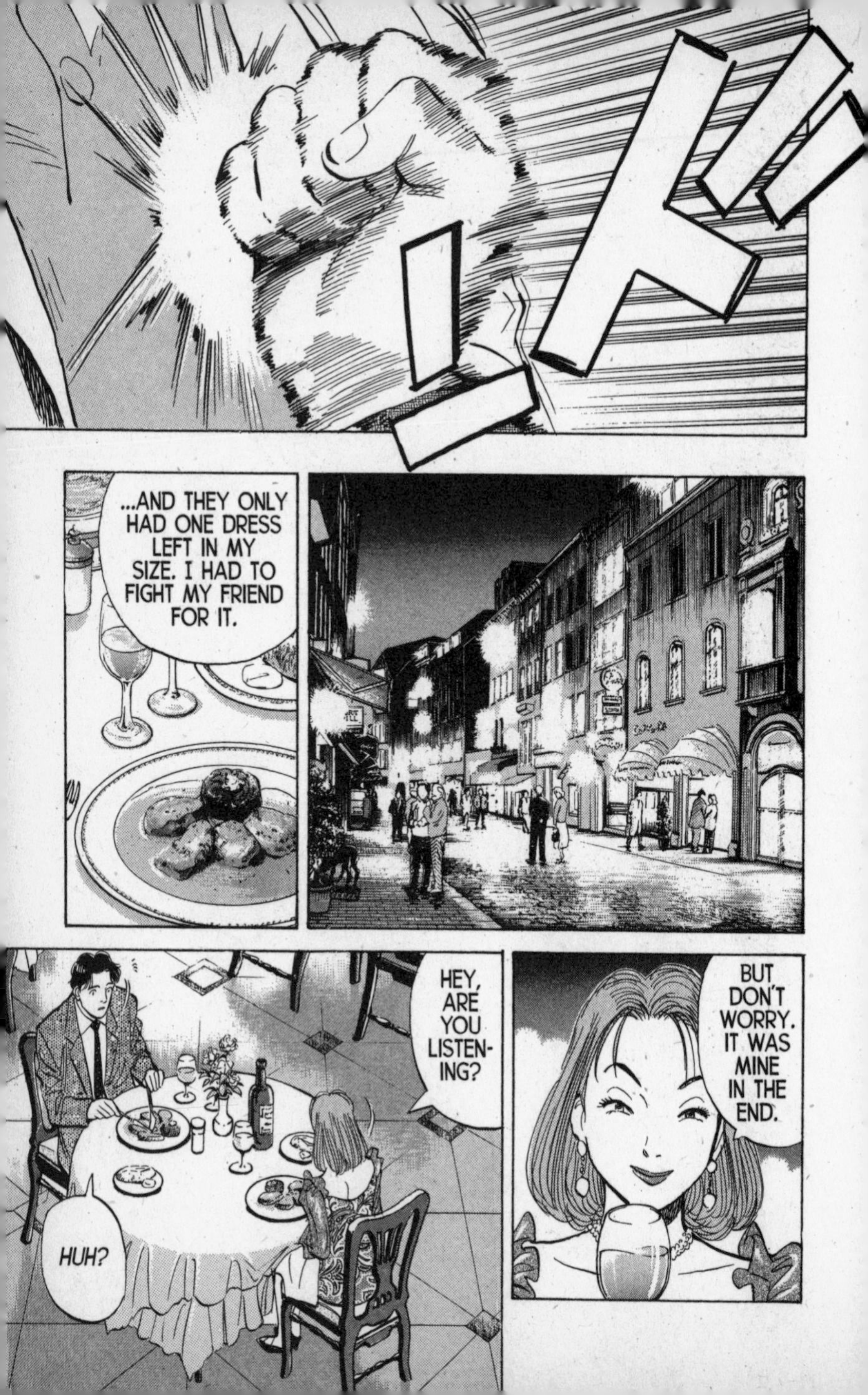
...AND THEY ONLY HAD ONE DRESS LEFT IN MY SIZE. I HAD TO FIGHT MY FRIEND FOR IT.
BUT DON'T WORRY. IT WAS MINE IN THE END.
HEY, ARE YOU LISTEN-ING?
HUH?

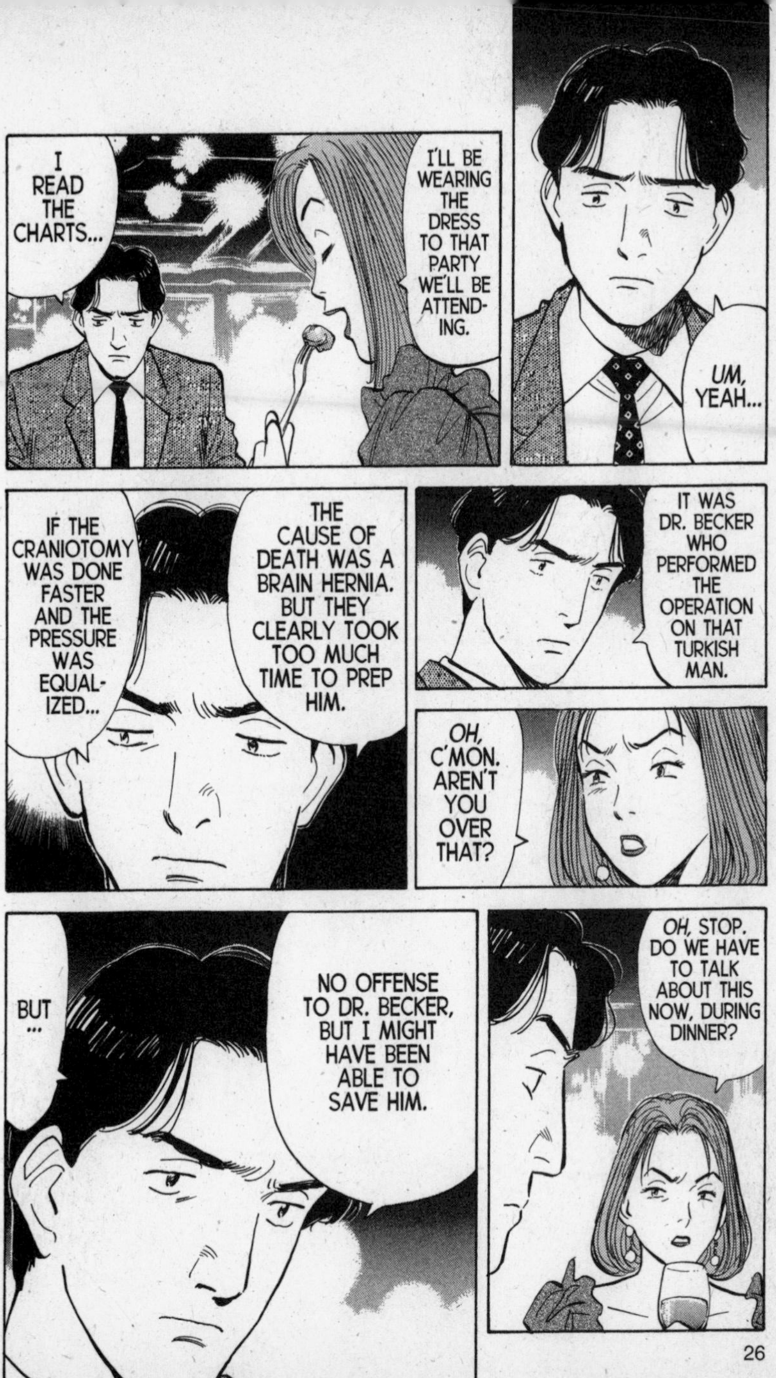
UM, YEAH...
I'LL BE WEARING THE DRESS TO THAT PARTY WE'LL BE ATTENDING.
I READ THE CHARTS...
IT WAS DR. BECKER WHO PERFORMED THE OPERATION ON THAT TURKISH MAN.
OH, C'MON. AREN'T YOU OVER THAT?
THE CAUSE OF DEATH WAS A BRAIN HERNIA. BUT THEY CLEARLY TOOK TOO MUCH TIME TO PREP HIM.
IF THE CRANIOTOMY WAS DONE FASTER AND THE PRESSURE WAS EQUALIZED...
OH, STOP. DO WE HAVE TO TALK ABOUT THIS NOW, DURING DINNER?
NO OFFENSE TO DR. BECKER, BUT I MIGHT HAVE BEEN ABLE TO SAVE HIM.
BUT ...

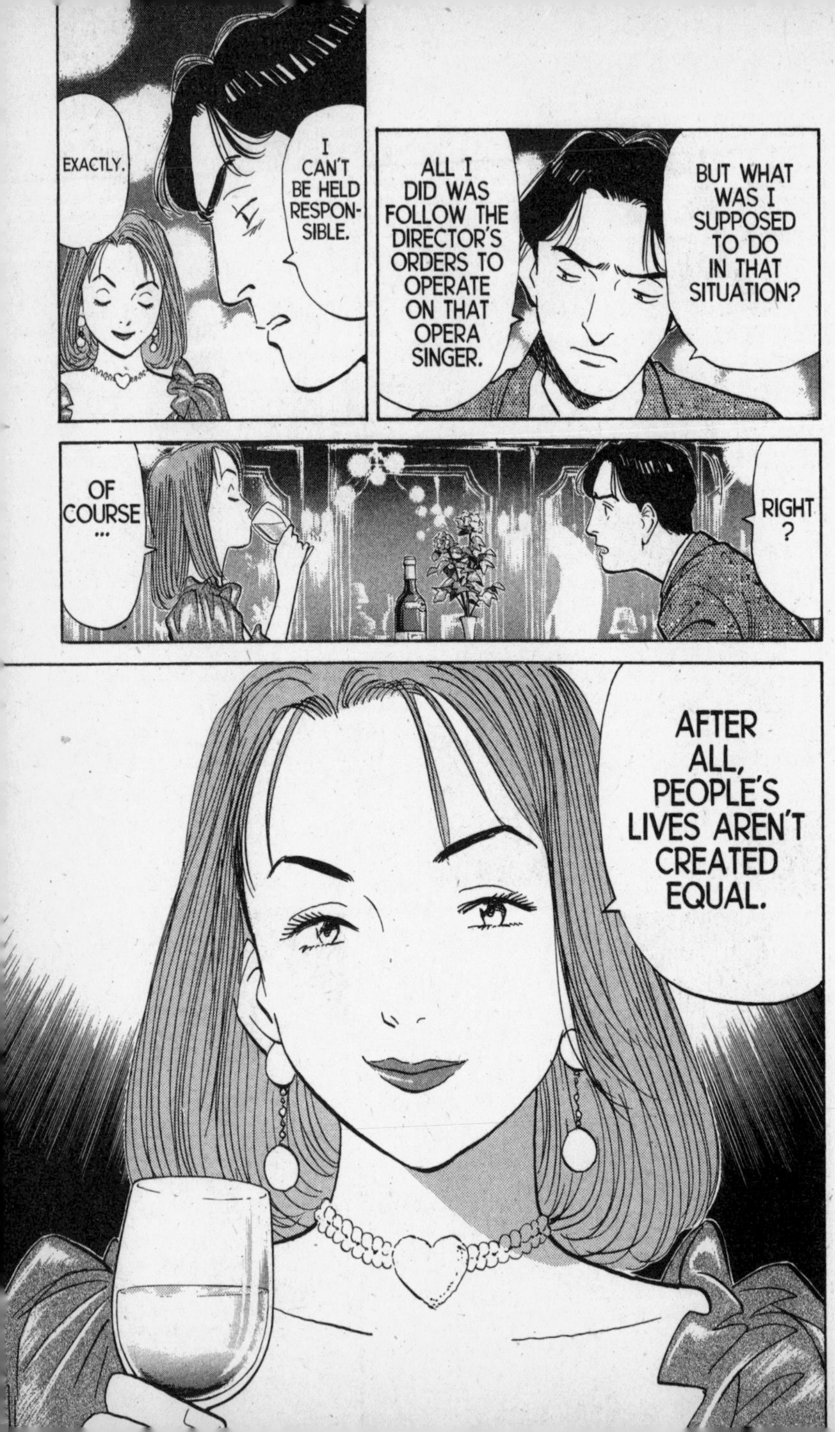
BUT WHAT WAS I SUPPOSED TO DO IN THAT SITUATION?
ALL I DID WAS FOLLOW THE DIRECTOR'S ORDERS TO OPERATE ON THAT OPERA SINGER.
I CAN'T BE HELD RESPON-SIBLE.
EXACTLY.
RIGHT?
OF COURSE...
AFTER ALL, PEOPLE'S LIVES AREN'T CREATED EQUAL.

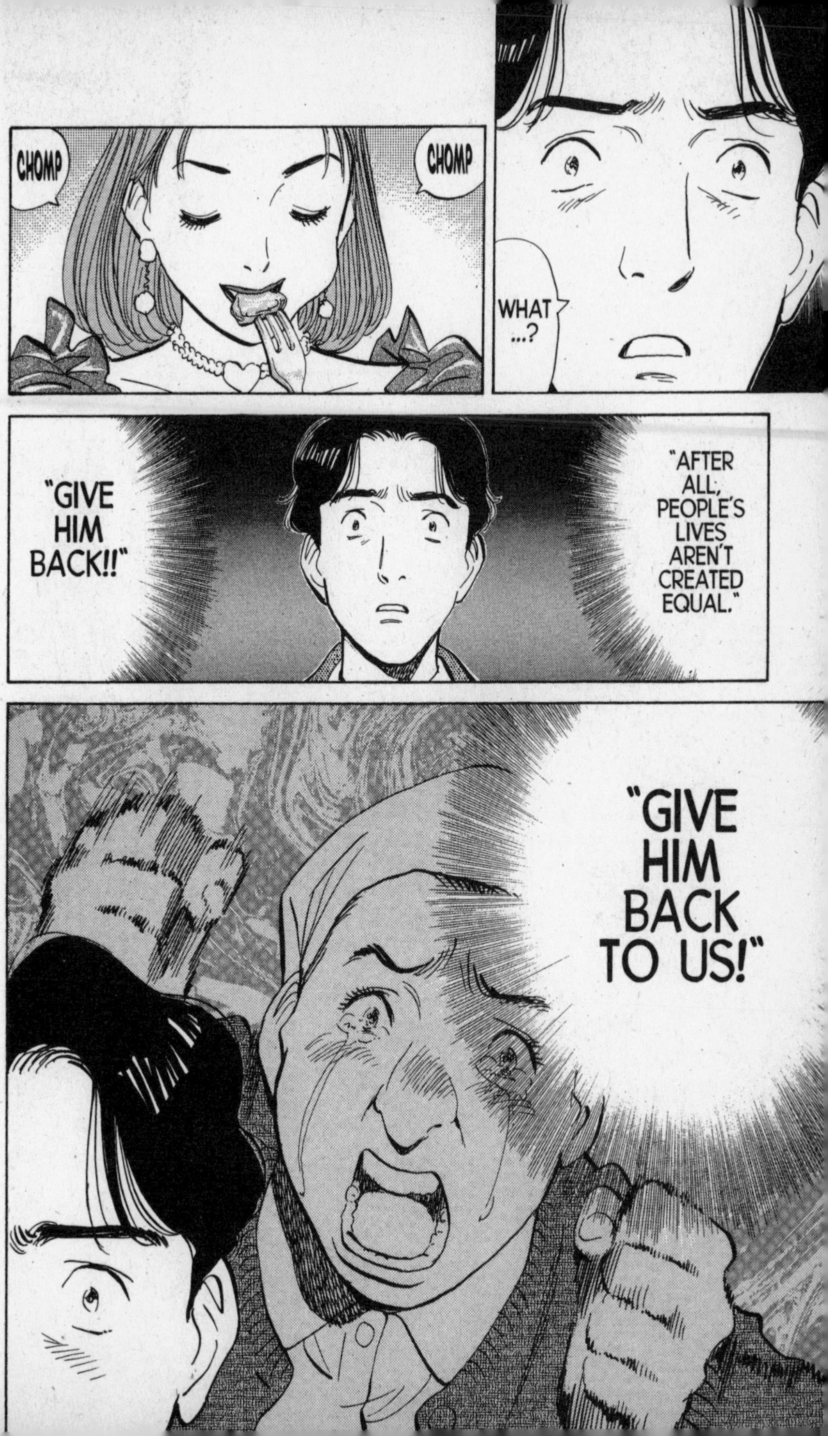
WHAT ...?
CHOMP
CHOMP
"AFTER ALL, PEOPLE'S LIVES AREN'T CREATED EQUAL."
"GIVE HIM BACK!!"
"GIVE HIM BACK TO US!"

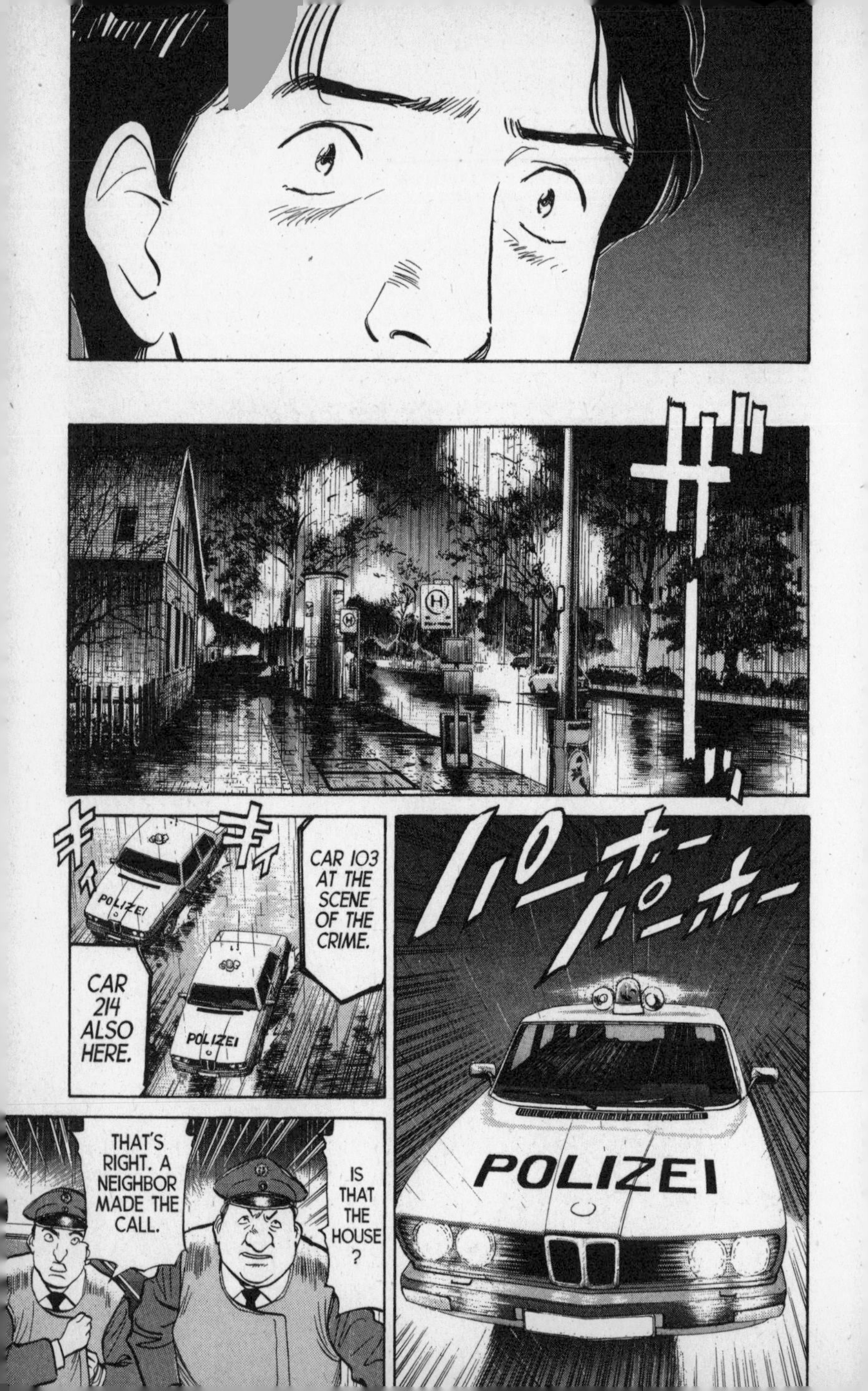
ザザーッ
パーポーパーポー
CAR 103 AT THE SCENE OF THE CRIME.
キキィ
CAR 214 ALSO HERE.
POLIZEI
IS THAT THE HOUSE?
THAT'S RIGHT. A NEIGHBOR MADE THE CALL.

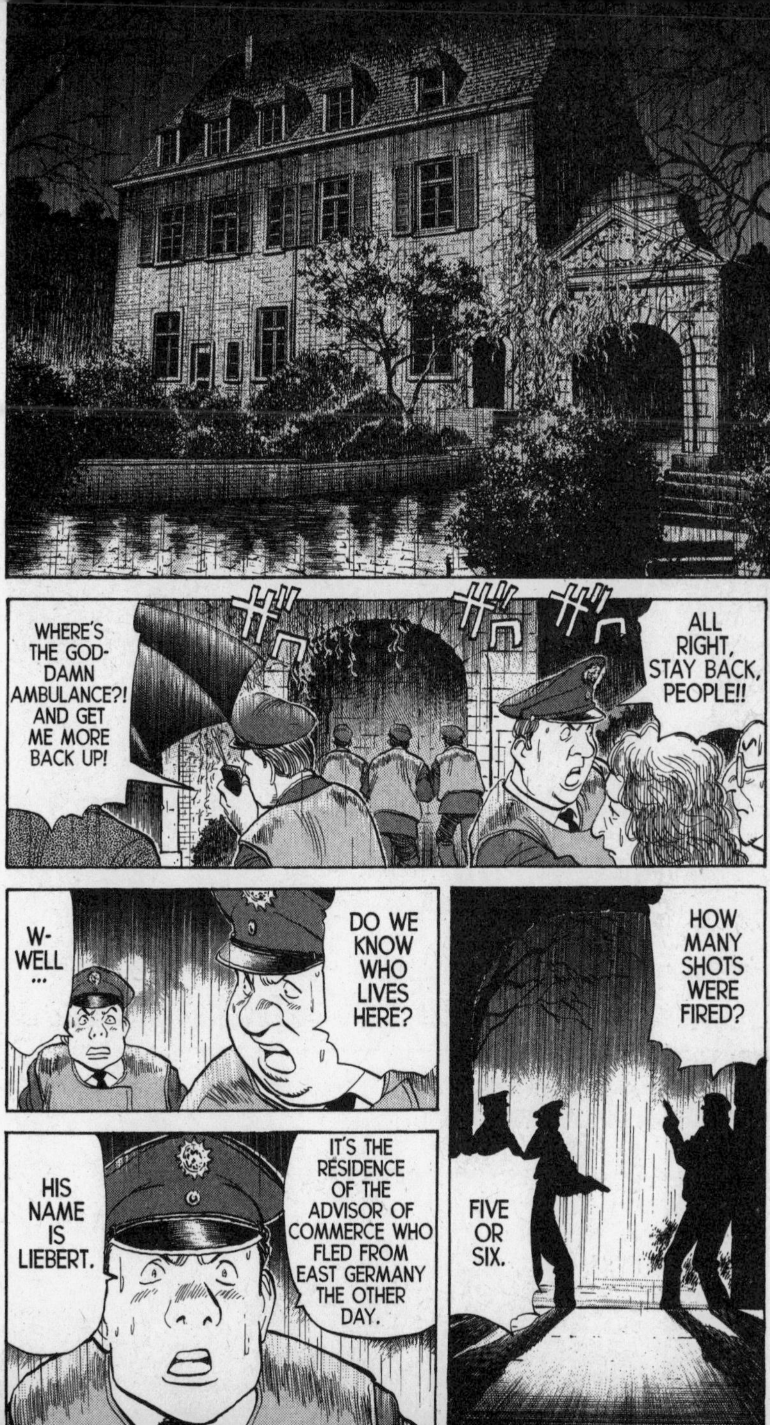
ALL RIGHT, STAY BACK, PEOPLE!!
WHERE'S THE GOD-DAMN AMBULANCE?! AND GET ME MORE BACK UP!
HOW MANY SHOTS WERE FIRED?
FIVE OR SIX.
DO WE KNOW WHO LIVES HERE?
W-WELL...
IT'S THE RESIDENCE OF THE ADVISOR OF COMMERCE WHO FLED FROM EAST GERMANY THE OTHER DAY.
HIS NAME IS LIEBERT.

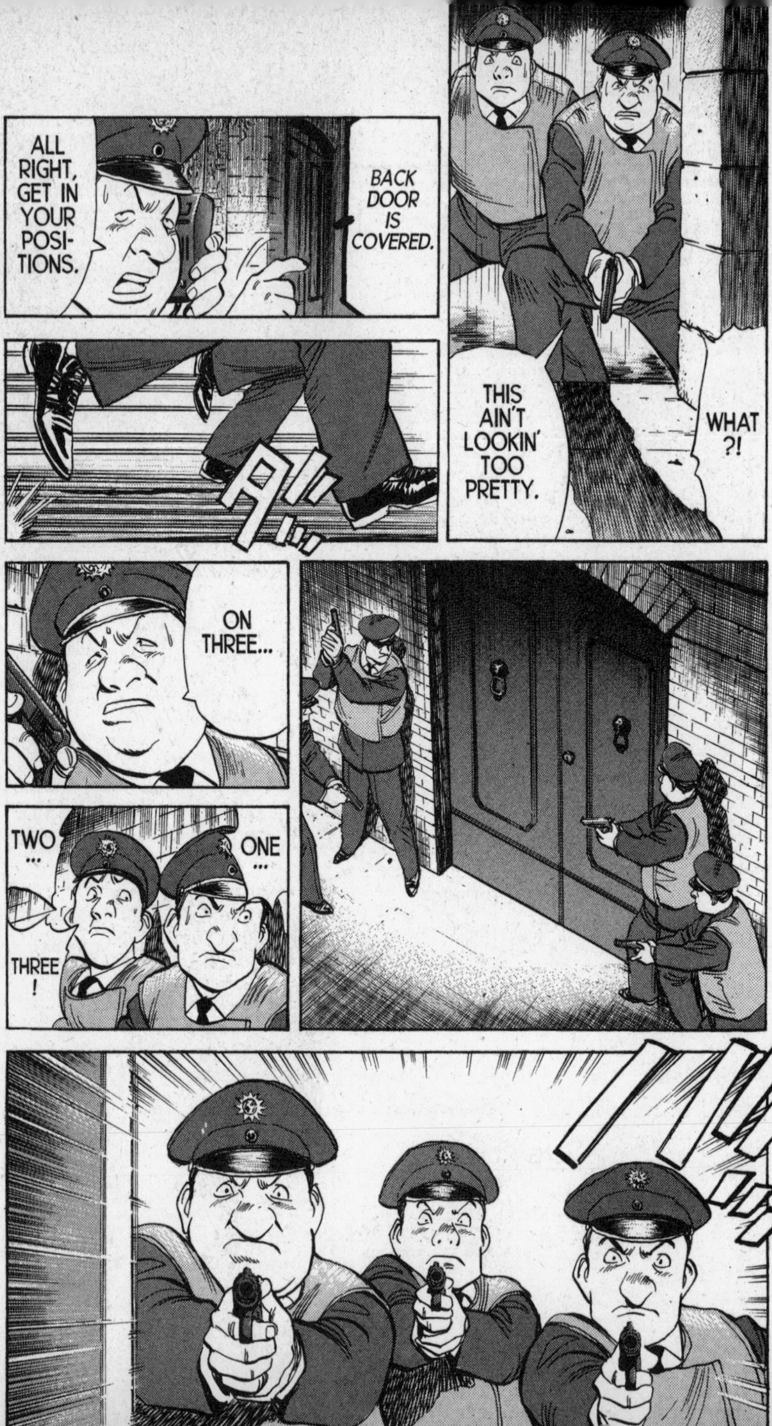
THIS AIN'T LOOKIN' TOO PRETTY.
WHAT ?!
BACK DOOR IS COVERED.
ALL RIGHT, GET IN YOUR POSI- TIONS.
ON THREE...
ONE ...
TWO ...
THREE !

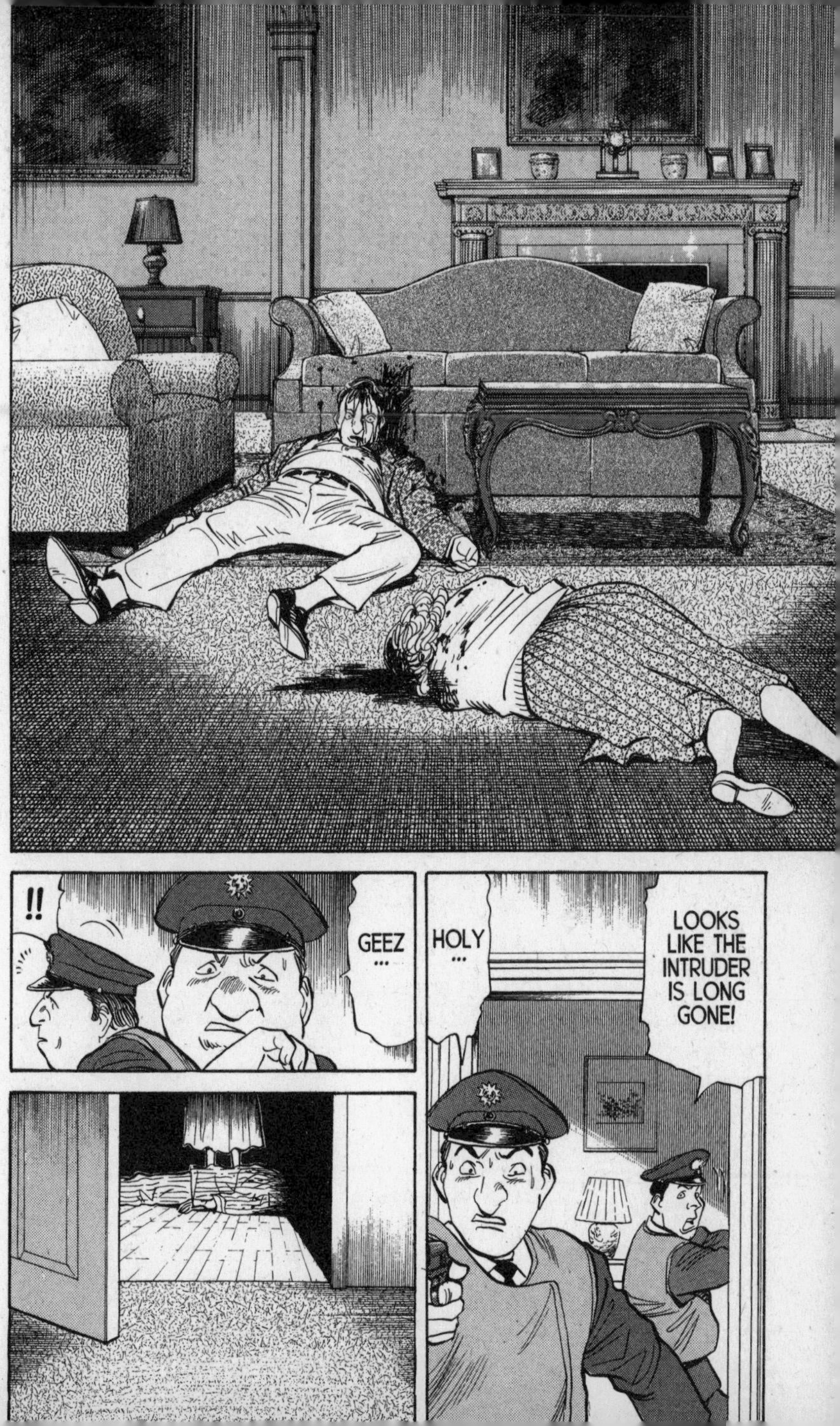
LOOKS LIKE THE INTRUDER IS LONG GONE!
HOLY...
!!
GEEZ...

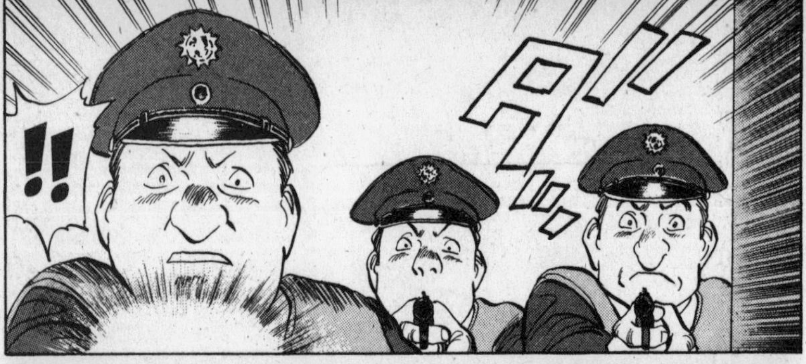
ダッ
!!

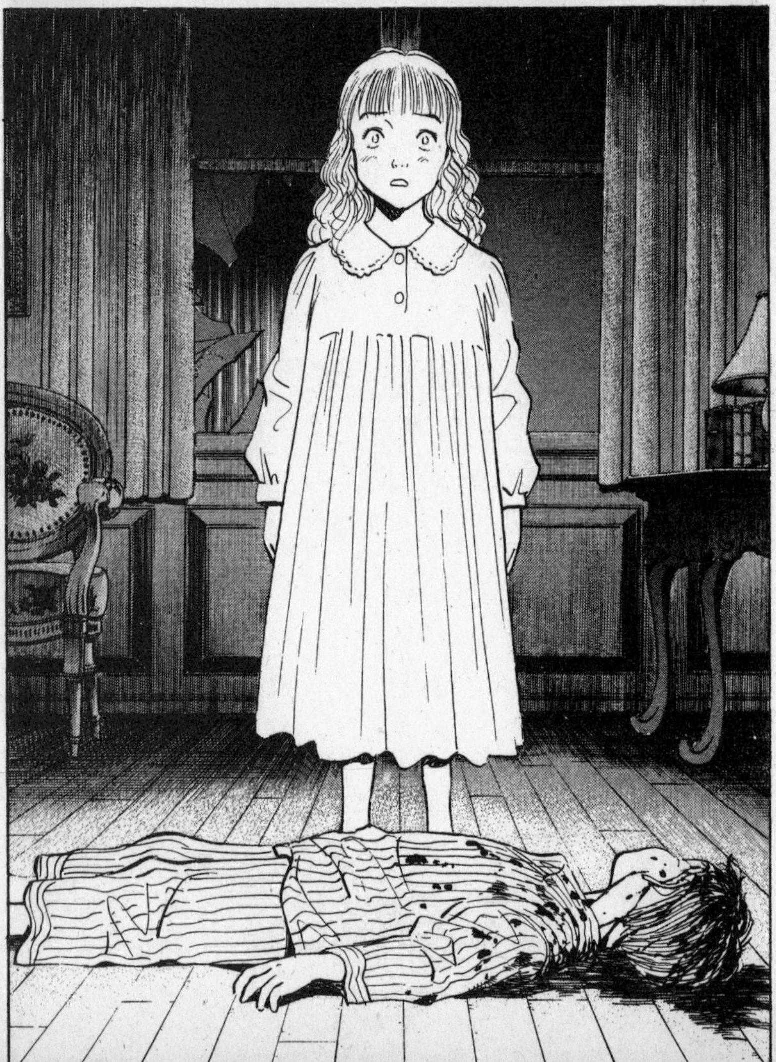

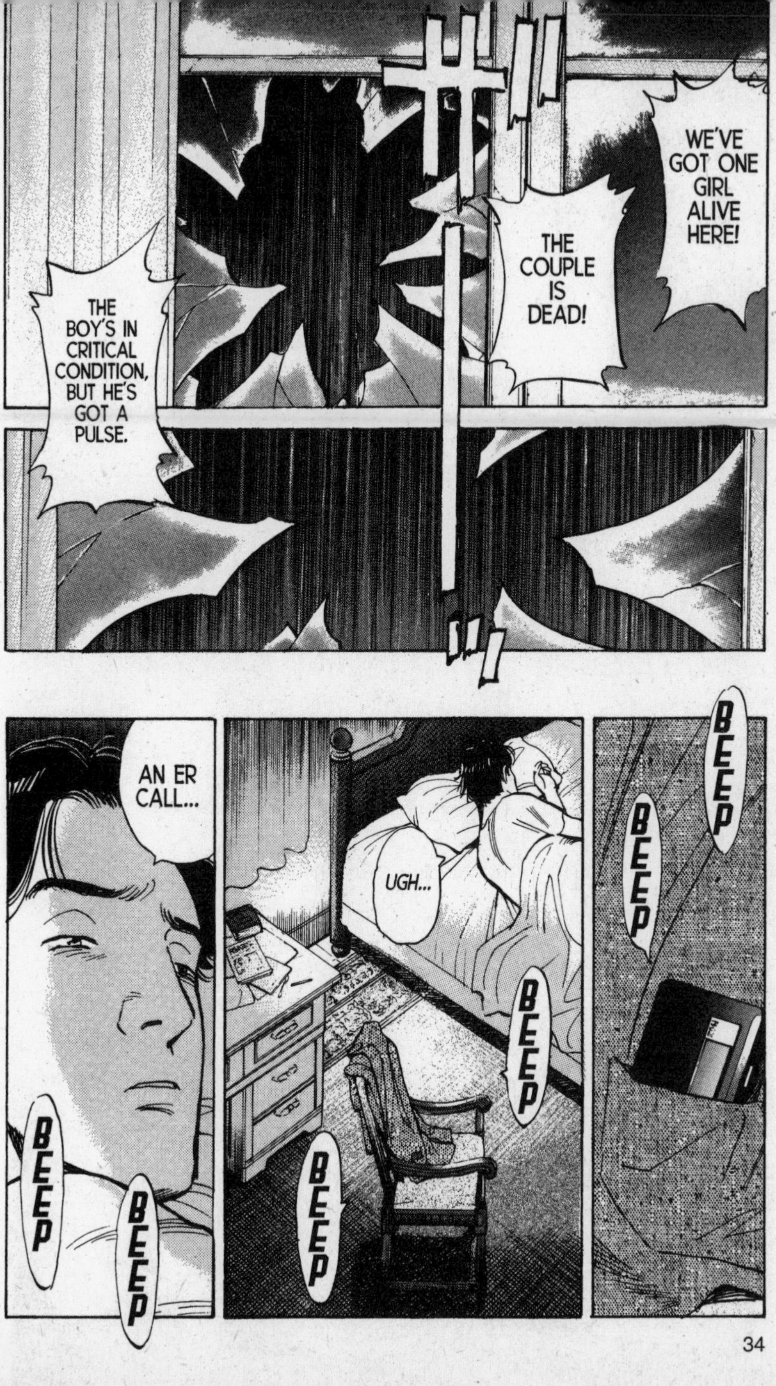
WE'VE GOT ONE GIRL ALIVE HERE!
THE COUPLE IS DEAD!
THE BOY'S IN CRITICAL CONDITION, BUT HE'S GOT A PULSE.
BEEP
BEEP
UGH...
BEEP
BEEP
AN ER CALL...
BEEP
BEEP

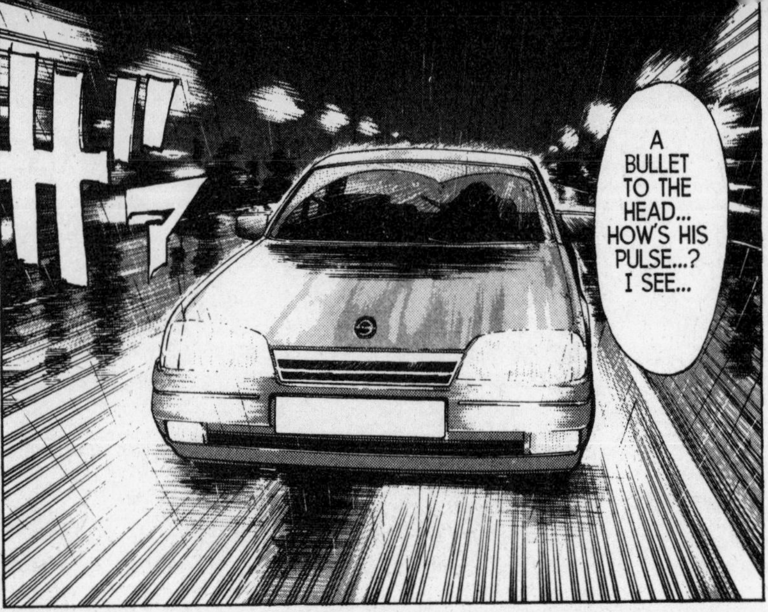
A BULLET TO THE HEAD... HOW'S HIS PULSE...? I SEE...

Chapter 2
Kill

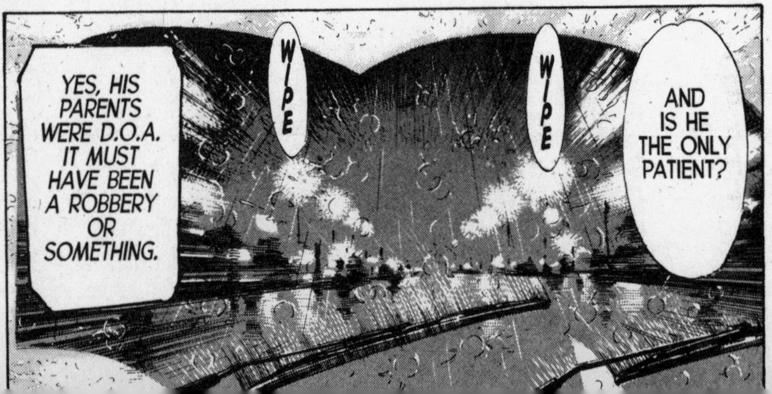
AND IS HE THE ONLY PATIENT?
WIPE
WIPE
YES, HIS PARENTS WERE D.O.A. IT MUST HAVE BEEN A ROBBERY OR SOMETHING.

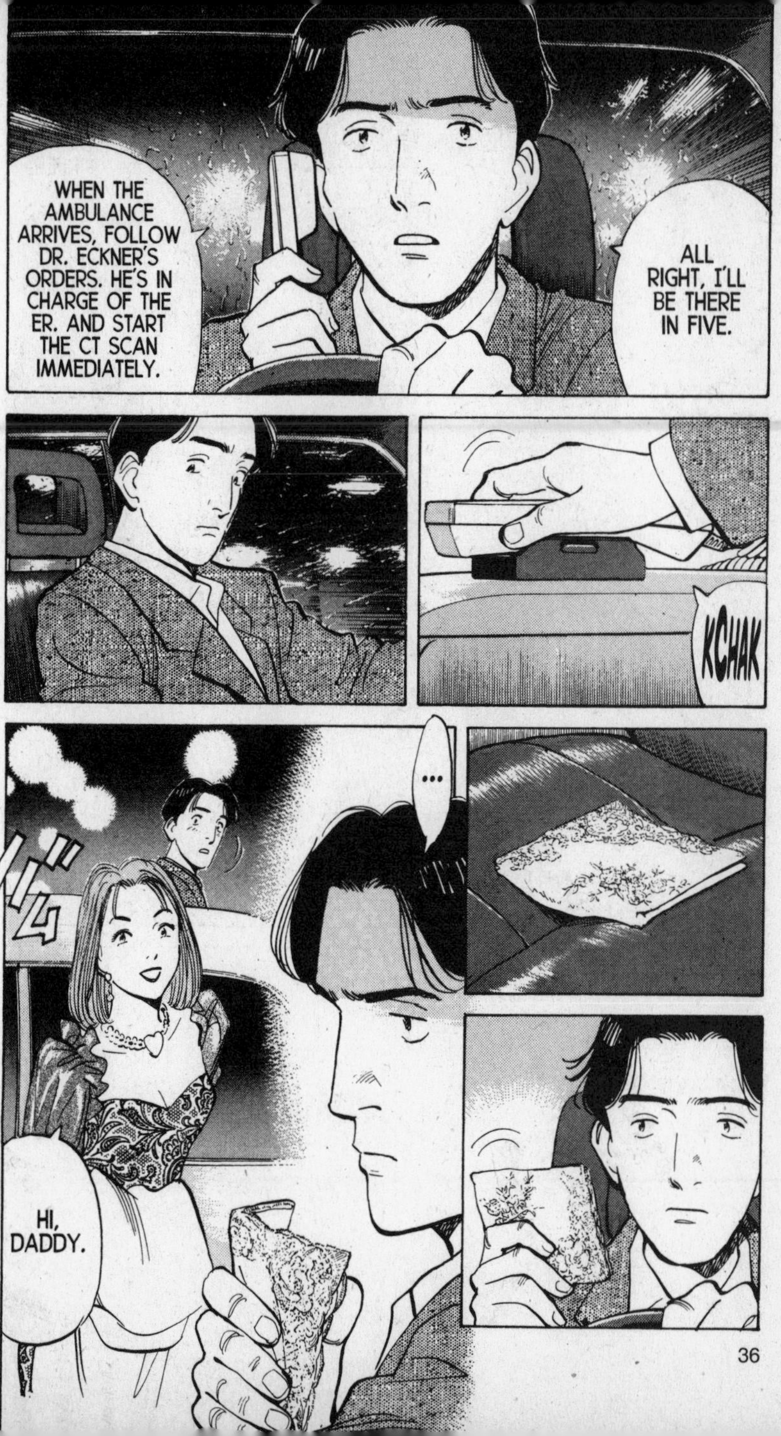
ALL RIGHT, I'LL BE THERE IN FIVE.
WHEN THE AMBULANCE ARRIVES, FOLLOW DR. ECKNER'S ORDERS. HE'S IN CHARGE OF THE ER. AND START THE CT SCAN IMMEDIATELY.
KCHAK
...
HI, DADDY.

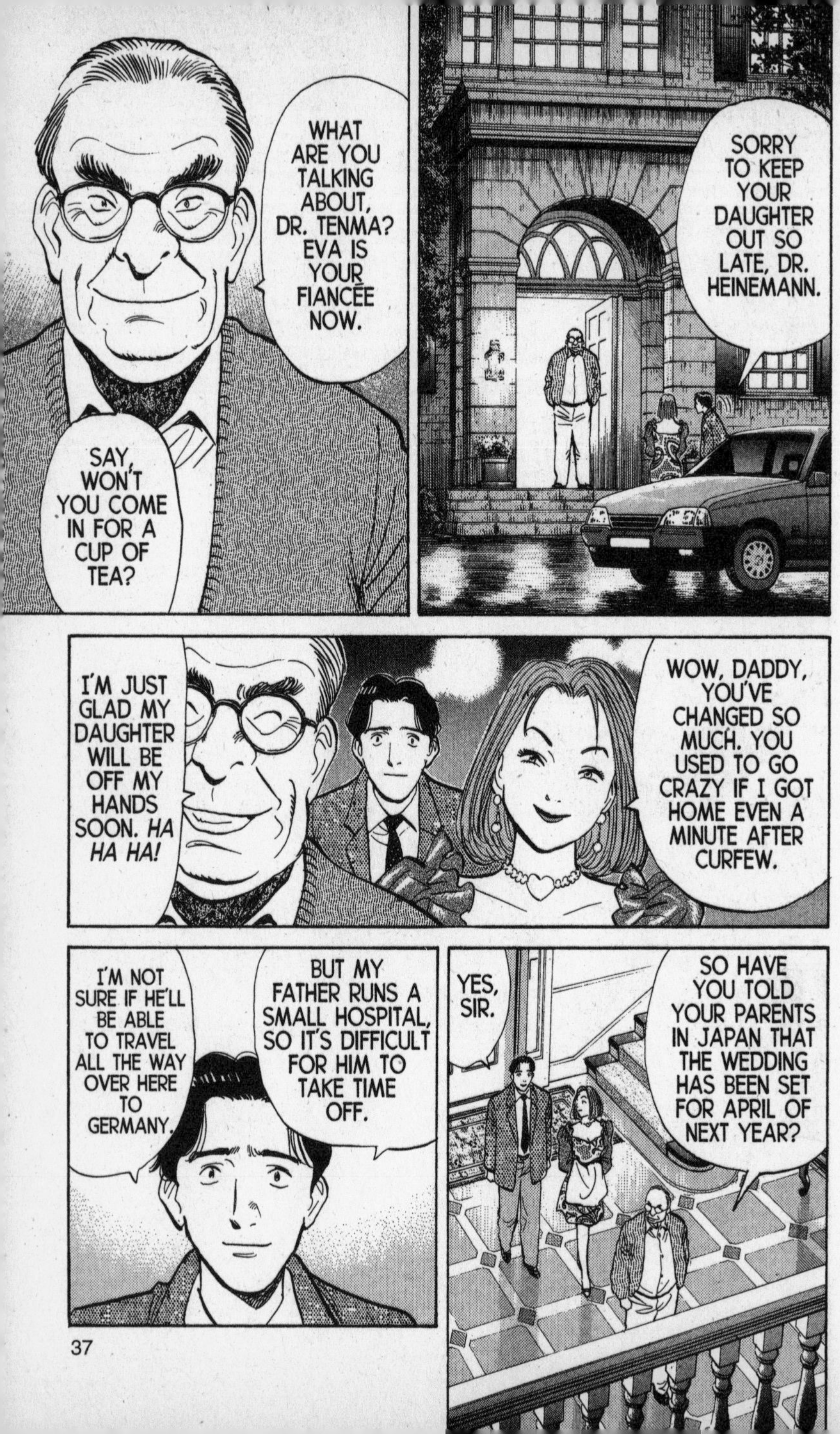
SORRY TO KEEP YOUR DAUGHTER OUT SO LATE, DR. HEINEMANN.
WHAT ARE YOU TALKING ABOUT, DR. TENMA? EVA IS YOUR FIANCÉE NOW.
SAY, WON'T YOU COME IN FOR A CUP OF TEA?
WOW, DADDY, YOU'VE CHANGED SO MUCH. YOU USED TO GO CRAZY IF I GOT HOME EVEN A MINUTE AFTER CURFEW.
I'M JUST GLAD MY DAUGHTER WILL BE OFF MY HANDS SOON. *HA HA HA!*
SO HAVE YOU TOLD YOUR PARENTS IN JAPAN THAT THE WEDDING HAS BEEN SET FOR APRIL OF NEXT YEAR?
YES, SIR.
BUT MY FATHER RUNS A SMALL HOSPITAL, SO IT'S DIFFICULT FOR HIM TO TAKE TIME OFF.
I'M NOT SURE IF HE'LL BE ABLE TO TRAVEL ALL THE WAY OVER HERE TO GERMANY.

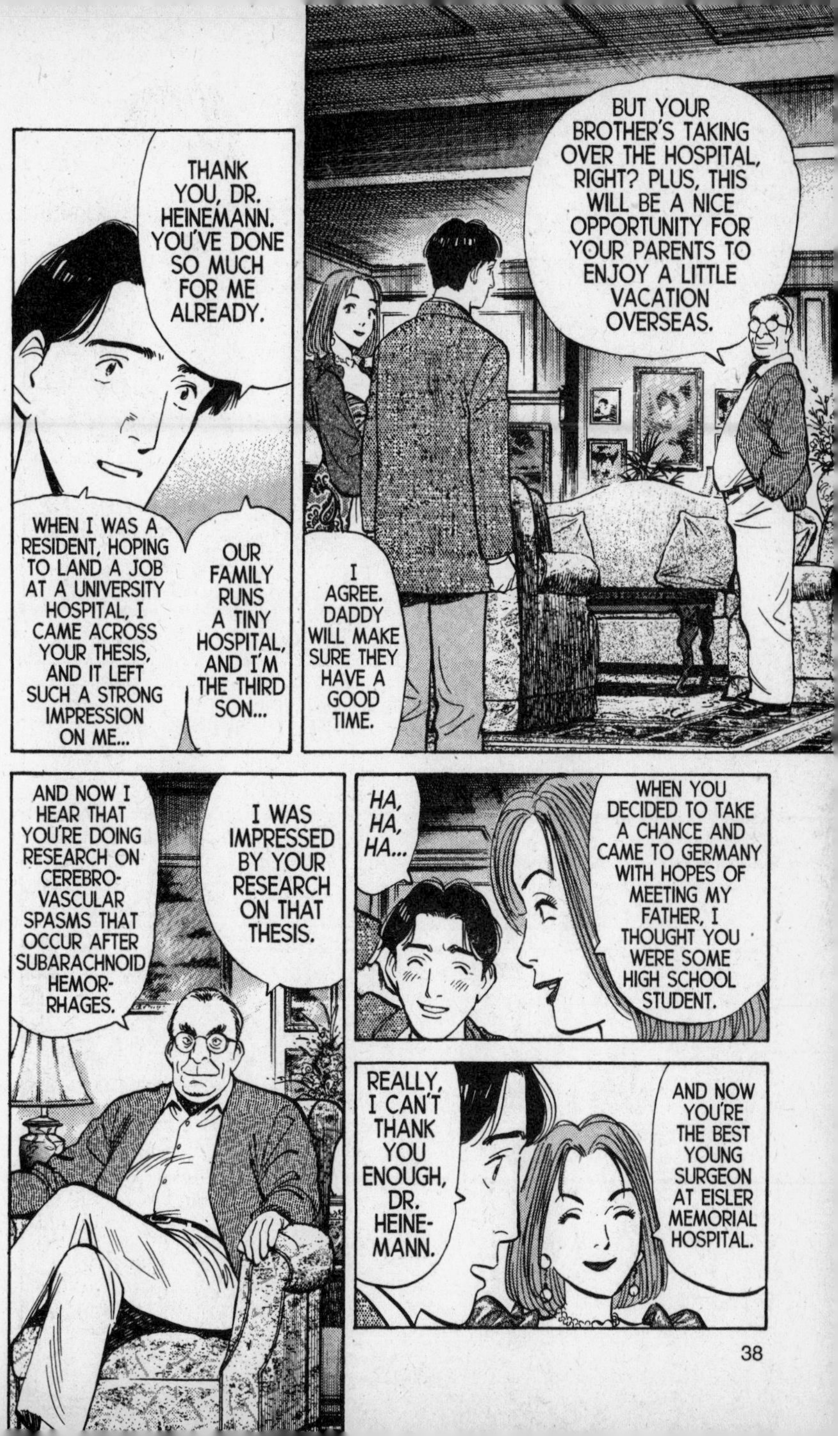
BUT YOUR BROTHER'S TAKING OVER THE HOSPITAL, RIGHT? PLUS, THIS WILL BE A NICE OPPORTUNITY FOR YOUR PARENTS TO ENJOY A LITTLE VACATION OVERSEAS.
I AGREE. DADDY WILL MAKE SURE THEY HAVE A GOOD TIME.
THANK YOU, DR. HEINEMANN. YOU'VE DONE SO MUCH FOR ME ALREADY.
OUR FAMILY RUNS A TINY HOSPITAL, AND I'M THE THIRD SON...
WHEN I WAS A RESIDENT, HOPING TO LAND A JOB AT A UNIVERSITY HOSPITAL, I CAME ACROSS YOUR THESIS, AND IT LEFT SUCH A STRONG IMPRESSION ON ME...
WHEN YOU DECIDED TO TAKE A CHANCE AND CAME TO GERMANY WITH HOPES OF MEETING MY FATHER, I THOUGHT YOU WERE SOME HIGH SCHOOL STUDENT.
HA, HA, HA...
AND NOW YOU'RE THE BEST YOUNG SURGEON AT EISLER MEMORIAL HOSPITAL.
REALLY, I CAN'T THANK YOU ENOUGH, DR. HEINE-MANN.
I WAS IMPRESSED BY YOUR RESEARCH ON THAT THESIS.
AND NOW I HEAR THAT YOU'RE DOING RESEARCH ON CEREBRO-VASCULAR SPASMS THAT OCCUR AFTER SUBARACHNOID HEMOR-RHAGES.

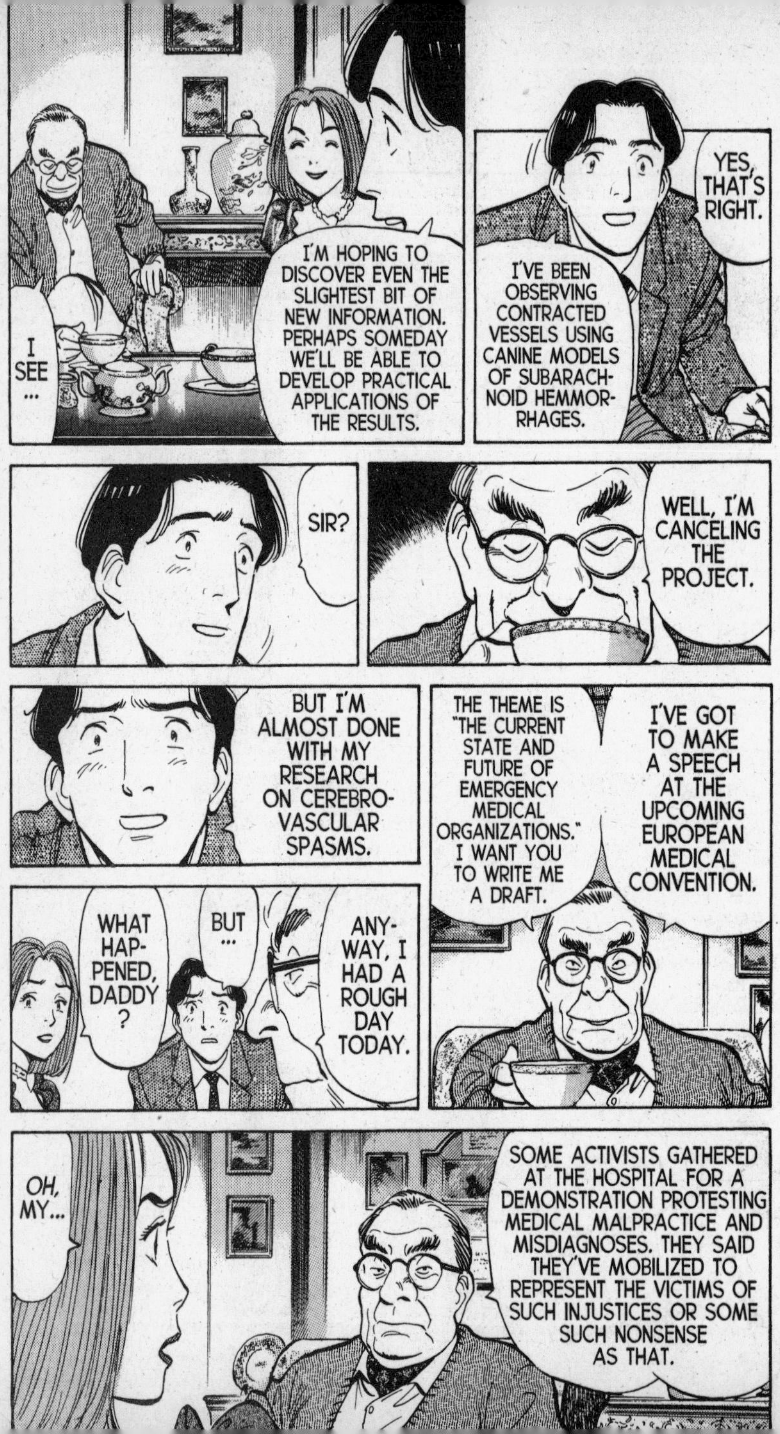
YES, THAT'S RIGHT.
I'VE BEEN OBSERVING CONTRACTED VESSELS USING CANINE MODELS OF SUBARACH-NOID HEMMOR-RHAGES.
I'M HOPING TO DISCOVER EVEN THE SLIGHTEST BIT OF NEW INFORMATION. PERHAPS SOMEDAY WE'LL BE ABLE TO DEVELOP PRACTICAL APPLICATIONS OF THE RESULTS.
I SEE ...
WELL, I'M CANCELING THE PROJECT.
SIR?
I'VE GOT TO MAKE A SPEECH AT THE UPCOMING EUROPEAN MEDICAL CONVENTION.
THE THEME IS "THE CURRENT STATE AND FUTURE OF EMERGENCY MEDICAL ORGANIZATIONS." I WANT YOU TO WRITE ME A DRAFT.
BUT I'M ALMOST DONE WITH MY RESEARCH ON CEREBRO-VASCULAR SPASMS.
ANY-WAY, I HAD A ROUGH DAY TODAY.
BUT ...
WHAT HAP-PENED, DADDY ?
SOME ACTIVISTS GATHERED AT THE HOSPITAL FOR A DEMONSTRATION PROTESTING MEDICAL MALPRACTICE AND MISDIAGNOSES. THEY SAID THEY'VE MOBILIZED TO REPRESENT THE VICTIMS OF SUCH INJUSTICES OR SOME SUCH NONSENSE AS THAT.
OH, MY...

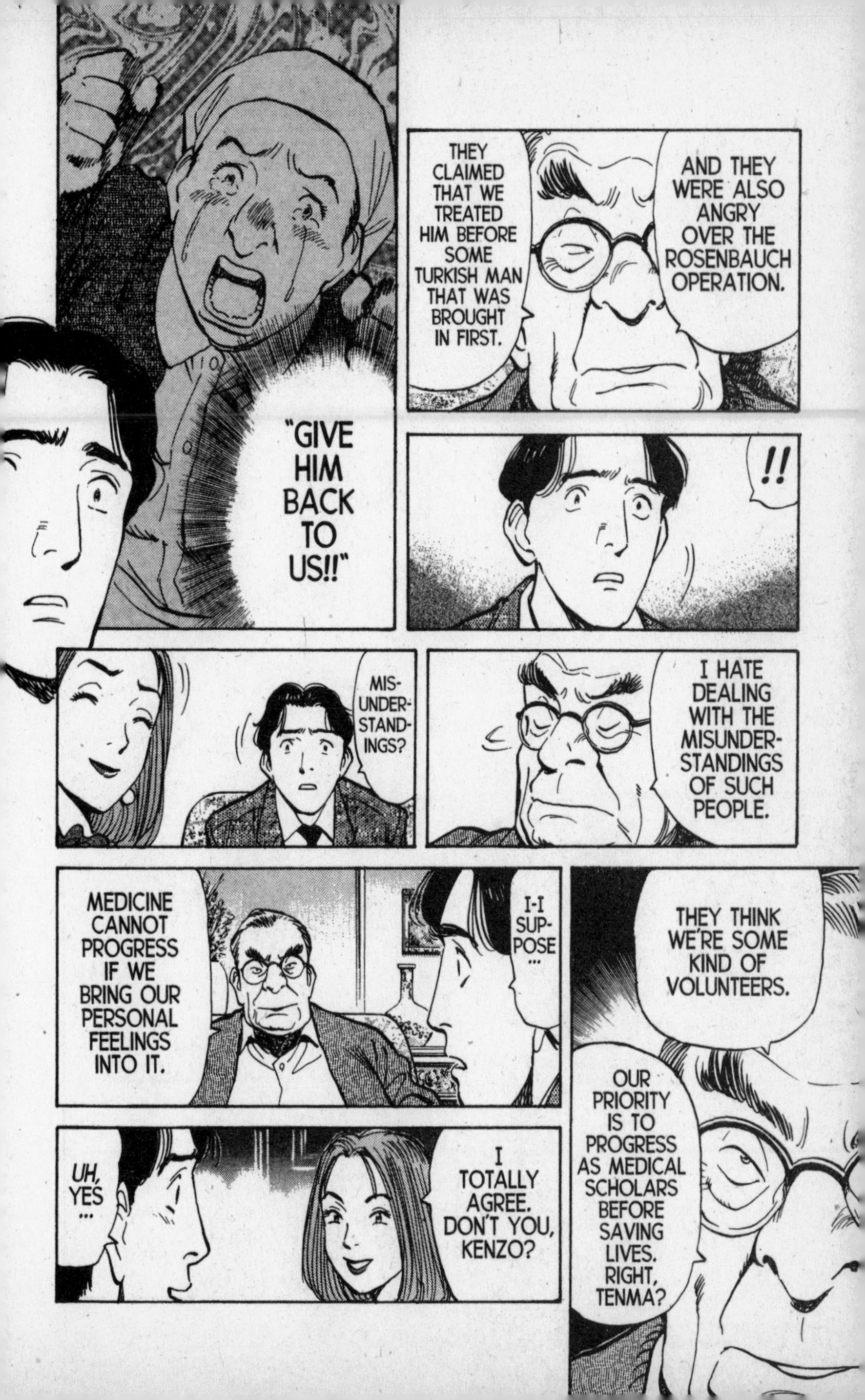

AND THEY WERE ALSO ANGRY OVER THE ROSENBAUCH OPERATION.
THEY CLAIMED THAT WE TREATED HIM BEFORE SOME TURKISH MAN THAT WAS BROUGHT IN FIRST.
!!
"GIVE HIM BACK TO US!!"
I HATE DEALING WITH THE MISUNDER-STANDINGS OF SUCH PEOPLE.
MIS-UNDER-STAND-INGS?
THEY THINK WE'RE SOME KIND OF VOLUNTEERS.
OUR PRIORITY IS TO PROGRESS AS MEDICAL SCHOLARS BEFORE SAVING LIVES. RIGHT, TENMA?
I-I SUP-POSE...
MEDICINE CANNOT PROGRESS IF WE BRING OUR PERSONAL FEELINGS INTO IT.
I TOTALLY AGREE. DON'T YOU, KENZO?
UH, YES...

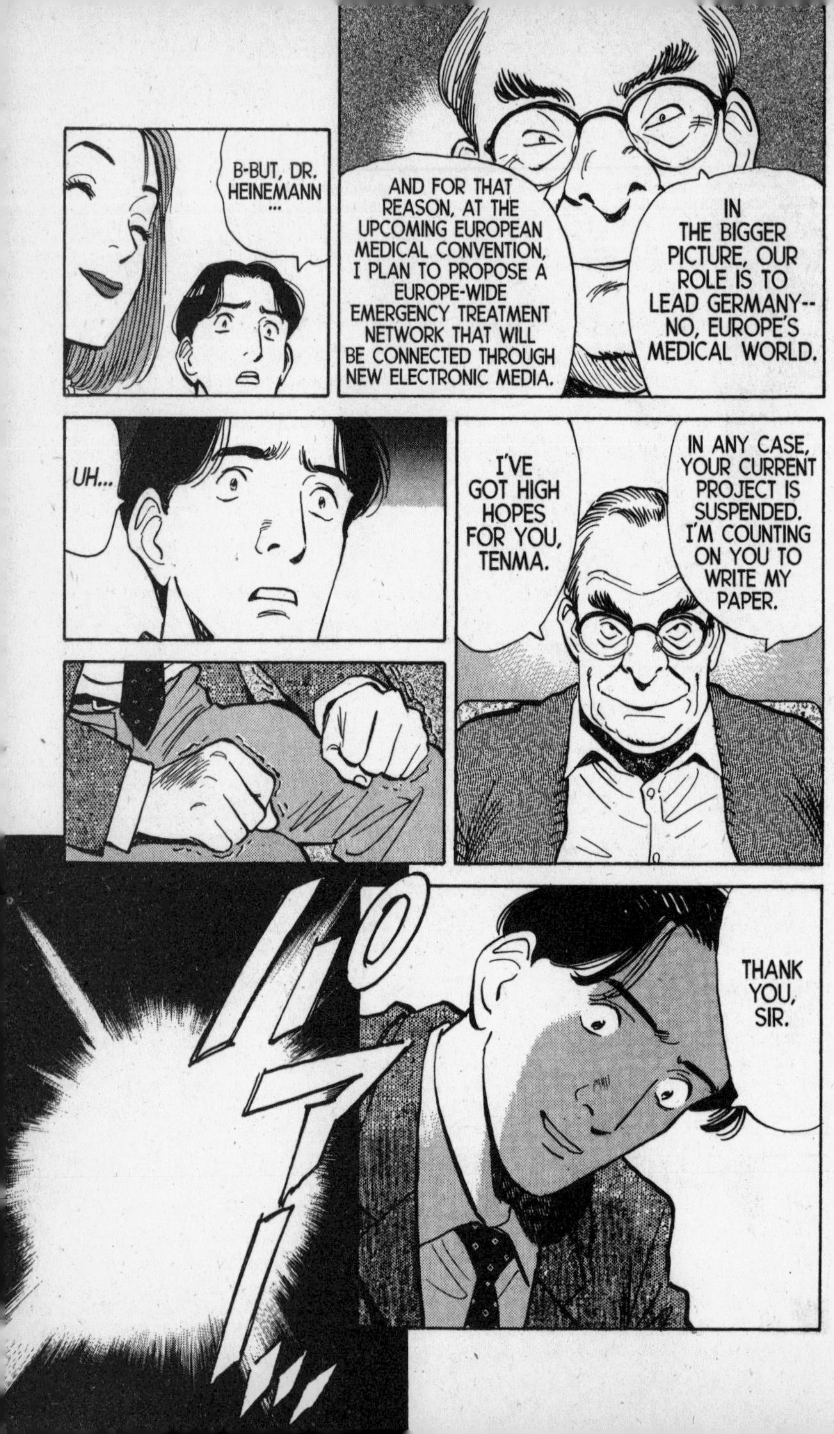
IN THE BIGGER PICTURE, OUR ROLE IS TO LEAD GERMANY-- NO, EUROPE'S MEDICAL WORLD.
AND FOR THAT REASON, AT THE UPCOMING EUROPEAN MEDICAL CONVENTION, I PLAN TO PROPOSE A EUROPE-WIDE EMERGENCY TREATMENT NETWORK THAT WILL BE CONNECTED THROUGH NEW ELECTRONIC MEDIA.
B-BUT, DR. HEINEMANN...
IN ANY CASE, YOUR CURRENT PROJECT IS SUSPENDED. I'M COUNTING ON YOU TO WRITE MY PAPER.
I'VE GOT HIGH HOPES FOR YOU, TENMA.
UH...
THANK YOU, SIR.

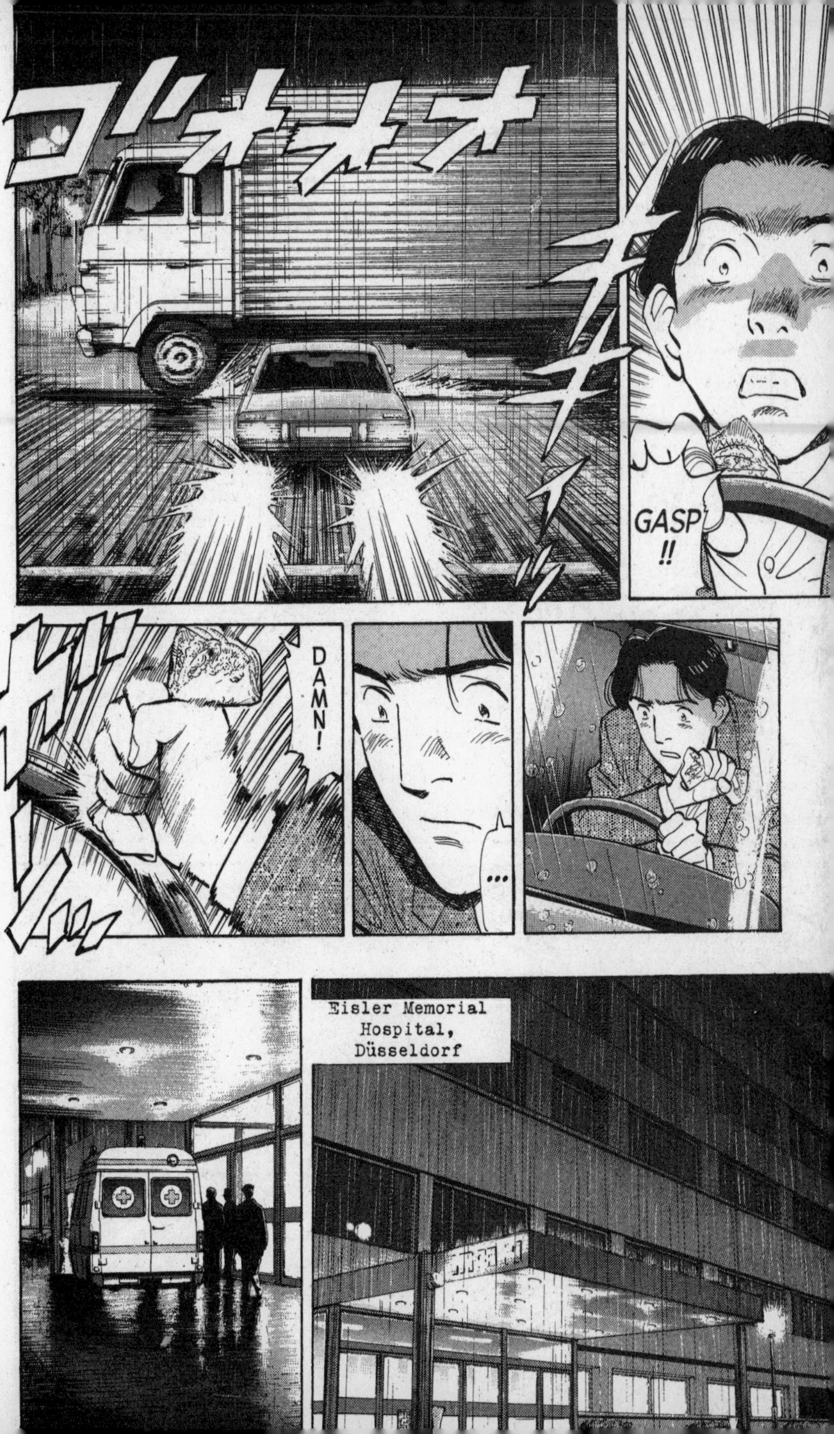
GASP!!
...
DAMN!
Eisler Memorial Hospital, Düsseldorf

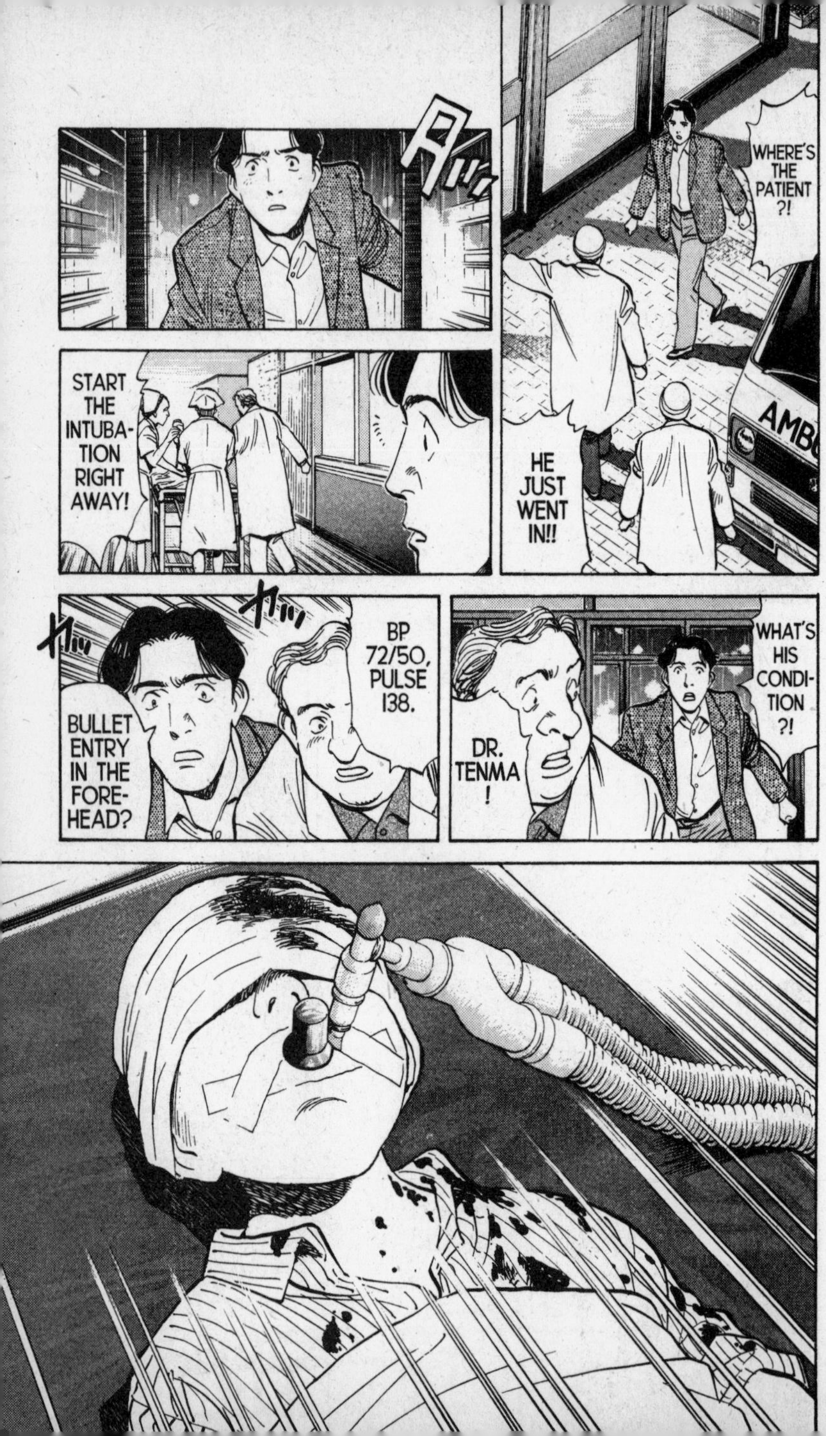
WHERE'S THE PATIENT ?!
HE JUST WENT IN!!
START THE INTUBATION RIGHT AWAY!
WHAT'S HIS CONDITION ?!
DR. TENMA!
BP 72/50, PULSE 138.
BULLET ENTRY IN THE FOREHEAD?

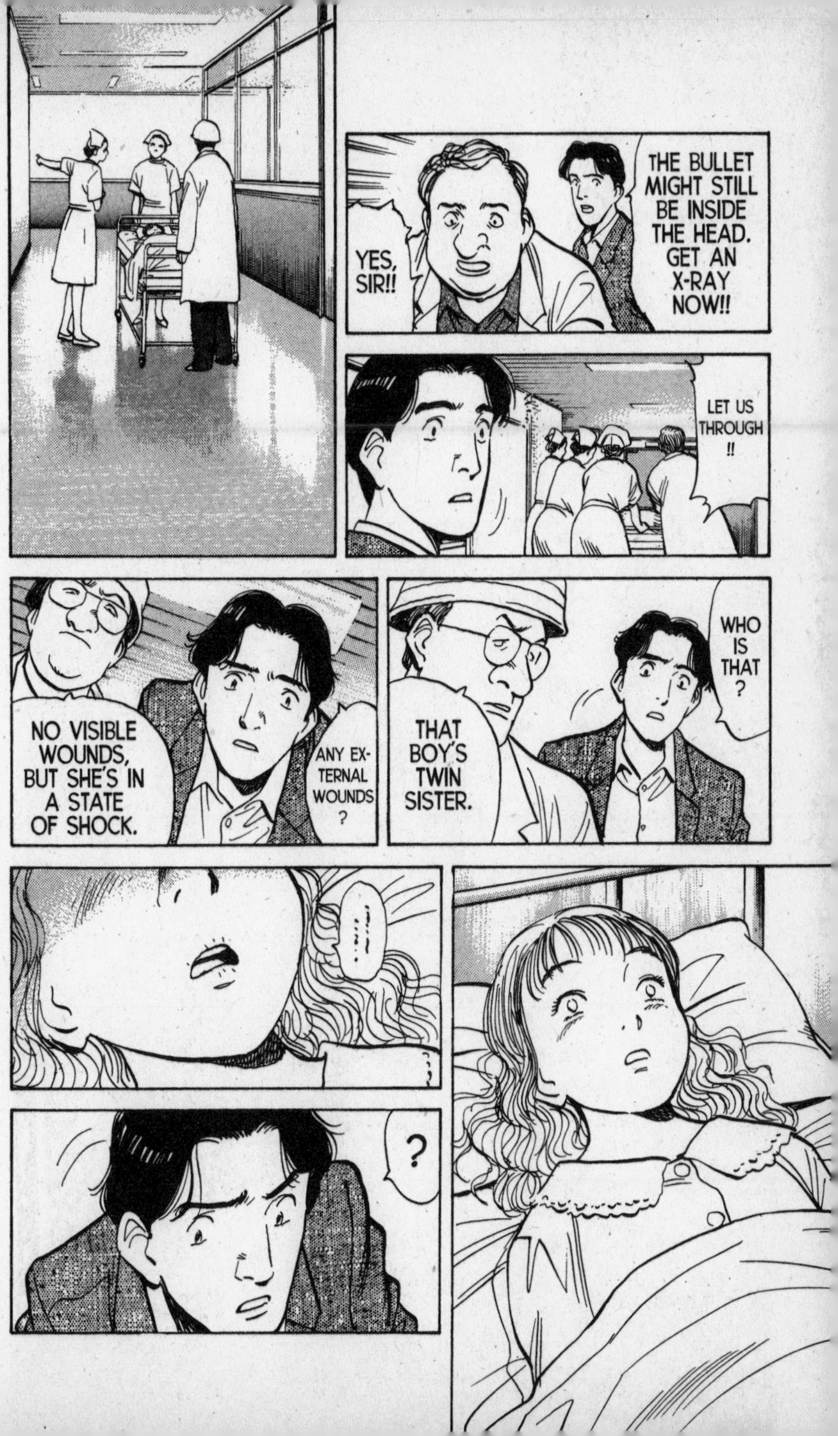
THE BULLET MIGHT STILL BE INSIDE THE HEAD. GET AN X-RAY NOW!!
YES, SIR!!
LET US THROUGH !!
WHO IS THAT ?
THAT BOY'S TWIN SISTER.
ANY EX-TERNAL WOUNDS ?
NO VISIBLE WOUNDS, BUT SHE'S IN A STATE OF SHOCK.
?

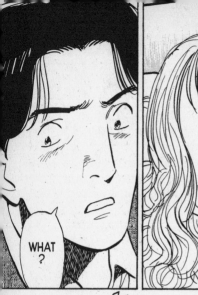

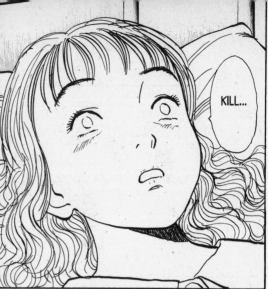

KILL...
WHAT?
DR. TENMA, THE CRANIAL SHOTS AND CT SCANS ARE READY IN THE X-RAY ROOM.
YES.
I'LL BE RIGHT THERE.

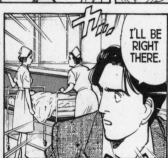

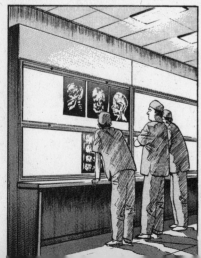

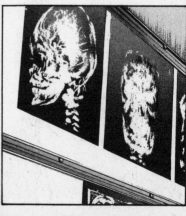

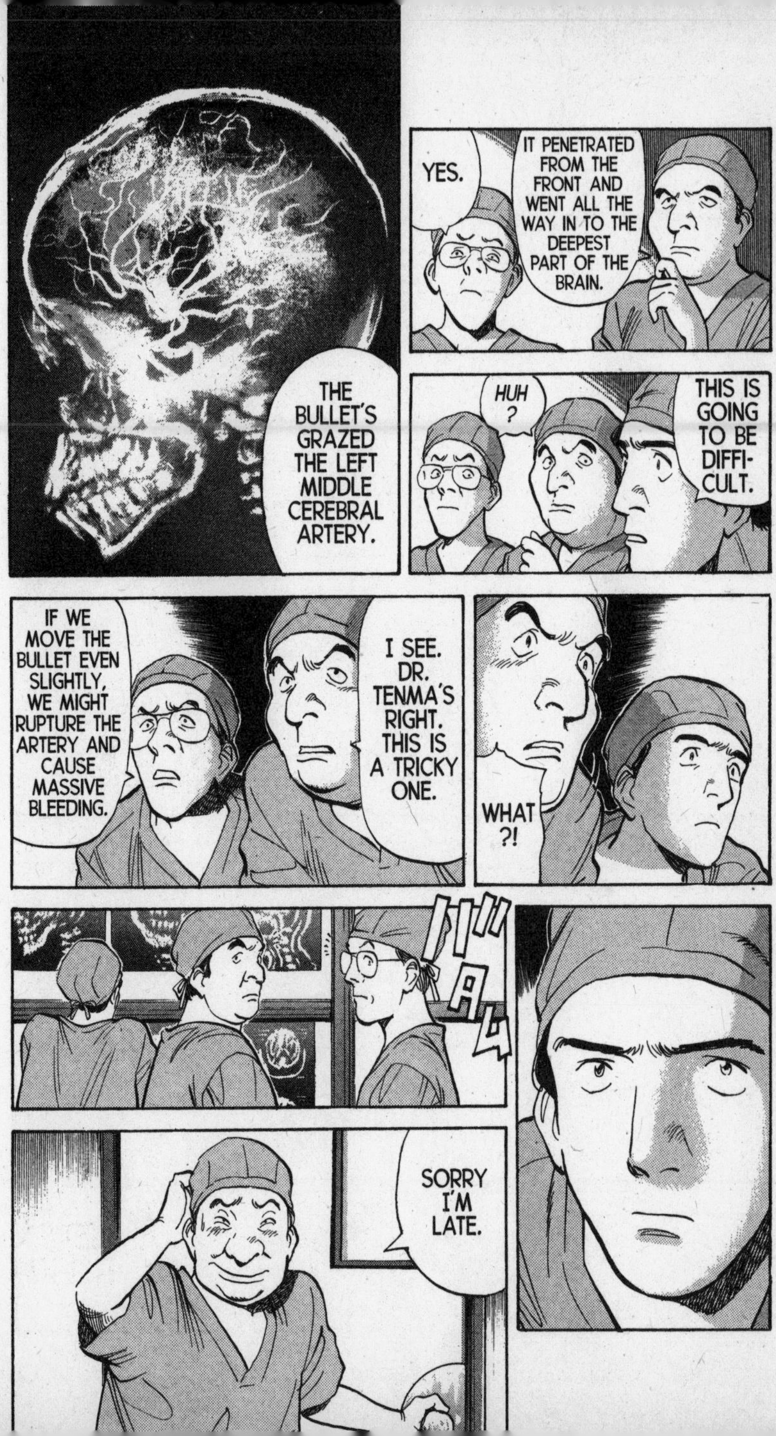
IT PENETRATED FROM THE FRONT AND WENT ALL THE WAY IN TO THE DEEPEST PART OF THE BRAIN.
YES.
THIS IS GOING TO BE DIFFI-CULT.
HUH?
THE BULLET'S GRAZED THE LEFT MIDDLE CEREBRAL ARTERY.
WHAT?!
I SEE. DR. TENMA'S RIGHT. THIS IS A TRICKY ONE.
IF WE MOVE THE BULLET EVEN SLIGHTLY, WE MIGHT RUPTURE THE ARTERY AND CAUSE MASSIVE BLEEDING.
SORRY I'M LATE.

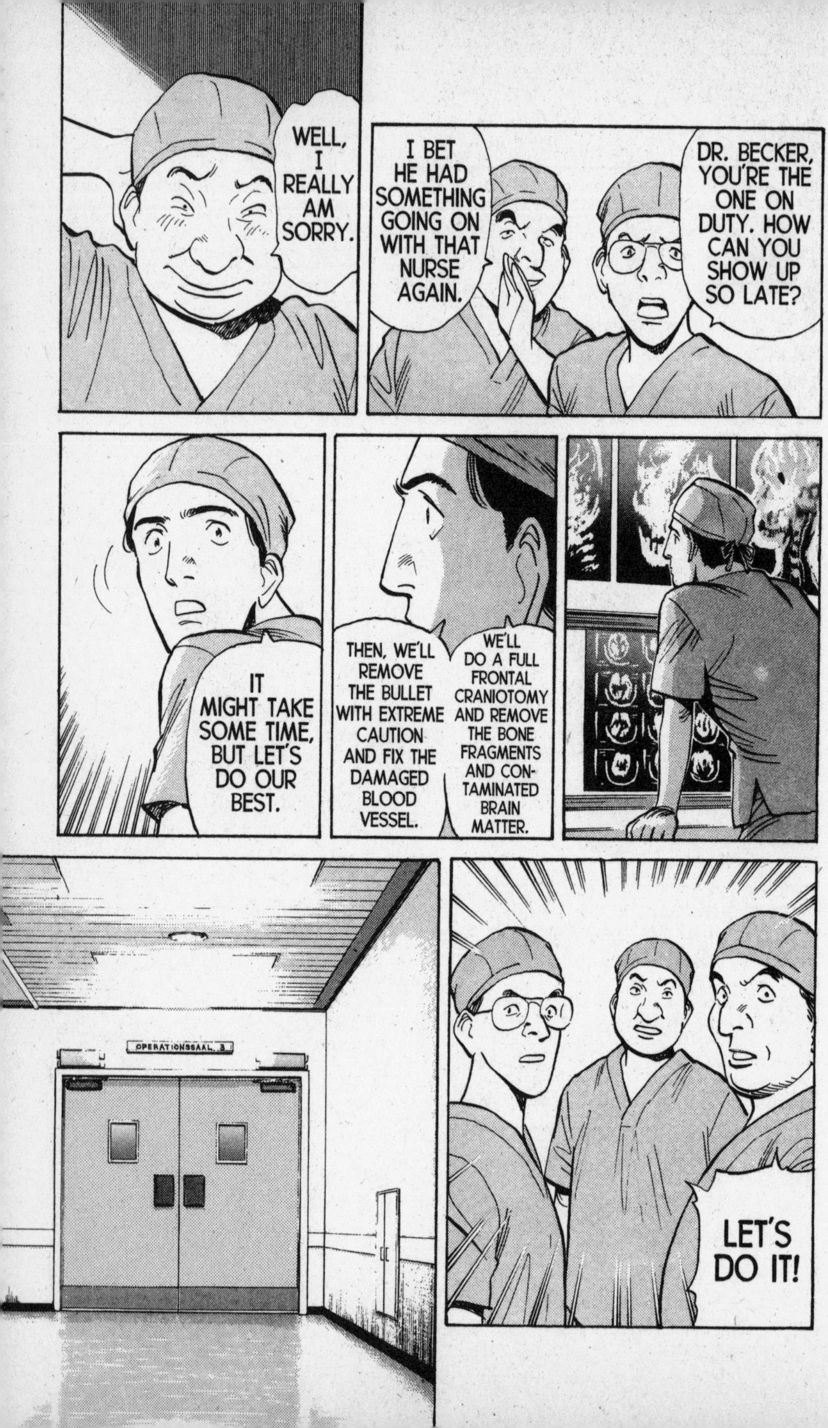
DR. BECKER, YOU'RE THE ONE ON DUTY. HOW CAN YOU SHOW UP SO LATE?
I BET HE HAD SOMETHING GOING ON WITH THAT NURSE AGAIN.
WELL, I REALLY AM SORRY.
WE'LL DO A FULL FRONTAL CRANIOTOMY AND REMOVE THE BONE FRAGMENTS AND CONTAMINATED BRAIN MATTER.
THEN, WE'LL REMOVE THE BULLET WITH EXTREME CAUTION AND FIX THE DAMAGED BLOOD VESSEL.
IT MIGHT TAKE SOME TIME, BUT LET'S DO OUR BEST.
LET'S DO IT!
OPERATIONSSAAL 3

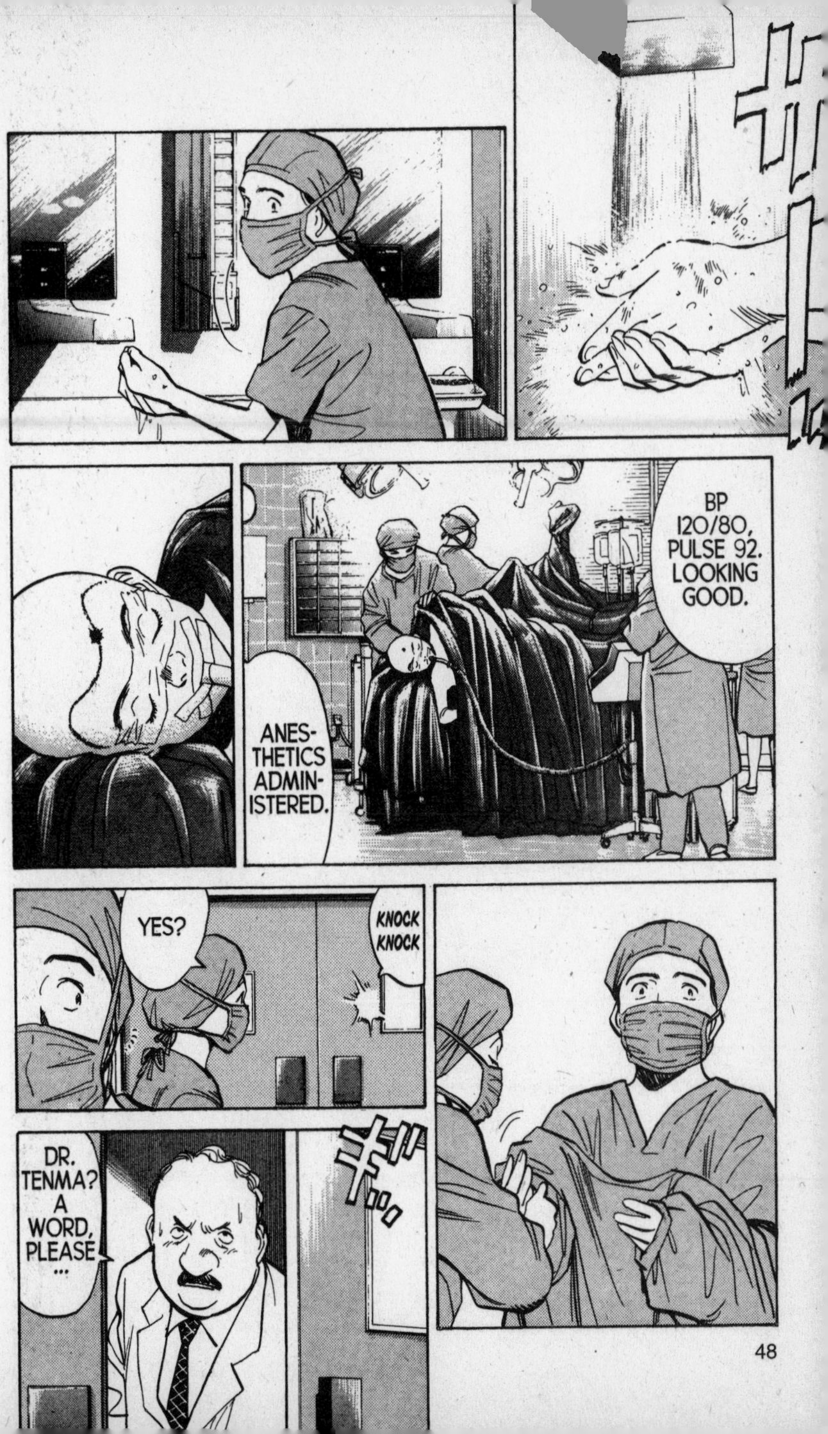
BP 120/80, PULSE 92. LOOKING GOOD.
ANES-THETICS ADMIN-ISTERED.
KNOCK KNOCK
YES?
DR. TENMA? A WORD, PLEASE ...

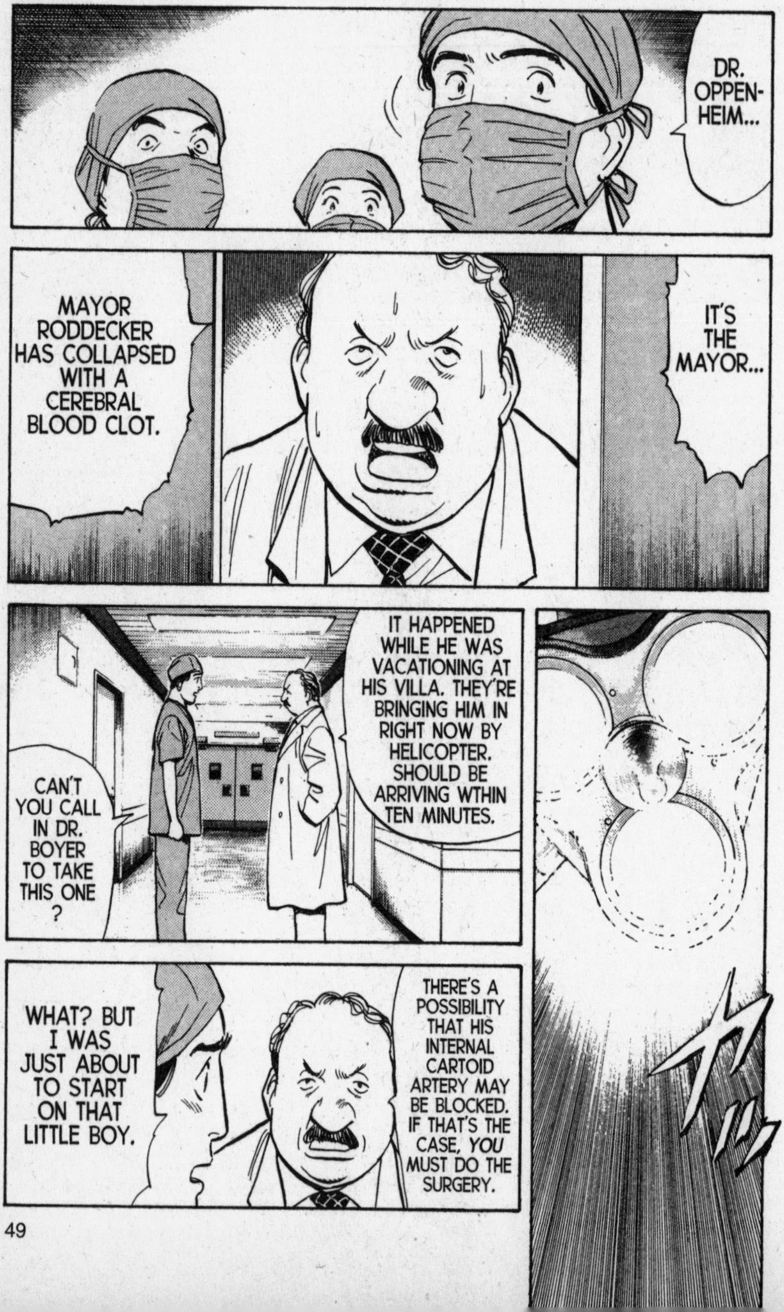
DR. OPPEN-HEIM...
IT'S THE MAYOR...
MAYOR RODDECKER HAS COLLAPSED WITH A CEREBRAL BLOOD CLOT.
IT HAPPENED WHILE HE WAS VACATIONING AT HIS VILLA. THEY'RE BRINGING HIM IN RIGHT NOW BY HELICOPTER. SHOULD BE ARRIVING WTHIN TEN MINUTES.
CAN'T YOU CALL IN DR. BOYER TO TAKE THIS ONE ?
THERE'S A POSSIBILITY THAT HIS INTERNAL CARTOID ARTERY MAY BE BLOCKED. IF THAT'S THE CASE, *YOU* MUST DO THE SURGERY.
WHAT? BUT I WAS JUST ABOUT TO START ON THAT LITTLE BOY.

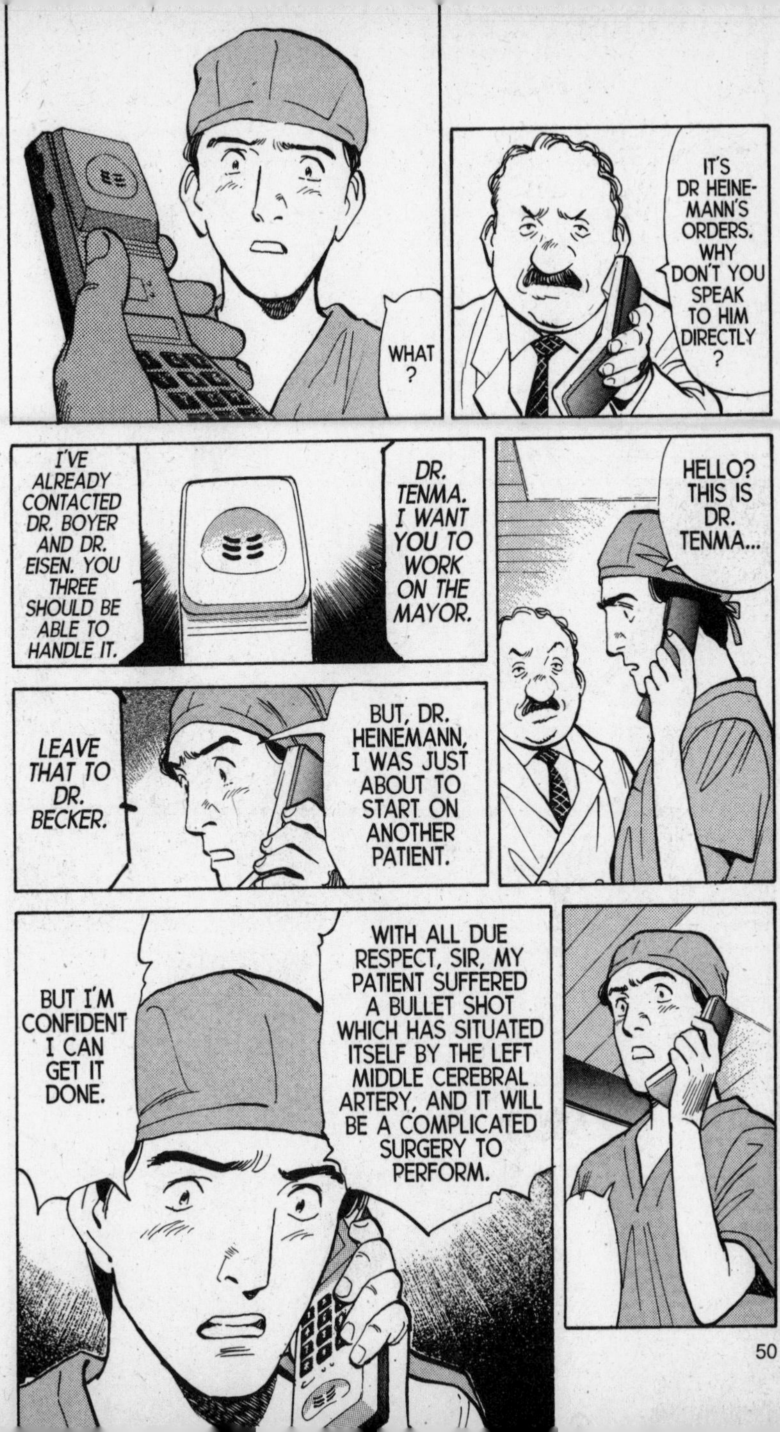
IT'S DR HEINE-MANN'S ORDERS. WHY DON'T YOU SPEAK TO HIM DIRECTLY ?
WHAT ?
HELLO? THIS IS DR. TENMA...
DR. TENMA. I WANT YOU TO WORK ON THE MAYOR.
I'VE ALREADY CONTACTED DR. BOYER AND DR. EISEN. YOU THREE SHOULD BE ABLE TO HANDLE IT.
BUT, DR. HEINEMANN, I WAS JUST ABOUT TO START ON ANOTHER PATIENT.
LEAVE THAT TO DR. BECKER.
WITH ALL DUE RESPECT, SIR, MY PATIENT SUFFERED A BULLET SHOT WHICH HAS SITUATED ITSELF BY THE LEFT MIDDLE CEREBRAL ARTERY, AND IT WILL BE A COMPLICATED SURGERY TO PERFORM.
BUT I'M CONFIDENT I CAN GET IT DONE.

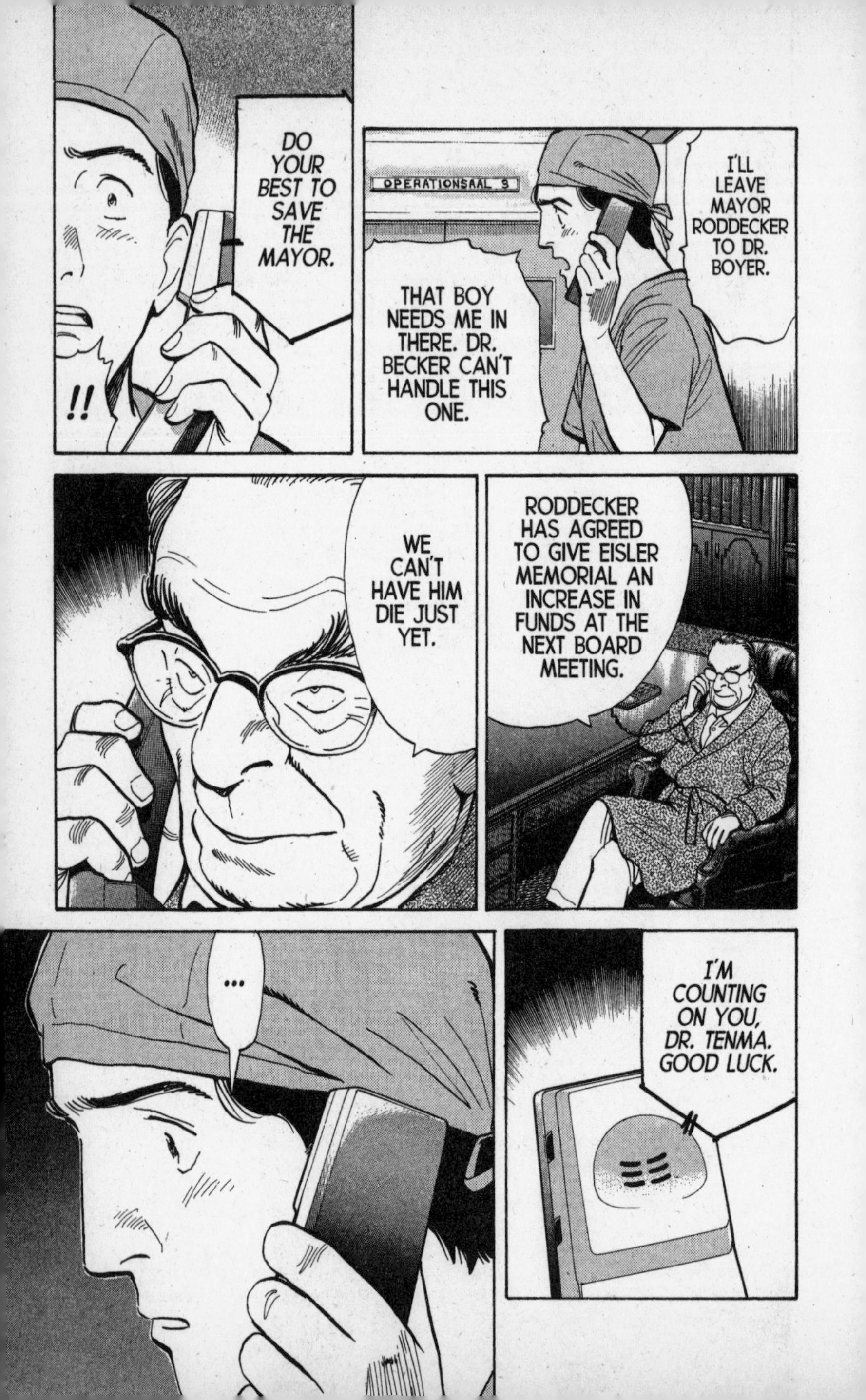
OPERATIONSAAL 3
I'LL LEAVE MAYOR RODDECKER TO DR. BOYER.
THAT BOY NEEDS ME IN THERE. DR. BECKER CAN'T HANDLE THIS ONE.
DO YOUR BEST TO SAVE THE MAYOR.
!!
RODDECKER HAS AGREED TO GIVE EISLER MEMORIAL AN INCREASE IN FUNDS AT THE NEXT BOARD MEETING.
WE CAN'T HAVE HIM DIE JUST YET.
I'M COUNTING ON YOU, DR. TENMA. GOOD LUCK.
...

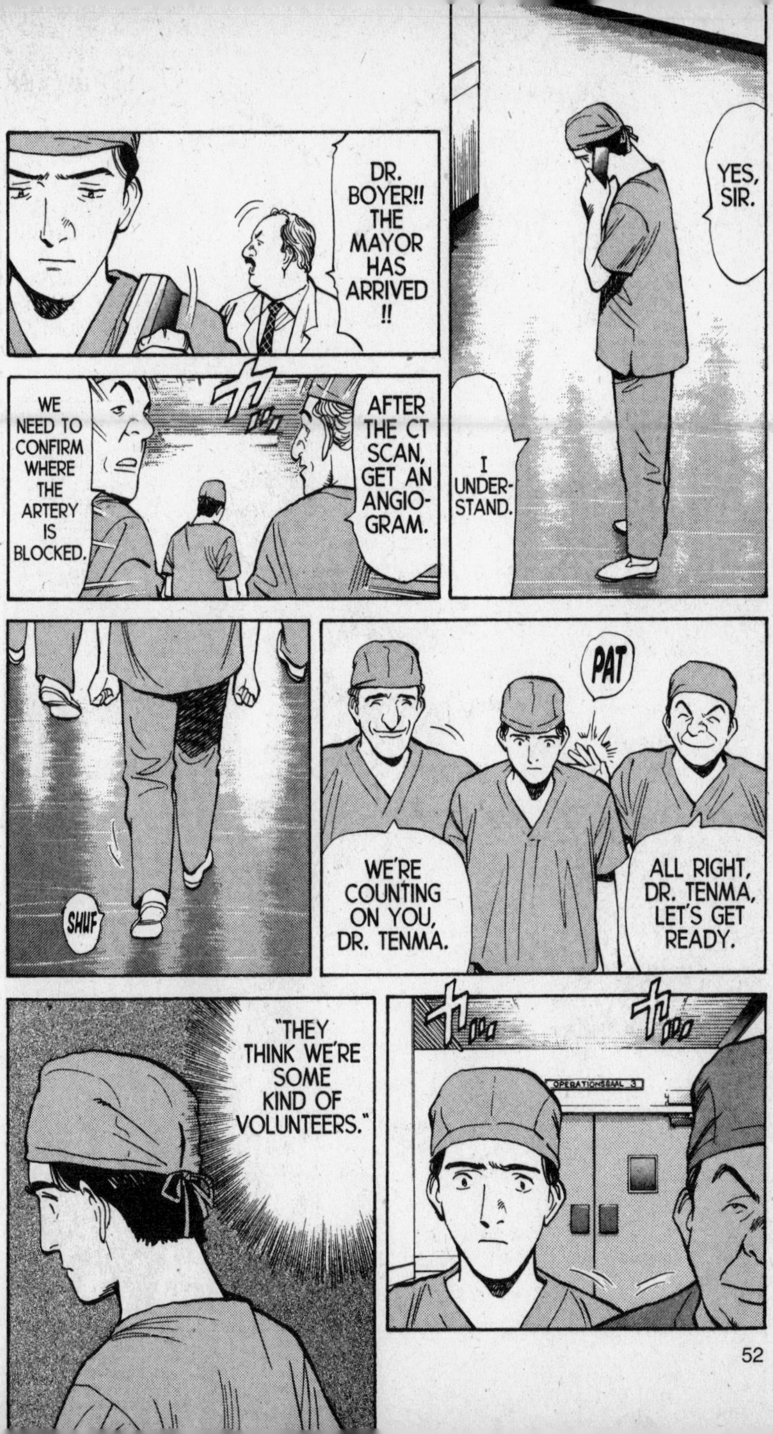
YES, SIR.
I UNDER-STAND.
DR. BOYER!! THE MAYOR HAS ARRIVED!!
AFTER THE CT SCAN, GET AN ANGIO-GRAM.
WE NEED TO CONFIRM WHERE THE ARTERY IS BLOCKED.
PAT
ALL RIGHT, DR. TENMA, LET'S GET READY.
WE'RE COUNTING ON YOU, DR. TENMA.
SHUF
OPERATIONSSAAL 3
"THEY THINK WE'RE SOME KIND OF VOLUNTEERS."

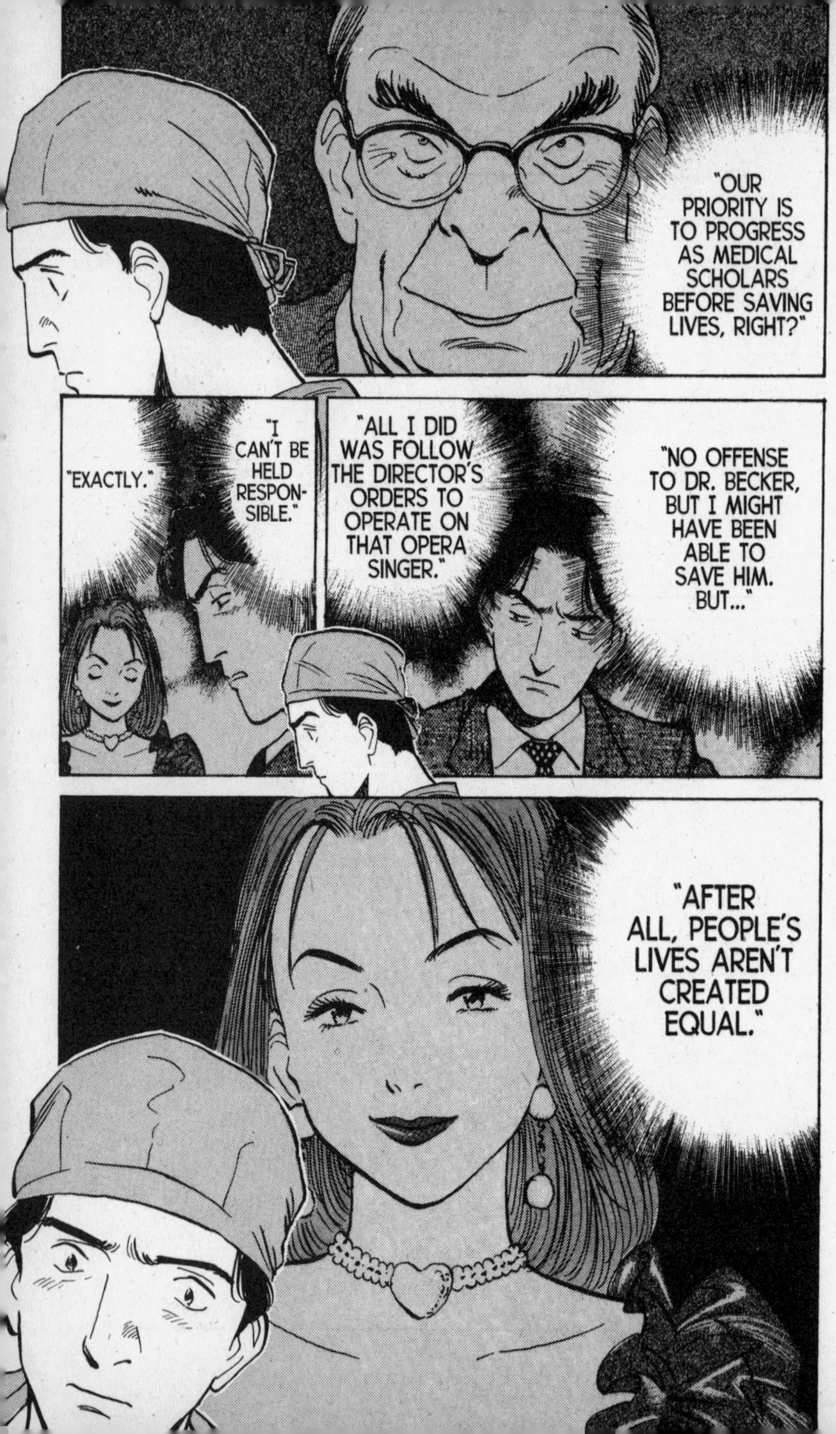
"OUR PRIORITY IS TO PROGRESS AS MEDICAL SCHOLARS BEFORE SAVING LIVES, RIGHT?"
"NO OFFENSE TO DR. BECKER, BUT I MIGHT HAVE BEEN ABLE TO SAVE HIM. BUT..."
"ALL I DID WAS FOLLOW THE DIRECTOR'S ORDERS TO OPERATE ON THAT OPERA SINGER."
"I CAN'T BE HELD RESPON-SIBLE."
"EXACTLY."
"AFTER ALL, PEOPLE'S LIVES AREN'T CREATED EQUAL."

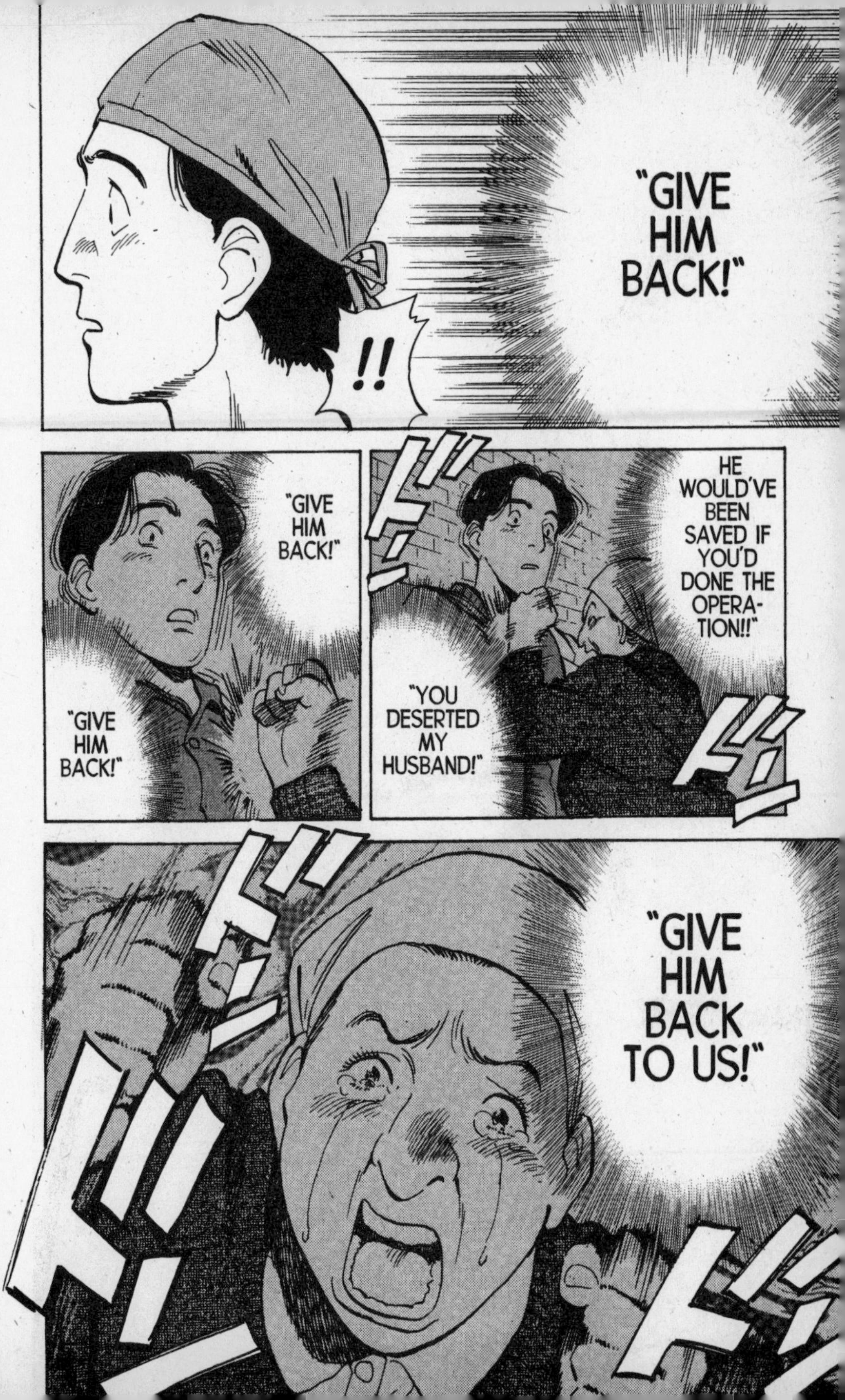
"GIVE HIM BACK!"
!!
HE WOULD'VE BEEN SAVED IF YOU'D DONE THE OPERATION!!"
"YOU DESERTED MY HUSBAND!"
"GIVE HIM BACK!"
"GIVE HIM BACK!"
"GIVE HIM BACK TO US!"

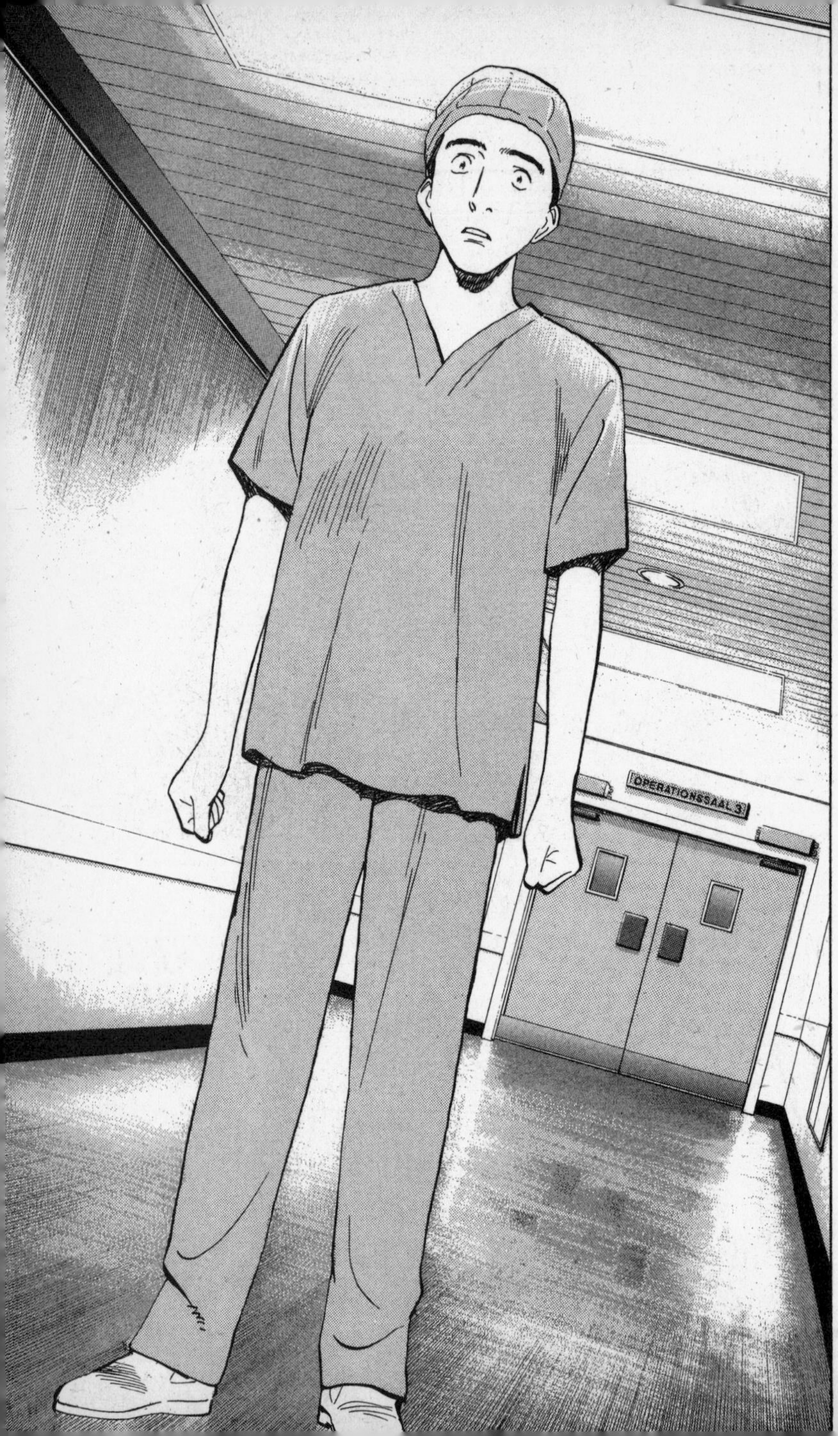
OPERATIONSSAAL 3

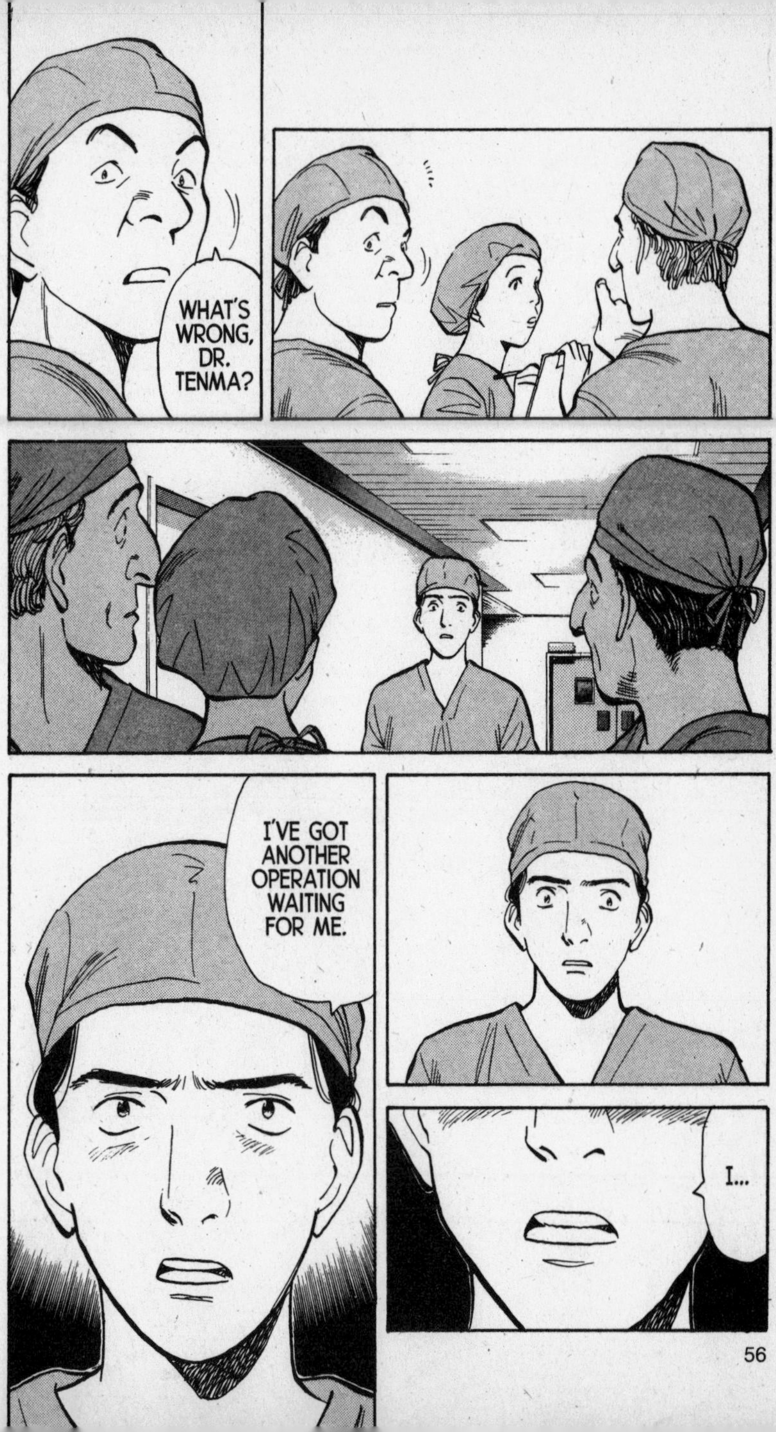
WHAT'S WRONG, DR. TENMA?
I...
I'VE GOT ANOTHER OPERATION WAITING FOR ME.

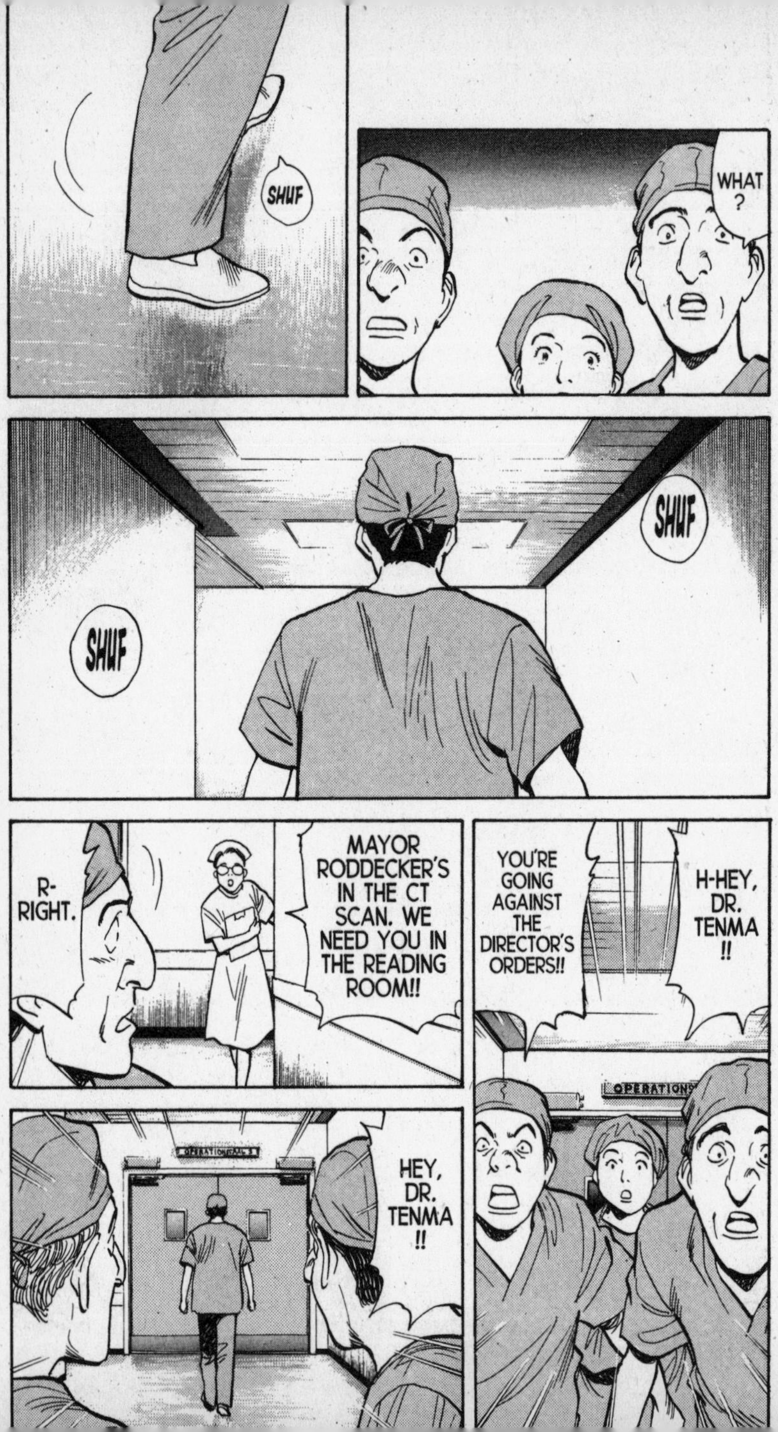
WHAT?
SHUF
SHUF
SHUF
H-HEY, DR. TENMA!!
YOU'RE GOING AGAINST THE DIRECTOR'S ORDERS!!
OPERATIONS
MAYOR RODDECKER'S IN THE CT SCAN. WE NEED YOU IN THE READING ROOM!!
R-RIGHT.
HEY, DR. TENMA!!

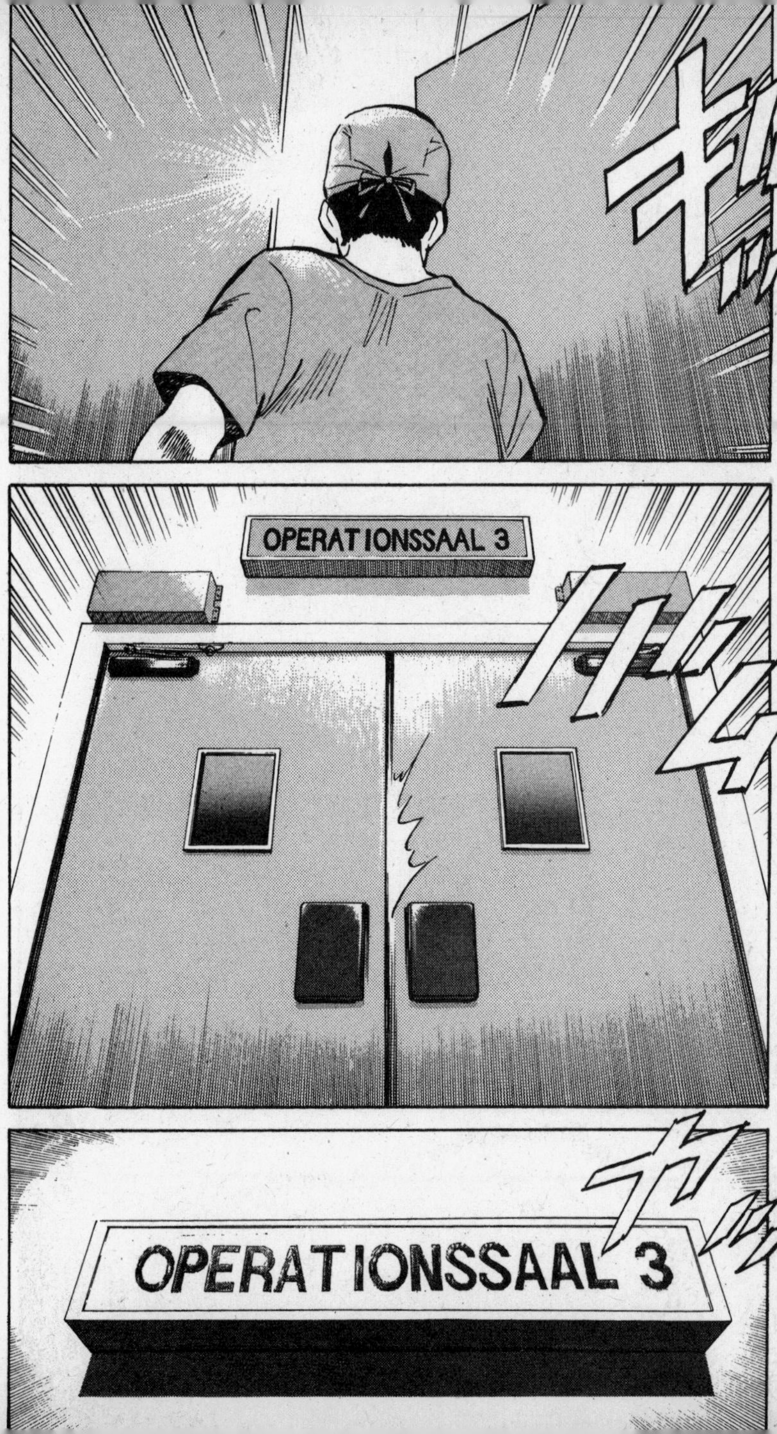
OPERATIONSSAAL 3
OPERATIONSSAAL 3

BEEP
BEEP
BEEP
HANG IN THERE, KID...
I'LL SAVE YOU!!
BEEP
BEEP
BEEP

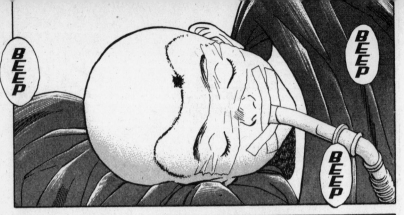

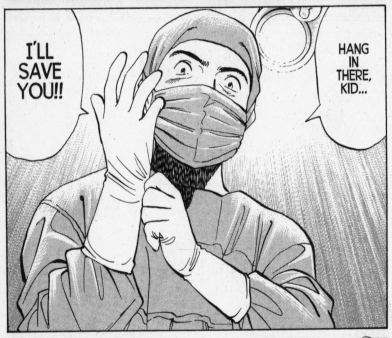

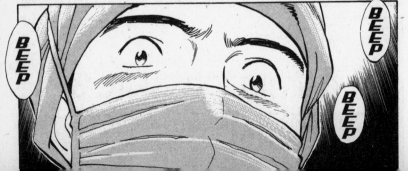

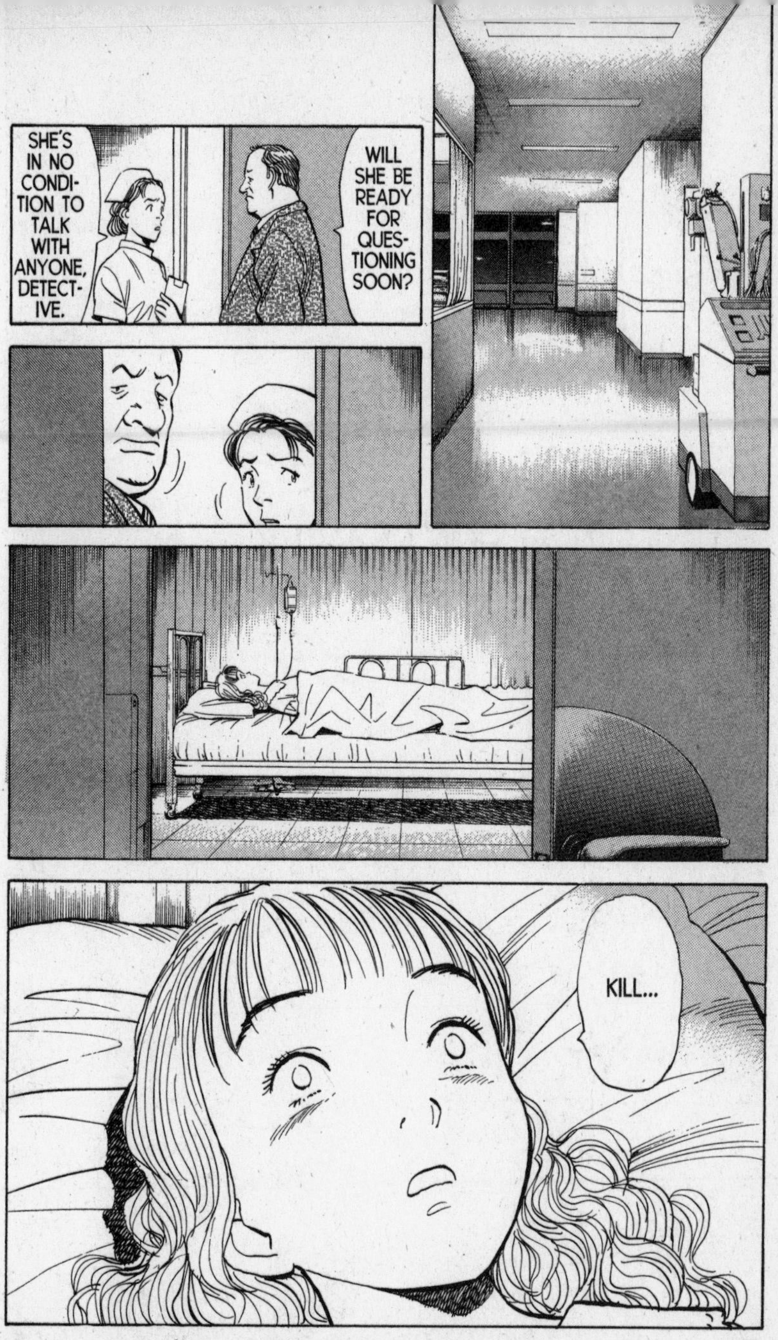
WILL SHE BE READY FOR QUES-TIONING SOON?
SHE'S IN NO CONDI-TION TO TALK WITH ANYONE, DETECT-IVE.
KILL...

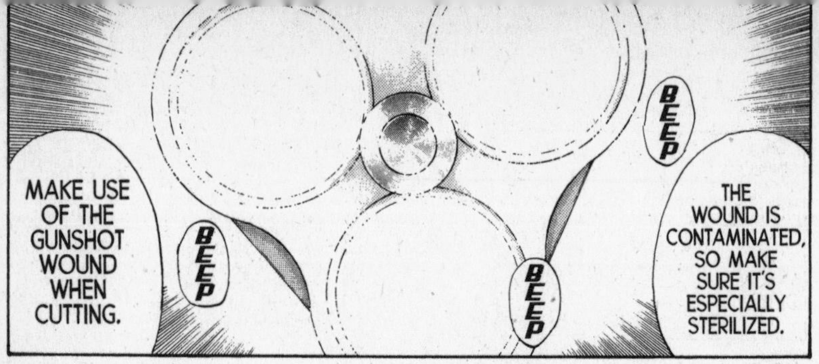
BEEP
THE WOUND IS CONTAMINATED, SO MAKE SURE IT'S ESPECIALLY STERILIZED.
BEEP
BEEP
MAKE USE OF THE GUNSHOT WOUND WHEN CUTTING.

Chapter 3
Downfall

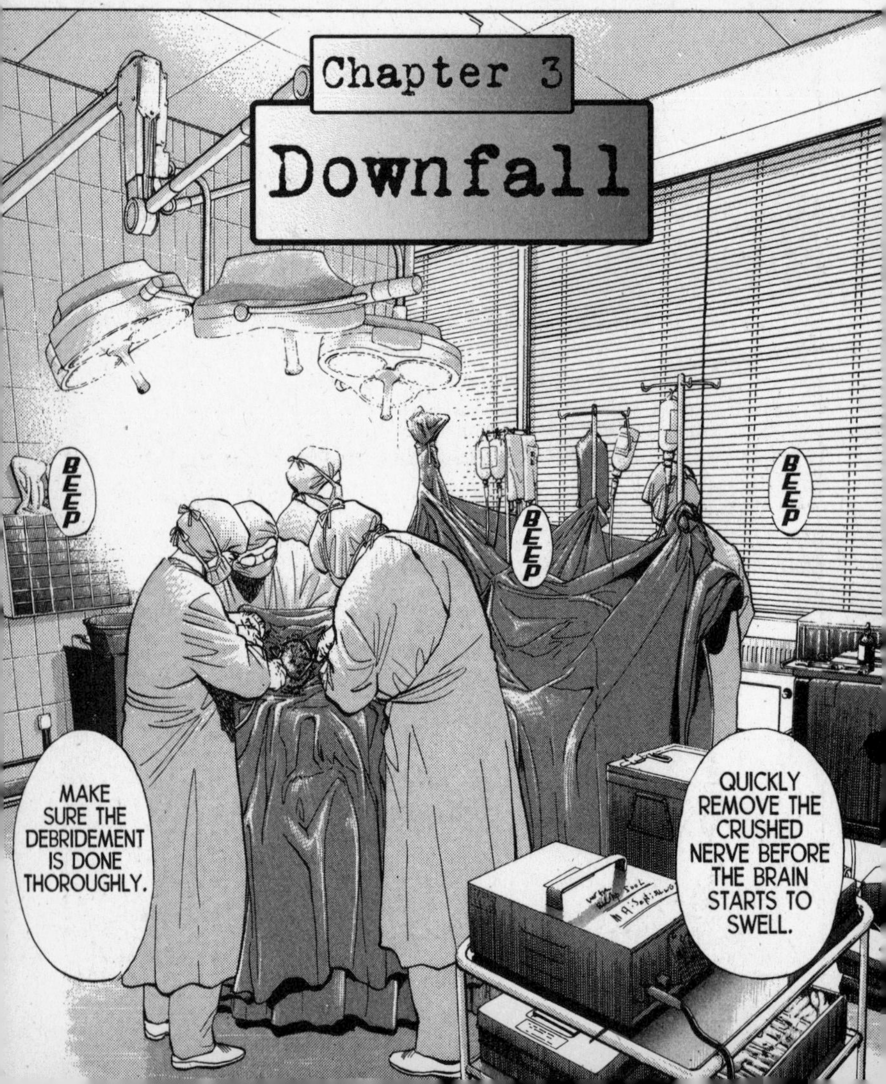
BEEP
BEEP
BEEP
QUICKLY REMOVE THE CRUSHED NERVE BEFORE THE BRAIN STARTS TO SWELL.
MAKE SURE THE DEBRIDEMENT IS DONE THOROUGHLY.

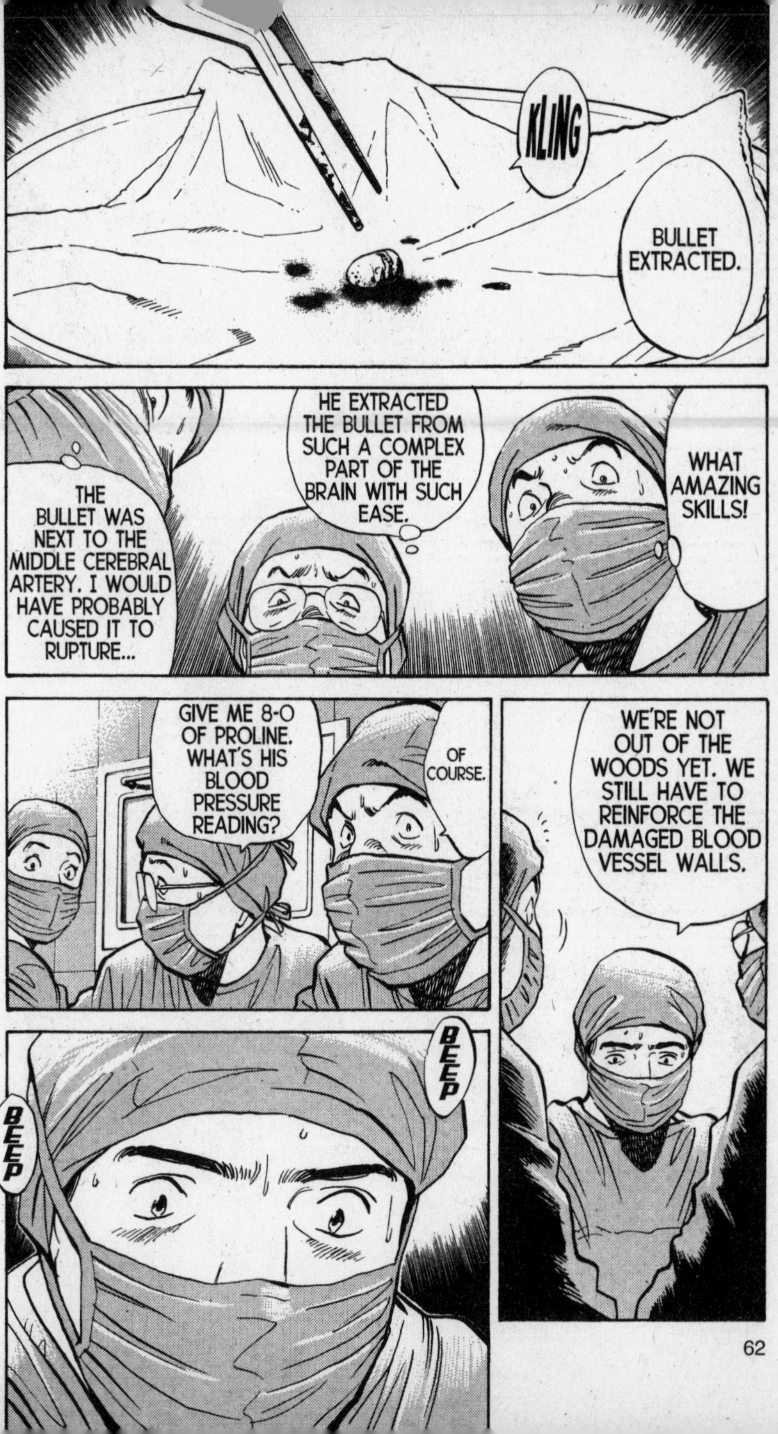
KLING
BULLET EXTRACTED.
WHAT AMAZING SKILLS!
HE EXTRACTED THE BULLET FROM SUCH A COMPLEX PART OF THE BRAIN WITH SUCH EASE.
THE BULLET WAS NEXT TO THE MIDDLE CEREBRAL ARTERY. I WOULD HAVE PROBABLY CAUSED IT TO RUPTURE...
WE'RE NOT OUT OF THE WOODS YET. WE STILL HAVE TO REINFORCE THE DAMAGED BLOOD VESSEL WALLS.
OF COURSE.
GIVE ME 8-O OF PROLINE. WHAT'S HIS BLOOD PRESSURE READING?
BEEP
BEEP

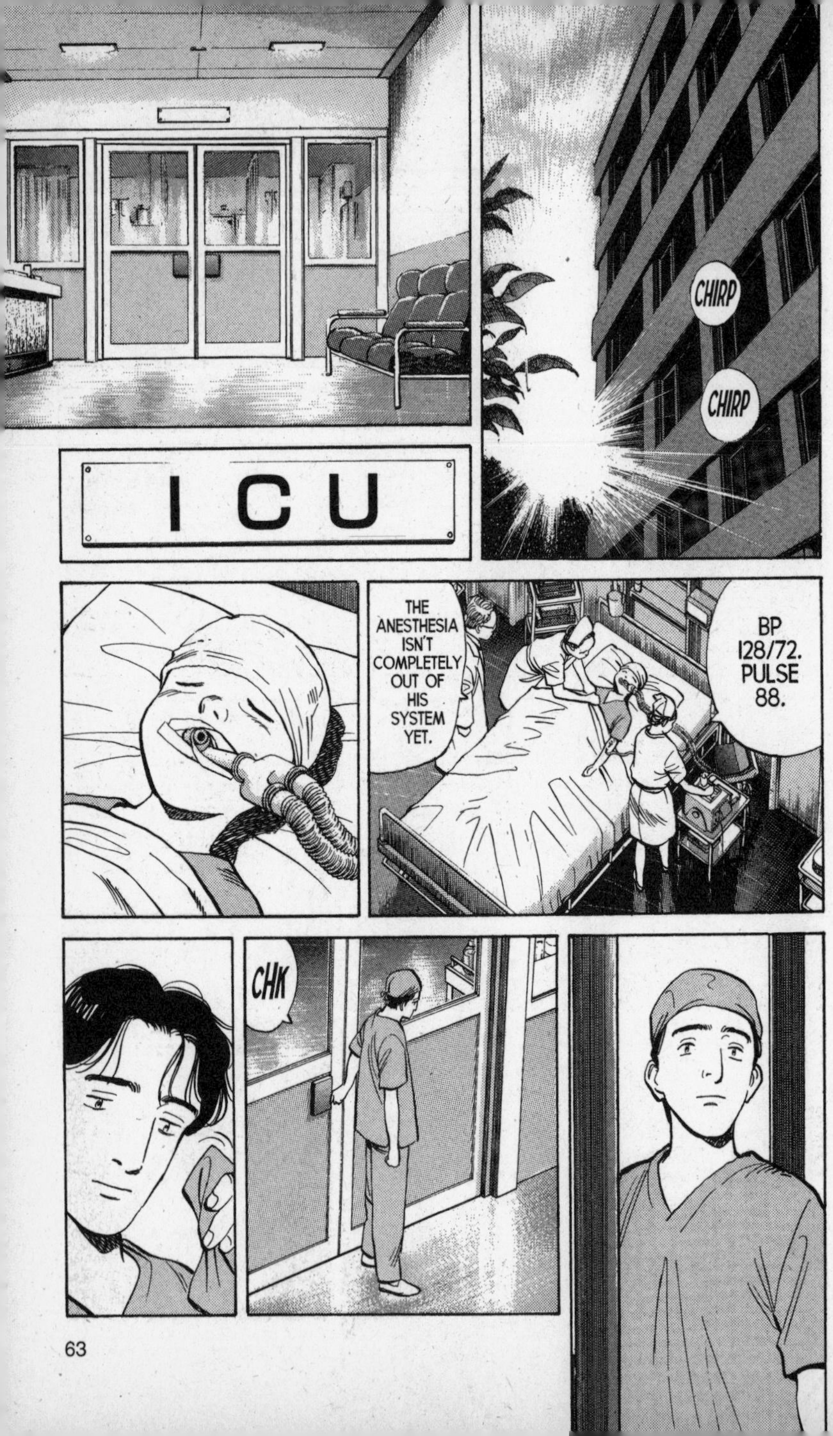
CHIRP
CHIRP
ICU
BP 128/72. PULSE 88.
THE ANESTHESIA ISN'T COMPLETELY OUT OF HIS SYSTEM YET.
CHK

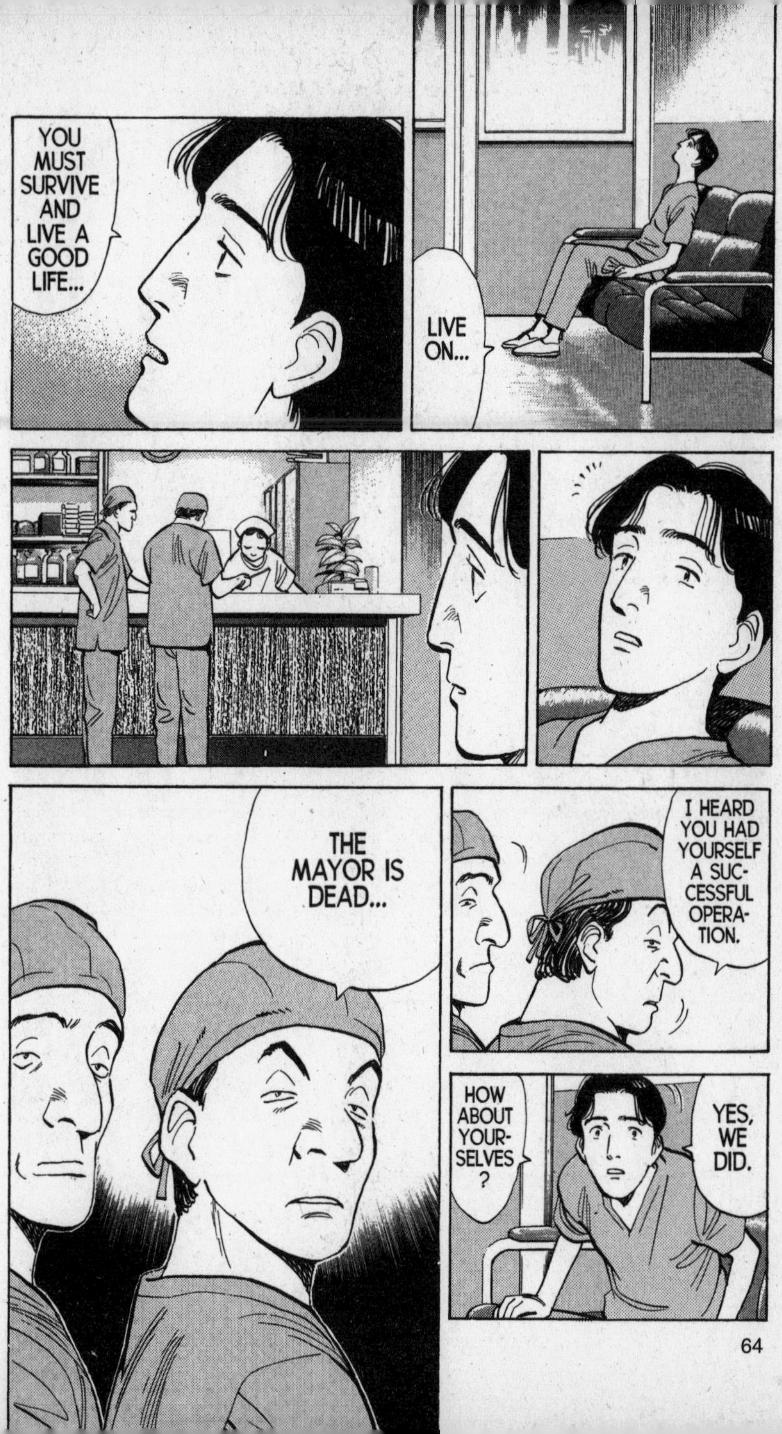
LIVE ON...
YOU MUST SURVIVE AND LIVE A GOOD LIFE...
I HEARD YOU HAD YOURSELF A SUC-CESSFUL OPERA-TION.
YES, WE DID.
HOW ABOUT YOUR-SELVES?
THE MAYOR IS DEAD...

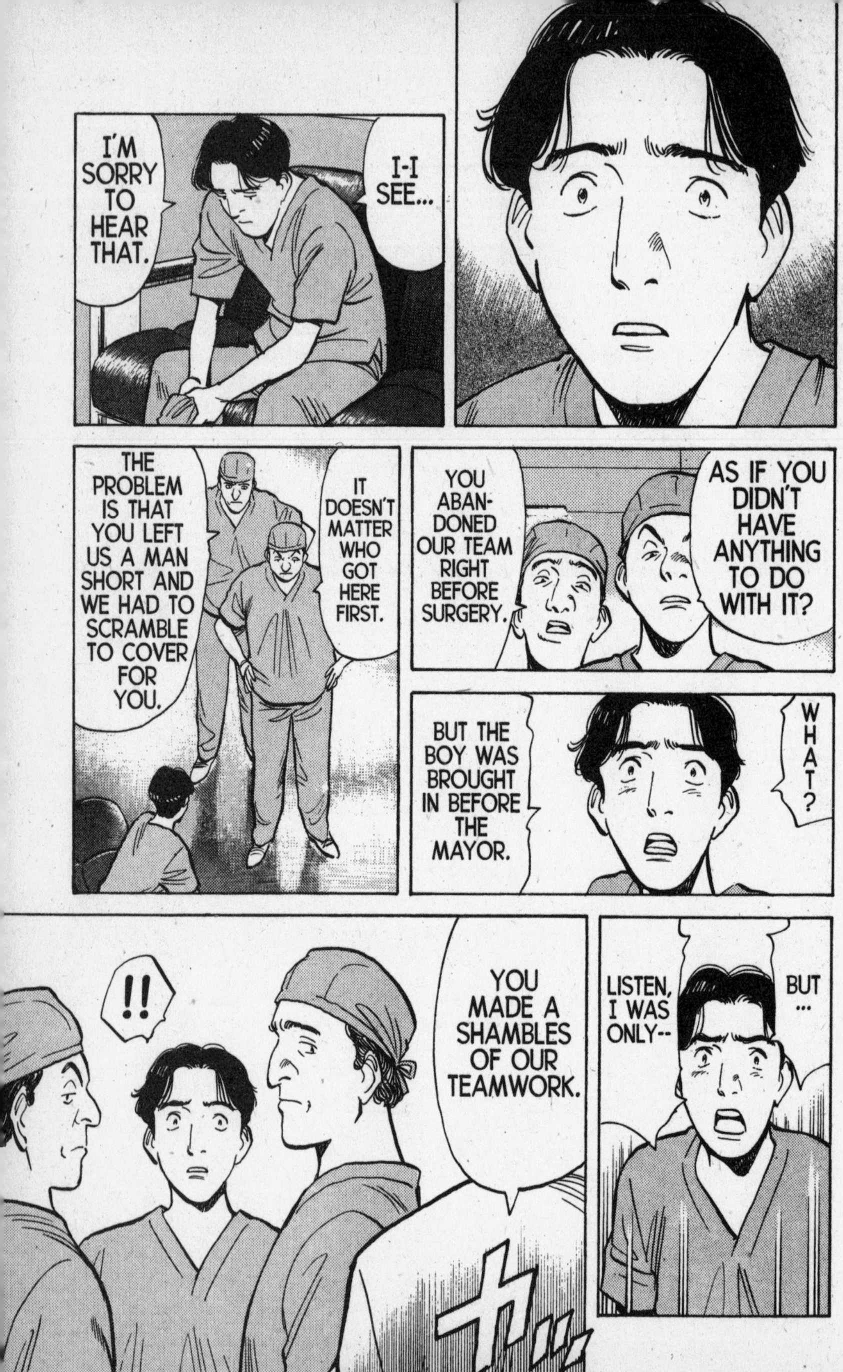
I-I SEE...
I'M SORRY TO HEAR THAT.
AS IF YOU DIDN'T HAVE ANYTHING TO DO WITH IT?
YOU ABAN-DONED OUR TEAM RIGHT BEFORE SURGERY.
WHAT?
BUT THE BOY WAS BROUGHT IN BEFORE THE MAYOR.
IT DOESN'T MATTER WHO GOT HERE FIRST.
THE PROBLEM IS THAT YOU LEFT US A MAN SHORT AND WE HAD TO SCRAMBLE TO COVER FOR YOU.
BUT ...
LISTEN, I WAS ONLY--
YOU MADE A SHAMBLES OF OUR TEAMWORK.
!!

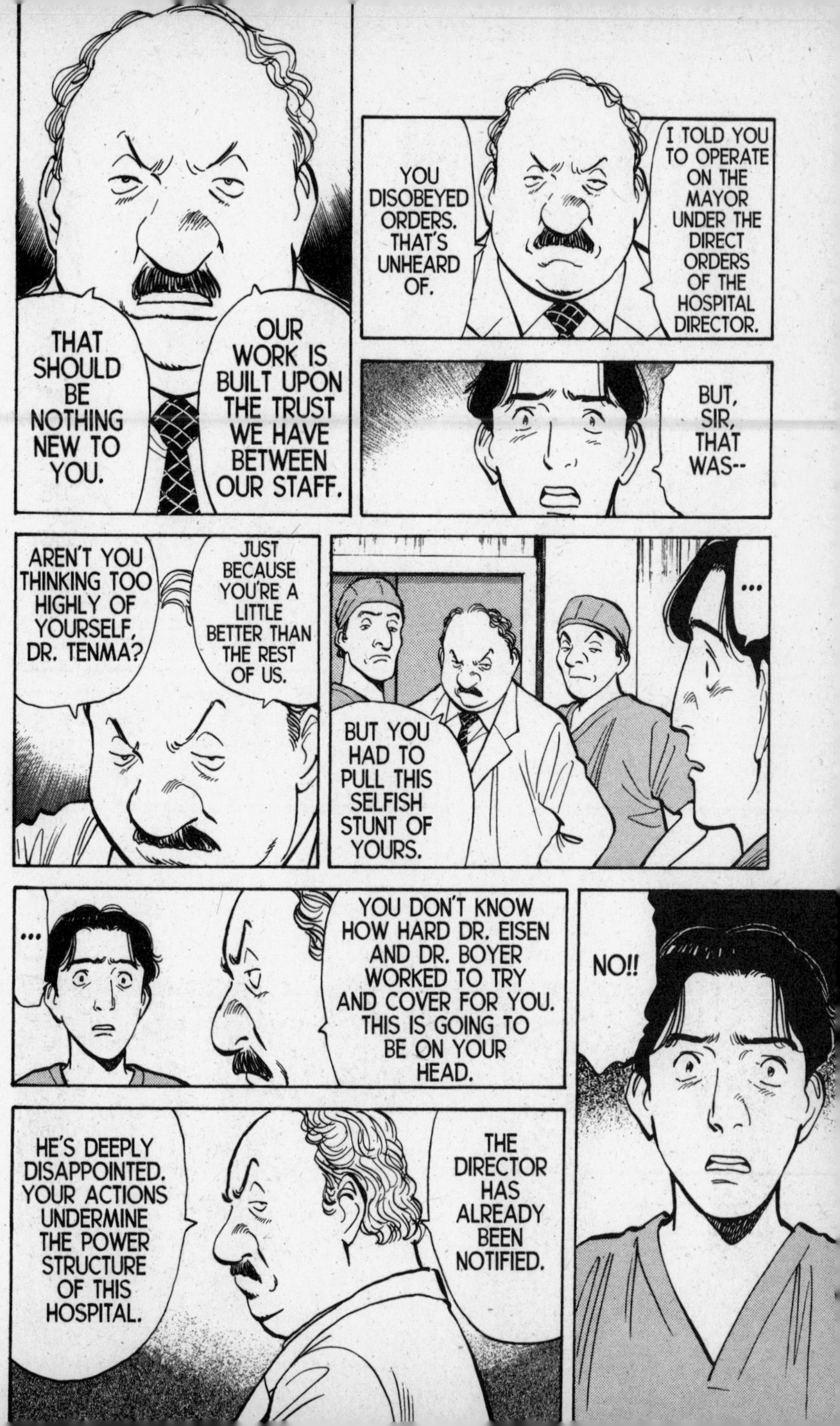
I TOLD YOU TO OPERATE ON THE MAYOR UNDER THE DIRECT ORDERS OF THE HOSPITAL DIRECTOR.
YOU DISOBEYED ORDERS. THAT'S UNHEARD OF.
BUT, SIR, THAT WAS--
OUR WORK IS BUILT UPON THE TRUST WE HAVE BETWEEN OUR STAFF.
THAT SHOULD BE NOTHING NEW TO YOU.
...
BUT YOU HAD TO PULL THIS SELFISH STUNT OF YOURS.
JUST BECAUSE YOU'RE A LITTLE BETTER THAN THE REST OF US.
AREN'T YOU THINKING TOO HIGHLY OF YOURSELF, DR. TENMA?
NO!!
YOU DON'T KNOW HOW HARD DR. EISEN AND DR. BOYER WORKED TO TRY AND COVER FOR YOU. THIS IS GOING TO BE ON YOUR HEAD.
...
THE DIRECTOR HAS ALREADY BEEN NOTIFIED.
HE'S DEEPLY DISAPPOINTED. YOUR ACTIONS UNDERMINE THE POWER STRUCTURE OF THIS HOSPITAL.

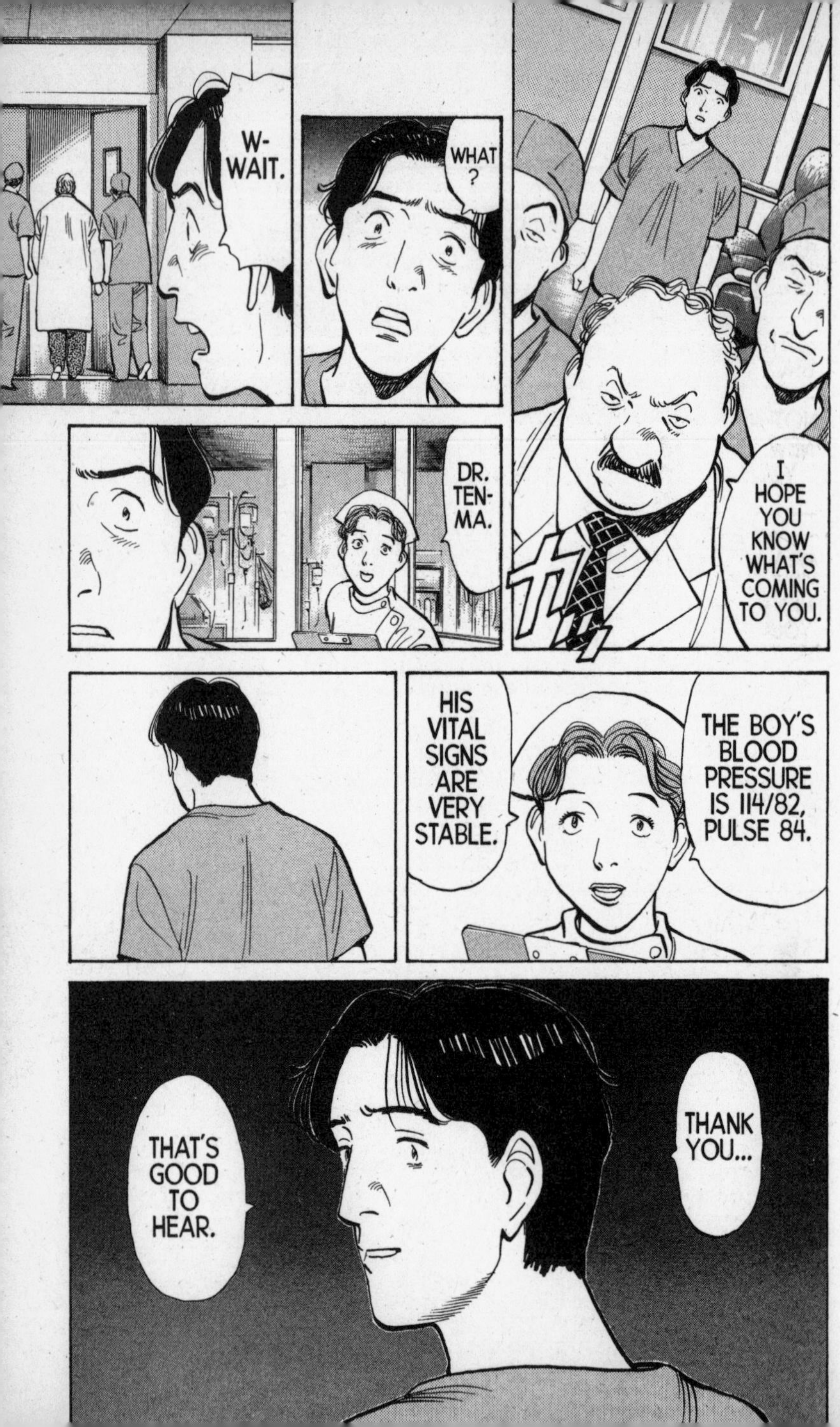
I HOPE YOU KNOW WHAT'S COMING TO YOU.
カッ
WHAT?
W-WAIT.
DR. TEN-MA.
THE BOY'S BLOOD PRESSURE IS 114/82, PULSE 84.
HIS VITAL SIGNS ARE VERY STABLE.
THANK YOU...
THAT'S GOOD TO HEAR.

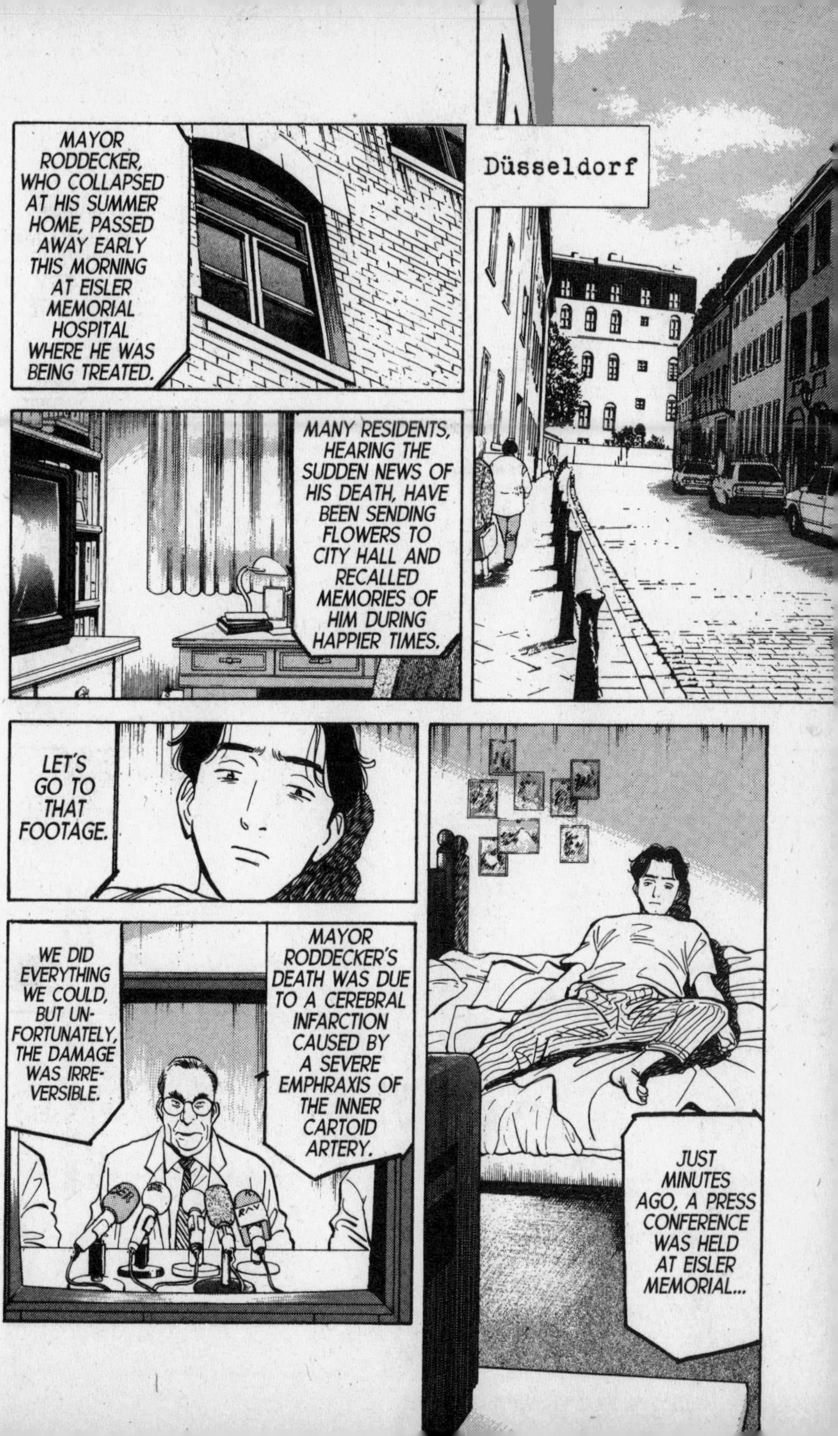
Düsseldorf
MAYOR RODDECKER, WHO COLLAPSED AT HIS SUMMER HOME, PASSED AWAY EARLY THIS MORNING AT EISLER MEMORIAL HOSPITAL WHERE HE WAS BEING TREATED.
MANY RESIDENTS, HEARING THE SUDDEN NEWS OF HIS DEATH, HAVE BEEN SENDING FLOWERS TO CITY HALL AND RECALLED MEMORIES OF HIM DURING HAPPIER TIMES.
JUST MINUTES AGO, A PRESS CONFERENCE WAS HELD AT EISLER MEMORIAL...
LET'S GO TO THAT FOOTAGE.
MAYOR RODDECKER'S DEATH WAS DUE TO A CEREBRAL INFARCTION CAUSED BY A SEVERE EMPHRAXIS OF THE INNER CARTOID ARTERY.
WE DID EVERYTHING WE COULD, BUT UN-FORTUNATELY, THE DAMAGE WAS IRRE-VERSIBLE.

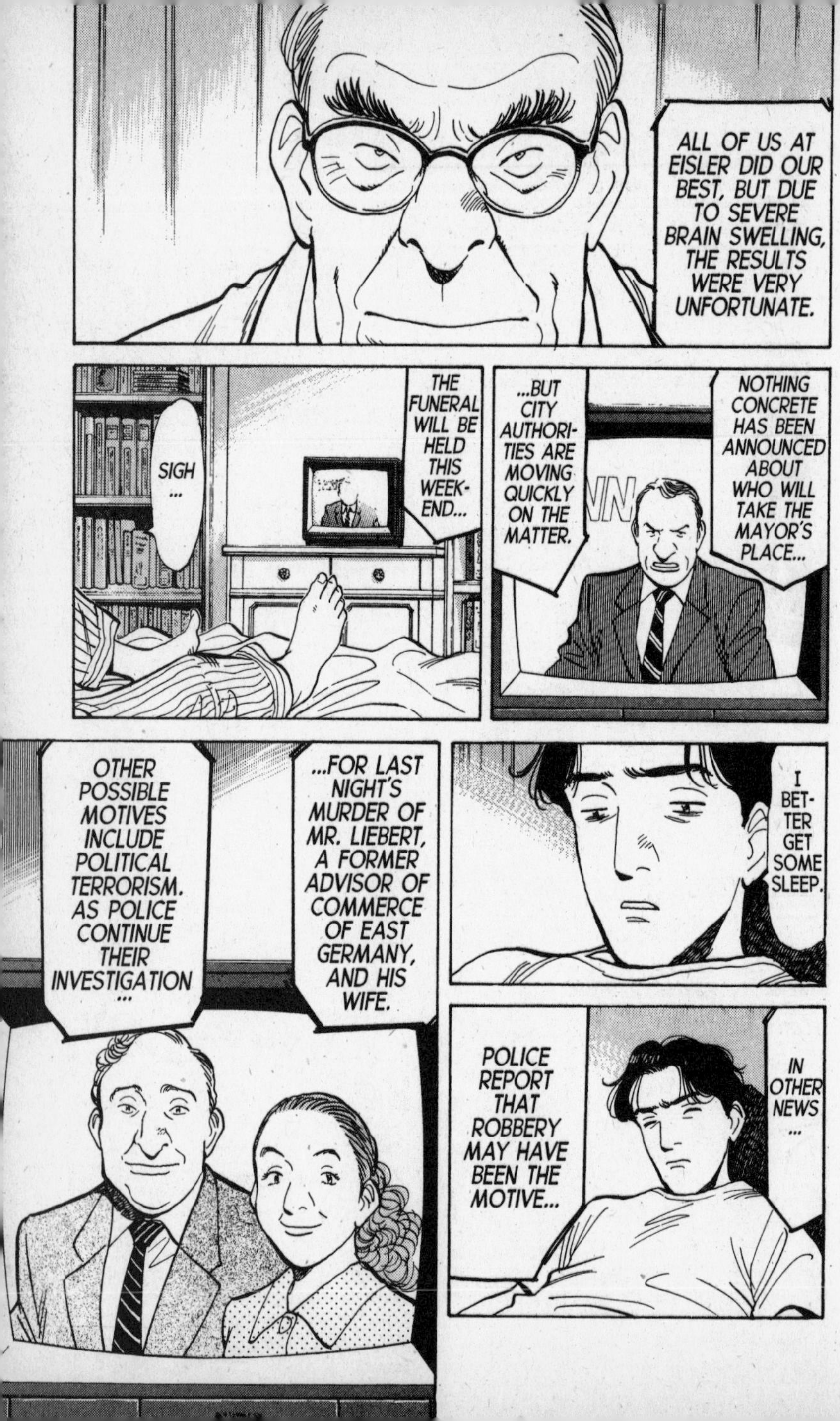
ALL OF US AT EISLER DID OUR BEST, BUT DUE TO SEVERE BRAIN SWELLING, THE RESULTS WERE VERY UNFORTUNATE.
NOTHING CONCRETE HAS BEEN ANNOUNCED ABOUT WHO WILL TAKE THE MAYOR'S PLACE...
...BUT CITY AUTHORITIES ARE MOVING QUICKLY ON THE MATTER.
THE FUNERAL WILL BE HELD THIS WEEKEND...
SIGH...
I BETTER GET SOME SLEEP.
IN OTHER NEWS...
POLICE REPORT THAT ROBBERY MAY HAVE BEEN THE MOTIVE...
...FOR LAST NIGHT'S MURDER OF MR. LIEBERT, A FORMER ADVISOR OF COMMERCE OF EAST GERMANY, AND HIS WIFE.
OTHER POSSIBLE MOTIVES INCLUDE POLITICAL TERRORISM. AS POLICE CONTINUE THEIR INVESTIGATION...

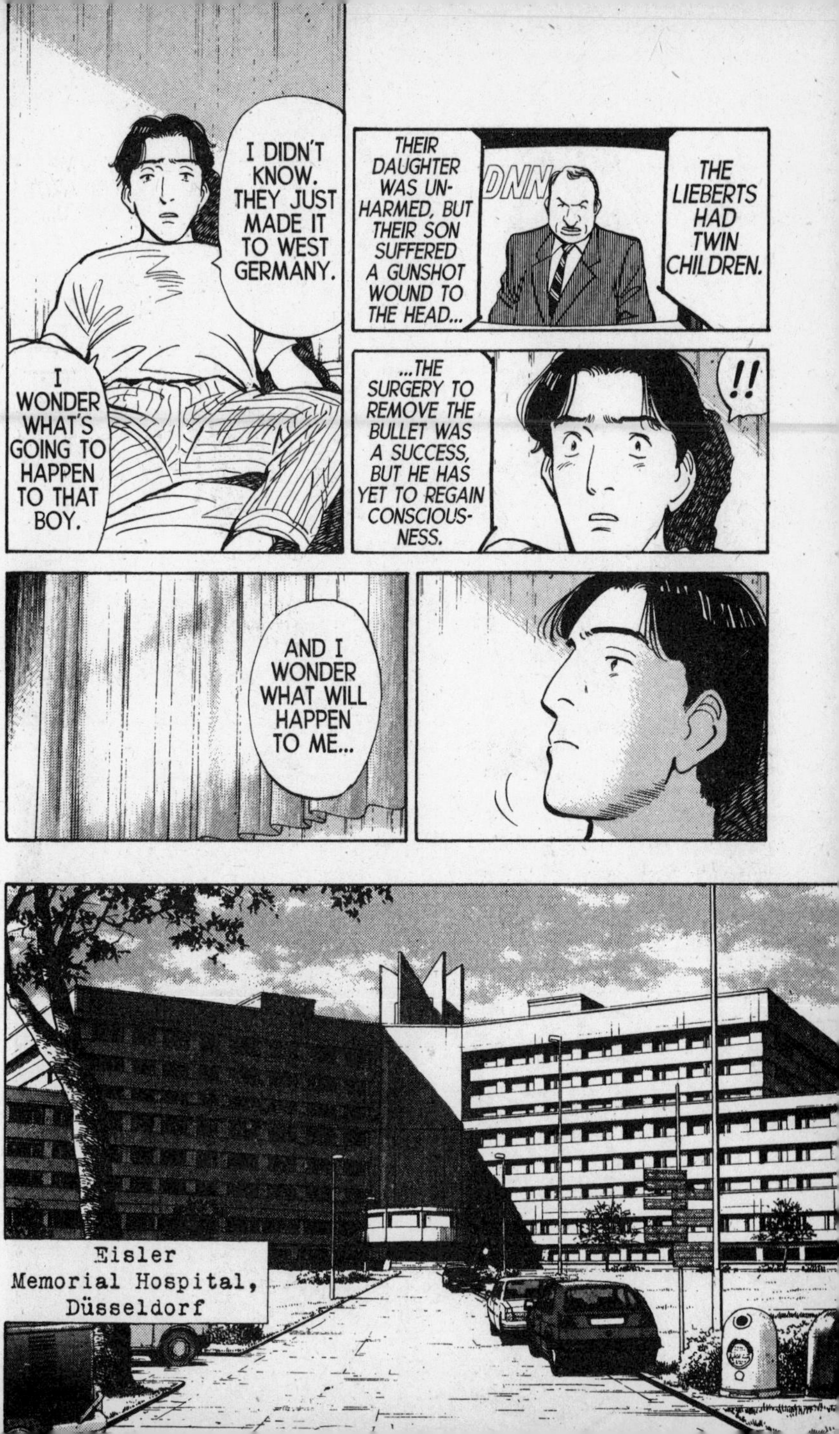
THE LIEBERTS HAD TWIN CHILDREN.
DNN
THEIR DAUGHTER WAS UN-HARMED, BUT THEIR SON SUFFERED A GUNSHOT WOUND TO THE HEAD...
!!
...THE SURGERY TO REMOVE THE BULLET WAS A SUCCESS, BUT HE HAS YET TO REGAIN CONSCIOUS-NESS.
I DIDN'T KNOW. THEY JUST MADE IT TO WEST GERMANY.
I WONDER WHAT'S GOING TO HAPPEN TO THAT BOY.
AND I WONDER WHAT WILL HAPPEN TO ME...
Eisler Memorial Hospital, Düsseldorf

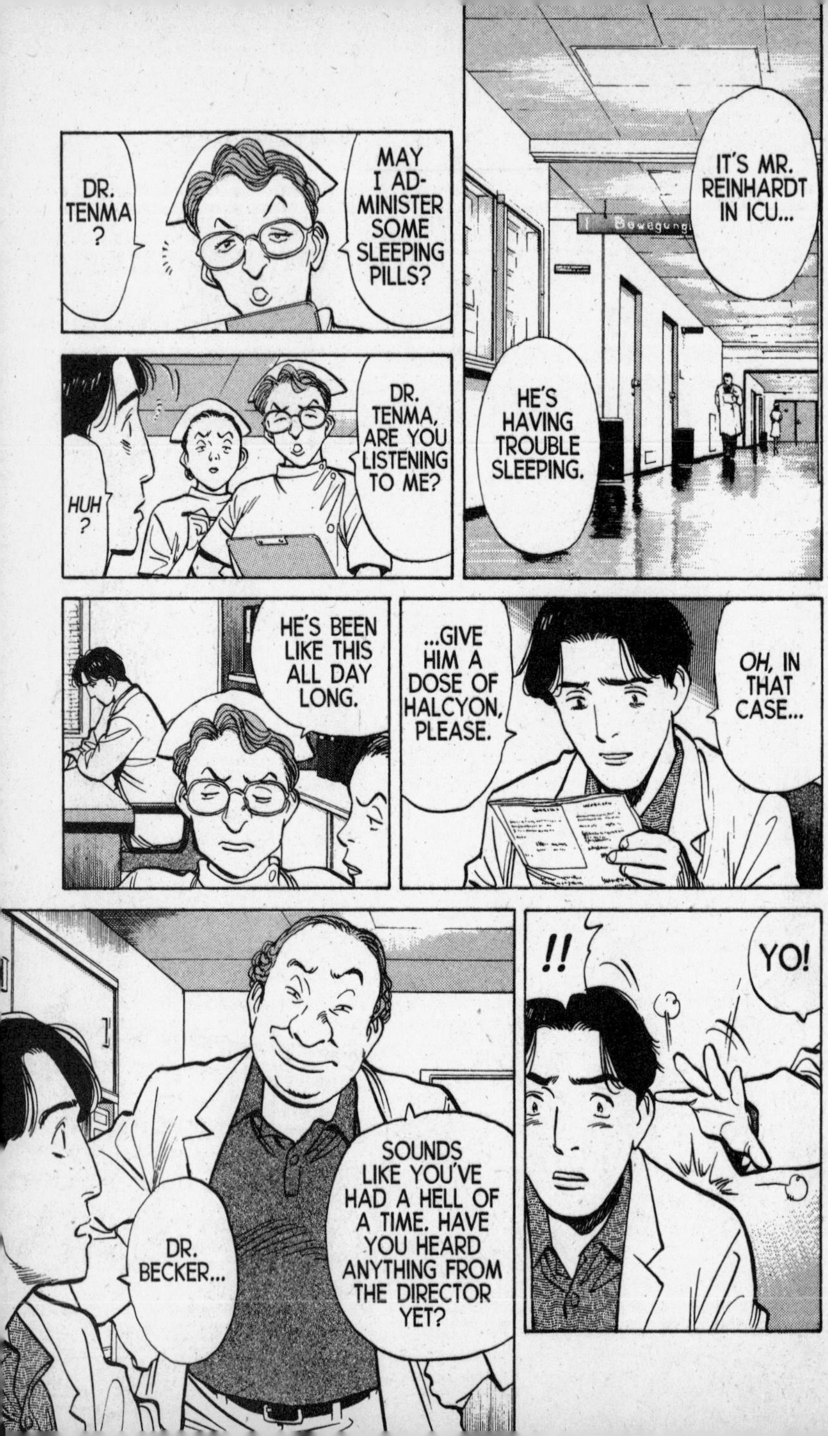
IT'S MR. REINHARDT IN ICU...
HE'S HAVING TROUBLE SLEEPING.
MAY I ADMINISTER SOME SLEEPING PILLS?
DR. TENMA?
DR. TENMA, ARE YOU LISTENING TO ME?
HUH?
OH, IN THAT CASE...
...GIVE HIM A DOSE OF HALCYON, PLEASE.
HE'S BEEN LIKE THIS ALL DAY LONG.
YO!
!!
SOUNDS LIKE YOU'VE HAD A HELL OF A TIME. HAVE YOU HEARD ANYTHING FROM THE DIRECTOR YET?
DR. BECKER...

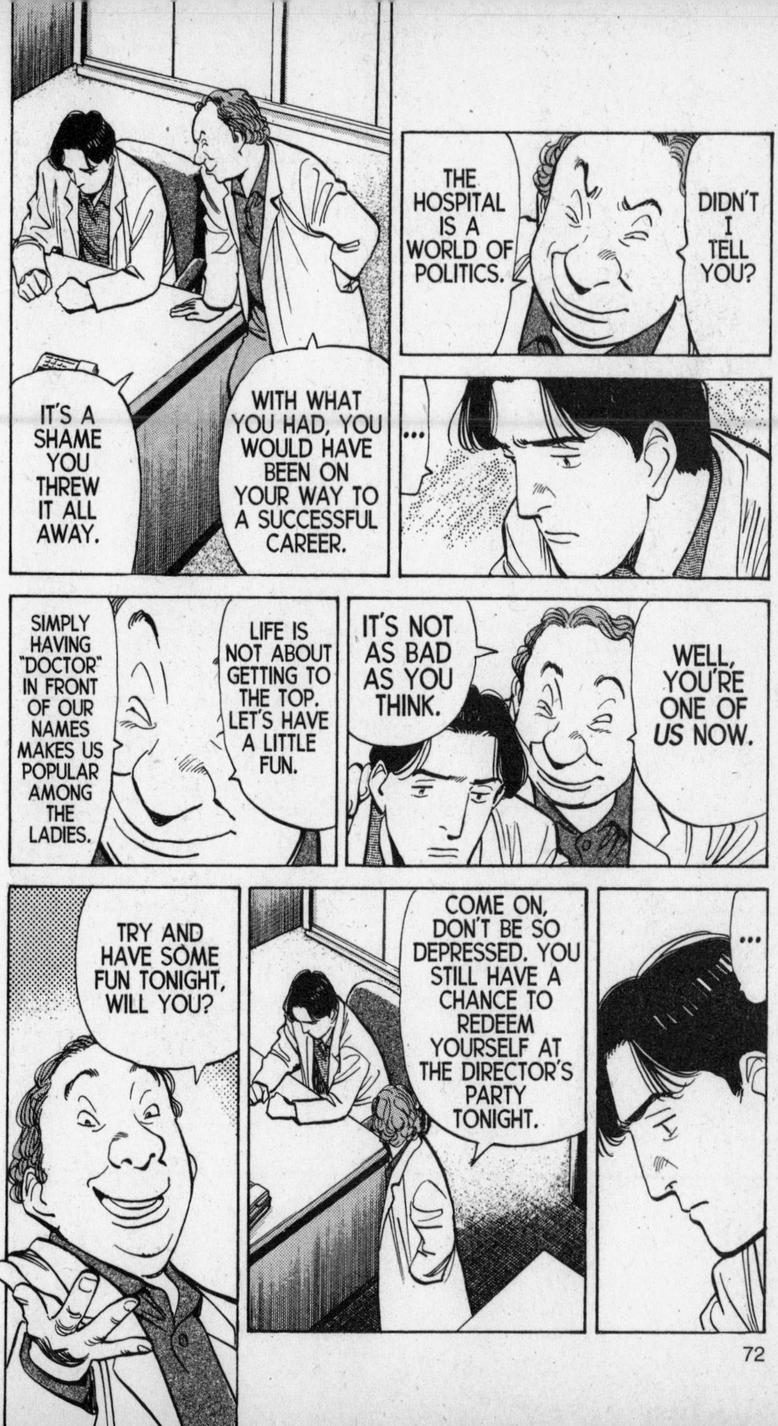
DIDN'T I TELL YOU?
THE HOSPITAL IS A WORLD OF POLITICS.
...
WITH WHAT YOU HAD, YOU WOULD HAVE BEEN ON YOUR WAY TO A SUCCESSFUL CAREER.
IT'S A SHAME YOU THREW IT ALL AWAY.
WELL, YOU'RE ONE OF *US* NOW.
IT'S NOT AS BAD AS YOU THINK.
LIFE IS NOT ABOUT GETTING TO THE TOP. LET'S HAVE A LITTLE FUN.
SIMPLY HAVING "DOCTOR" IN FRONT OF OUR NAMES MAKES US POPULAR AMONG THE LADIES.
...
COME ON, DON'T BE SO DEPRESSED. YOU STILL HAVE A CHANCE TO REDEEM YOURSELF AT THE DIRECTOR'S PARTY TONIGHT.
TRY AND HAVE SOME FUN TONIGHT, WILL YOU?

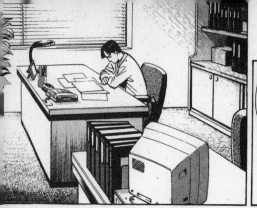

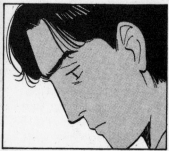

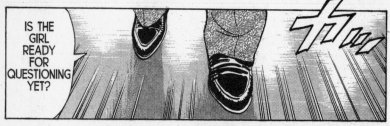

IS THE GIRL READY FOR QUESTIONING YET?
THAT'S THE LEAST OF OUR CONCERNS RIGHT NOW, DETECTIVE.
WHAT?
THAT GIRL HAS TO GET HER REST...
...BUT SHE KEEPS GETTING OUT OF HER ROOM AND WANDERING AROUND THE HOSPITAL.
HMM?
PIT
PAT

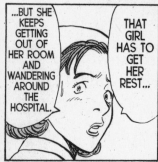

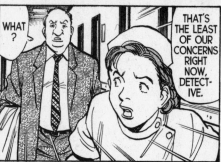

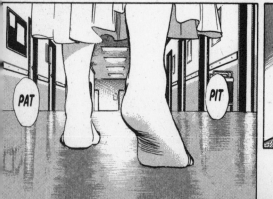

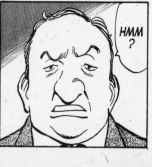

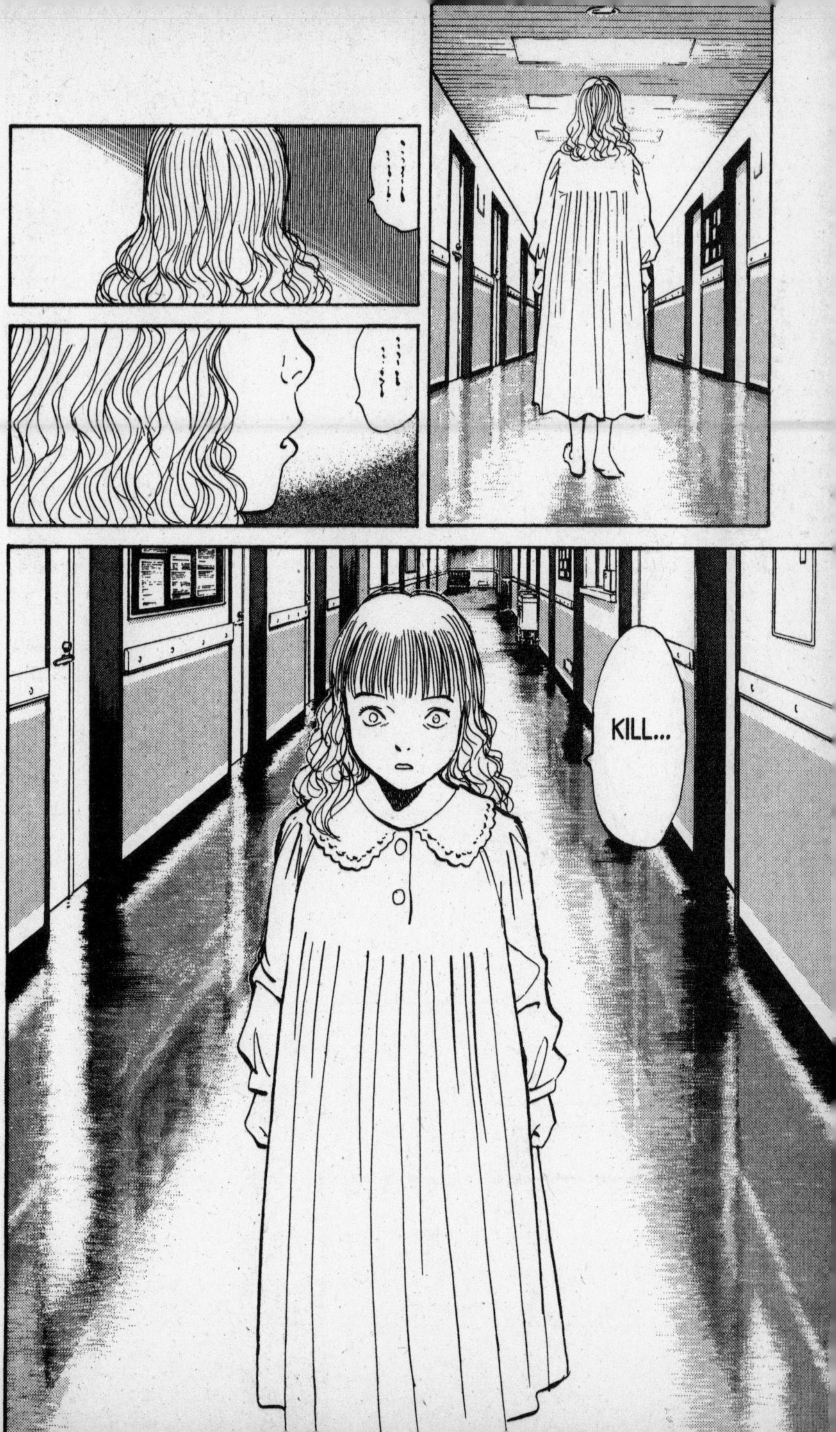
KILL...

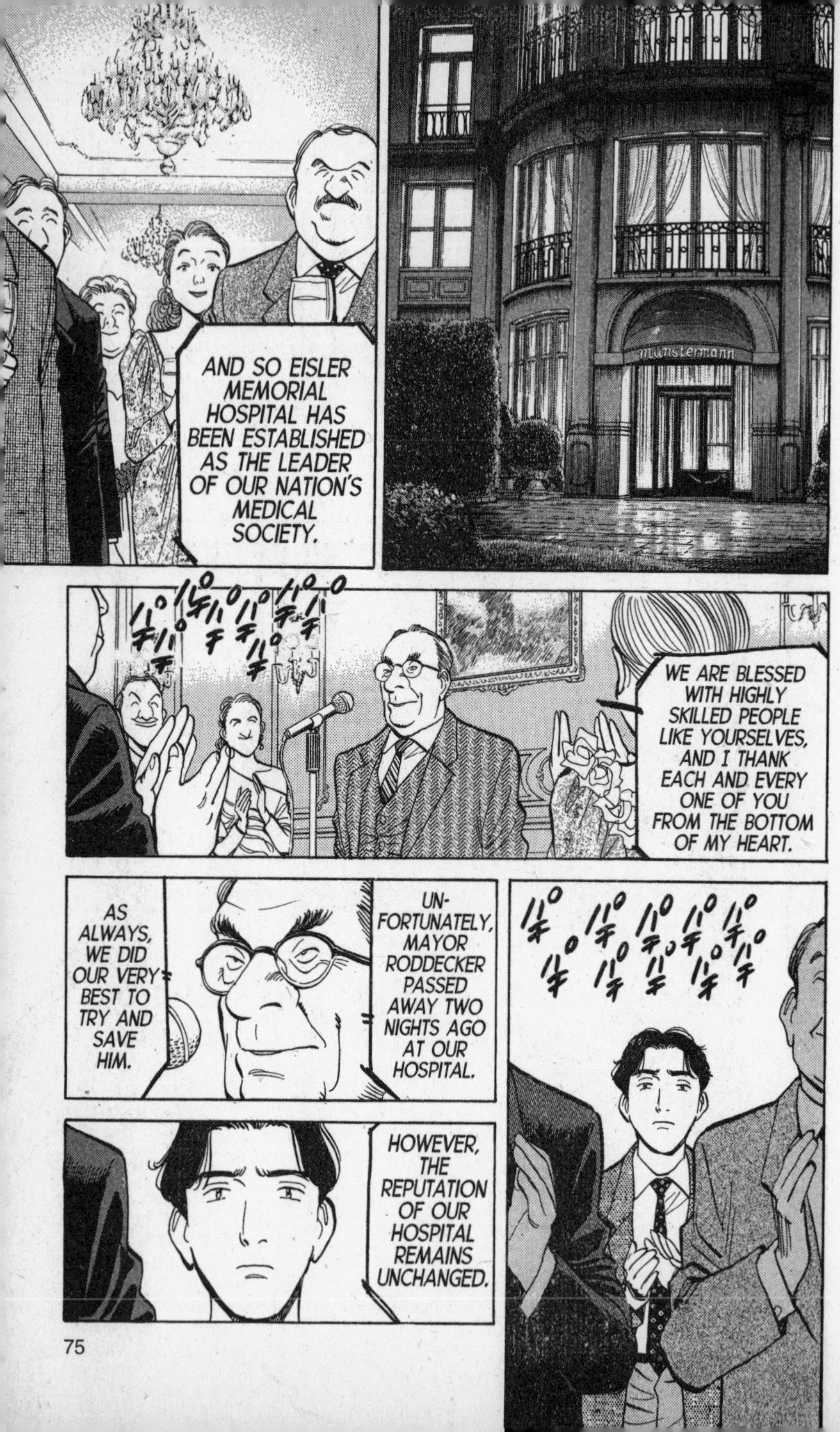
AND SO EISLER MEMORIAL HOSPITAL HAS BEEN ESTABLISHED AS THE LEADER OF OUR NATION'S MEDICAL SOCIETY.
パチパチパチパチ
WE ARE BLESSED WITH HIGHLY SKILLED PEOPLE LIKE YOURSELVES, AND I THANK EACH AND EVERY ONE OF YOU FROM THE BOTTOM OF MY HEART.
パチパチパチパチ
UN-FORTUNATELY, MAYOR RODDECKER PASSED AWAY TWO NIGHTS AGO AT OUR HOSPITAL.
AS ALWAYS, WE DID OUR VERY BEST TO TRY AND SAVE HIM.
HOWEVER, THE REPUTATION OF OUR HOSPITAL REMAINS UNCHANGED.

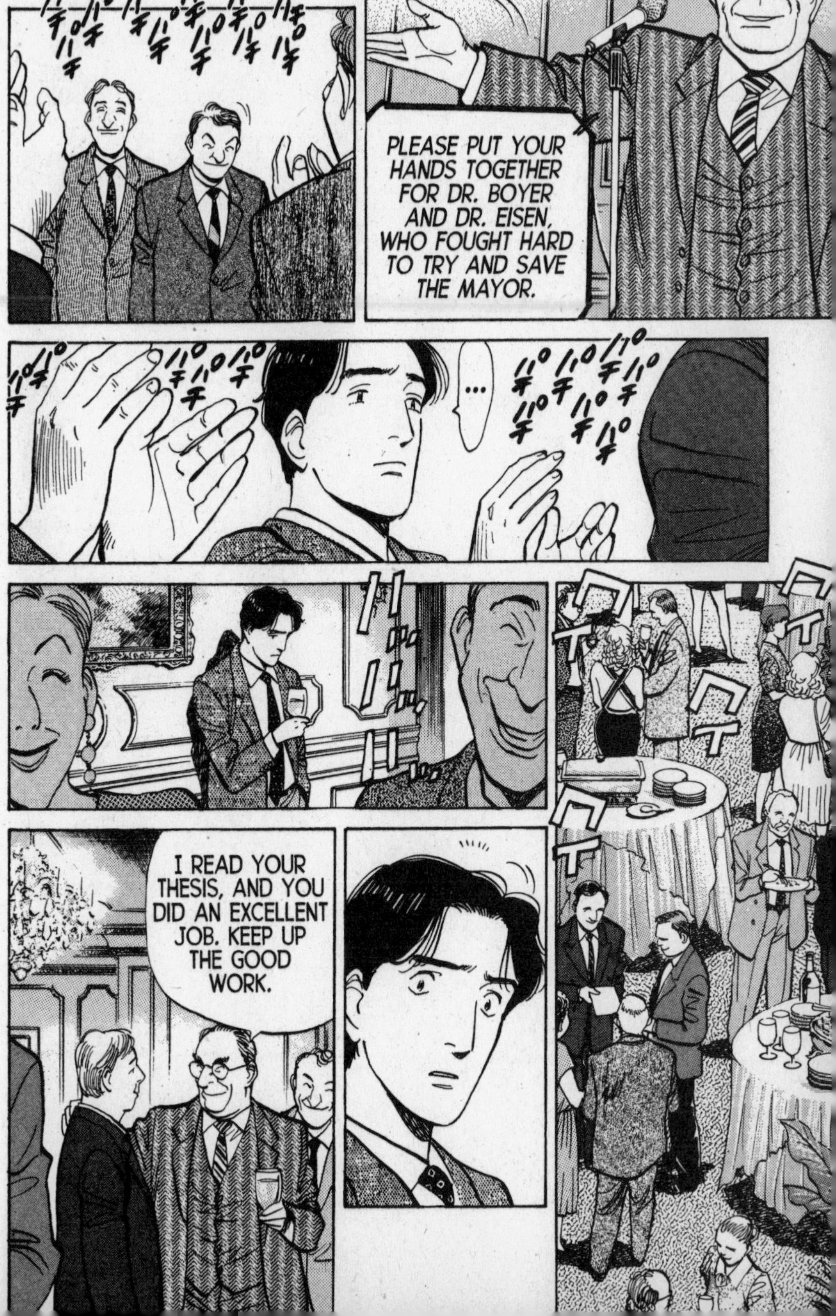
PLEASE PUT YOUR HANDS TOGETHER FOR DR. BOYER AND DR. EISEN, WHO FOUGHT HARD TO TRY AND SAVE THE MAYOR.
...
I READ YOUR THESIS, AND YOU DID AN EXCELLENT JOB. KEEP UP THE GOOD WORK.

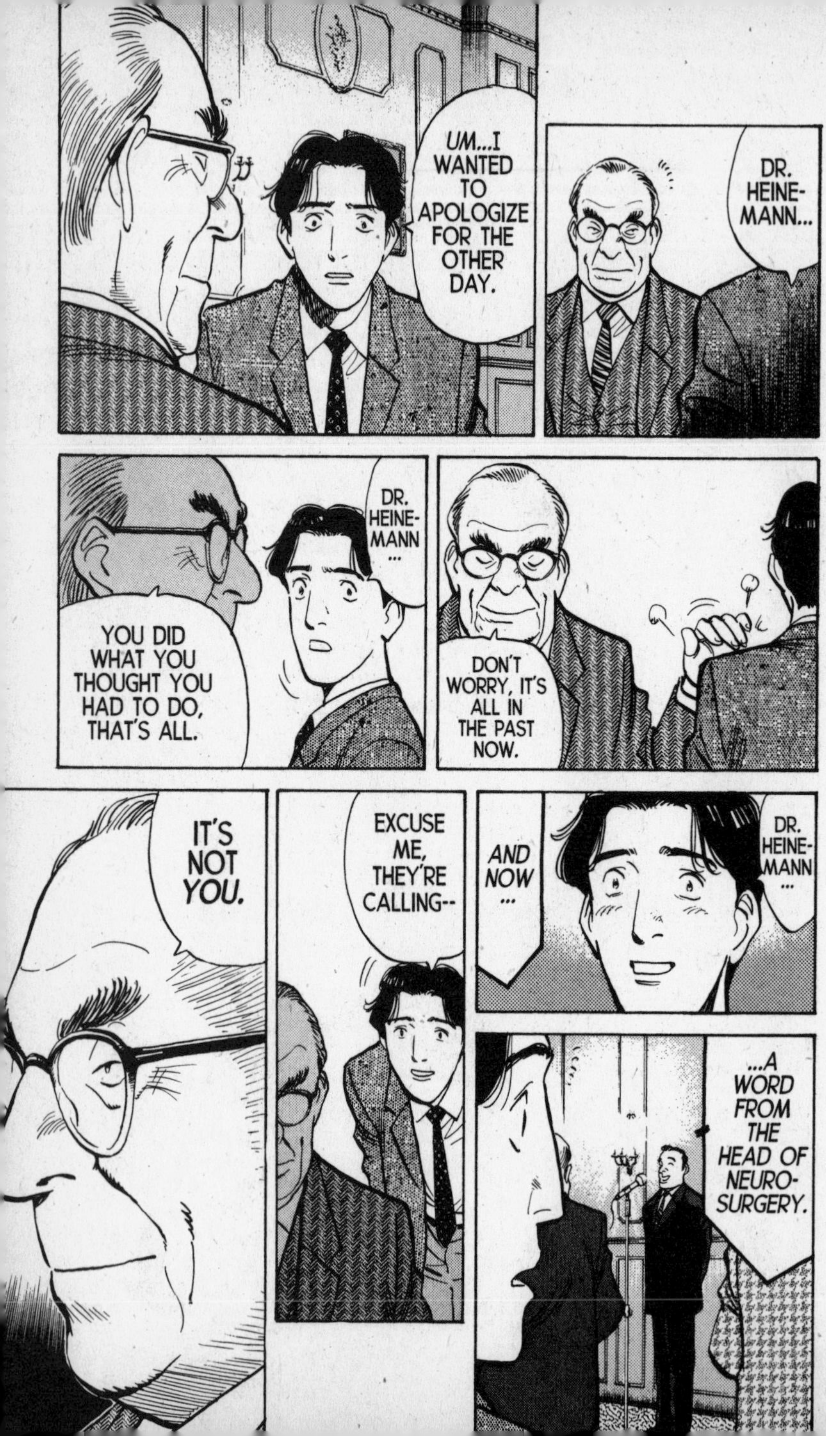
DR. HEINE-MANN...
UM...I WANTED TO APOLOGIZE FOR THE OTHER DAY.
DON'T WORRY, IT'S ALL IN THE PAST NOW.
DR. HEINE-MANN...
YOU DID WHAT YOU THOUGHT YOU HAD TO DO, THAT'S ALL.
DR. HEINE-MANN...
AND NOW...
...A WORD FROM THE HEAD OF NEURO-SURGERY.
EXCUSE ME, THEY'RE CALLING--
IT'S NOT YOU.

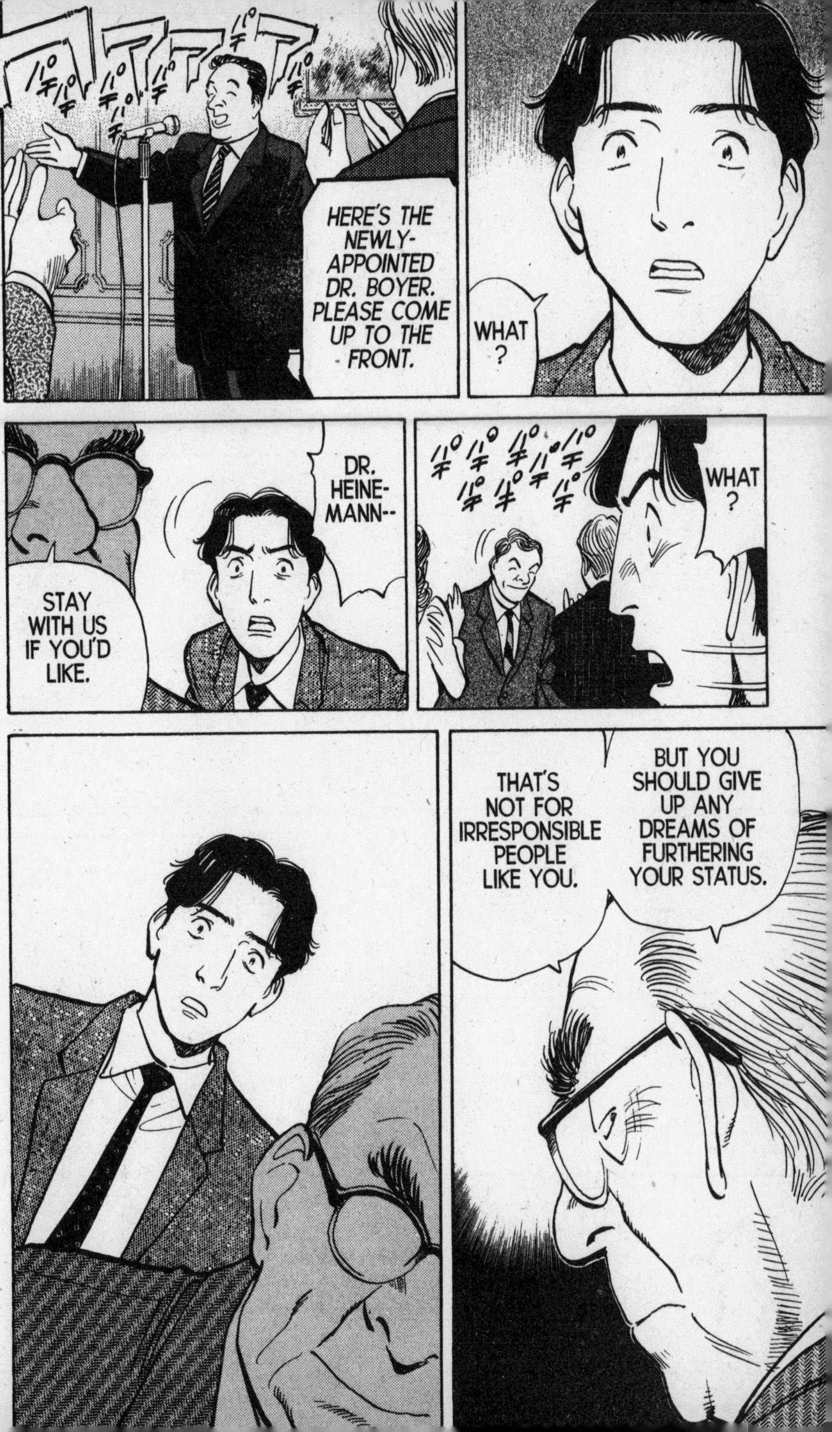
WHAT ?
パチパチ
HERE'S THE NEWLY-APPOINTED DR. BOYER. PLEASE COME UP TO THE FRONT.
パチパチ
WHAT ?
DR. HEINE-MANN--
STAY WITH US IF YOU'D LIKE.
BUT YOU SHOULD GIVE UP ANY DREAMS OF FURTHERING YOUR STATUS.
THAT'S NOT FOR IRRESPONSIBLE PEOPLE LIKE YOU.

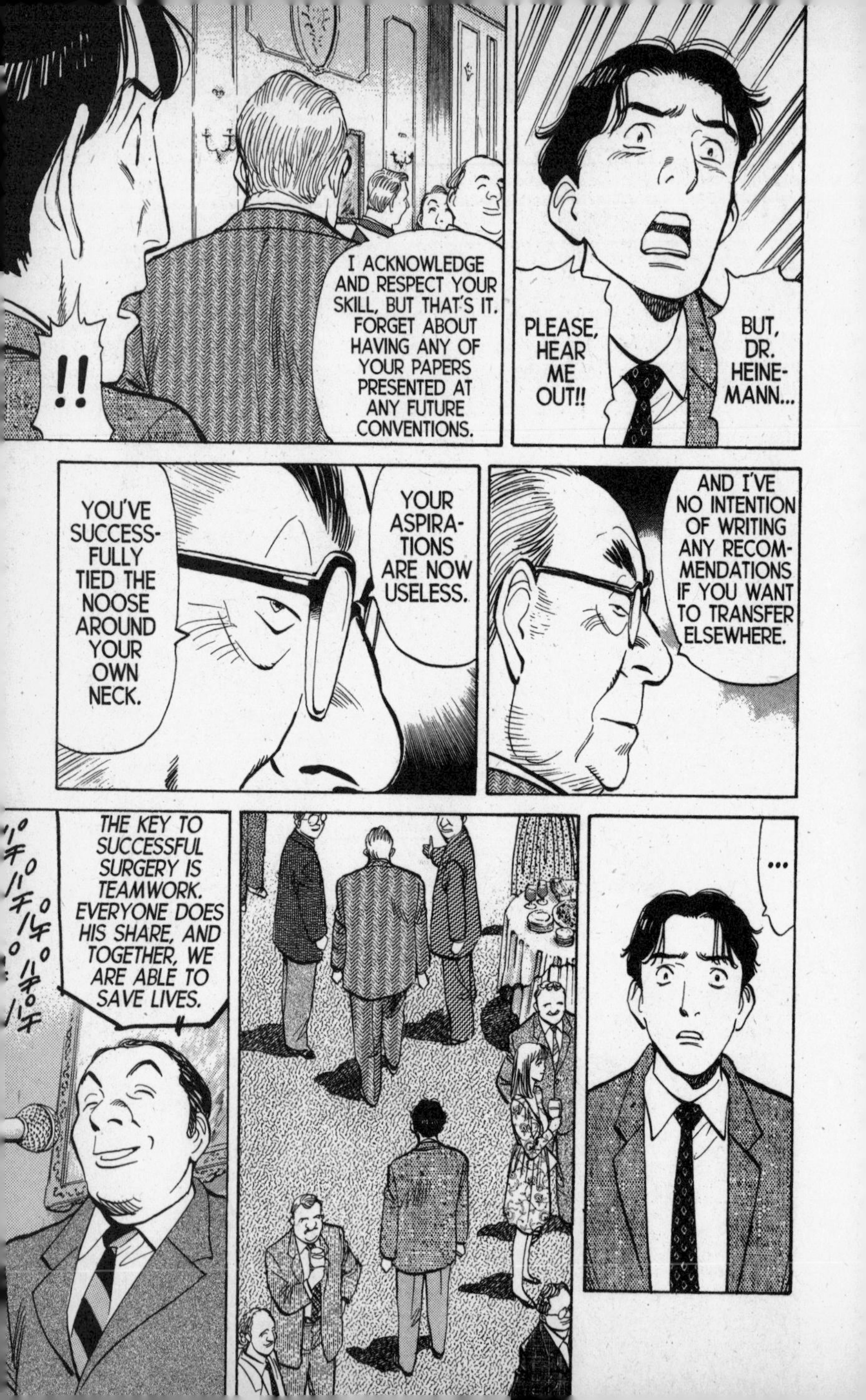
BUT, DR. HEINEMANN...
PLEASE, HEAR ME OUT!!
I ACKNOWLEDGE AND RESPECT YOUR SKILL, BUT THAT'S IT. FORGET ABOUT HAVING ANY OF YOUR PAPERS PRESENTED AT ANY FUTURE CONVENTIONS.
!!
AND I'VE NO INTENTION OF WRITING ANY RECOMMENDATIONS IF YOU WANT TO TRANSFER ELSEWHERE.
YOUR ASPIRATIONS ARE NOW USELESS.
YOU'VE SUCCESSFULLY TIED THE NOOSE AROUND YOUR OWN NECK.
...
THE KEY TO SUCCESSFUL SURGERY IS TEAMWORK. EVERYONE DOES HIS SHARE, AND TOGETHER, WE ARE ABLE TO SAVE LIVES.

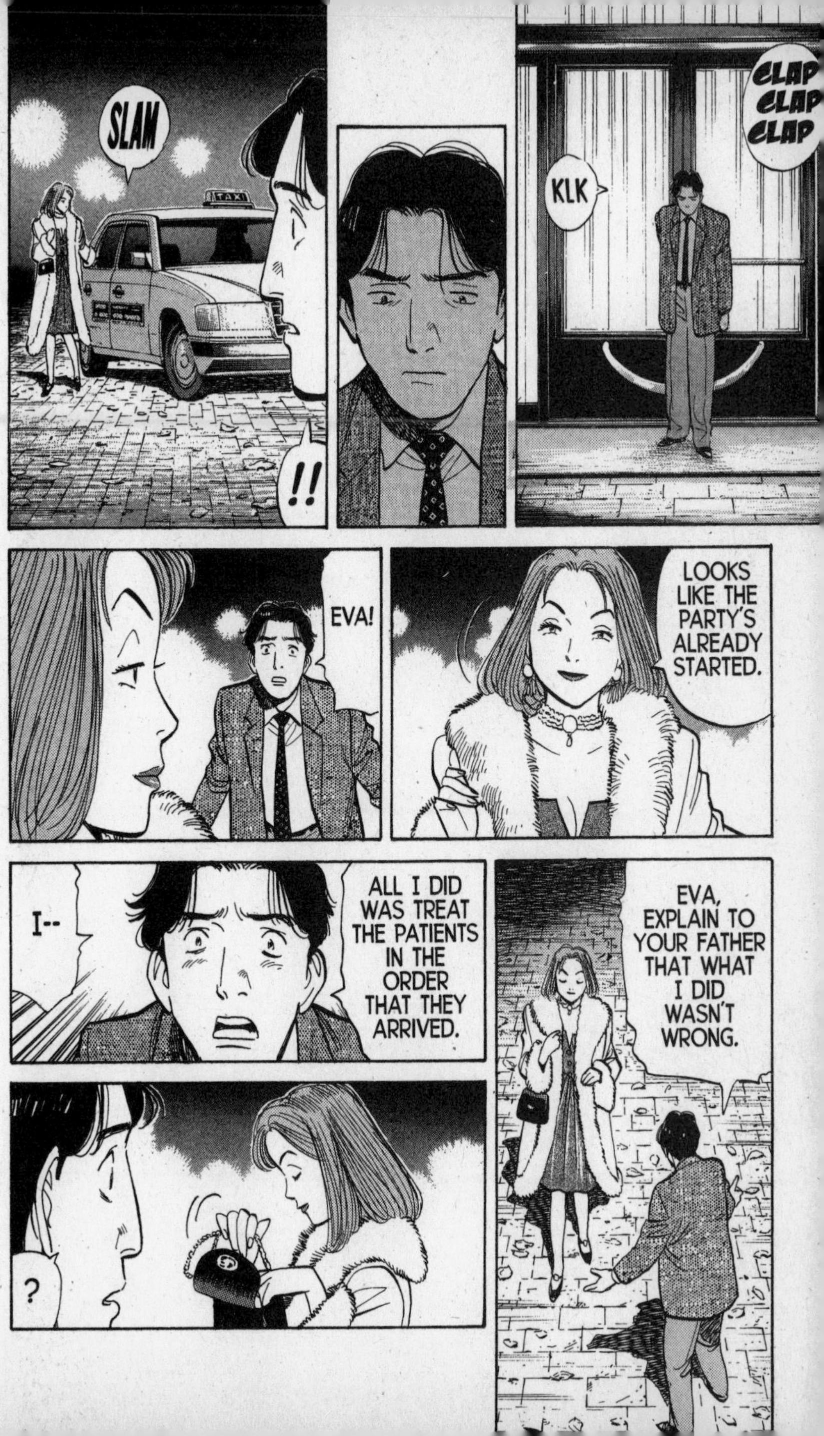
CLAP CLAP CLAP
KLK
SLAM
!!
LOOKS LIKE THE PARTY'S ALREADY STARTED.
EVA!
EVA, EXPLAIN TO YOUR FATHER THAT WHAT I DID WASN'T WRONG.
ALL I DID WAS TREAT THE PATIENTS IN THE ORDER THAT THEY ARRIVED.
I--
?

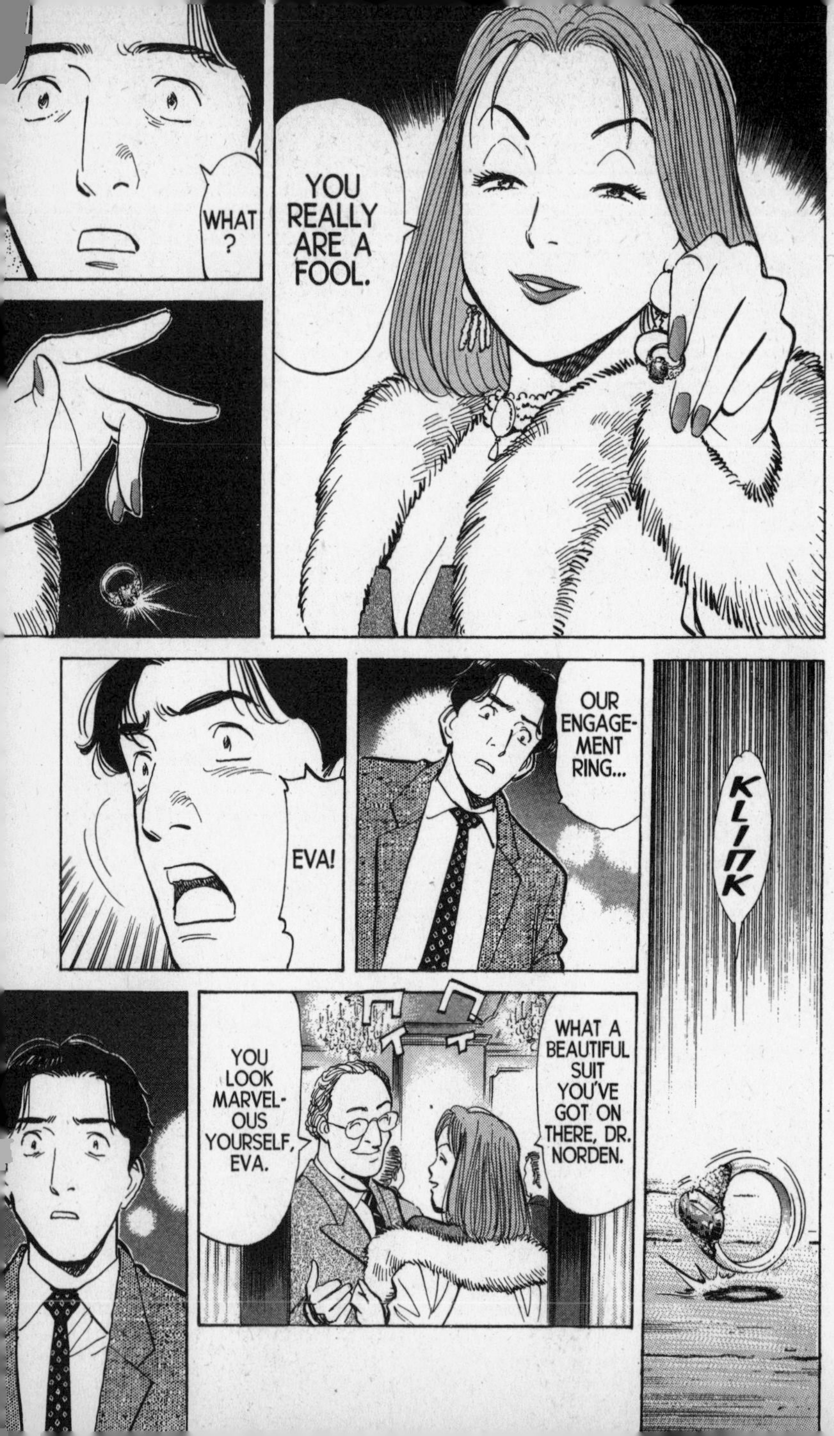
YOU REALLY ARE A FOOL.
WHAT?
KLINK
OUR ENGAGEMENT RING...
EVA!
WHAT A BEAUTIFUL SUIT YOU'VE GOT ON THERE, DR. NORDEN.
YOU LOOK MARVELOUS YOURSELF, EVA.

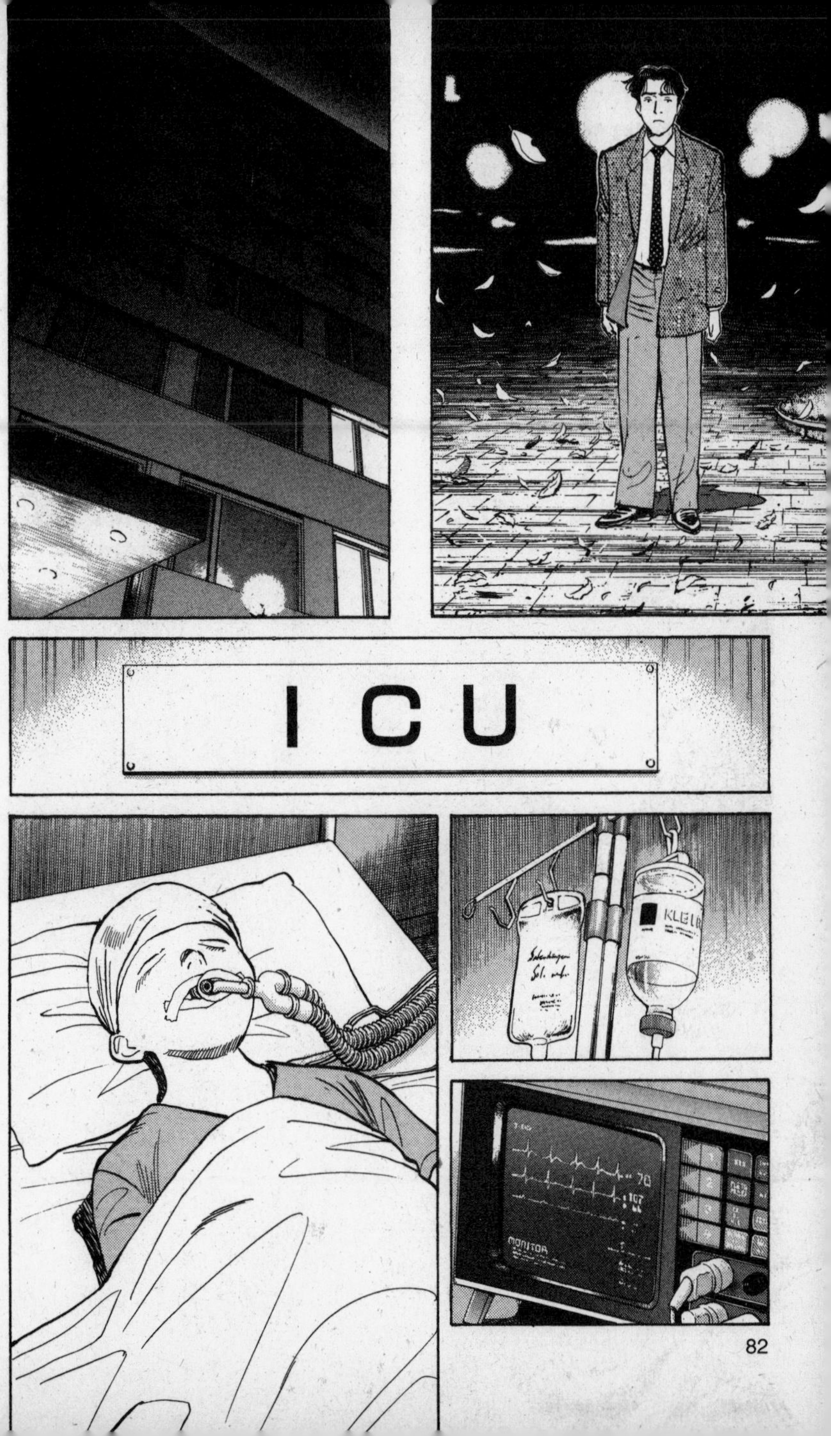
ICU
MONITOR

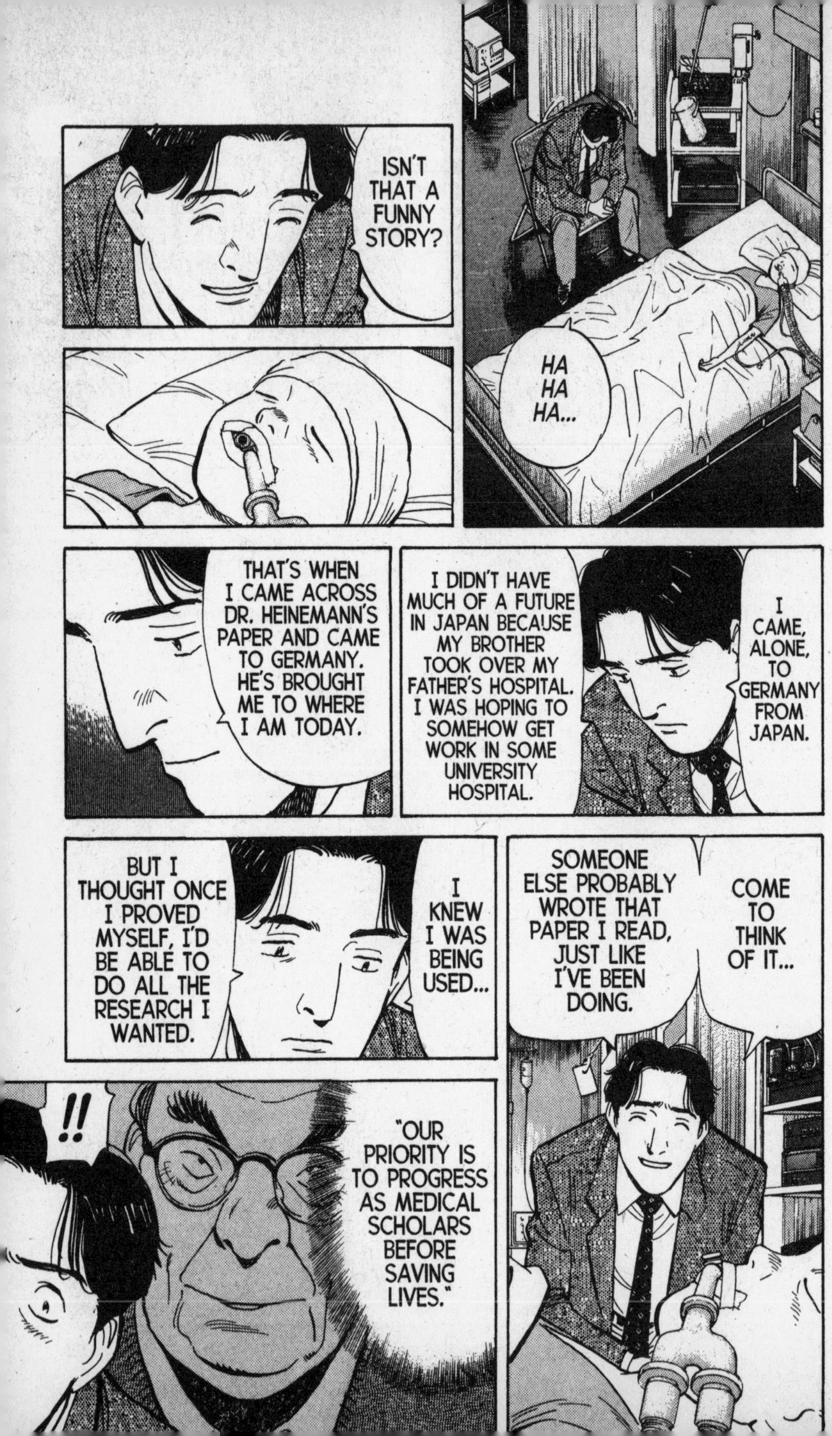
HA HA HA...
ISN'T THAT A FUNNY STORY?
I CAME, ALONE, TO GERMANY FROM JAPAN.
I DIDN'T HAVE MUCH OF A FUTURE IN JAPAN BECAUSE MY BROTHER TOOK OVER MY FATHER'S HOSPITAL. I WAS HOPING TO SOMEHOW GET WORK IN SOME UNIVERSITY HOSPITAL.
THAT'S WHEN I CAME ACROSS DR. HEINEMANN'S PAPER AND CAME TO GERMANY. HE'S BROUGHT ME TO WHERE I AM TODAY.
COME TO THINK OF IT...
SOMEONE ELSE PROBABLY WROTE THAT PAPER I READ, JUST LIKE I'VE BEEN DOING.
I KNEW I WAS BEING USED...
BUT I THOUGHT ONCE I PROVED MYSELF, I'D BE ABLE TO DO ALL THE RESEARCH I WANTED.
"OUR PRIORITY IS TO PROGRESS AS MEDICAL SCHOLARS BEFORE SAVING LIVES."
!!

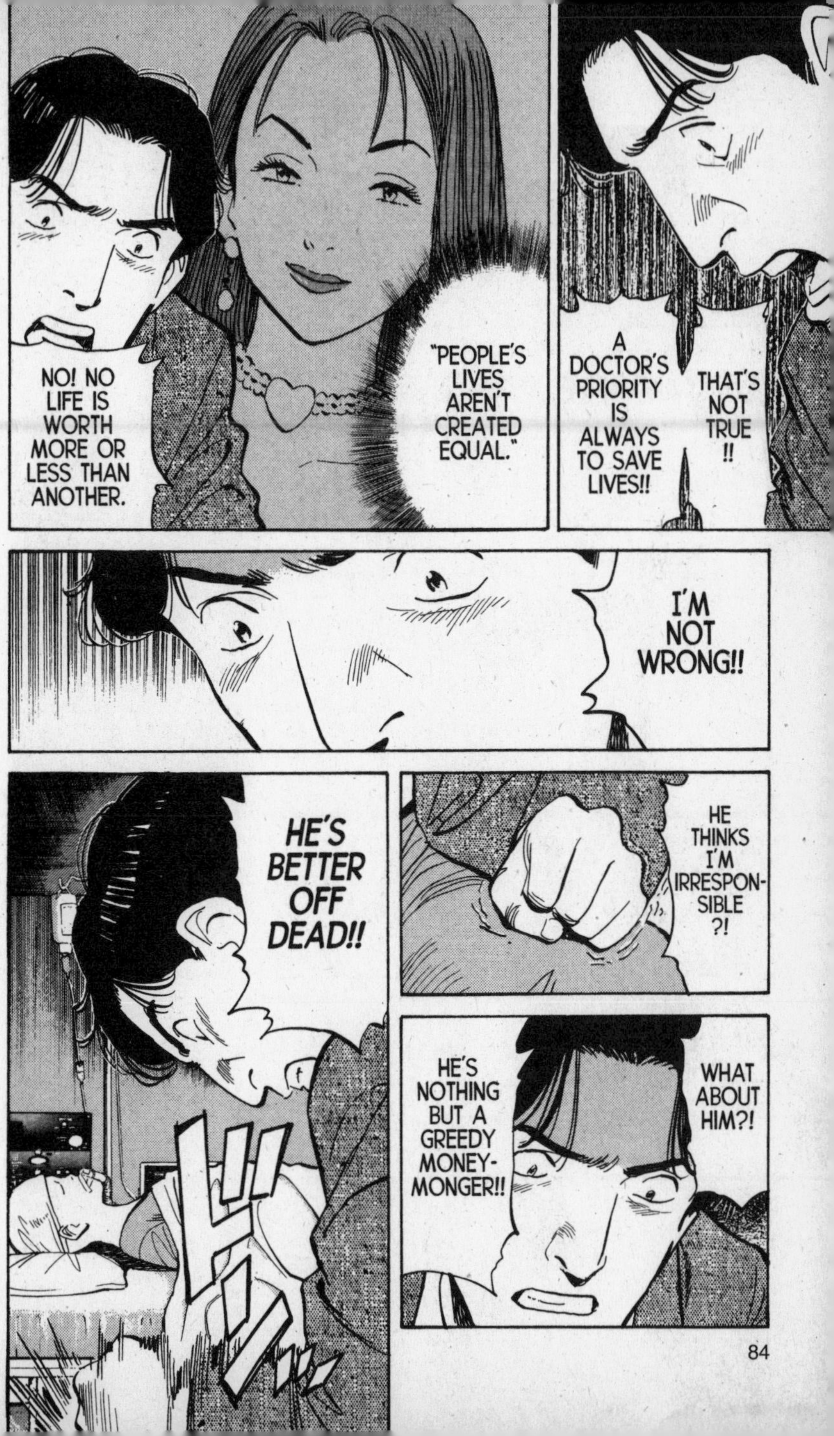
THAT'S NOT TRUE !!
A DOCTOR'S PRIORITY IS ALWAYS TO SAVE LIVES!!
"PEOPLE'S LIVES AREN'T CREATED EQUAL."
NO! NO LIFE IS WORTH MORE OR LESS THAN ANOTHER.
I'M NOT WRONG!!
HE THINKS I'M IRRESPON-SIBLE ?!
WHAT ABOUT HIM?!
HE'S NOTHING BUT A GREEDY MONEY-MONGER!!
HE'S BETTER OFF DEAD!!

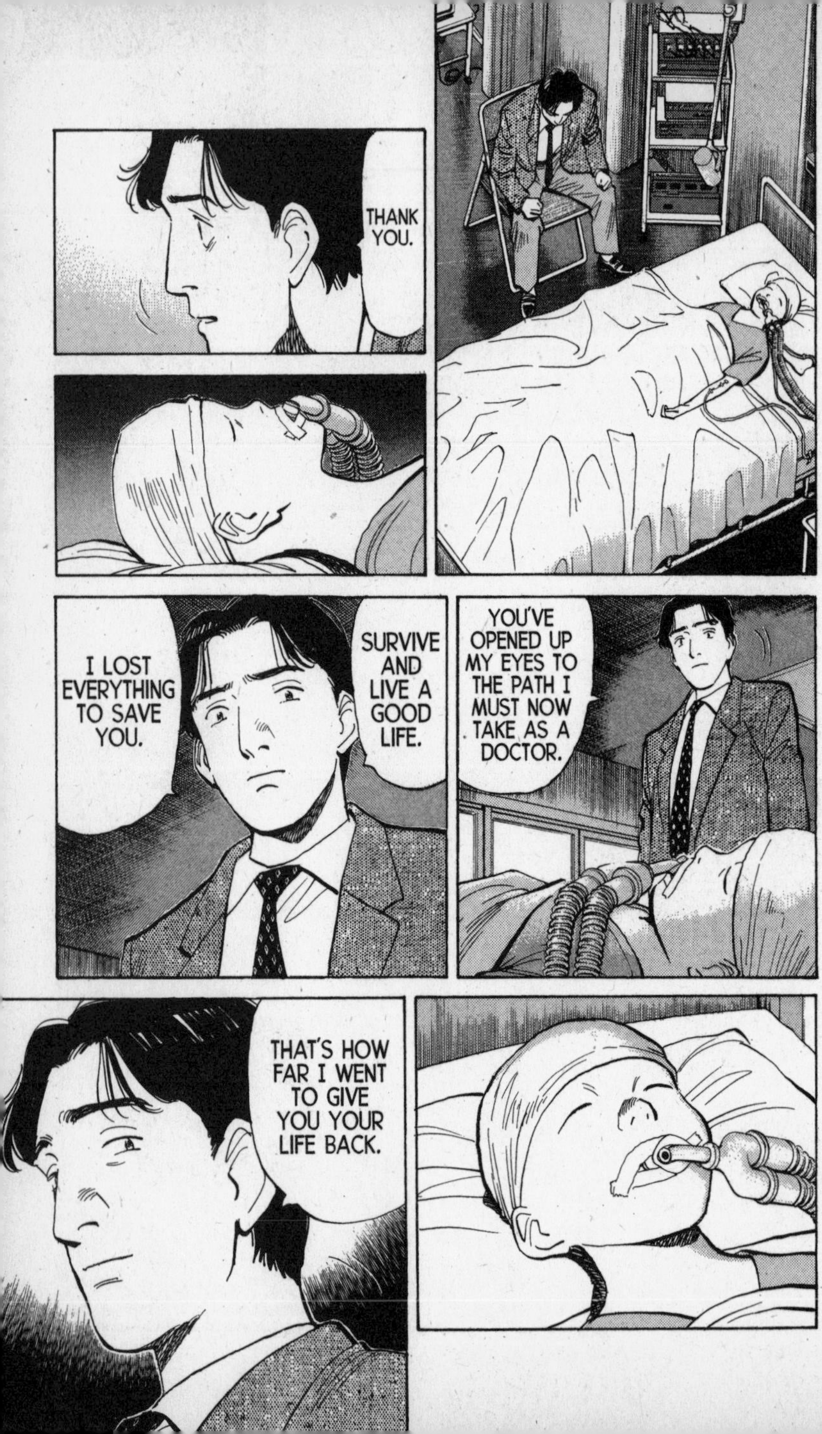
THANK YOU.
YOU'VE OPENED UP MY EYES TO THE PATH I MUST NOW TAKE AS A DOCTOR.
SURVIVE AND LIVE A GOOD LIFE.
I LOST EVERYTHING TO SAVE YOU.
THAT'S HOW FAR I WENT TO GIVE YOU YOUR LIFE BACK.

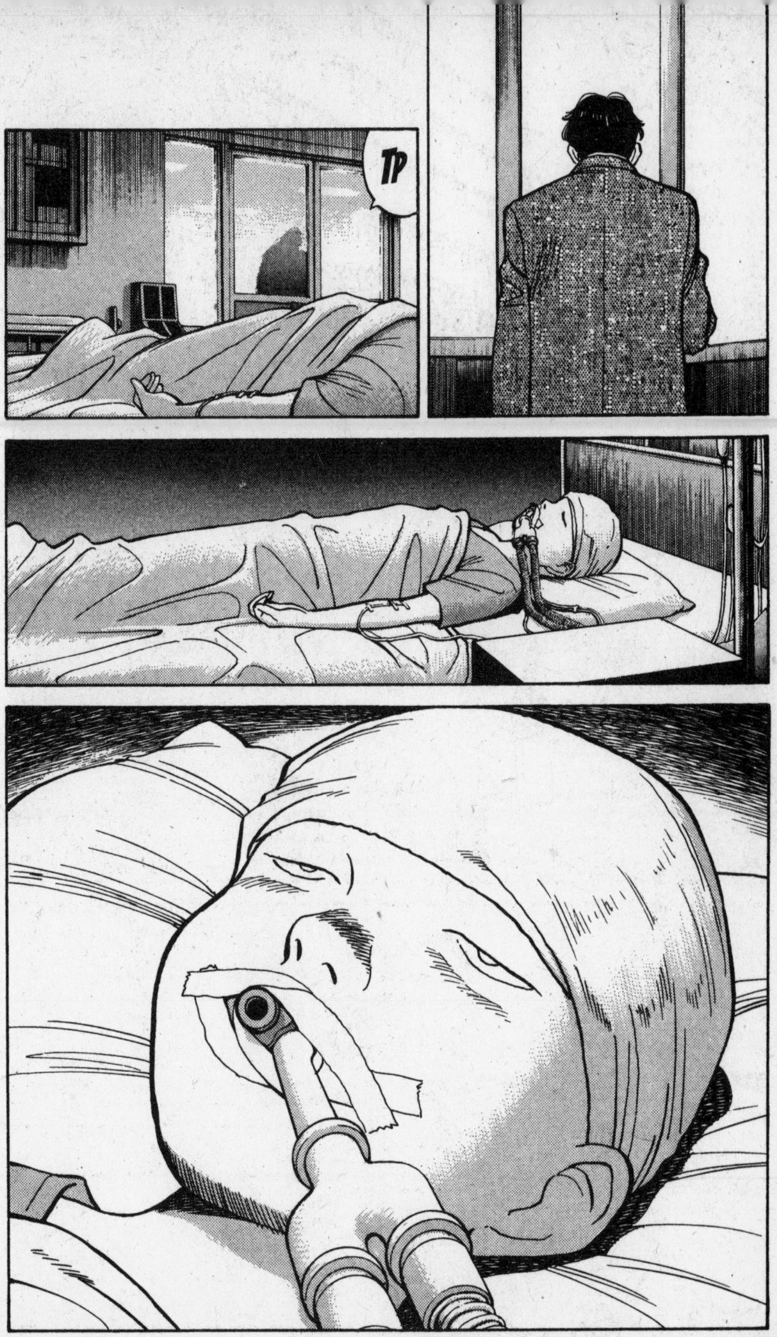
TP

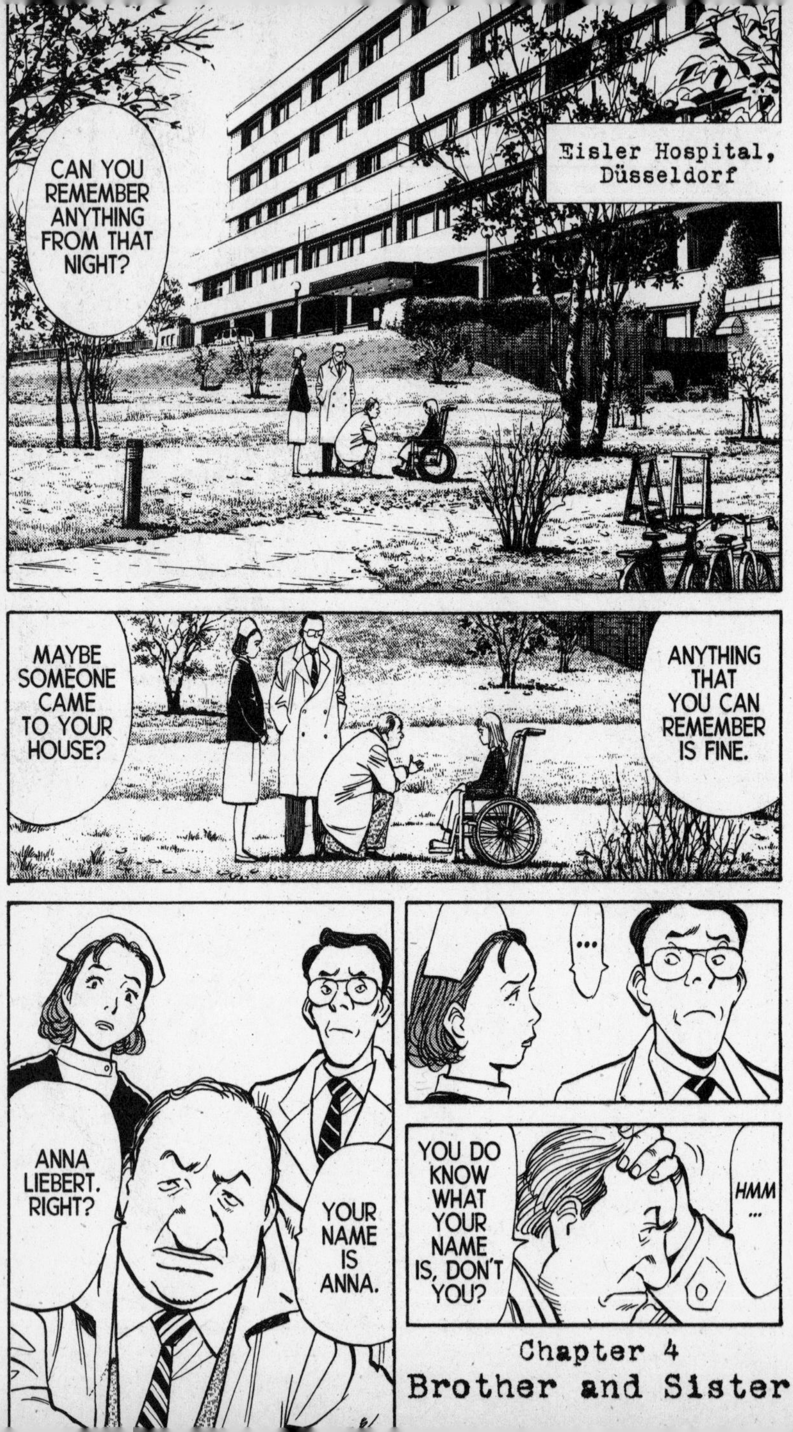
Eisler Hospital, Düsseldorf
CAN YOU REMEMBER ANYTHING FROM THAT NIGHT?
ANYTHING THAT YOU CAN REMEMBER IS FINE.
MAYBE SOMEONE CAME TO YOUR HOUSE?
...
HMM...
YOU DO KNOW WHAT YOUR NAME IS, DON'T YOU?
YOUR NAME IS ANNA.
ANNA LIEBERT. RIGHT?

Chapter 4
Brother and Sister

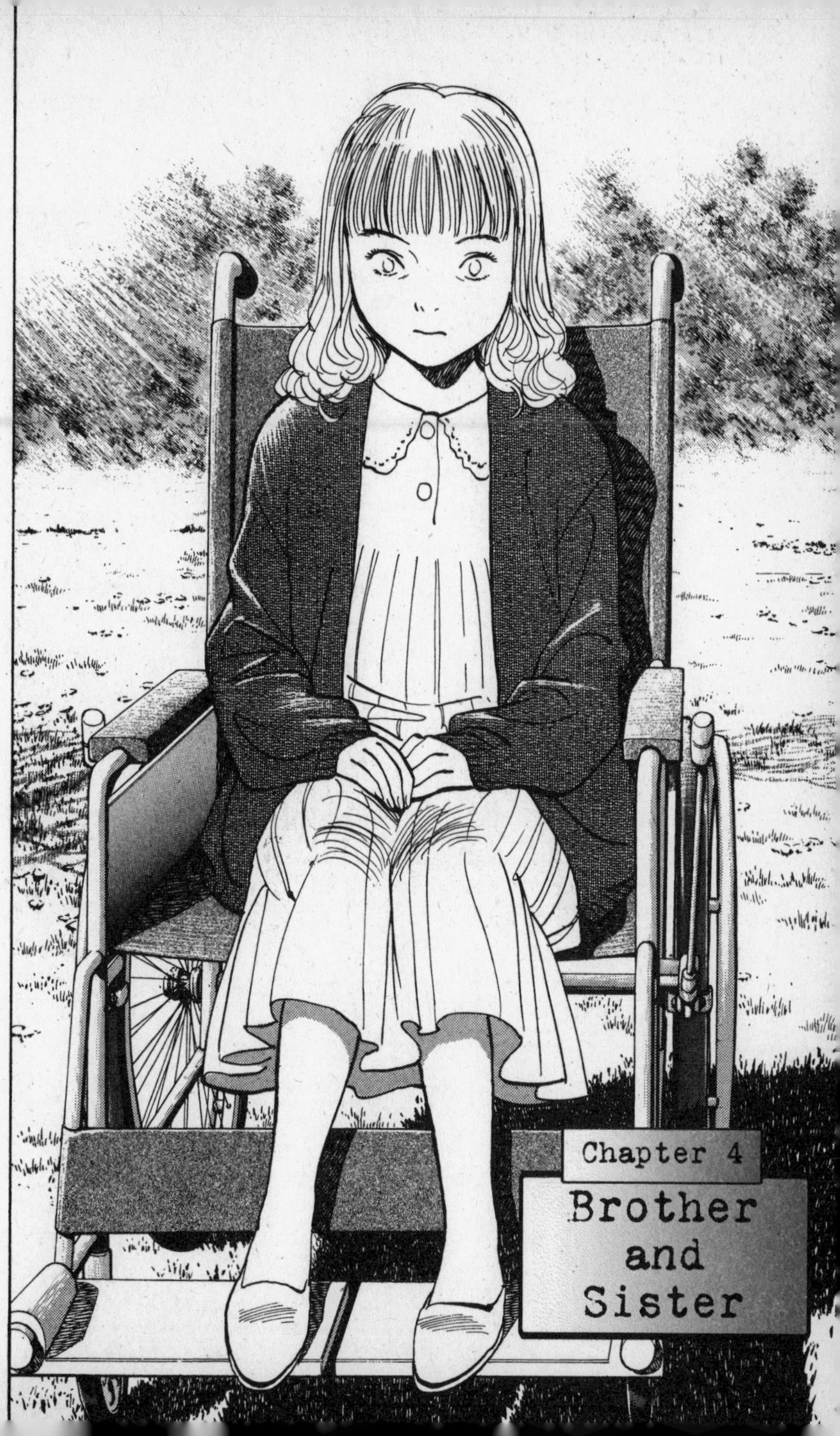
Chapter 4
Brother and Sister

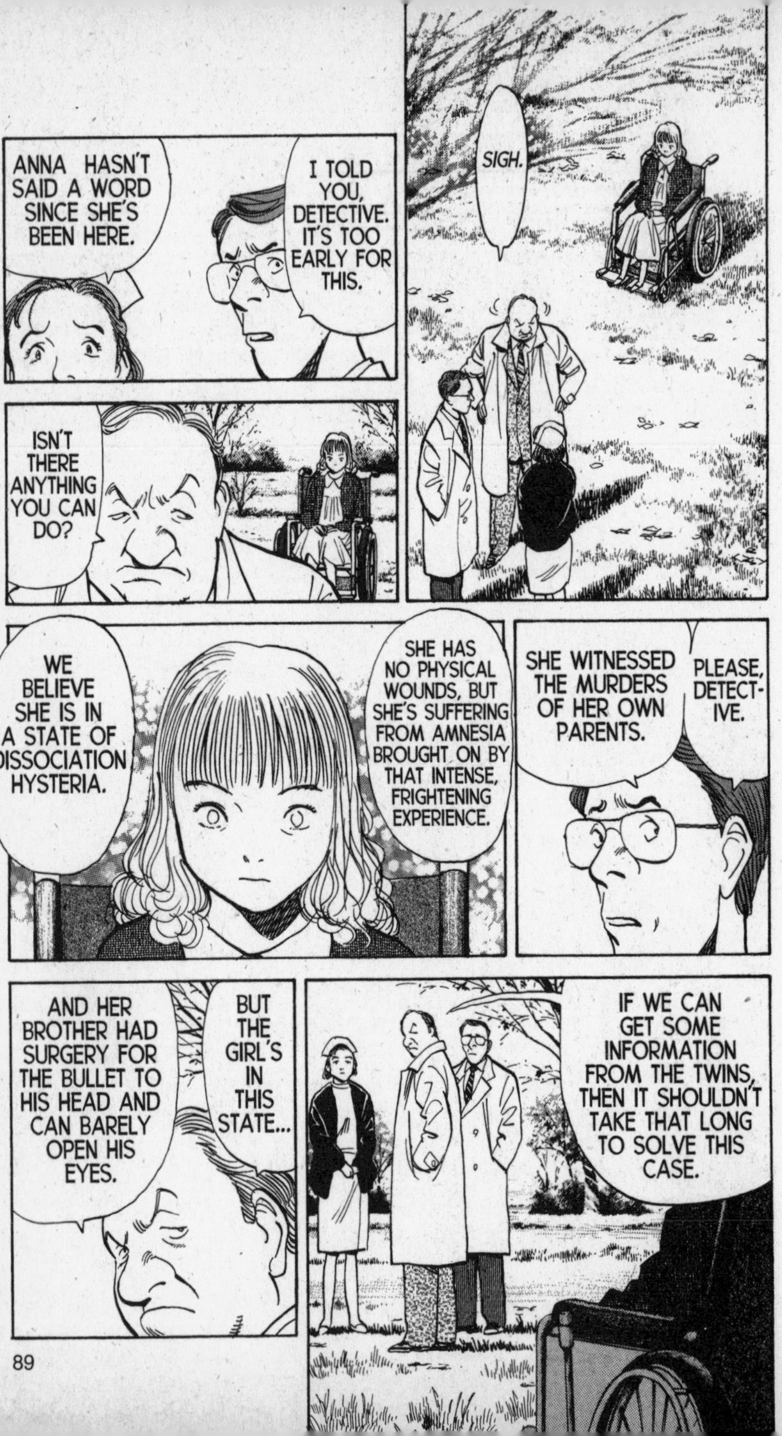
SIGH.
I TOLD YOU, DETECTIVE. IT'S TOO EARLY FOR THIS.
ANNA HASN'T SAID A WORD SINCE SHE'S BEEN HERE.
ISN'T THERE ANYTHING YOU CAN DO?
PLEASE, DETECT-IVE.
SHE WITNESSED THE MURDERS OF HER OWN PARENTS.
SHE HAS NO PHYSICAL WOUNDS, BUT SHE'S SUFFERING FROM AMNESIA BROUGHT ON BY THAT INTENSE, FRIGHTENING EXPERIENCE.
WE BELIEVE SHE IS IN A STATE OF DISSOCIATION HYSTERIA.
IF WE CAN GET SOME INFORMATION FROM THE TWINS, THEN IT SHOULDN'T TAKE THAT LONG TO SOLVE THIS CASE.
BUT THE GIRL'S IN THIS STATE...
AND HER BROTHER HAD SURGERY FOR THE BULLET TO HIS HEAD AND CAN BARELY OPEN HIS EYES.

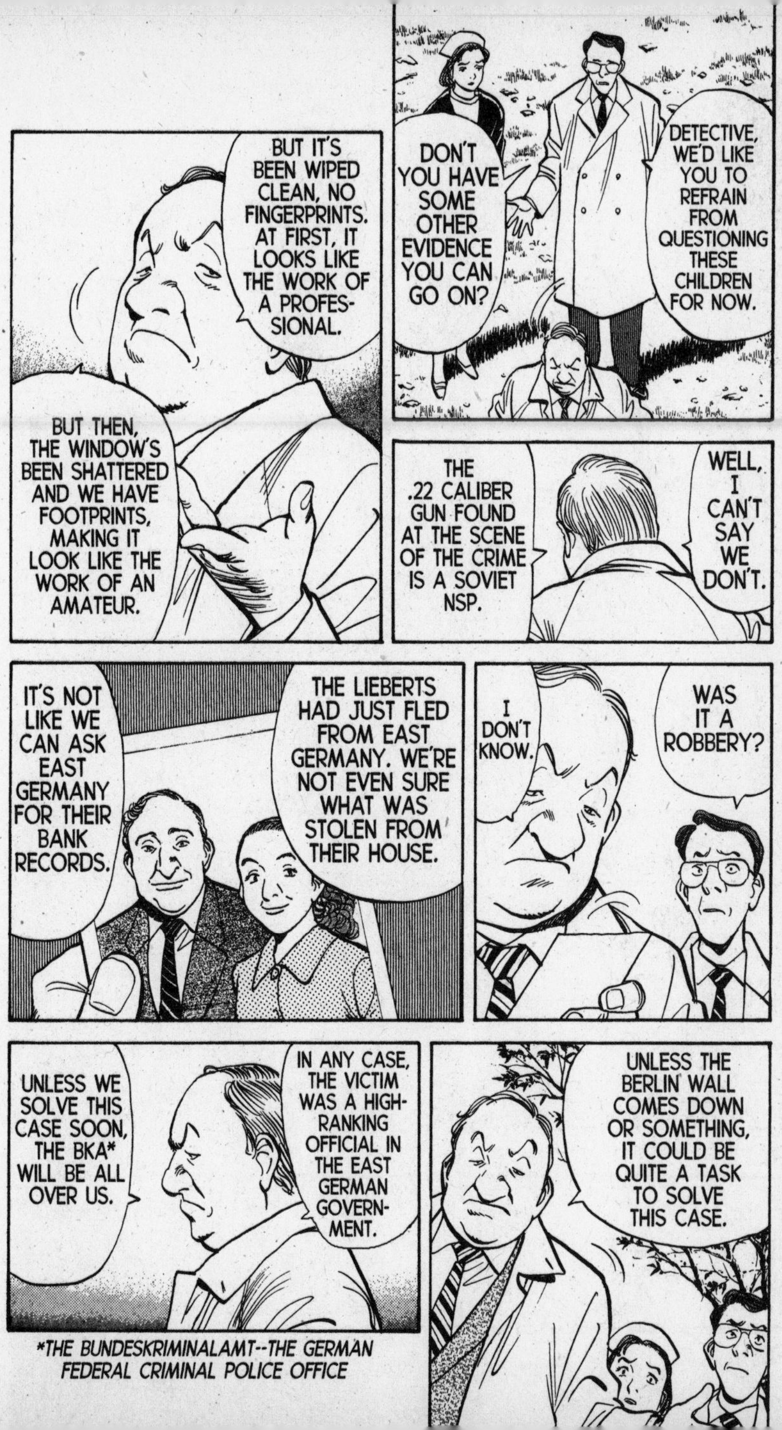
DETECTIVE, WE'D LIKE YOU TO REFRAIN FROM QUESTIONING THESE CHILDREN FOR NOW.
DON'T YOU HAVE SOME OTHER EVIDENCE YOU CAN GO ON?
WELL, I CAN'T SAY WE DON'T.
THE .22 CALIBER GUN FOUND AT THE SCENE OF THE CRIME IS A SOVIET NSP.
BUT IT'S BEEN WIPED CLEAN, NO FINGERPRINTS. AT FIRST, IT LOOKS LIKE THE WORK OF A PROFES-SIONAL.
BUT THEN, THE WINDOW'S BEEN SHATTERED AND WE HAVE FOOTPRINTS, MAKING IT LOOK LIKE THE WORK OF AN AMATEUR.
WAS IT A ROBBERY?
I DON'T KNOW.
THE LIEBERTS HAD JUST FLED FROM EAST GERMANY. WE'RE NOT EVEN SURE WHAT WAS STOLEN FROM THEIR HOUSE.
IT'S NOT LIKE WE CAN ASK EAST GERMANY FOR THEIR BANK RECORDS.
UNLESS THE BERLIN WALL COMES DOWN OR SOMETHING, IT COULD BE QUITE A TASK TO SOLVE THIS CASE.
IN ANY CASE, THE VICTIM WAS A HIGH-RANKING OFFICIAL IN THE EAST GERMAN GOVERN-MENT.
UNLESS WE SOLVE THIS CASE SOON, THE BKA* WILL BE ALL OVER US.

THE BUNDESKRIMINALAMT--THE GERMAN FEDERAL CRIMINAL POLICE OFFICE

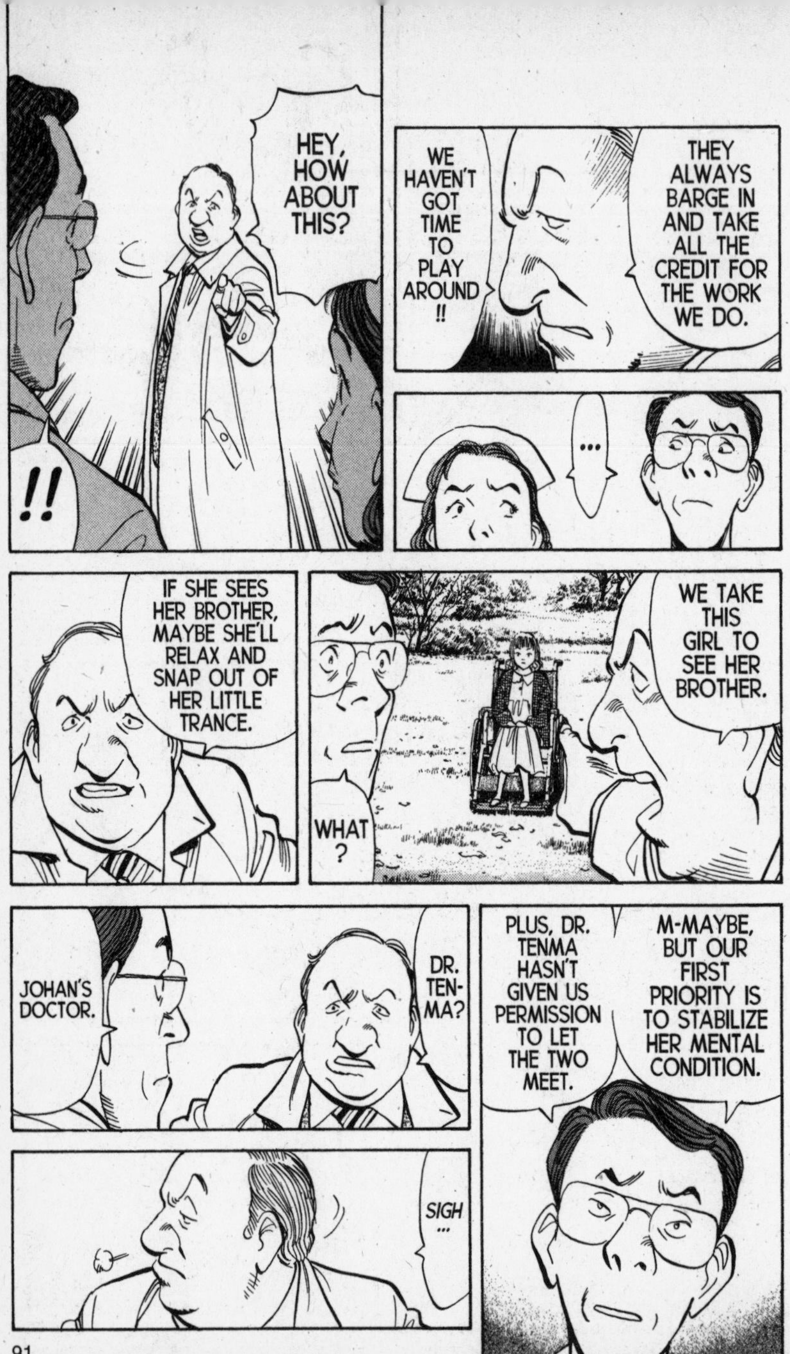
THEY ALWAYS BARGE IN AND TAKE ALL THE CREDIT FOR THE WORK WE DO.
WE HAVEN'T GOT TIME TO PLAY AROUND!!
...
HEY, HOW ABOUT THIS?
!!
WE TAKE THIS GIRL TO SEE HER BROTHER.
WHAT?
IF SHE SEES HER BROTHER, MAYBE SHE'LL RELAX AND SNAP OUT OF HER LITTLE TRANCE.
M-MAYBE, BUT OUR FIRST PRIORITY IS TO STABILIZE HER MENTAL CONDITION.
PLUS, DR. TENMA HASN'T GIVEN US PERMISSION TO LET THE TWO MEET.
DR. TEN-MA?
JOHAN'S DOCTOR.
SIGH...

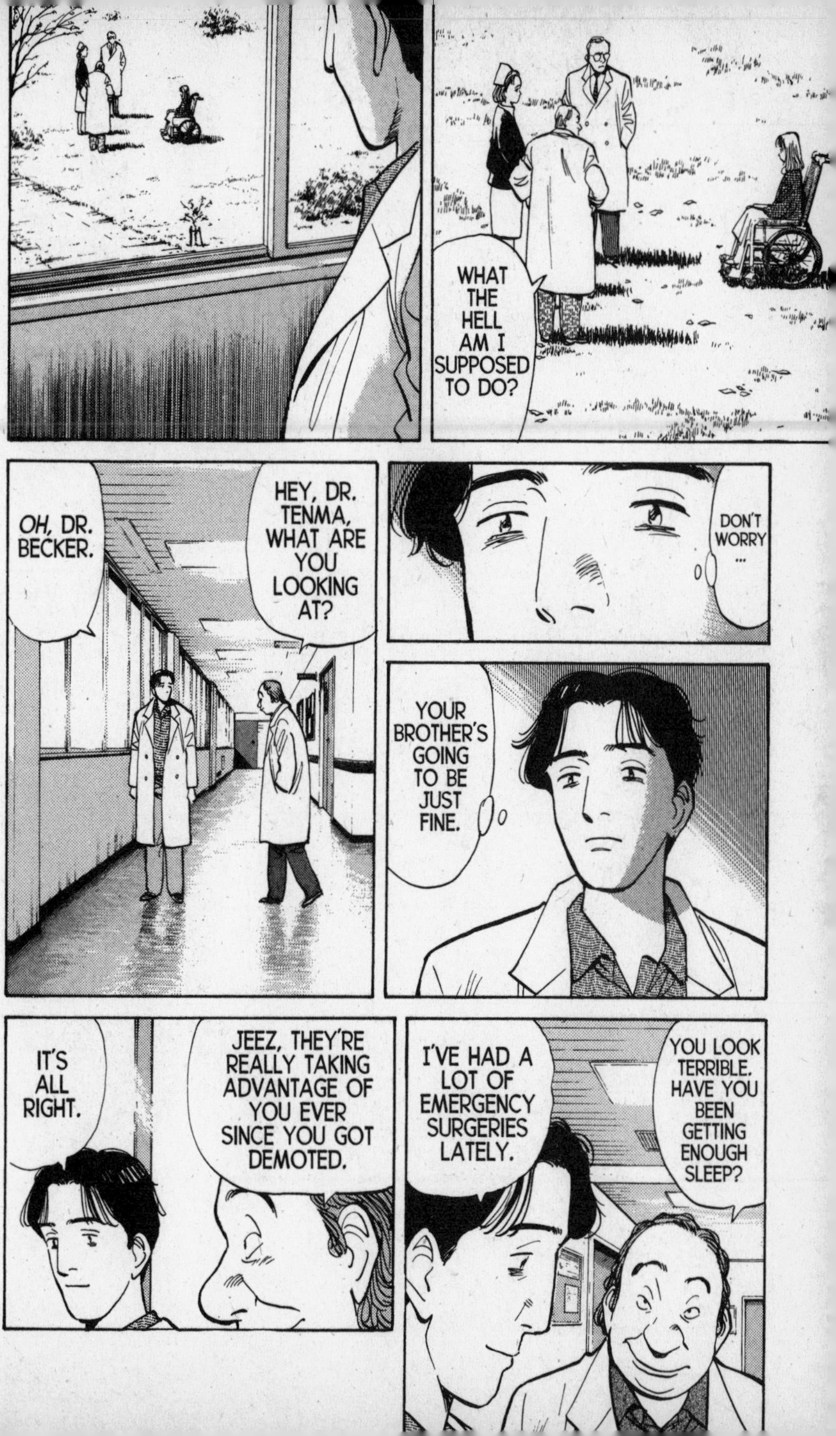
WHAT THE HELL AM I SUPPOSED TO DO?
DON'T WORRY...
YOUR BROTHER'S GOING TO BE JUST FINE.
HEY, DR. TENMA, WHAT ARE YOU LOOKING AT?
OH, DR. BECKER.
YOU LOOK TERRIBLE. HAVE YOU BEEN GETTING ENOUGH SLEEP?
I'VE HAD A LOT OF EMERGENCY SURGERIES LATELY.
JEEZ, THEY'RE REALLY TAKING ADVANTAGE OF YOU EVER SINCE YOU GOT DEMOTED.
IT'S ALL RIGHT.

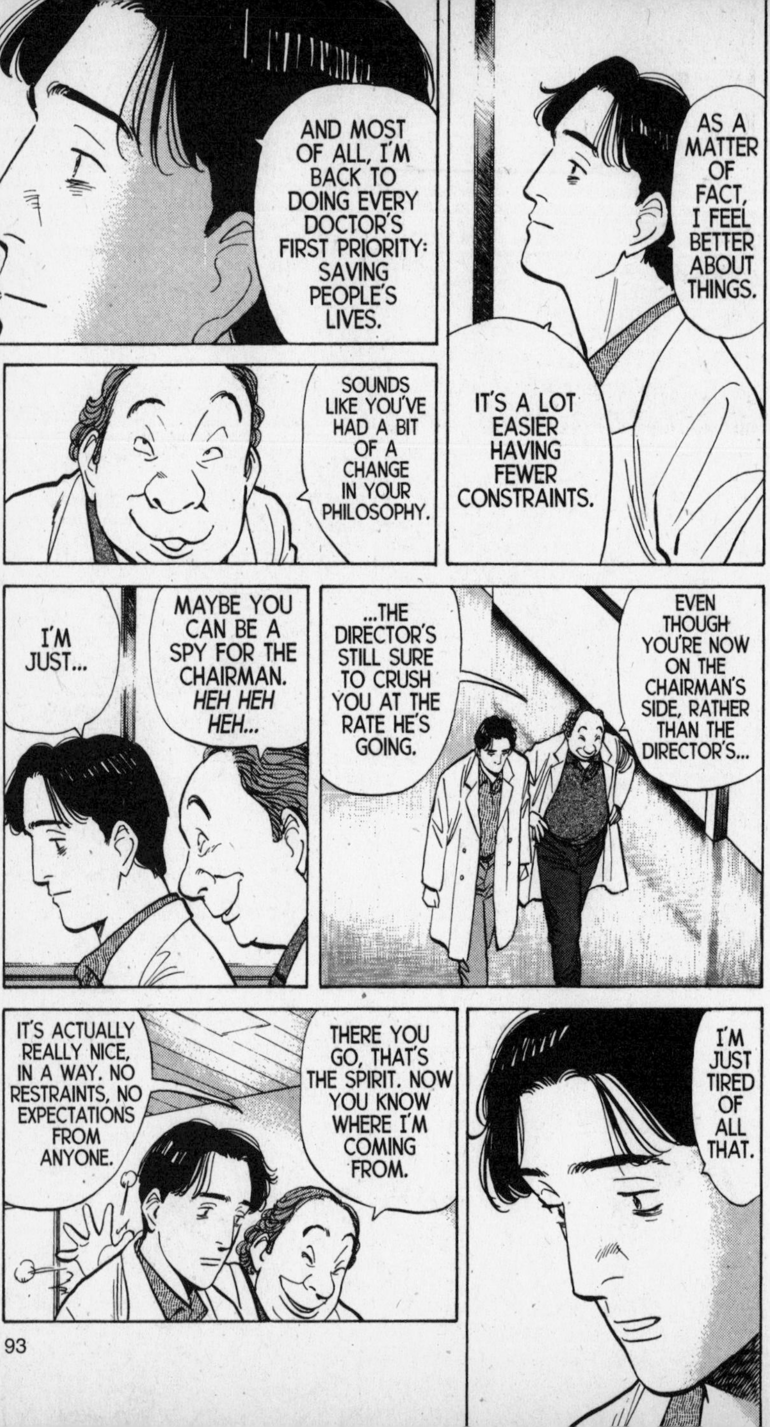
AS A MATTER OF FACT, I FEEL BETTER ABOUT THINGS.
IT'S A LOT EASIER HAVING FEWER CONSTRAINTS.
AND MOST OF ALL, I'M BACK TO DOING EVERY DOCTOR'S FIRST PRIORITY: SAVING PEOPLE'S LIVES.
SOUNDS LIKE YOU'VE HAD A BIT OF A CHANGE IN YOUR PHILOSOPHY.
EVEN THOUGH YOU'RE NOW ON THE CHAIRMAN'S SIDE, RATHER THAN THE DIRECTOR'S...
...THE DIRECTOR'S STILL SURE TO CRUSH YOU AT THE RATE HE'S GOING.
MAYBE YOU CAN BE A SPY FOR THE CHAIRMAN. *HEH HEH HEH...*
I'M JUST...
I'M JUST TIRED OF ALL THAT.
IT'S ACTUALLY REALLY NICE, IN A WAY. NO RESTRAINTS, NO EXPECTATIONS FROM ANYONE.
THERE YOU GO, THAT'S THE SPIRIT. NOW YOU KNOW WHERE I'M COMING FROM.

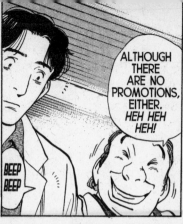

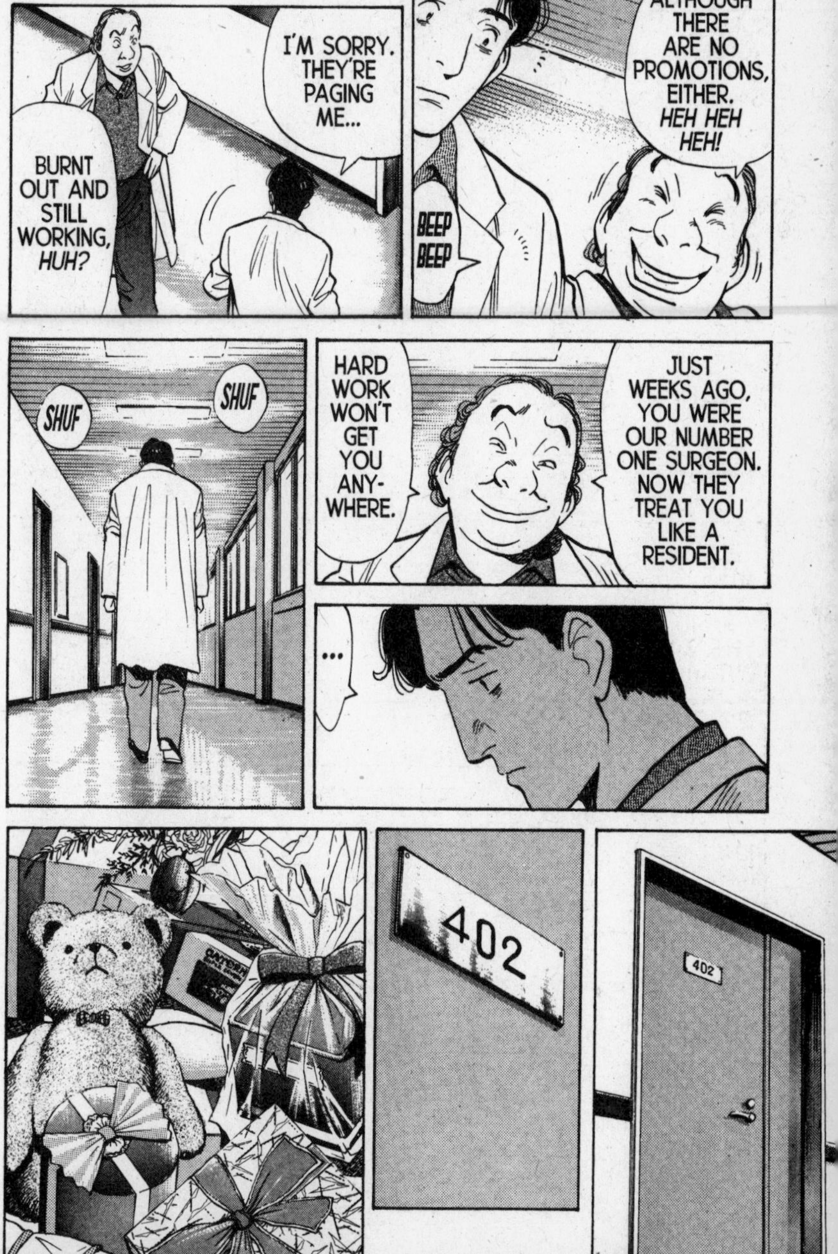
ALTHOUGH THERE ARE NO PROMOTIONS, EITHER. *HEH HEH HEH!*
BEEP BEEP
I'M SORRY. THEY'RE PAGING ME...
BURNT OUT AND STILL WORKING, *HUH?*
JUST WEEKS AGO, YOU WERE OUR NUMBER ONE SURGEON. NOW THEY TREAT YOU LIKE A RESIDENT.
HARD WORK WON'T GET YOU ANY-WHERE.
...
SHUF
SHUF
402
402

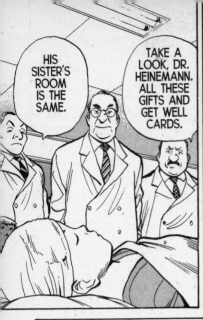

TAKE A LOOK, DR. HEINEMANN. ALL THESE GIFTS AND GET WELL CARDS.
HIS SISTER'S ROOM IS THE SAME.
THE PRESS PUTS OUT A SOB STORY ABOUT HOW THESE KIDS ARE ORPHANED, AND THIS IS WHAT HAPPENS.
ALL THE WHILE, THE HOSPITAL HASN'T FIGURED OUT WHO'S GOING TO PAY THEIR BILLS.
THE POLICE PRESENCE IS STARTING TO MAKE THE OTHER PATIENTS UNEASY, TOO.
THAT'S NOT ALL.
THERE'S A POSSIBILITY THAT THE MURDER OF THEIR PARENTS WAS THE WORK OF TERRORISTS. THEY MAY COME TO THE HOSPITAL TO GET THESE KIDS.
REALLY, THAT'S THE LAST THING WE NEED.
NOW, NOW.

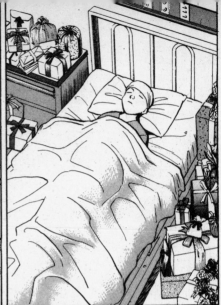

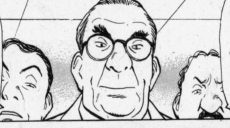

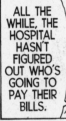

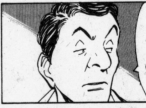

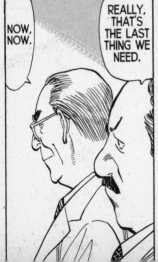

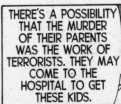

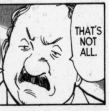

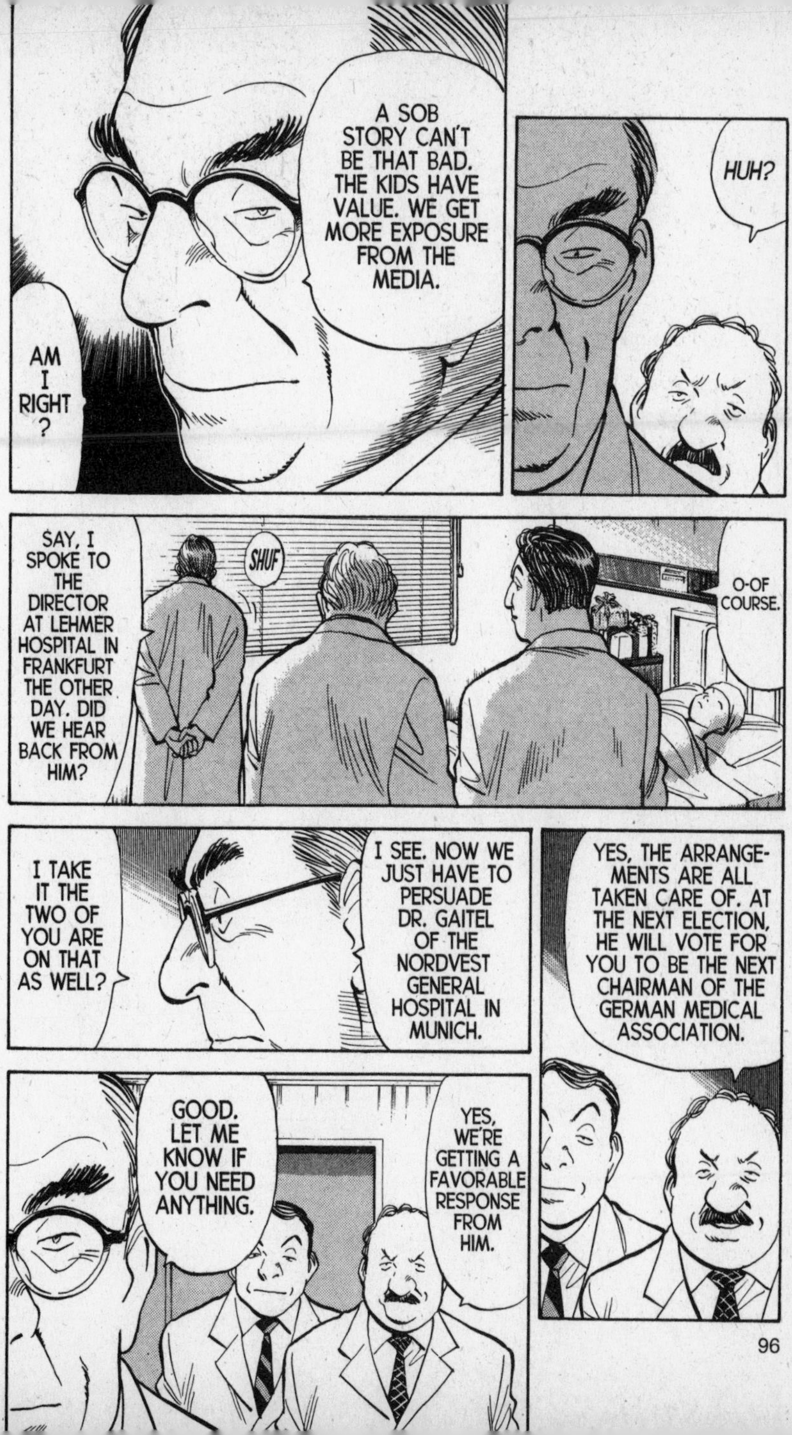
HUH?
A SOB STORY CAN'T BE THAT BAD. THE KIDS HAVE VALUE. WE GET MORE EXPOSURE FROM THE MEDIA.
AM I RIGHT?
O-OF COURSE.
SHUF
SAY, I SPOKE TO THE DIRECTOR AT LEHMER HOSPITAL IN FRANKFURT THE OTHER DAY. DID WE HEAR BACK FROM HIM?
YES, THE ARRANGEMENTS ARE ALL TAKEN CARE OF. AT THE NEXT ELECTION, HE WILL VOTE FOR YOU TO BE THE NEXT CHAIRMAN OF THE GERMAN MEDICAL ASSOCIATION.
I SEE. NOW WE JUST HAVE TO PERSUADE DR. GAITEL OF THE NORDVEST GENERAL HOSPITAL IN MUNICH.
I TAKE IT THE TWO OF YOU ARE ON THAT AS WELL?
YES, WE'RE GETTING A FAVORABLE RESPONSE FROM HIM.
GOOD. LET ME KNOW IF YOU NEED ANYTHING.

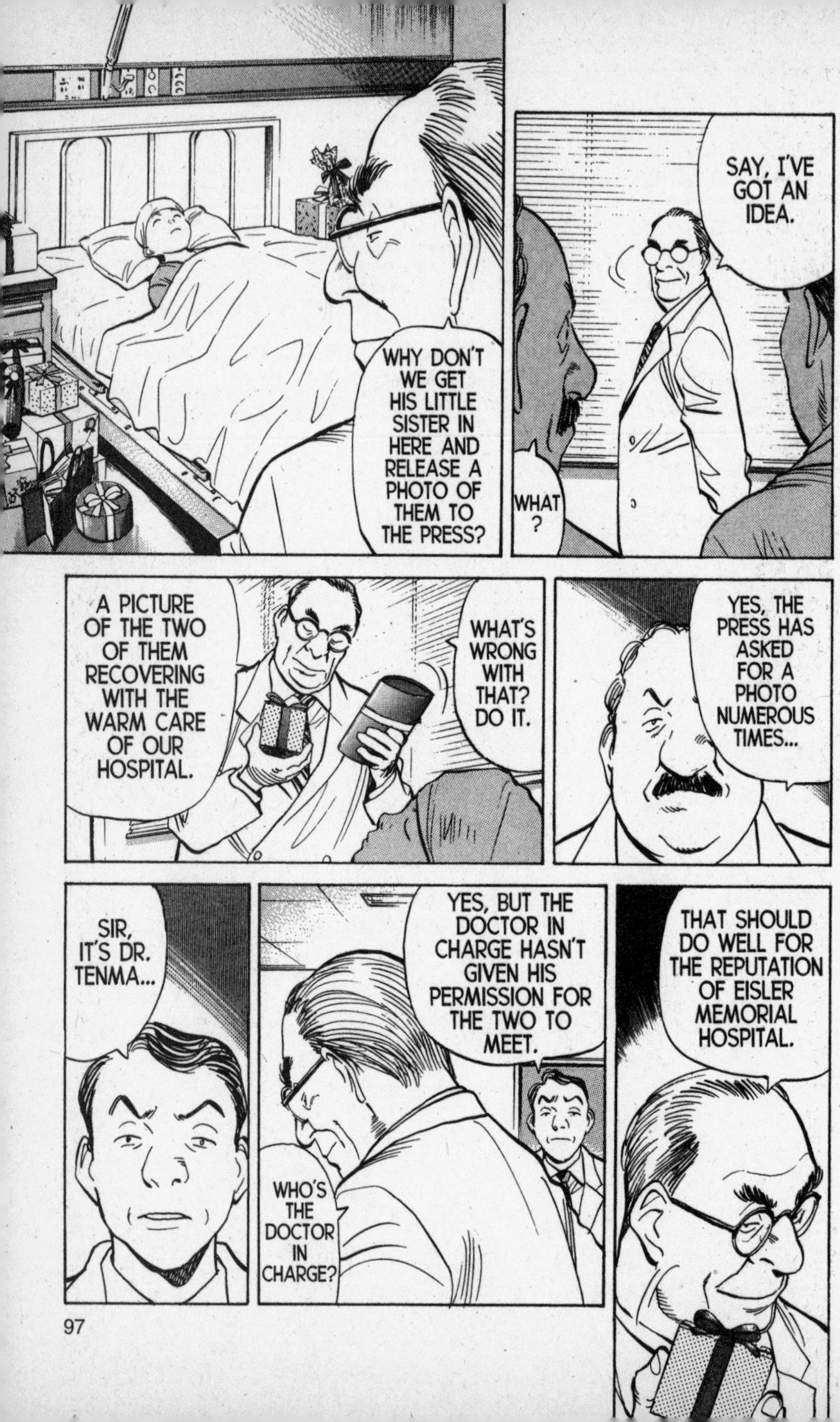
SAY, I'VE GOT AN IDEA.
WHAT?
WHY DON'T WE GET HIS LITTLE SISTER IN HERE AND RELEASE A PHOTO OF THEM TO THE PRESS?
YES, THE PRESS HAS ASKED FOR A PHOTO NUMEROUS TIMES...
WHAT'S WRONG WITH THAT? DO IT.
A PICTURE OF THE TWO OF THEM RECOVERING WITH THE WARM CARE OF OUR HOSPITAL.
THAT SHOULD DO WELL FOR THE REPUTATION OF EISLER MEMORIAL HOSPITAL.
YES, BUT THE DOCTOR IN CHARGE HASN'T GIVEN HIS PERMISSION FOR THE TWO TO MEET.
WHO'S THE DOCTOR IN CHARGE?
SIR, IT'S DR. TENMA...

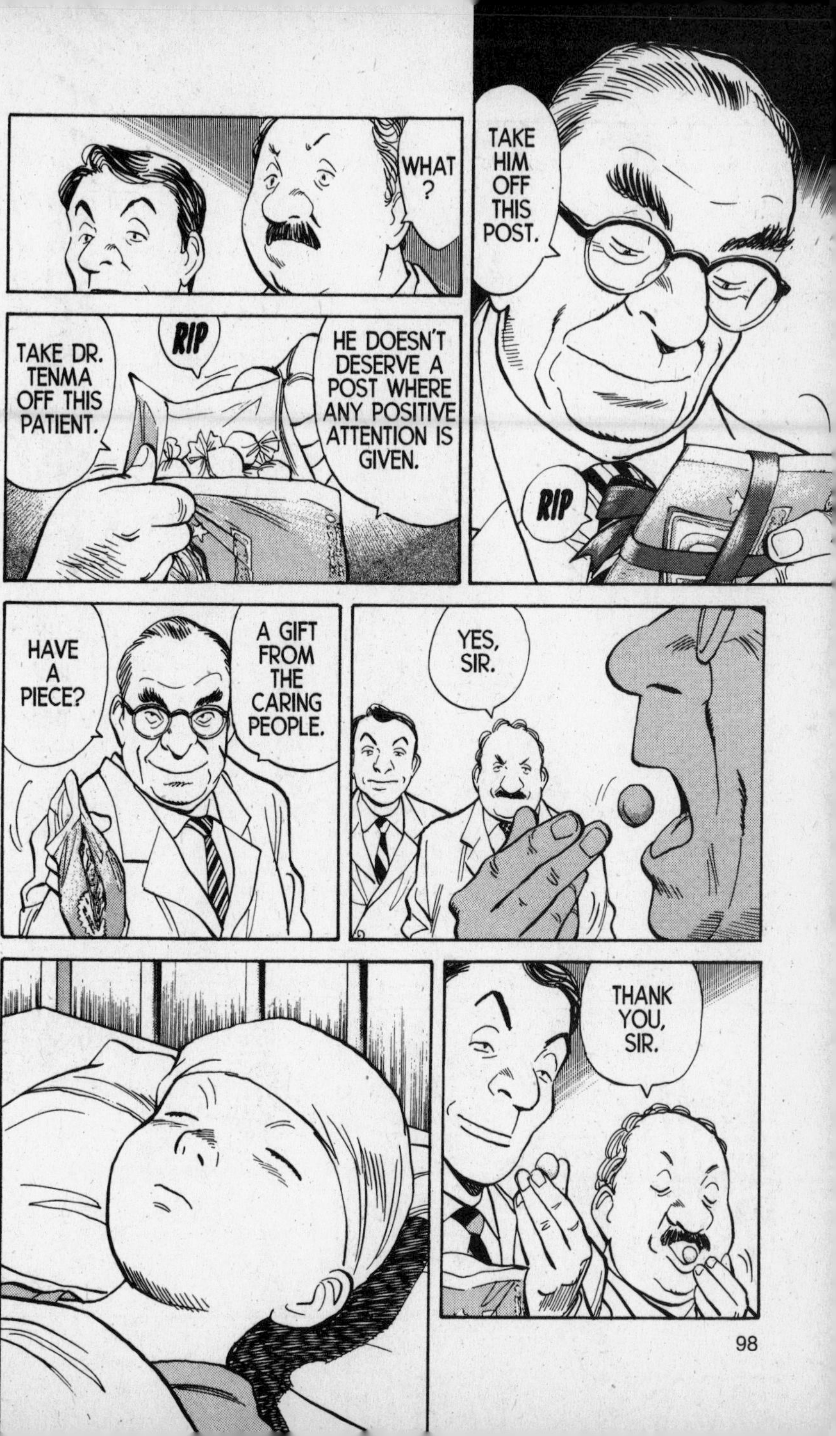
TAKE HIM OFF THIS POST.
RIP
WHAT?
HE DOESN'T DESERVE A POST WHERE ANY POSITIVE ATTENTION IS GIVEN.
RIP
TAKE DR. TENMA OFF THIS PATIENT.
YES, SIR.
A GIFT FROM THE CARING PEOPLE.
HAVE A PIECE?
THANK YOU, SIR.

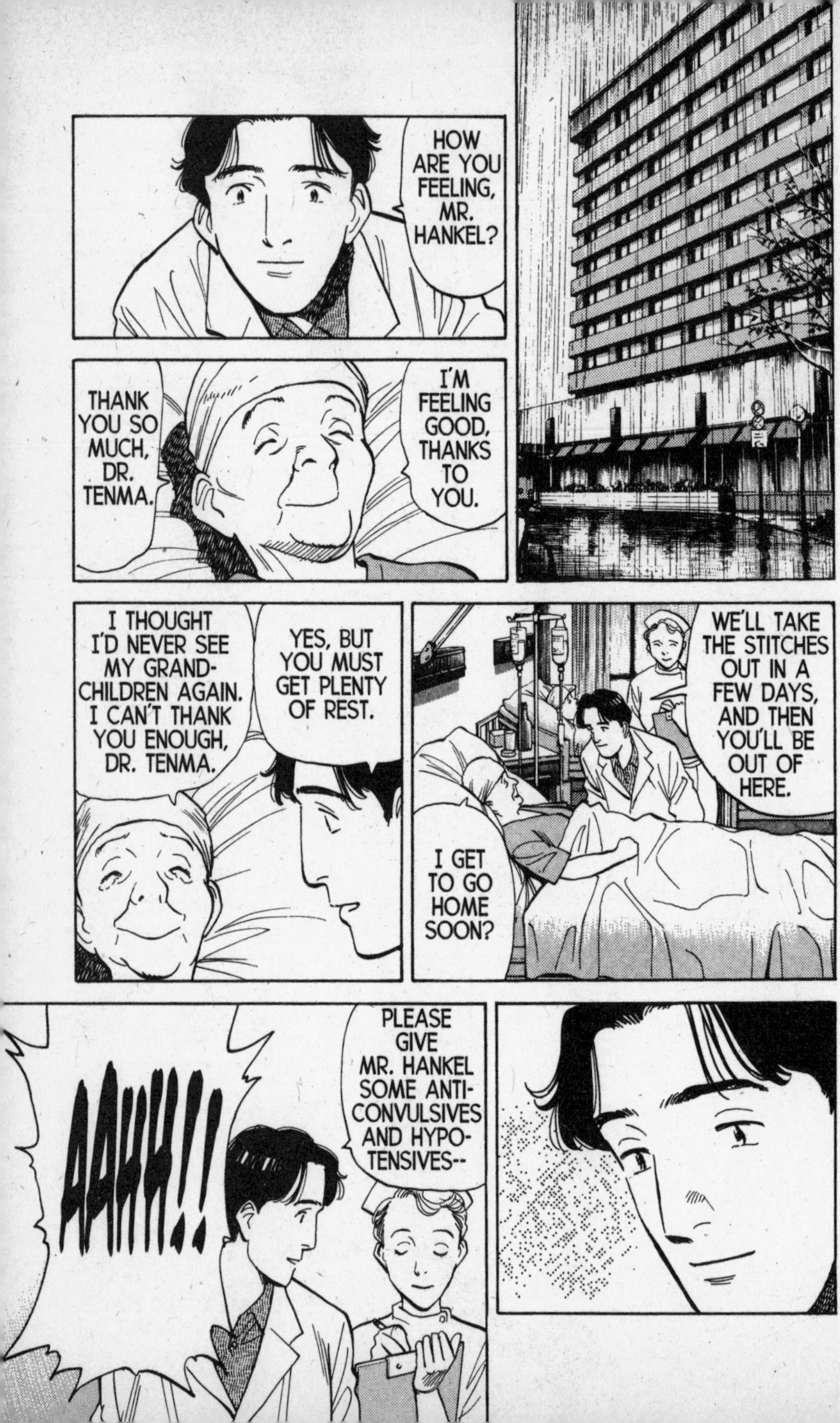
HOW ARE YOU FEELING, MR. HANKEL?
I'M FEELING GOOD, THANKS TO YOU.
THANK YOU SO MUCH, DR. TENMA.
WE'LL TAKE THE STITCHES OUT IN A FEW DAYS, AND THEN YOU'LL BE OUT OF HERE.
I GET TO GO HOME SOON?
YES, BUT YOU MUST GET PLENTY OF REST.
I THOUGHT I'D NEVER SEE MY GRAND-CHILDREN AGAIN. I CAN'T THANK YOU ENOUGH, DR. TENMA.
PLEASE GIVE MR. HANKEL SOME ANTI-CONVULSIVES AND HYPO-TENSIVES--
AAHH!!

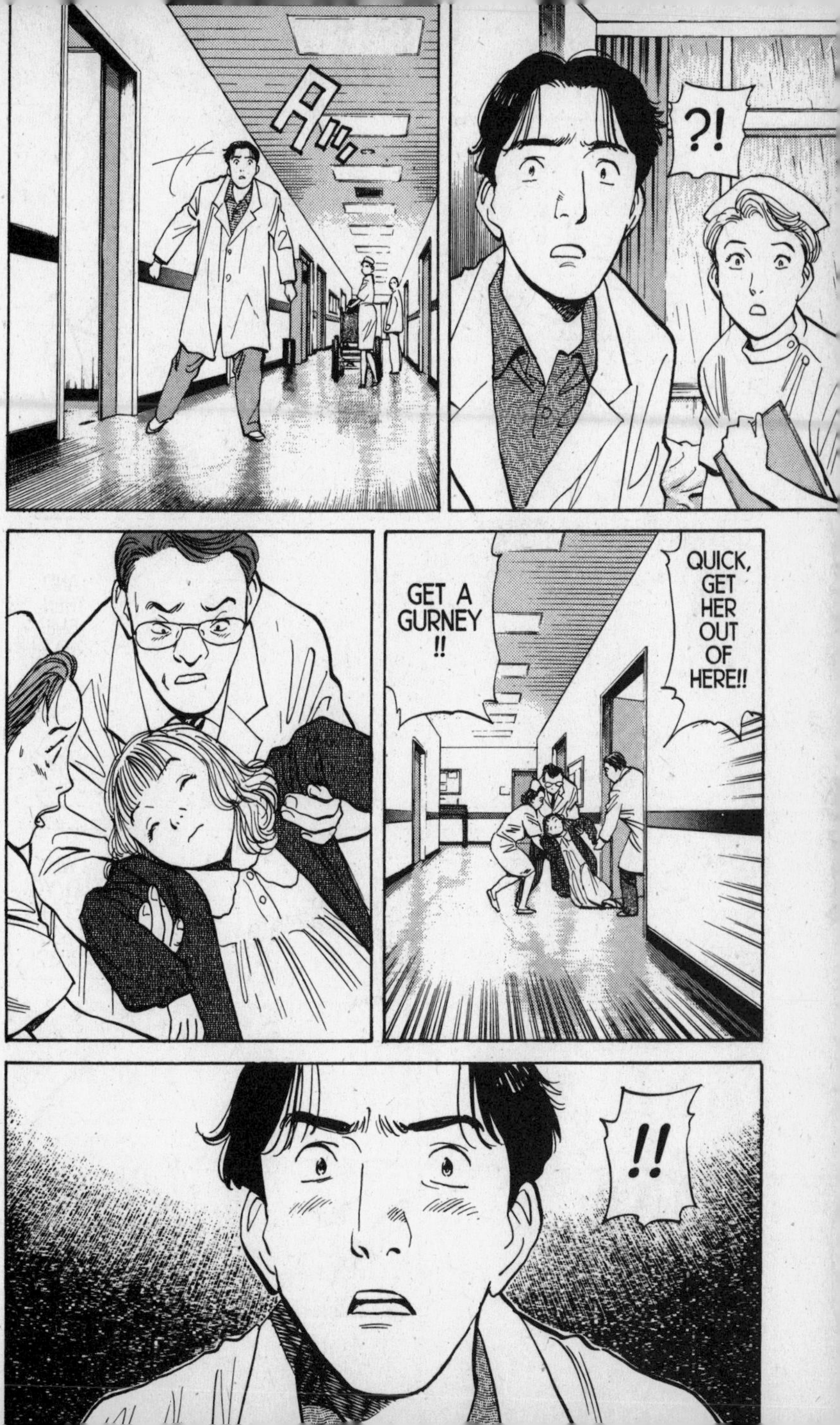
?!
QUICK, GET HER OUT OF HERE!!
GET A GURNEY !!
!!

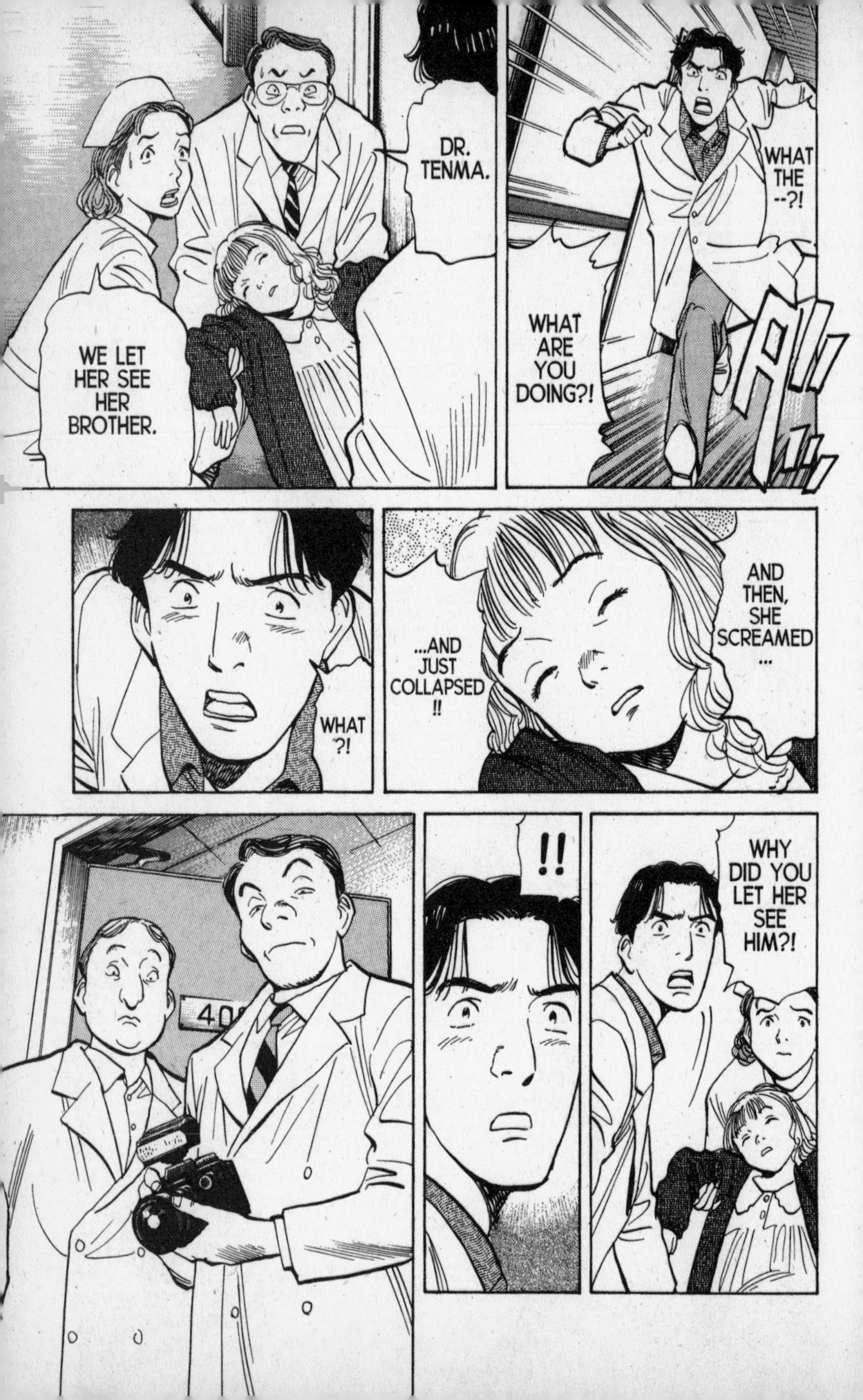
WHAT THE --?!
WHAT ARE YOU DOING?!
DR. TENMA.
WE LET HER SEE HER BROTHER.
AND THEN, SHE SCREAMED ...
...AND JUST COLLAPSED !!
WHAT ?!
WHY DID YOU LET HER SEE HIM?!
!!

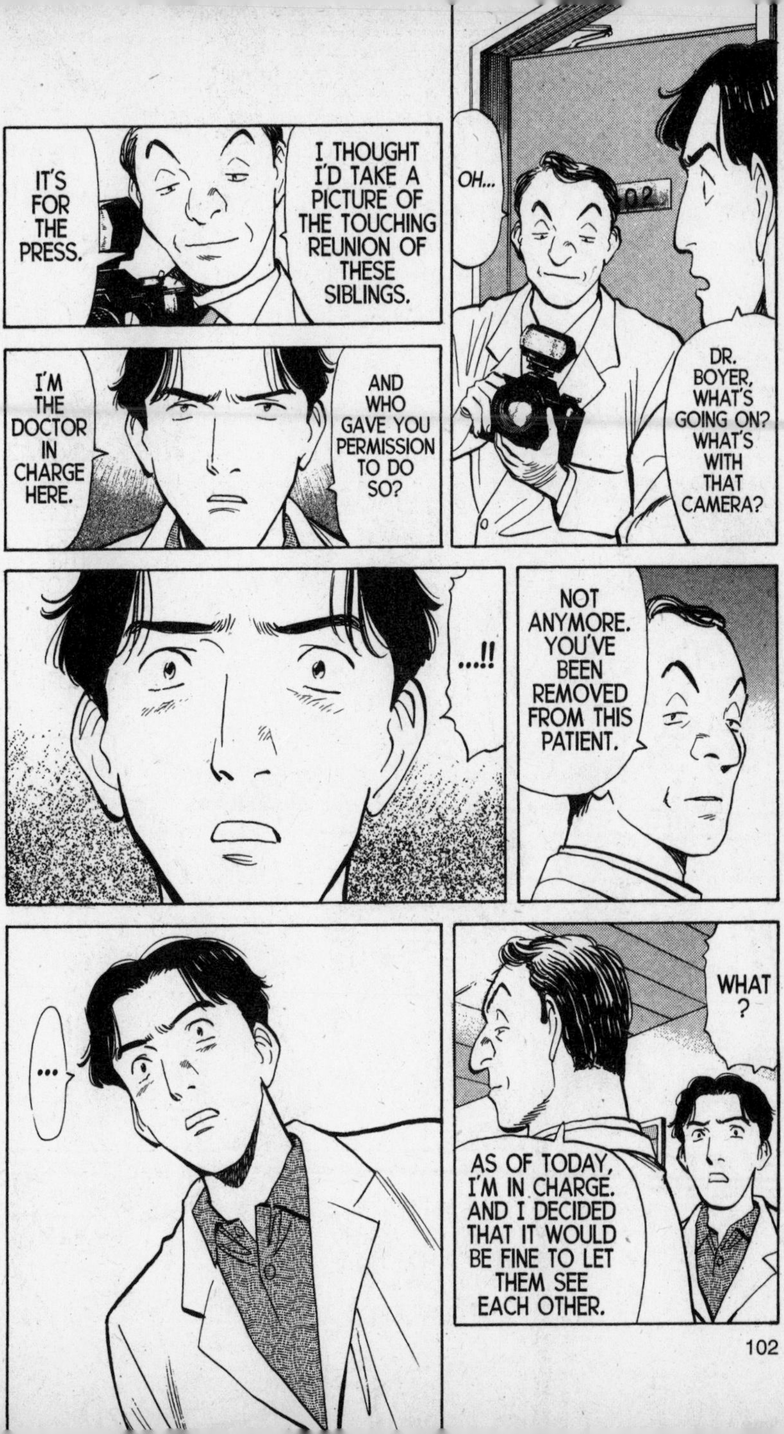
OH...
DR. BOYER, WHAT'S GOING ON? WHAT'S WITH THAT CAMERA?
I THOUGHT I'D TAKE A PICTURE OF THE TOUCHING REUNION OF THESE SIBLINGS.
IT'S FOR THE PRESS.
AND WHO GAVE YOU PERMISSION TO DO SO?
I'M THE DOCTOR IN CHARGE HERE.
NOT ANYMORE. YOU'VE BEEN REMOVED FROM THIS PATIENT.
...!!
WHAT?
AS OF TODAY, I'M IN CHARGE. AND I DECIDED THAT IT WOULD BE FINE TO LET THEM SEE EACH OTHER.
...

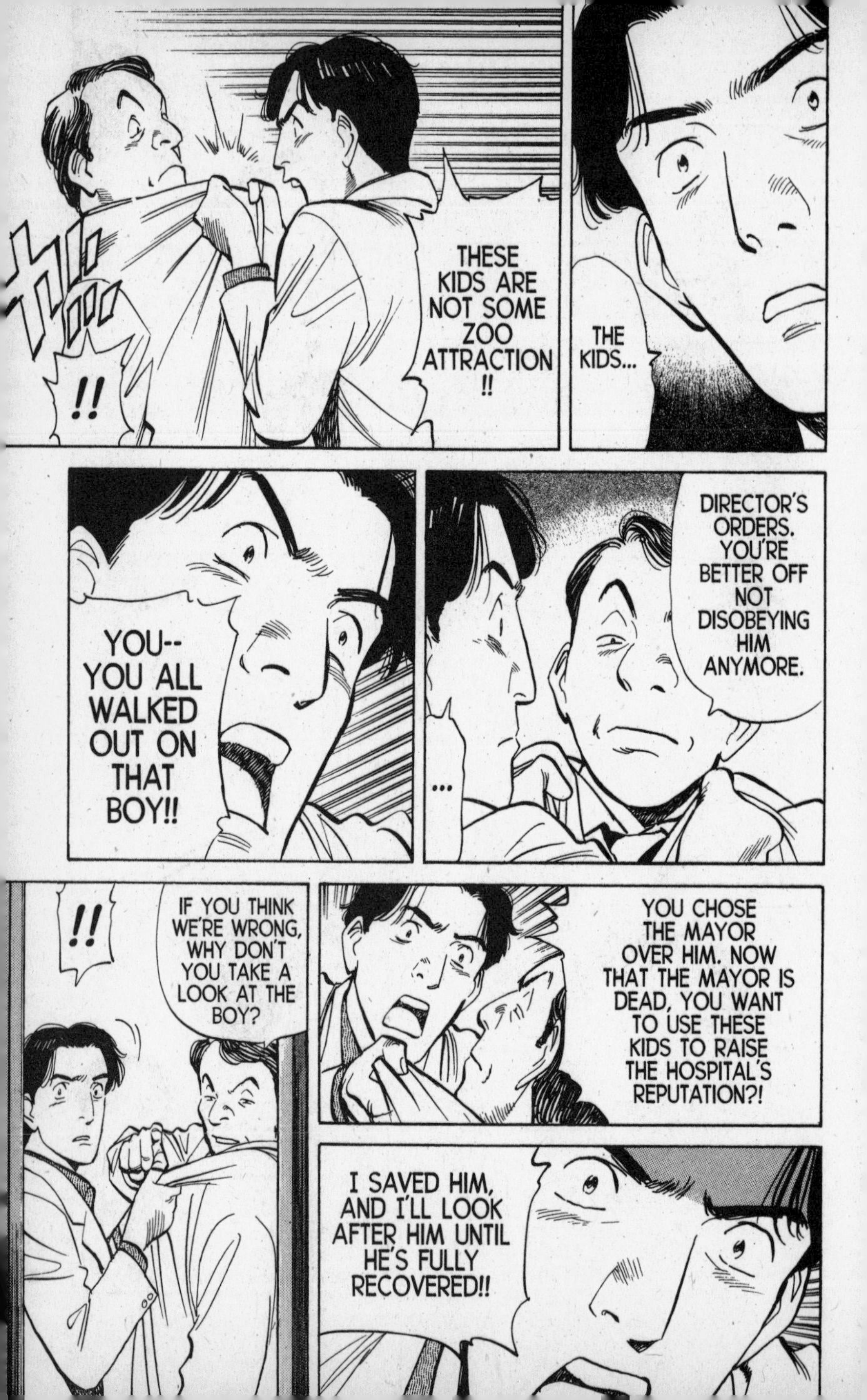
THE KIDS...
THESE KIDS ARE NOT SOME ZOO ATTRACTION !!
!!
DIRECTOR'S ORDERS. YOU'RE BETTER OFF NOT DISOBEYING HIM ANYMORE.
...
YOU-- YOU ALL WALKED OUT ON THAT BOY!!
YOU CHOSE THE MAYOR OVER HIM. NOW THAT THE MAYOR IS DEAD, YOU WANT TO USE THESE KIDS TO RAISE THE HOSPITAL'S REPUTATION?!
I SAVED HIM, AND I'LL LOOK AFTER HIM UNTIL HE'S FULLY RECOVERED!!
IF YOU THINK WE'RE WRONG, WHY DON'T YOU TAKE A LOOK AT THE BOY?
!!

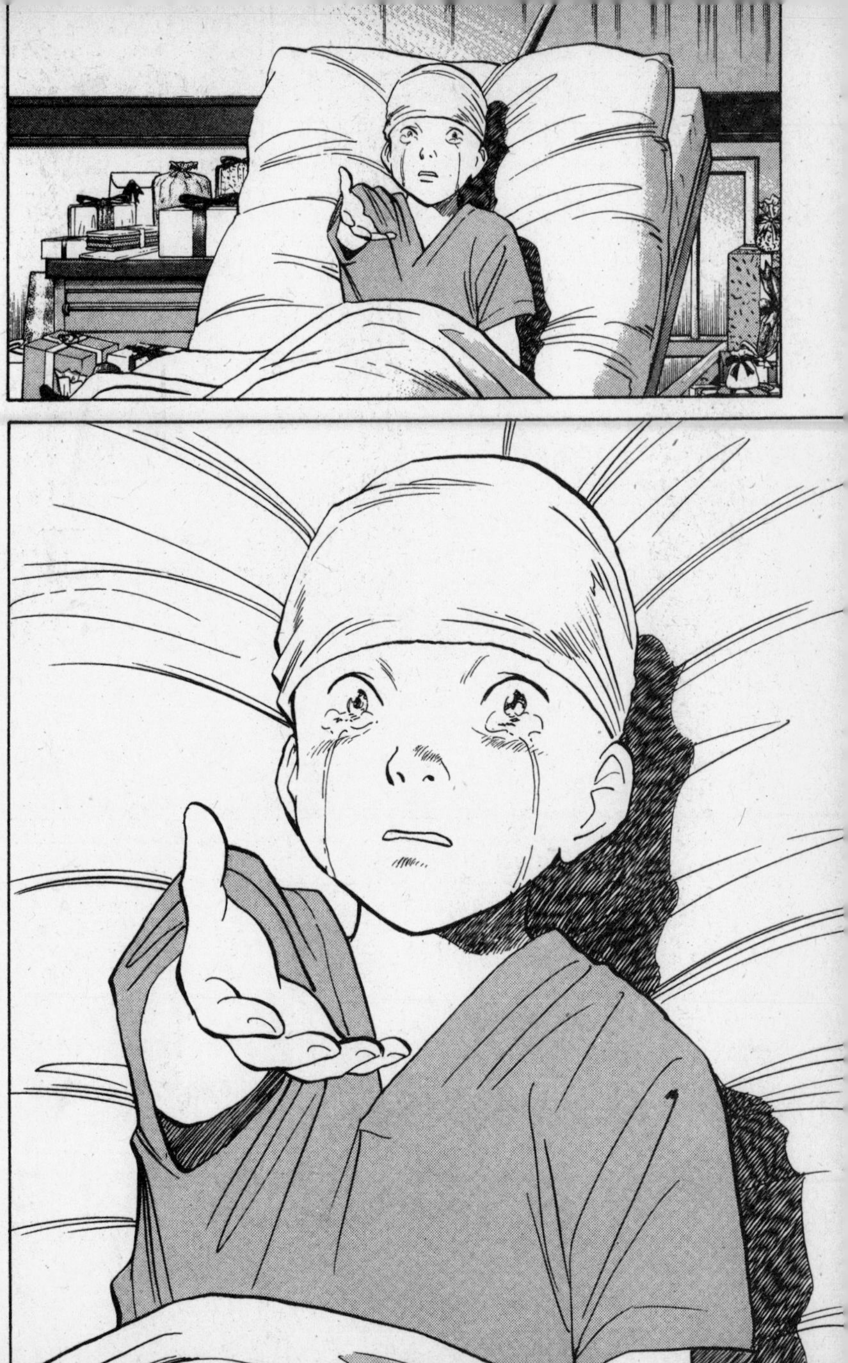

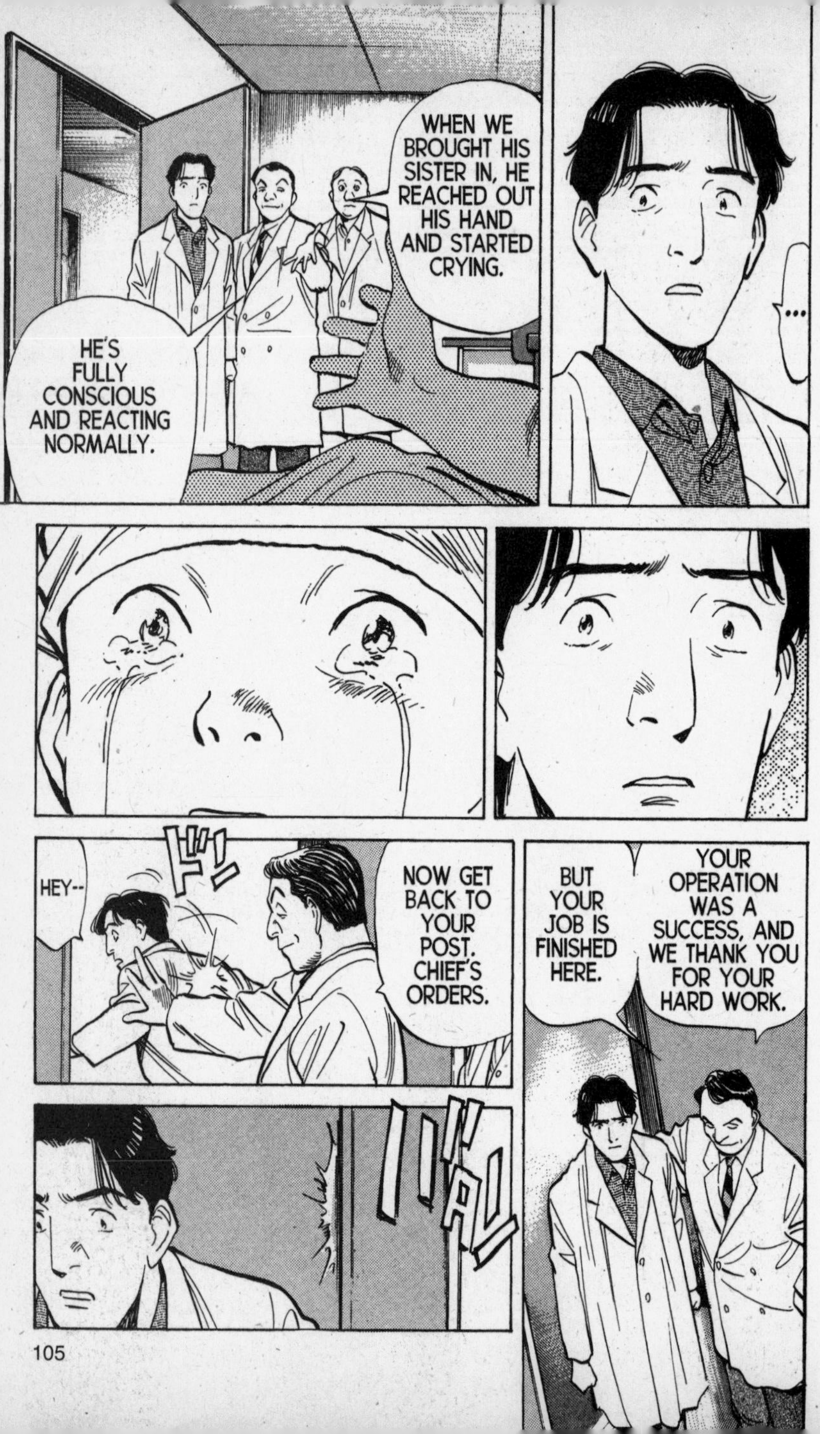
...
WHEN WE BROUGHT HIS SISTER IN, HE REACHED OUT HIS HAND AND STARTED CRYING.
HE'S FULLY CONSCIOUS AND REACTING NORMALLY.
YOUR OPERATION WAS A SUCCESS, AND WE THANK YOU FOR YOUR HARD WORK.
BUT YOUR JOB IS FINISHED HERE.
NOW GET BACK TO YOUR POST. CHIEF'S ORDERS.
HEY--

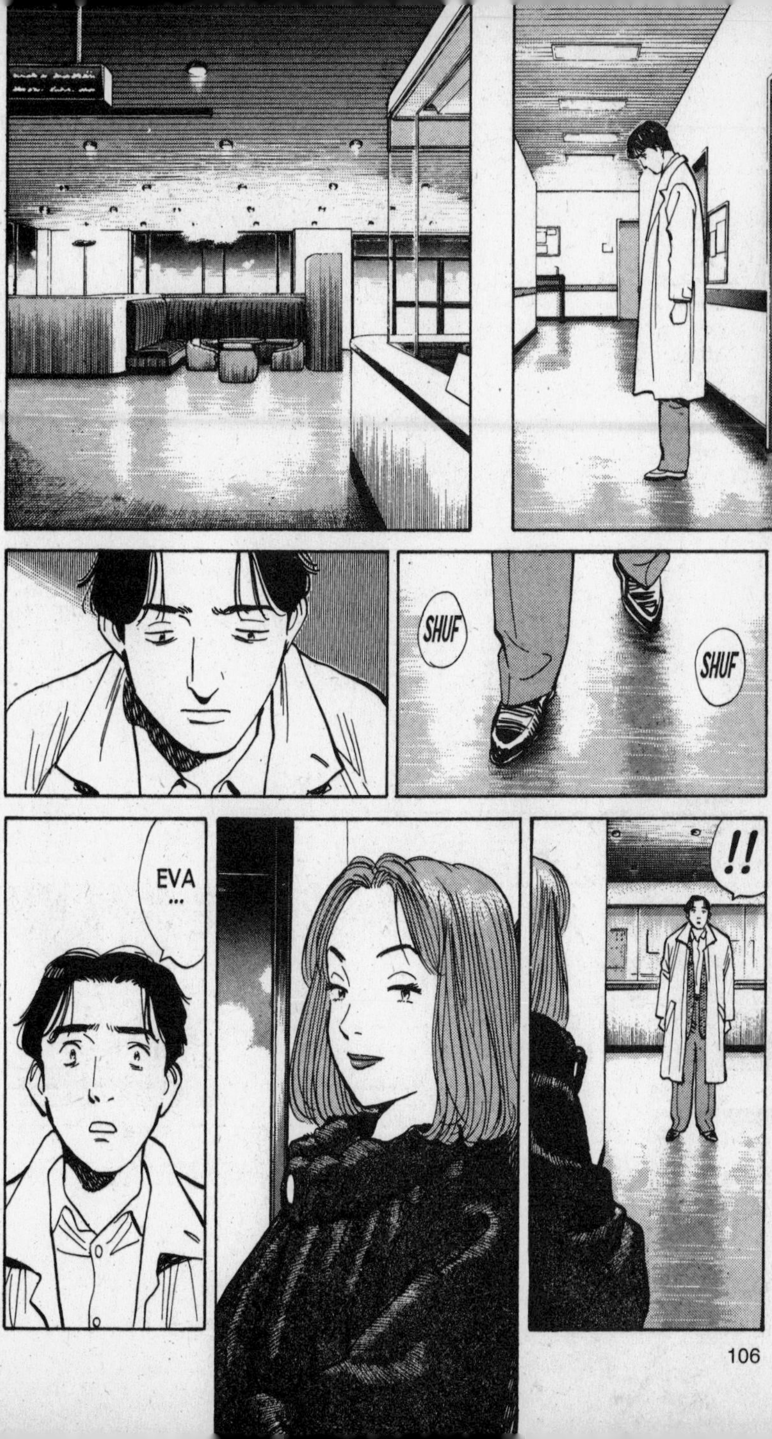
SHUF
SHUF
!!
EVA ...

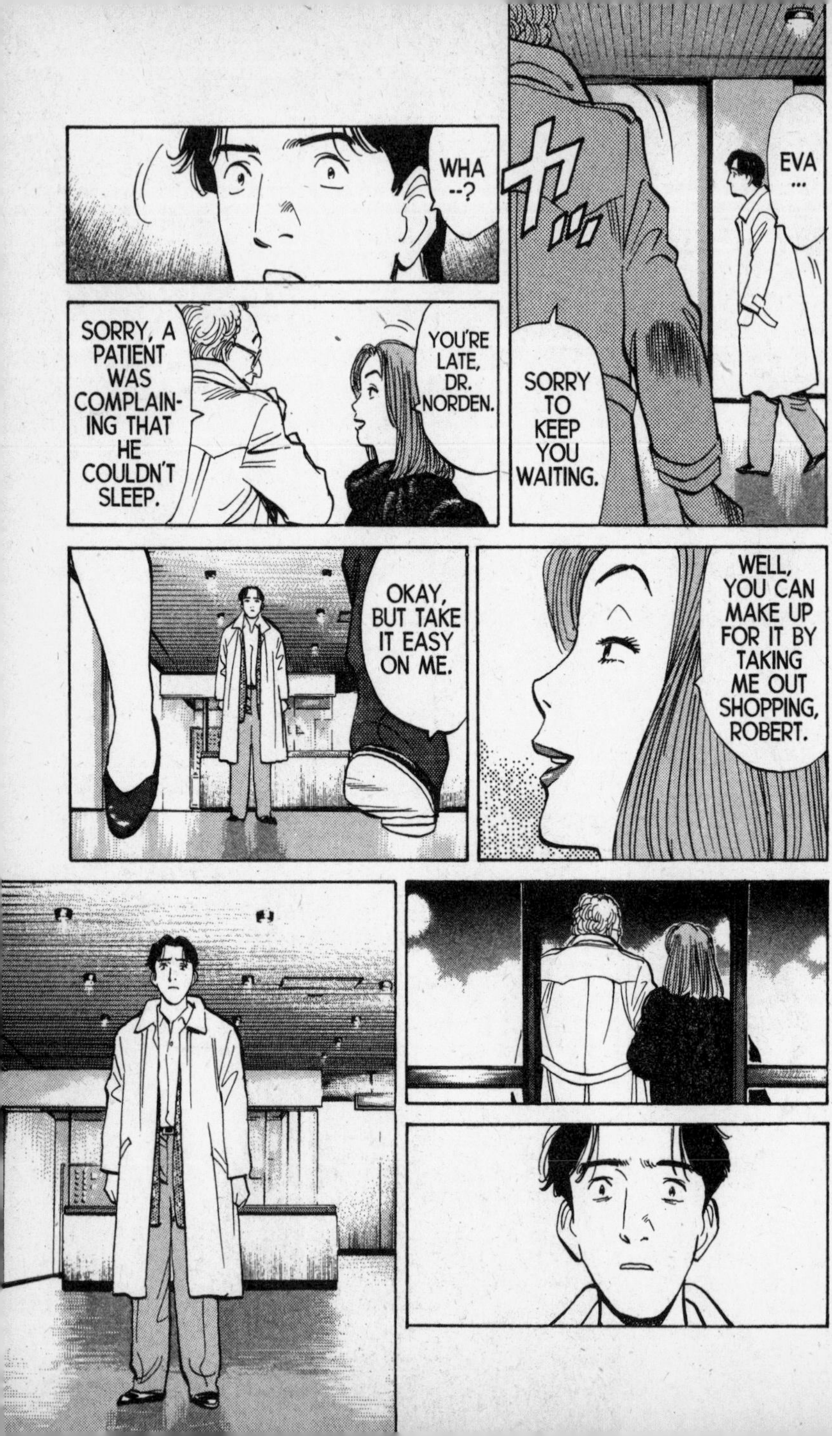
EVA ...
ガッ
SORRY TO KEEP YOU WAITING.
WHA --?
YOU'RE LATE, DR. NORDEN.
SORRY, A PATIENT WAS COMPLAIN-ING THAT HE COULDN'T SLEEP.
WELL, YOU CAN MAKE UP FOR IT BY TAKING ME OUT SHOPPING, ROBERT.
OKAY, BUT TAKE IT EASY ON ME.

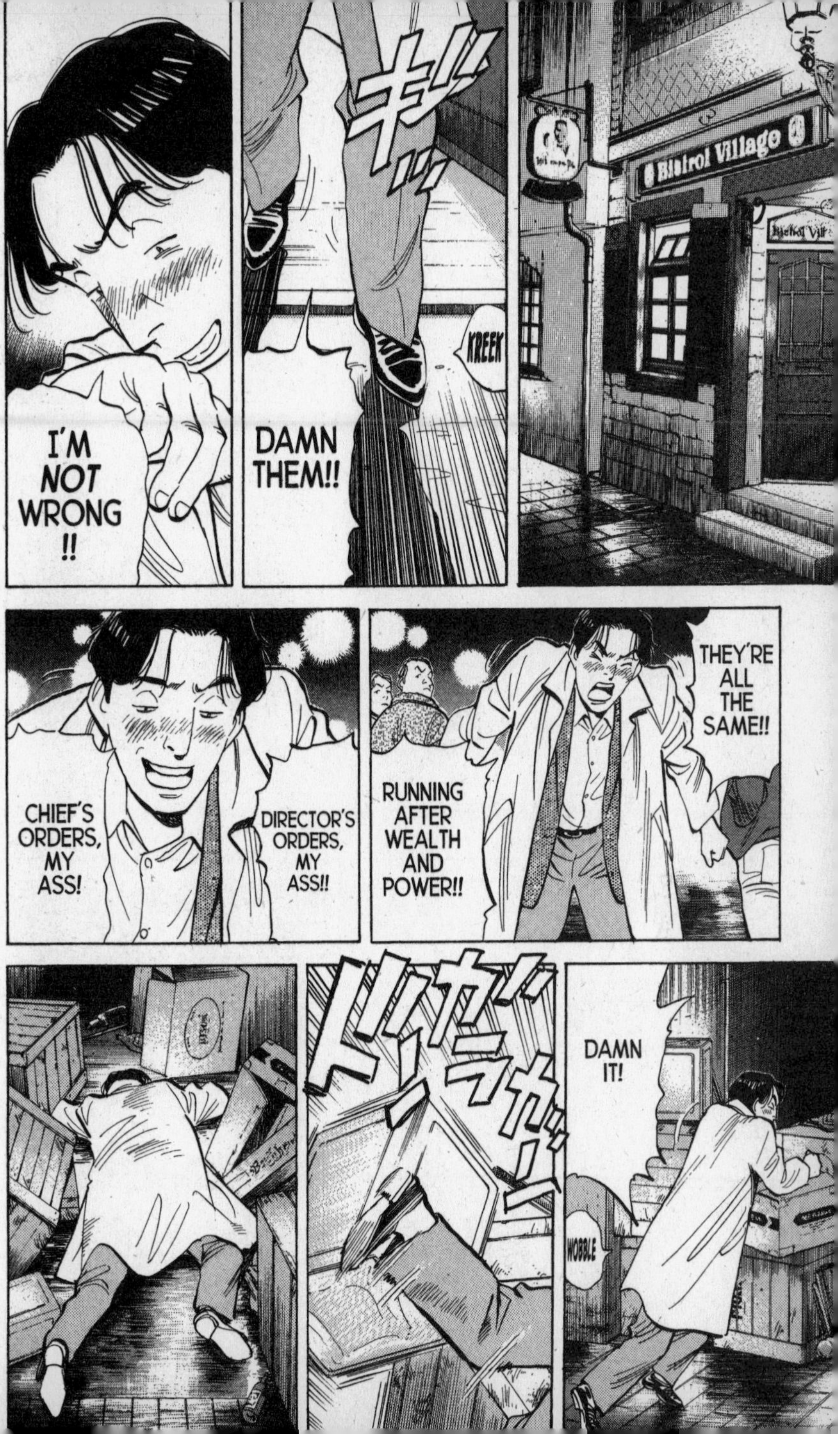
KREEK
DAMN THEM!!
I'M *NOT* WRONG !!
THEY'RE ALL THE SAME!!
RUNNING AFTER WEALTH AND POWER!!
DIRECTOR'S ORDERS, MY ASS!!
CHIEF'S ORDERS, MY ASS!
DAMN IT!
WOBBLE

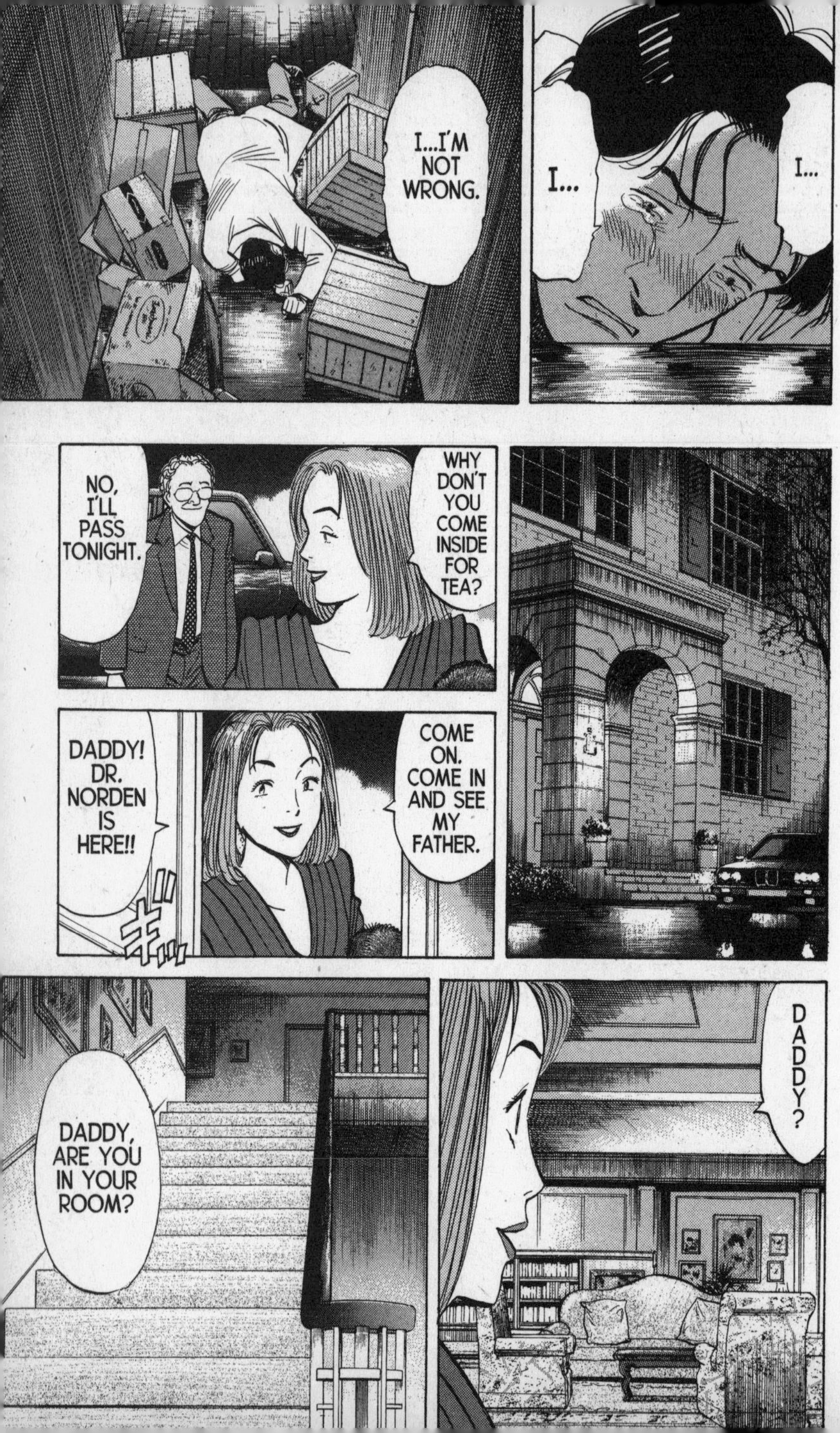
I...
I...
I...I'M NOT WRONG.
WHY DON'T YOU COME INSIDE FOR TEA?
NO, I'LL PASS TONIGHT.
COME ON. COME IN AND SEE MY FATHER.
DADDY! DR. NORDEN IS HERE!!
DADDY?
DADDY, ARE YOU IN YOUR ROOM?

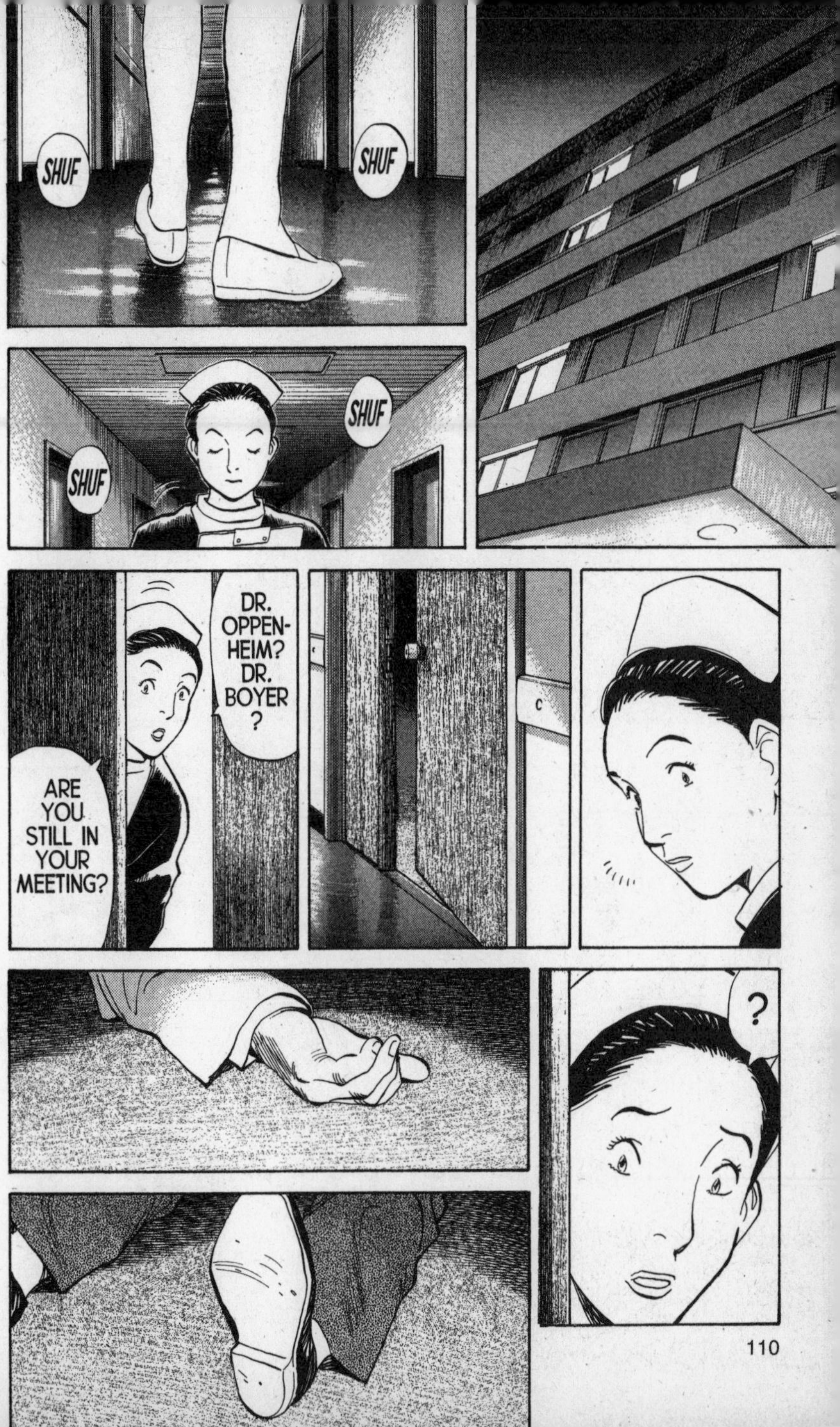
SHUF
SHUF
SHUF
SHUF
DR. OPPEN-HEIM? DR. BOYER ?
ARE YOU STILL IN YOUR MEETING?
?

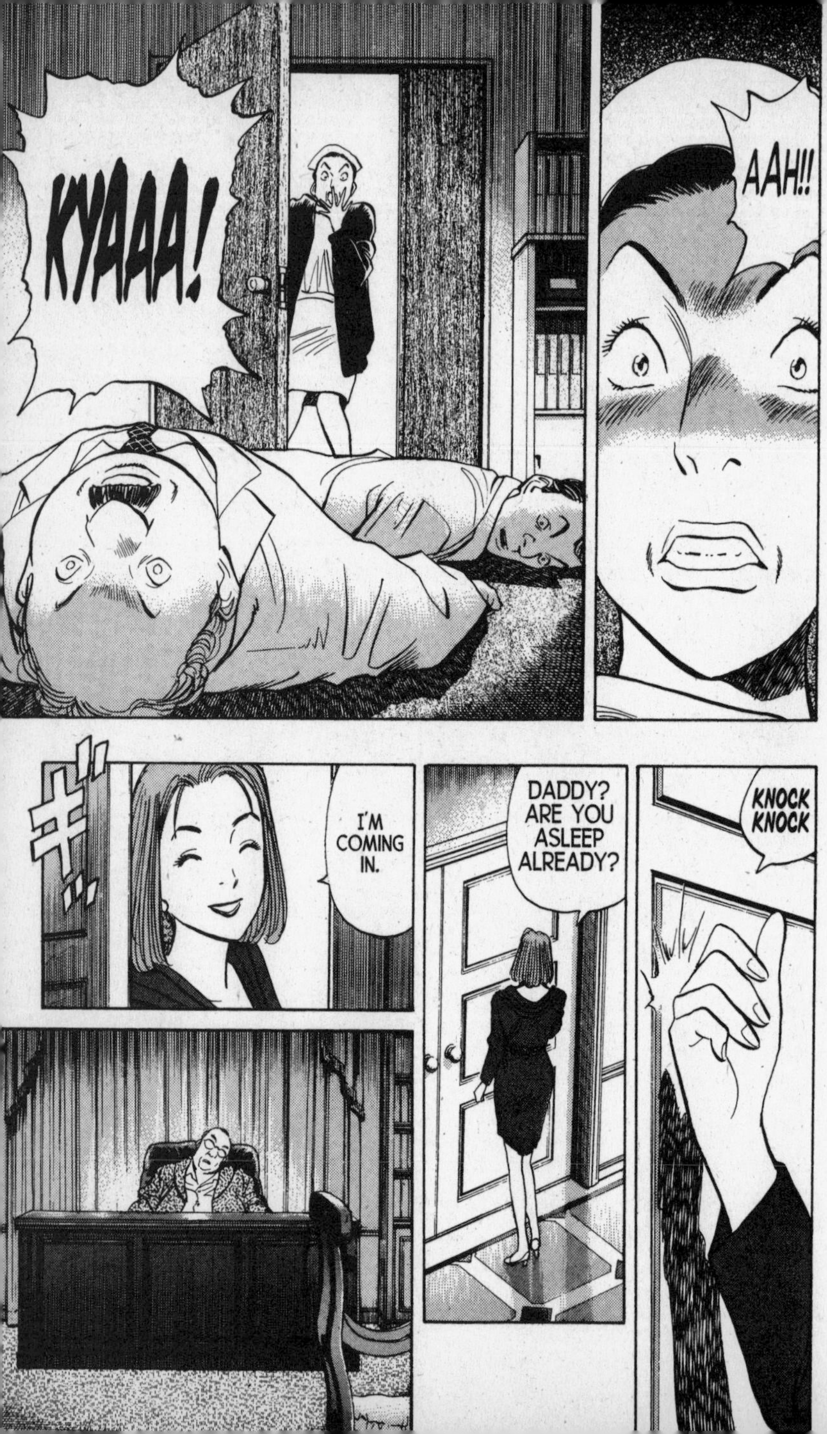
AAH!!
KYAAA!
KNOCK KNOCK
DADDY? ARE YOU ASLEEP ALREADY?
I'M COMING IN.

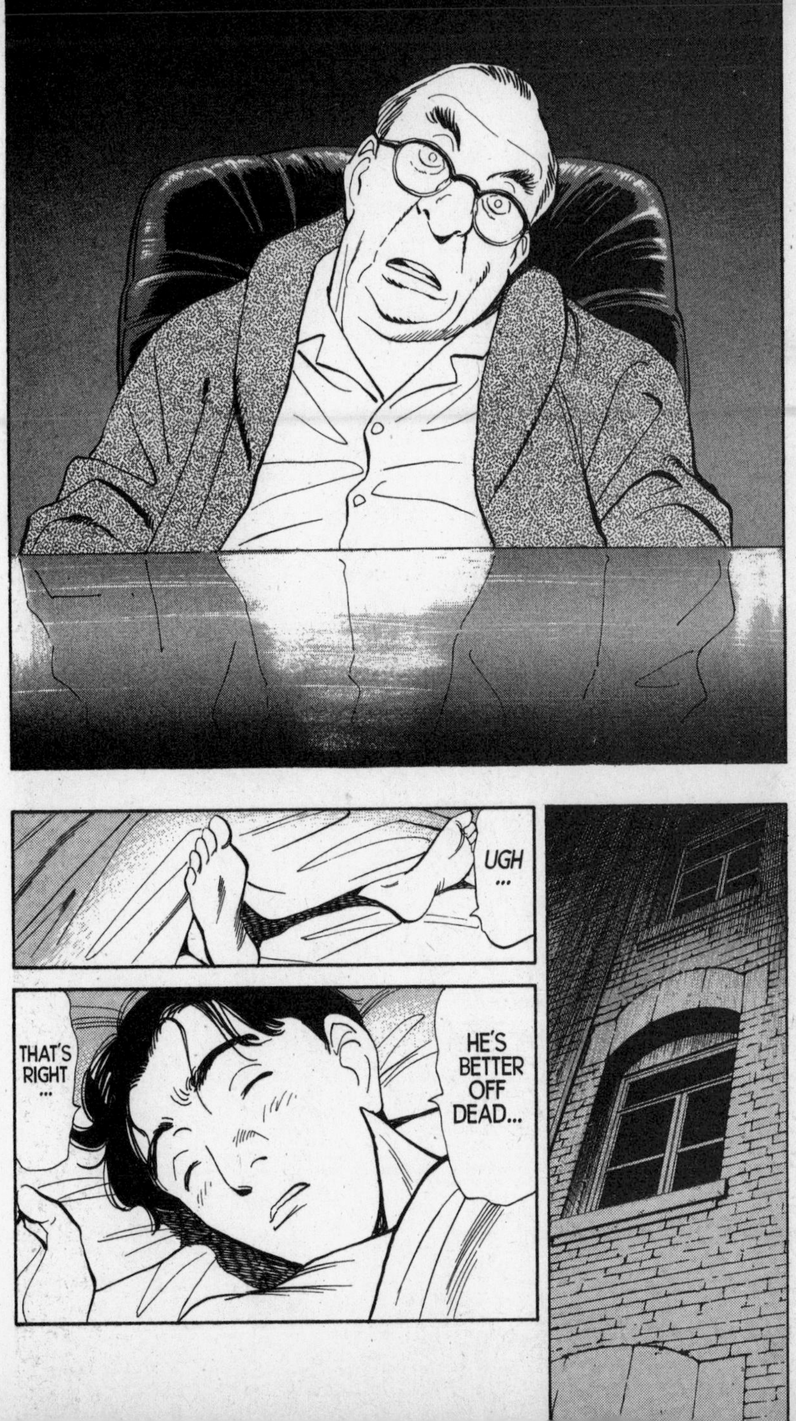
UGH...
HE'S BETTER OFF DEAD...
THAT'S RIGHT...

Chapter 5
Murder

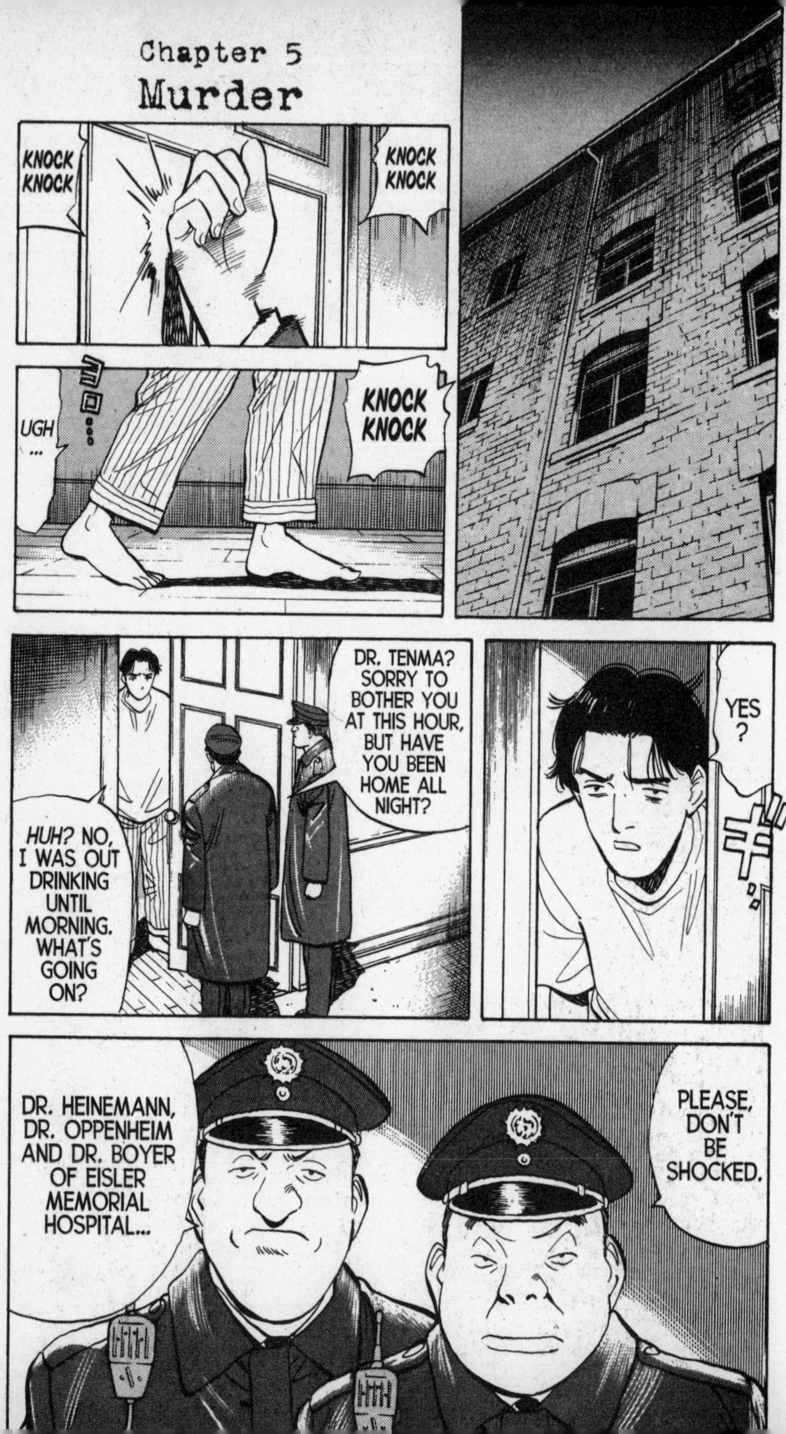

KNOCK KNOCK
KNOCK KNOCK
KNOCK KNOCK
UGH ...
YES ?
DR. TENMA? SORRY TO BOTHER YOU AT THIS HOUR, BUT HAVE YOU BEEN HOME ALL NIGHT?
HUH? NO, I WAS OUT DRINKING UNTIL MORNING. WHAT'S GOING ON?
PLEASE, DON'T BE SHOCKED.
DR. HEINEMANN, DR. OPPENHEIM AND DR. BOYER OF EISLER MEMORIAL HOSPITAL...

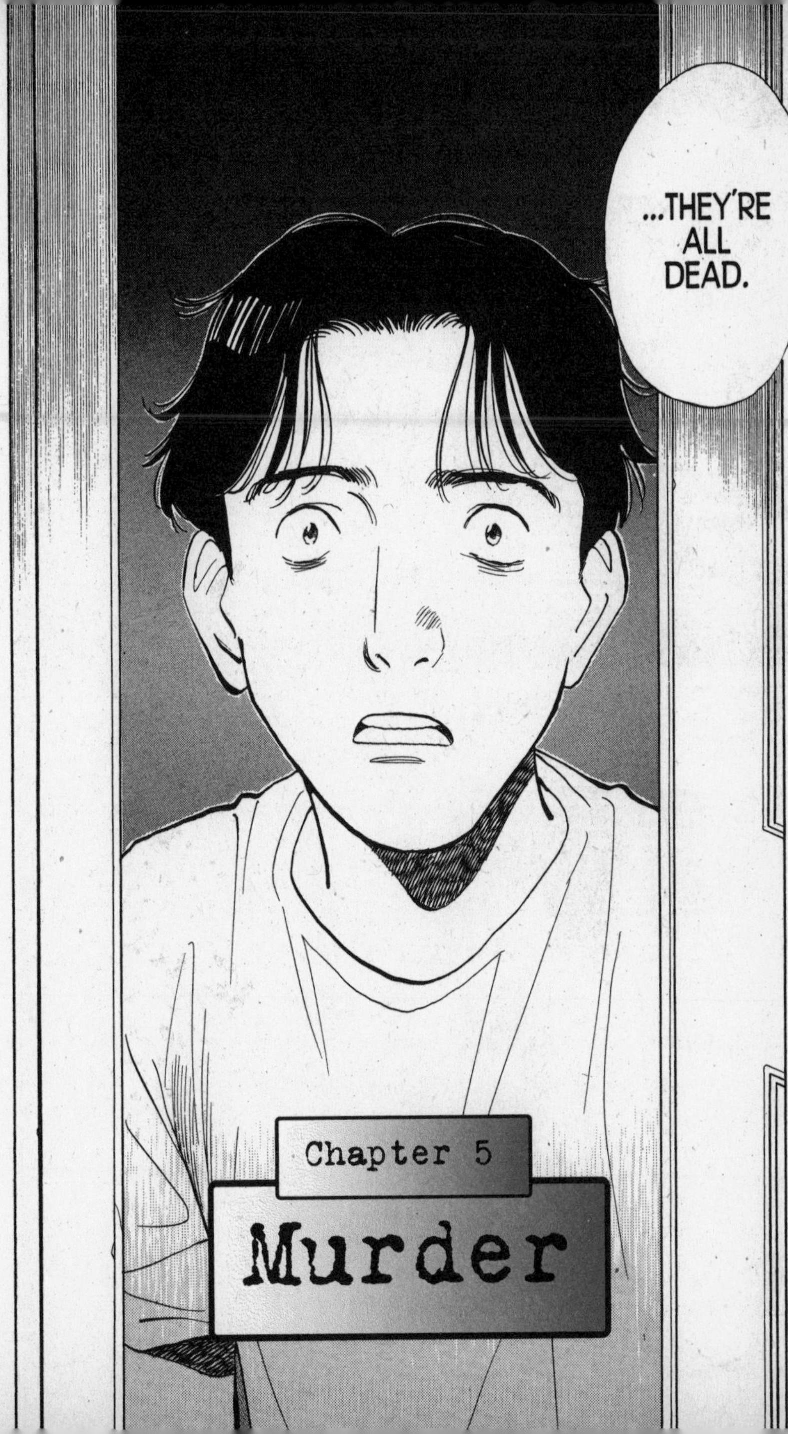
...THEY'RE ALL DEAD.
Chapter 5
Murder

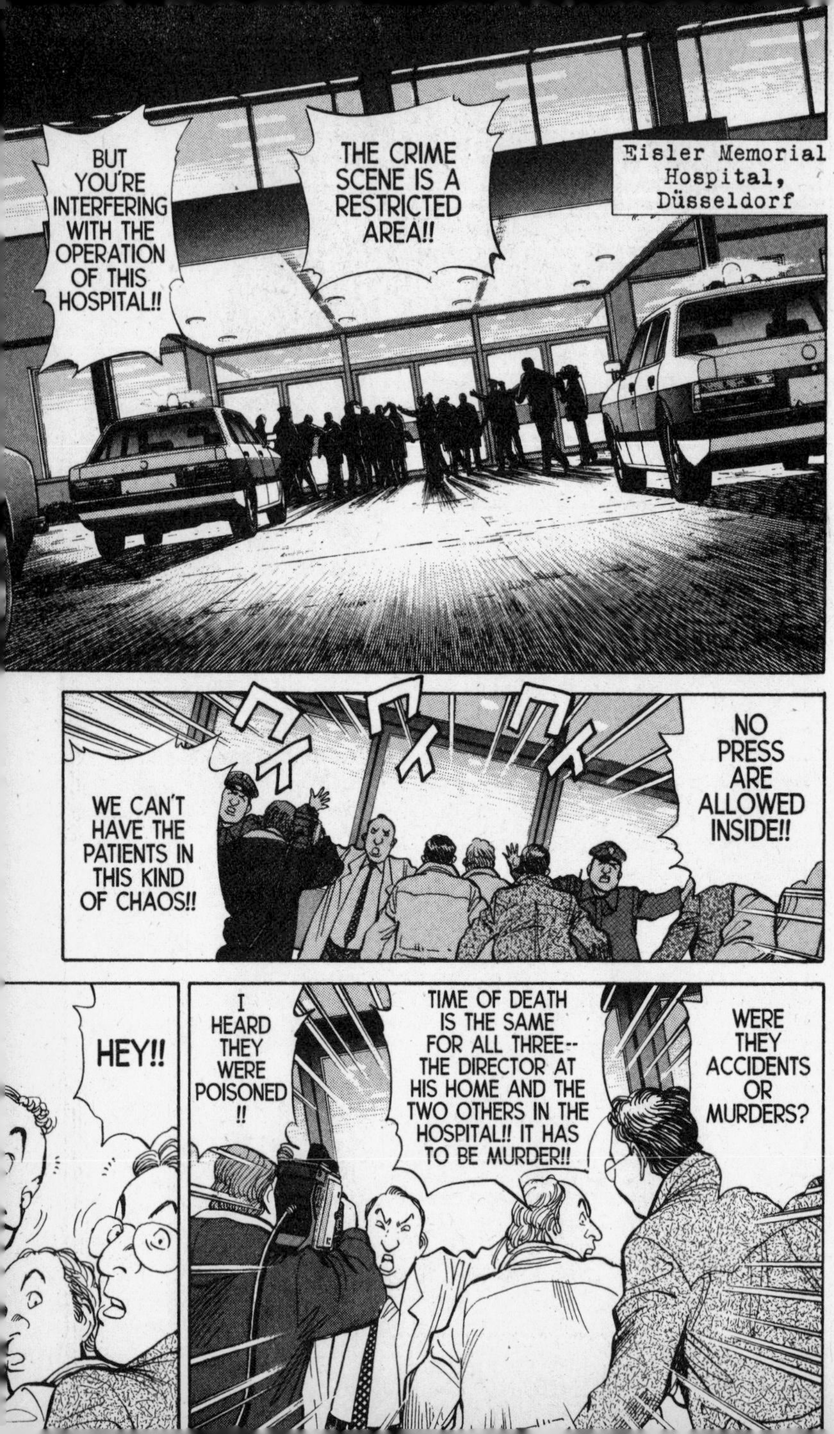
Eisler Memorial Hospital, Düsseldorf
THE CRIME SCENE IS A RESTRICTED AREA!!
BUT YOU'RE INTERFERING WITH THE OPERATION OF THIS HOSPITAL!!
NO PRESS ARE ALLOWED INSIDE!!
WE CAN'T HAVE THE PATIENTS IN THIS KIND OF CHAOS!!
WERE THEY ACCIDENTS OR MURDERS?
TIME OF DEATH IS THE SAME FOR ALL THREE-- THE DIRECTOR AT HIS HOME AND THE TWO OTHERS IN THE HOSPITAL!! IT HAS TO BE MURDER!!
I HEARD THEY WERE POISONED!!
HEY!!

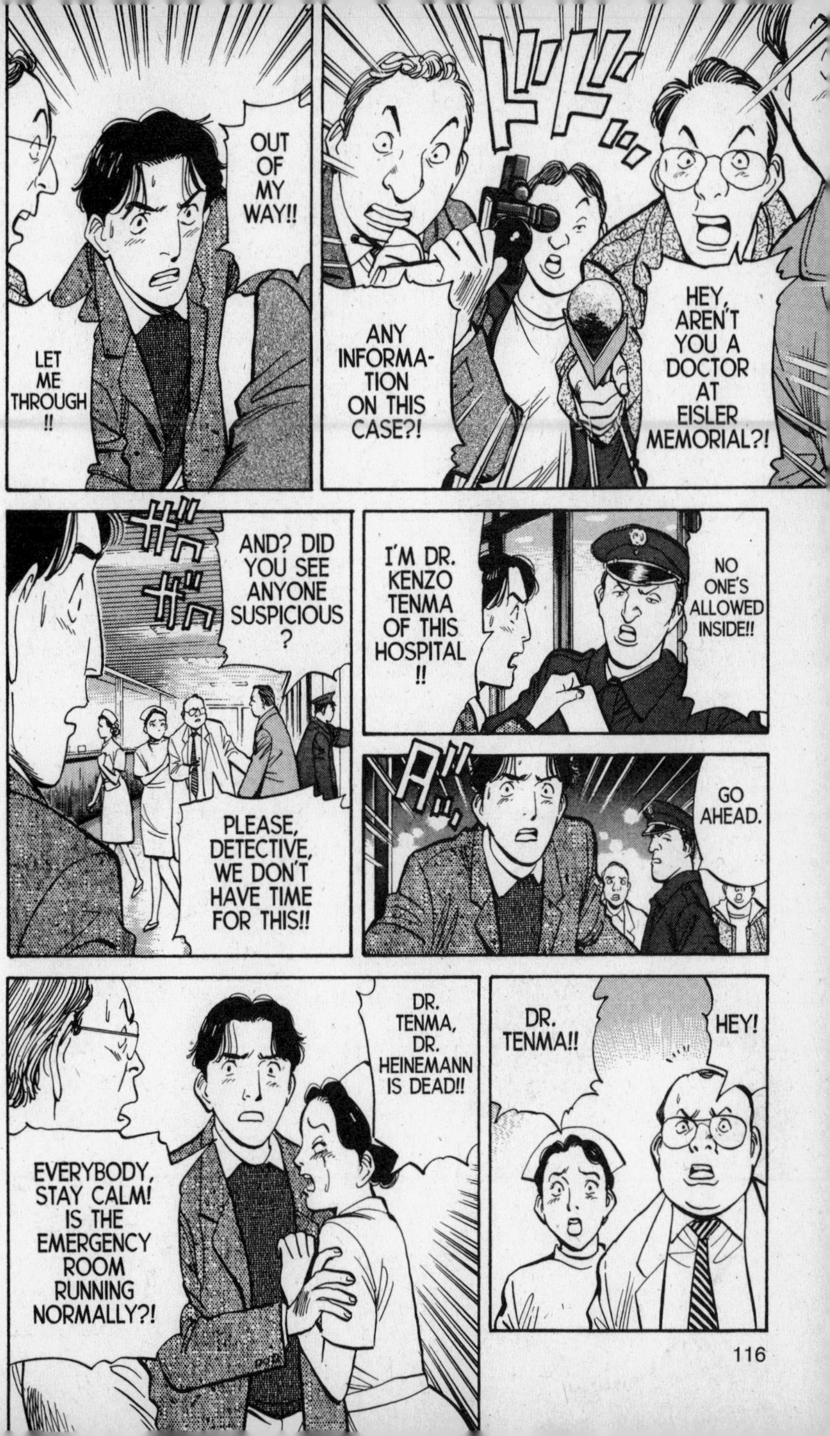
HEY, AREN'T YOU A DOCTOR AT EISLER MEMORIAL?!
ANY INFORMATION ON THIS CASE?!
OUT OF MY WAY!!
LET ME THROUGH!!
NO ONE'S ALLOWED INSIDE!!
I'M DR. KENZO TENMA OF THIS HOSPITAL!!
GO AHEAD.
AND? DID YOU SEE ANYONE SUSPICIOUS?
PLEASE, DETECTIVE, WE DON'T HAVE TIME FOR THIS!!
HEY!
DR. TENMA!!
DR. TENMA, DR. HEINEMANN IS DEAD!!
EVERYBODY, STAY CALM! IS THE EMERGENCY ROOM RUNNING NORMALLY?!

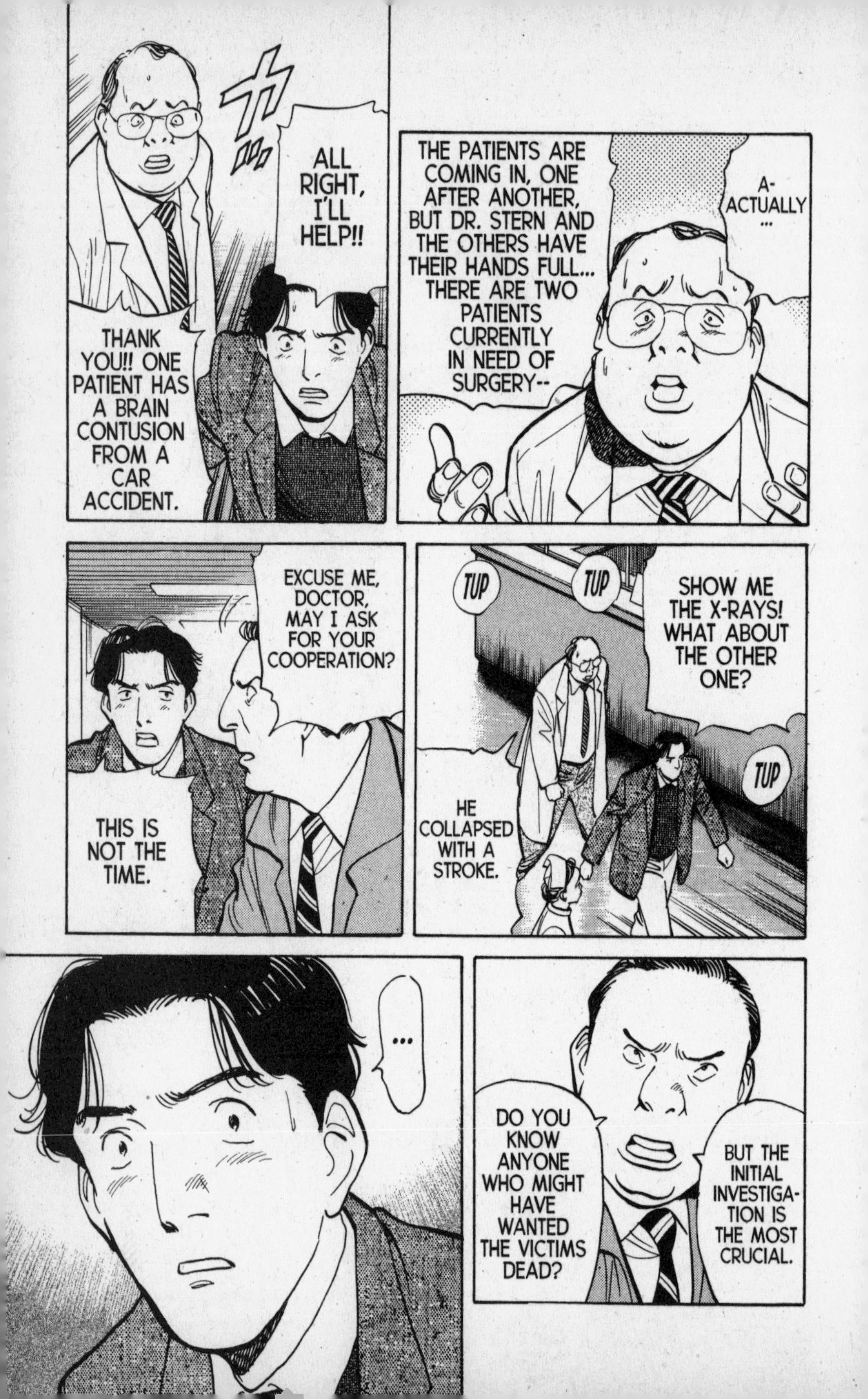
A-ACTUALLY...
THE PATIENTS ARE COMING IN, ONE AFTER ANOTHER, BUT DR. STERN AND THE OTHERS HAVE THEIR HANDS FULL... THERE ARE TWO PATIENTS CURRENTLY IN NEED OF SURGERY--
ALL RIGHT, I'LL HELP!!
THANK YOU!! ONE PATIENT HAS A BRAIN CONTUSION FROM A CAR ACCIDENT.
TUP
TUP
SHOW ME THE X-RAYS! WHAT ABOUT THE OTHER ONE?
TUP
HE COLLAPSED WITH A STROKE.
EXCUSE ME, DOCTOR, MAY I ASK FOR YOUR COOPERATION?
THIS IS NOT THE TIME.
BUT THE INITIAL INVESTIGA-TION IS THE MOST CRUCIAL.
DO YOU KNOW ANYONE WHO MIGHT HAVE WANTED THE VICTIMS DEAD?
...

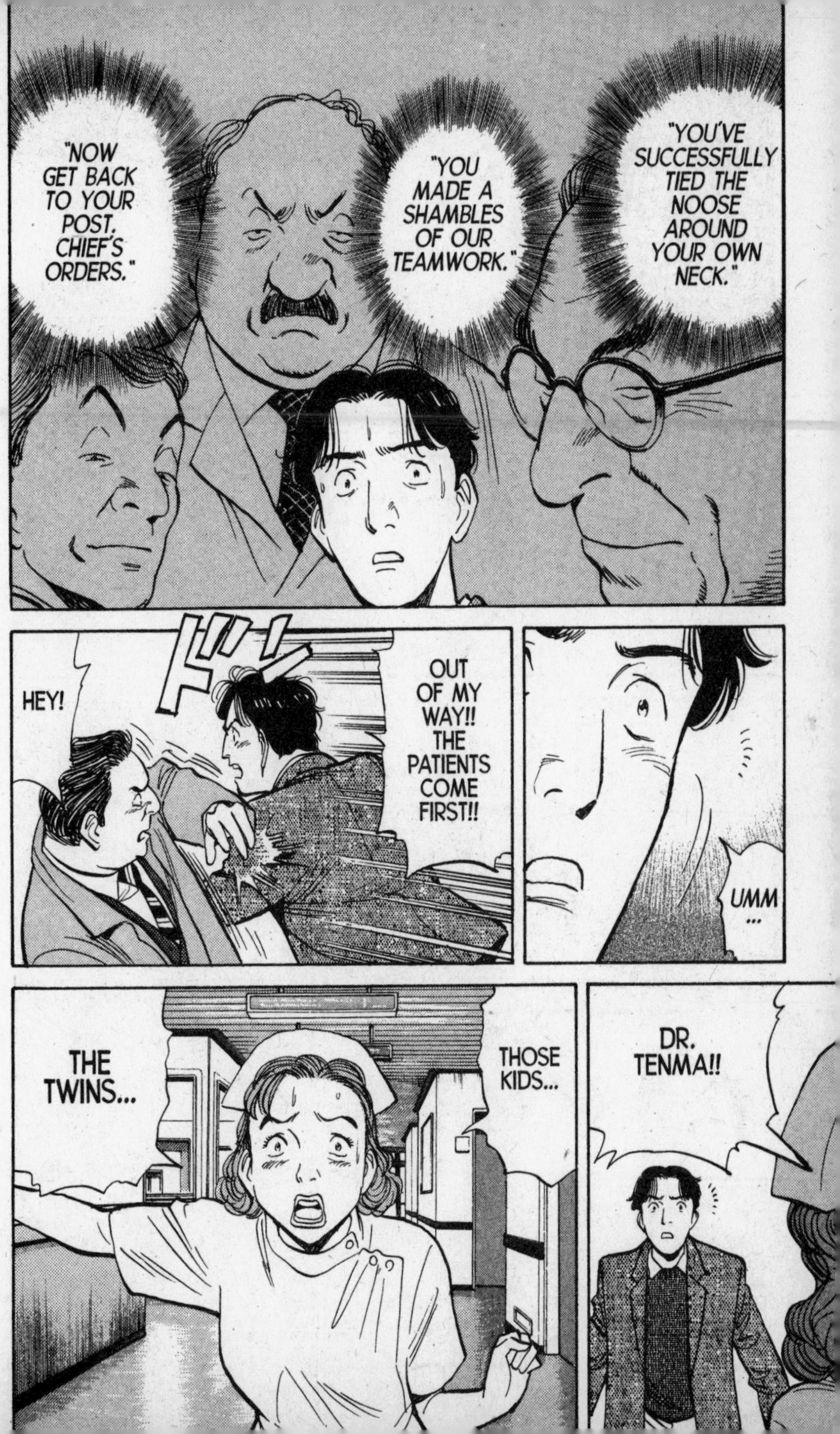
"YOU'VE SUCCESSFULLY TIED THE NOOSE AROUND YOUR OWN NECK."
"YOU MADE A SHAMBLES OF OUR TEAMWORK."
"NOW GET BACK TO YOUR POST. CHIEF'S ORDERS."
UMM ...
OUT OF MY WAY!! THE PATIENTS COME FIRST!!
HEY!
DR. TENMA!!
THOSE KIDS...
THE TWINS...

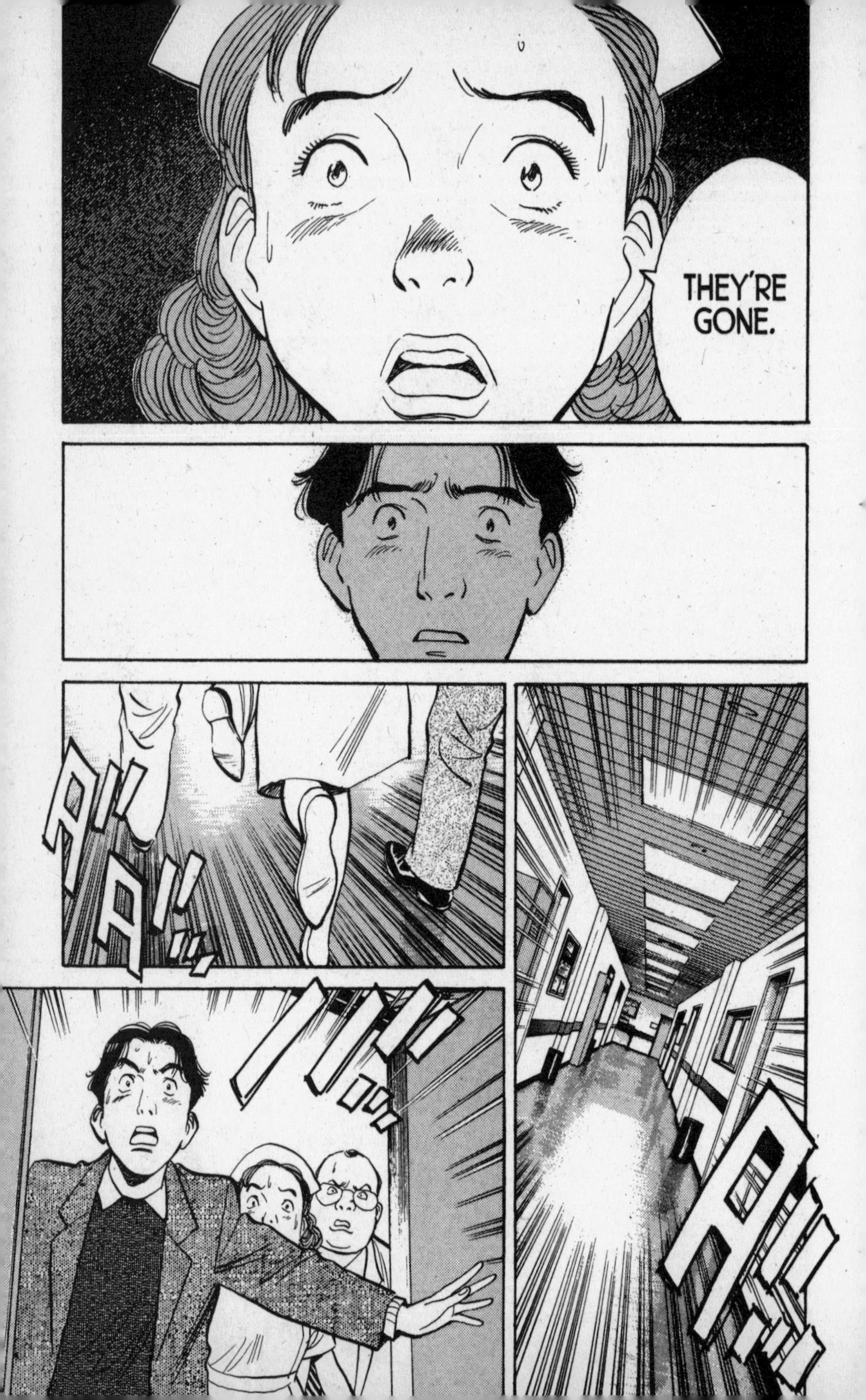
THEY'RE GONE.

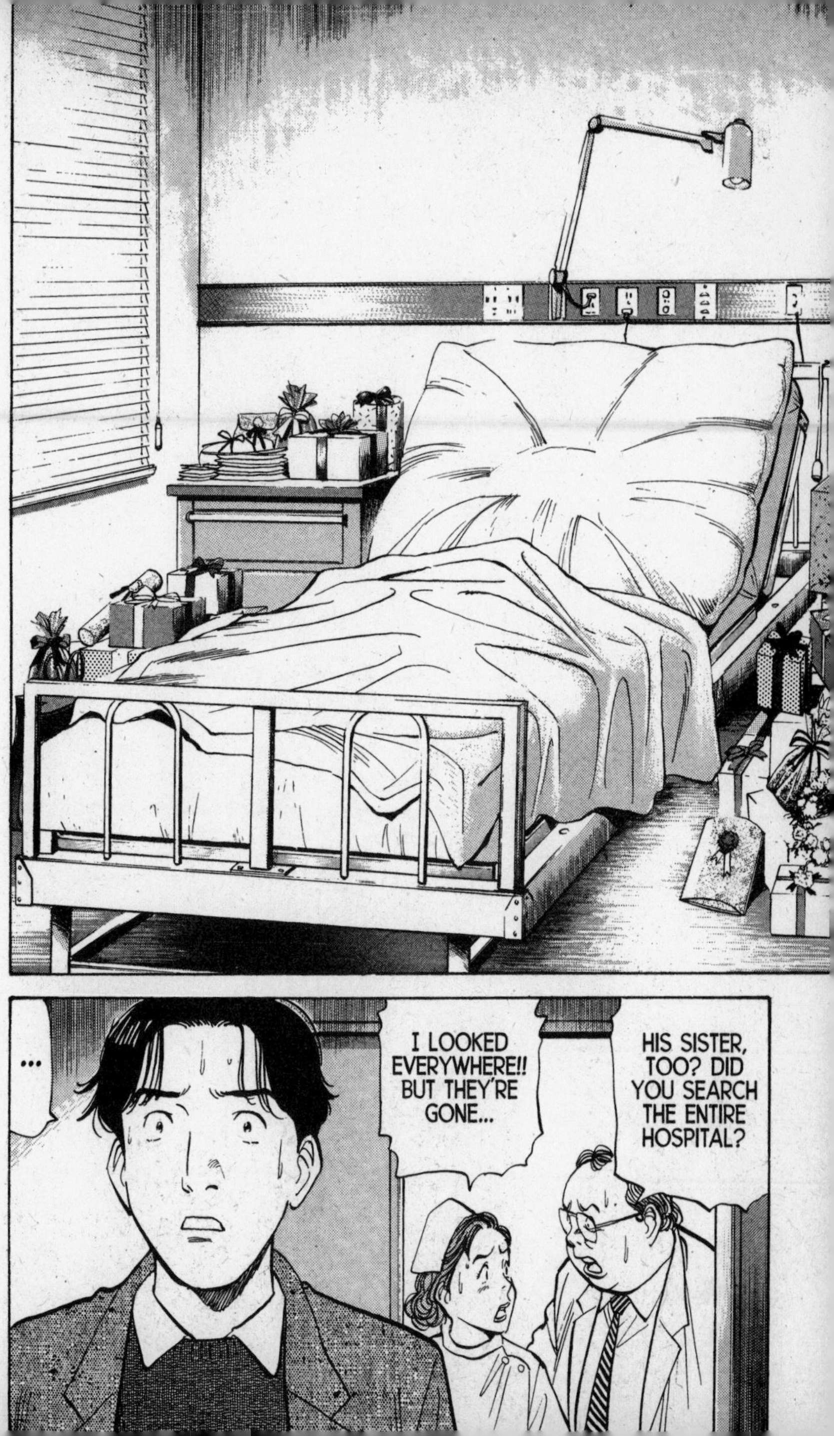
HIS SISTER, TOO? DID YOU SEARCH THE ENTIRE HOSPITAL?
I LOOKED EVERYWHERE!! BUT THEY'RE GONE...
...

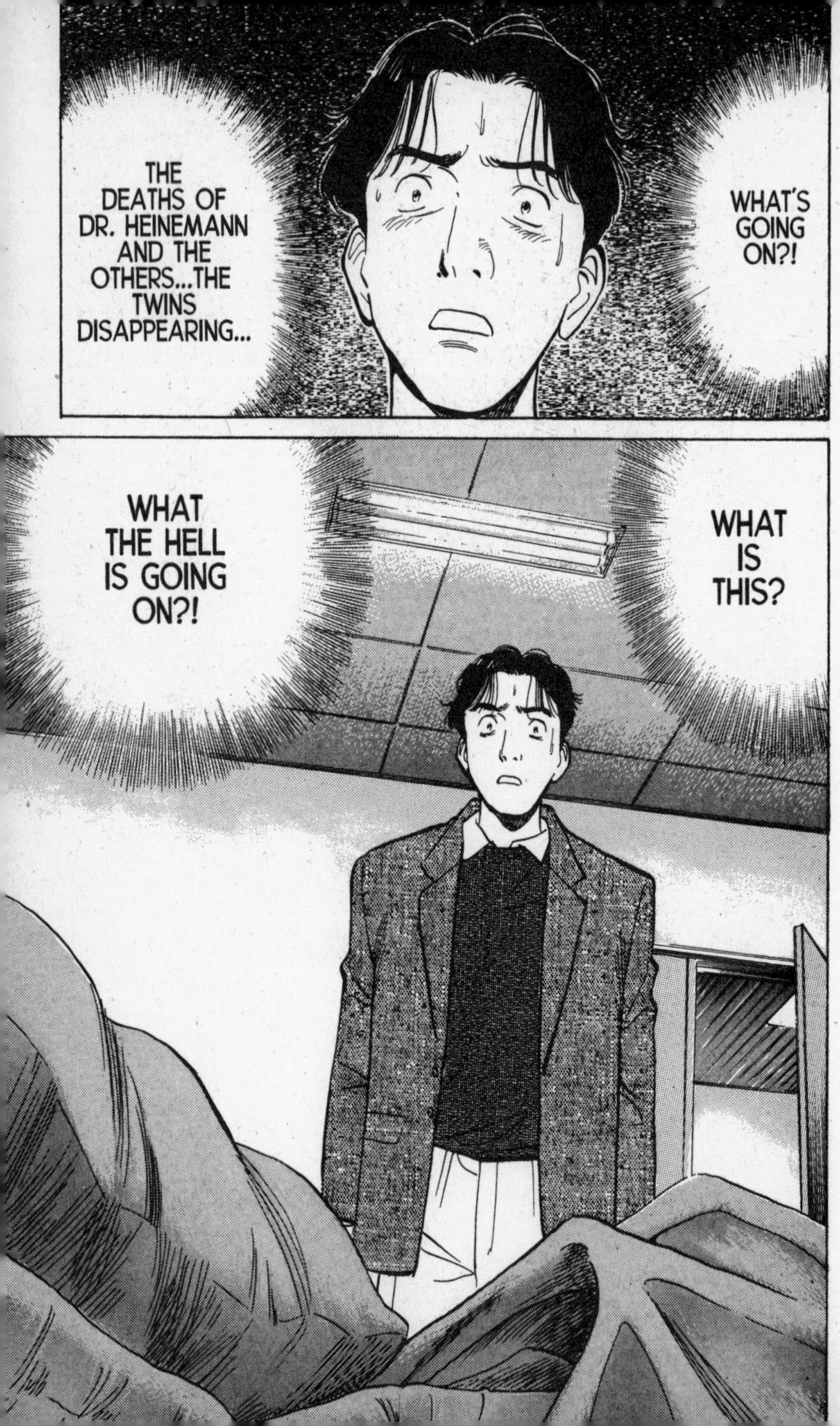
WHAT'S GOING ON?!
THE DEATHS OF DR. HEINEMANN AND THE OTHERS...THE TWINS DISAPPEARING...
WHAT IS THIS?
WHAT THE HELL IS GOING ON?!

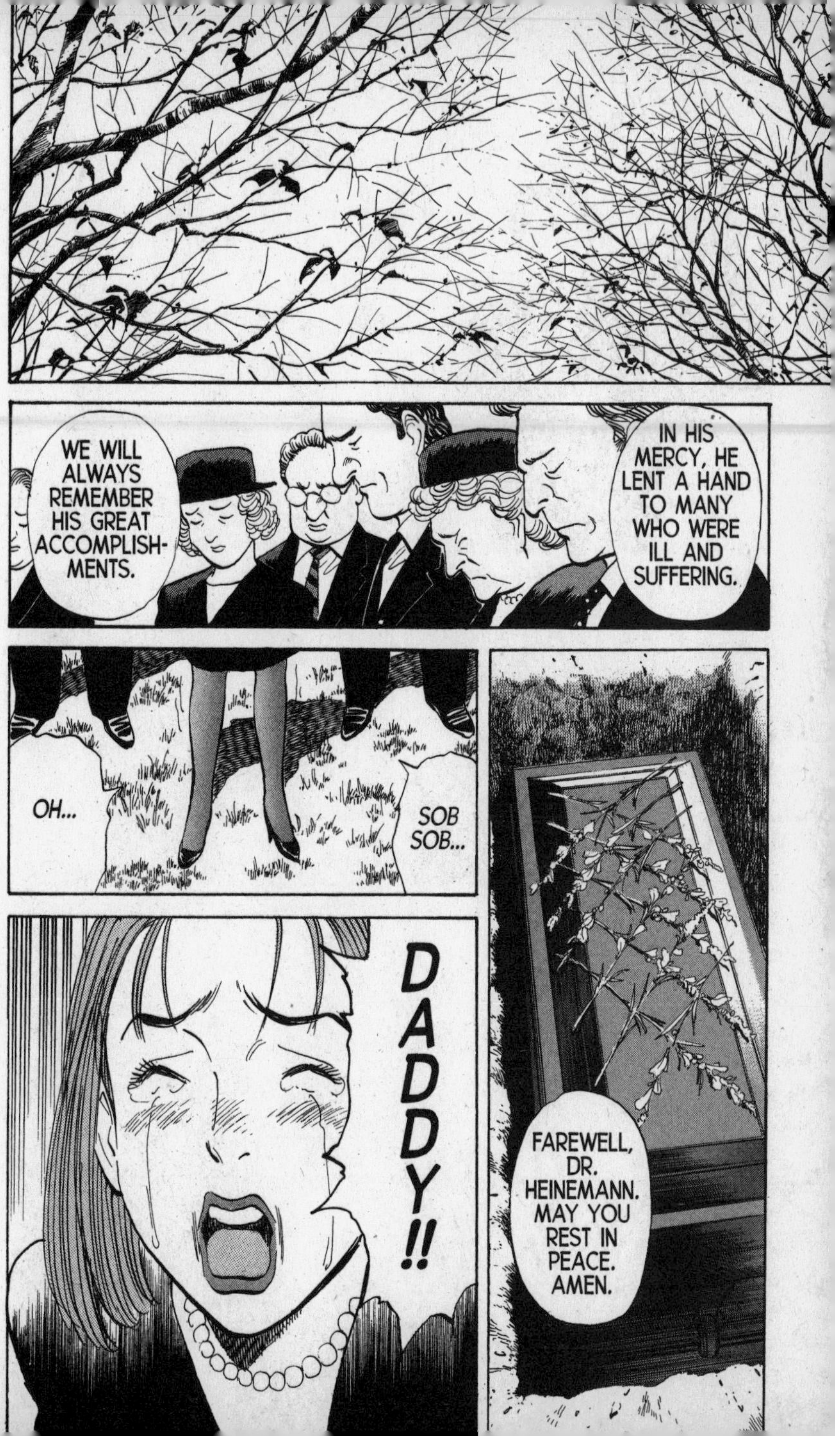
IN HIS MERCY, HE LENT A HAND TO MANY WHO WERE ILL AND SUFFERING.
WE WILL ALWAYS REMEMBER HIS GREAT ACCOMPLISHMENTS.
FAREWELL, DR. HEINEMANN. MAY YOU REST IN PEACE. AMEN.
SOB SOB...
OH...
DADDY!!

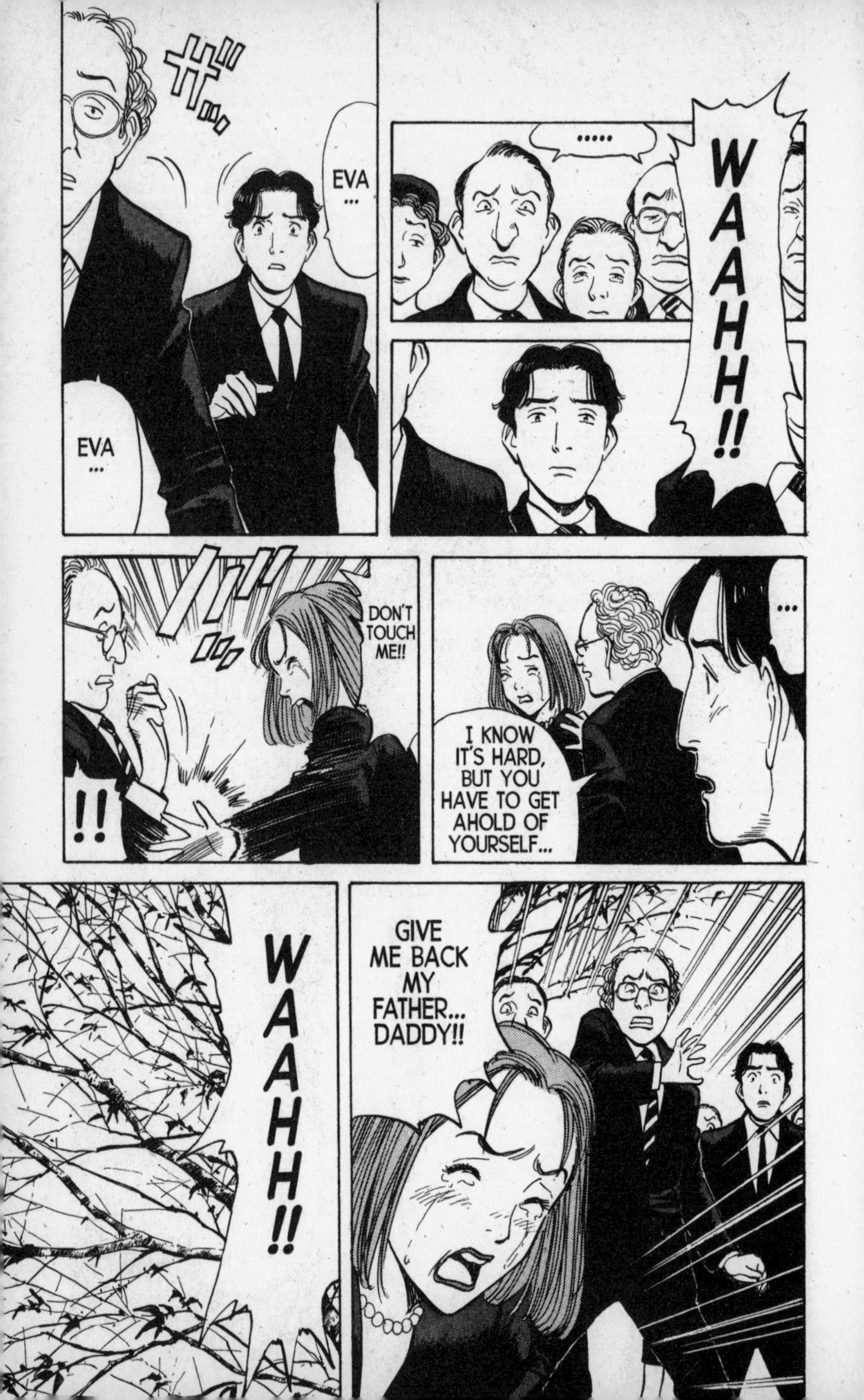

......
WAAHH!!
EVA ...
EVA ...
...
I KNOW IT'S HARD, BUT YOU HAVE TO GET AHOLD OF YOURSELF...
DON'T TOUCH ME!!
!!
GIVE ME BACK MY FATHER... DADDY!!
WAAHH!!

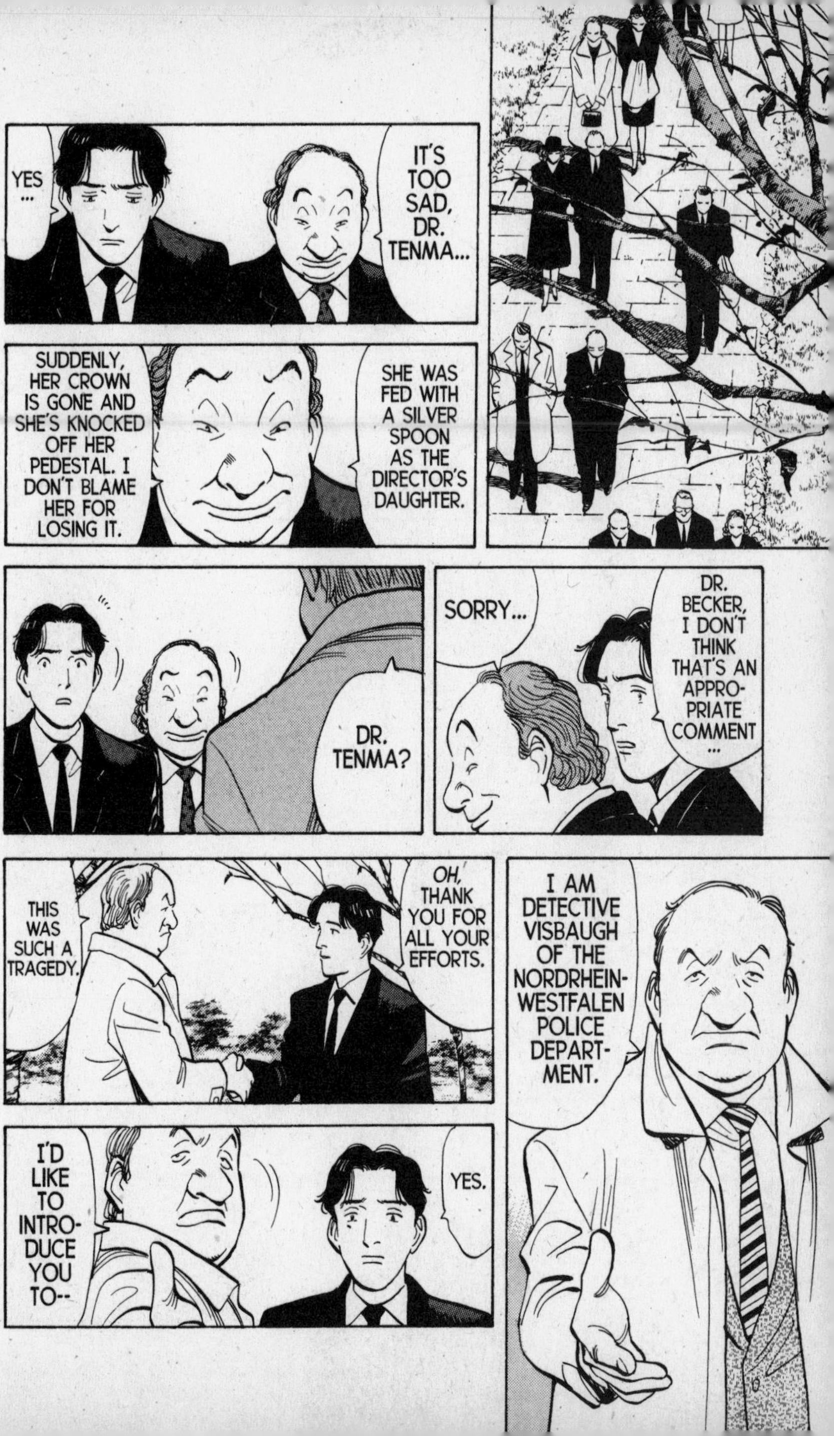
IT'S TOO SAD, DR. TENMA...
YES...
SHE WAS FED WITH A SILVER SPOON AS THE DIRECTOR'S DAUGHTER.
SUDDENLY, HER CROWN IS GONE AND SHE'S KNOCKED OFF HER PEDESTAL. I DON'T BLAME HER FOR LOSING IT.
DR. BECKER, I DON'T THINK THAT'S AN APPROPRIATE COMMENT...
SORRY...
DR. TENMA?
OH, THANK YOU FOR ALL YOUR EFFORTS.
THIS WAS SUCH A TRAGEDY.
YES.
I'D LIKE TO INTRODUCE YOU TO--
I AM DETECTIVE VISBAUGH OF THE NORDRHEIN-WESTFALEN POLICE DEPARTMENT.

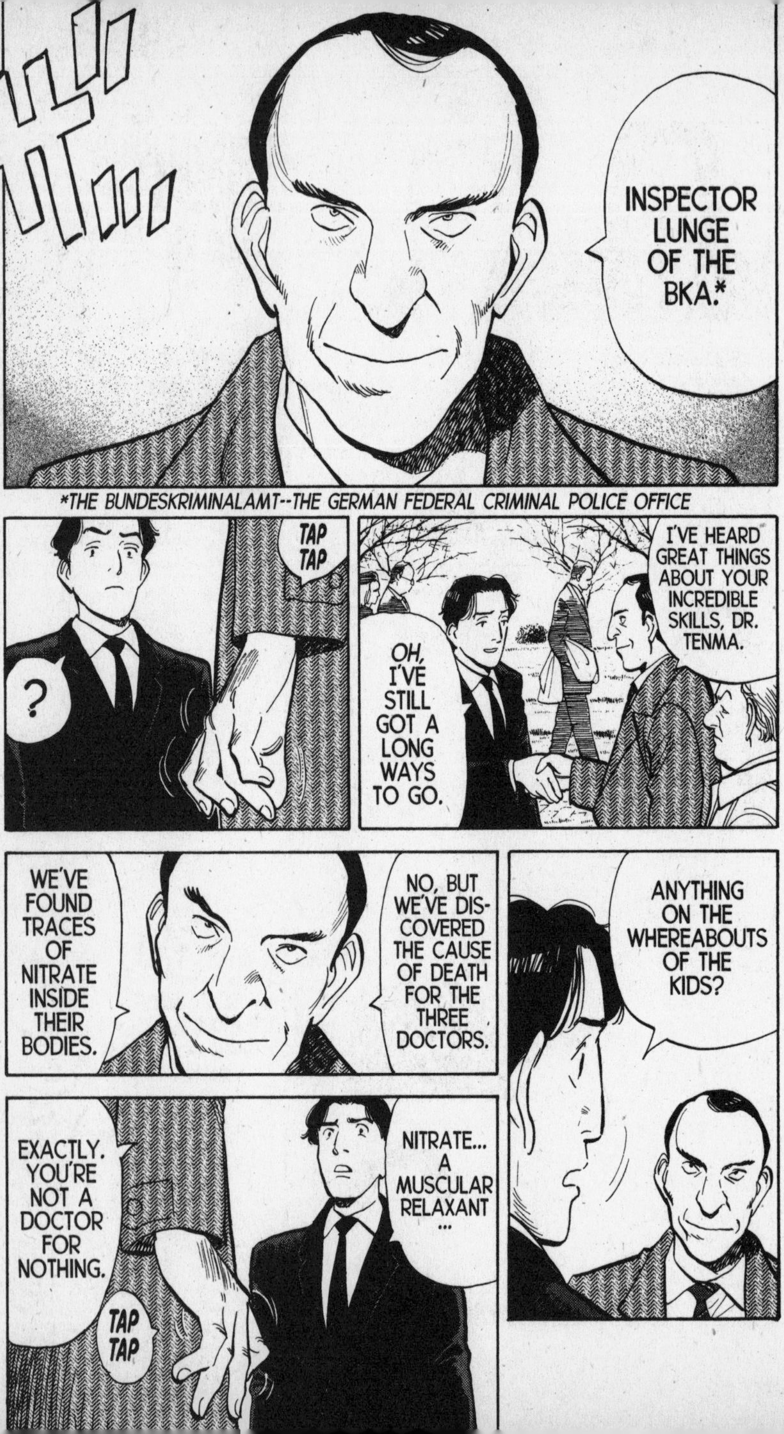
INSPECTOR LUNGE OF THE BKA.*
I'VE HEARD GREAT THINGS ABOUT YOUR INCREDIBLE SKILLS, DR. TENMA.
OH, I'VE STILL GOT A LONG WAYS TO GO.
TAP TAP
?
ANYTHING ON THE WHEREABOUTS OF THE KIDS?
NO, BUT WE'VE DIS-COVERED THE CAUSE OF DEATH FOR THE THREE DOCTORS.
WE'VE FOUND TRACES OF NITRATE INSIDE THEIR BODIES.
NITRATE... A MUSCULAR RELAXANT ...
EXACTLY. YOU'RE NOT A DOCTOR FOR NOTHING.
TAP TAP

*THE BUNDESKRIMINALAMT--THE GERMAN FEDERAL CRIMINAL POLICE OFFICE

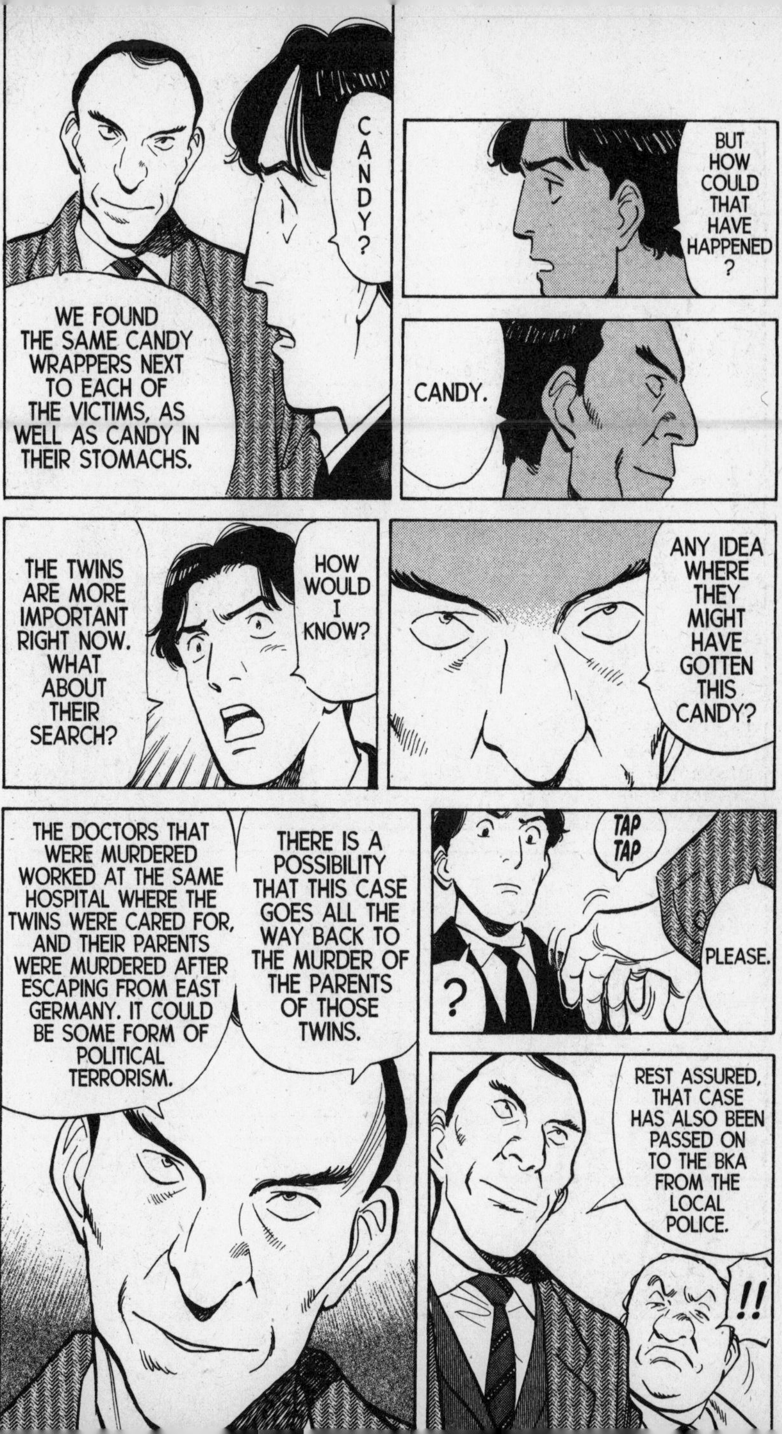

WE FOUND THE SAME CANDY WRAPPERS NEXT TO EACH OF THE VICTIMS, AS WELL AS CANDY IN THEIR STOMACHS.
CANDY?
BUT HOW COULD THAT HAVE HAPPENED?
CANDY.
THE TWINS ARE MORE IMPORTANT RIGHT NOW. WHAT ABOUT THEIR SEARCH?
HOW WOULD I KNOW?
ANY IDEA WHERE THEY MIGHT HAVE GOTTEN THIS CANDY?
THE DOCTORS THAT WERE MURDERED WORKED AT THE SAME HOSPITAL WHERE THE TWINS WERE CARED FOR, AND THEIR PARENTS WERE MURDERED AFTER ESCAPING FROM EAST GERMANY. IT COULD BE SOME FORM OF POLITICAL TERRORISM.
THERE IS A POSSIBILITY THAT THIS CASE GOES ALL THE WAY BACK TO THE MURDER OF THE PARENTS OF THOSE TWINS.
?
TAP TAP
PLEASE.
REST ASSURED, THAT CASE HAS ALSO BEEN PASSED ON TO THE BKA FROM THE LOCAL POLICE.
!!

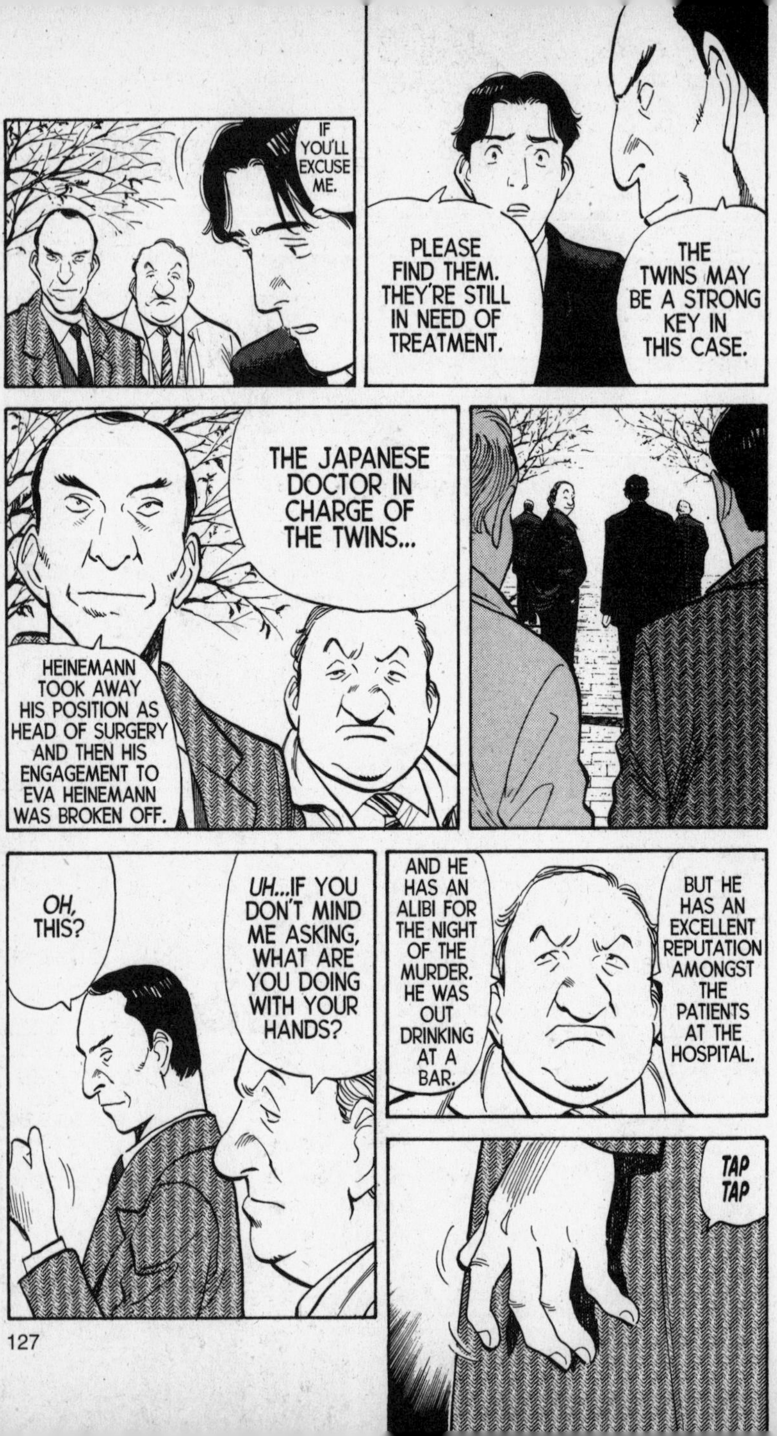
THE TWINS MAY BE A STRONG KEY IN THIS CASE.
PLEASE FIND THEM. THEY'RE STILL IN NEED OF TREATMENT.
IF YOU'LL EXCUSE ME.
THE JAPANESE DOCTOR IN CHARGE OF THE TWINS...
HEINEMANN TOOK AWAY HIS POSITION AS HEAD OF SURGERY AND THEN HIS ENGAGEMENT TO EVA HEINEMANN WAS BROKEN OFF.
BUT HE HAS AN EXCELLENT REPUTATION AMONGST THE PATIENTS AT THE HOSPITAL.
AND HE HAS AN ALIBI FOR THE NIGHT OF THE MURDER. HE WAS OUT DRINKING AT A BAR.
TAP TAP
*UH...*IF YOU DON'T MIND ME ASKING, WHAT ARE YOU DOING WITH YOUR HANDS?
OH, THIS?

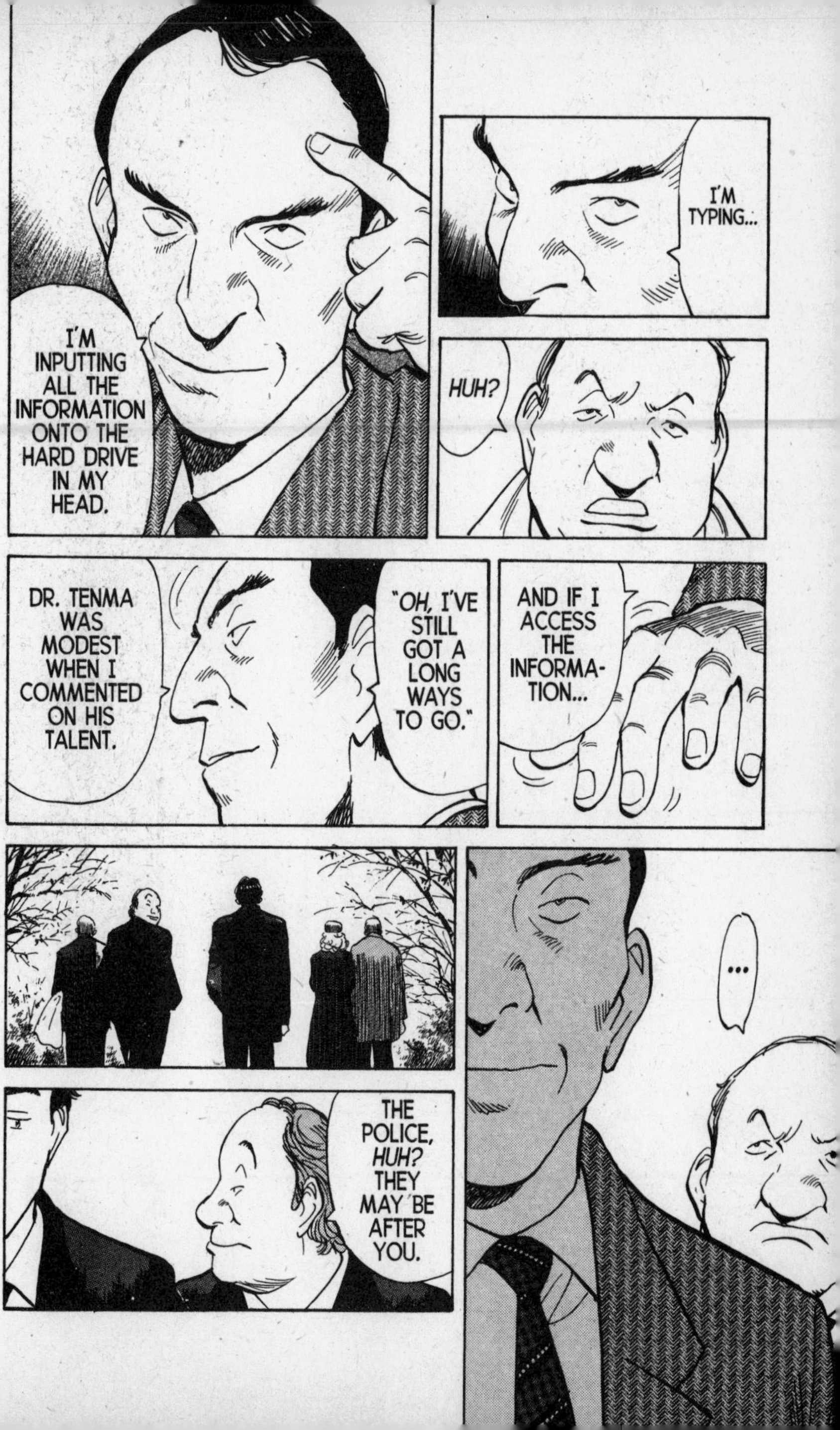
I'M TYPING...
HUH?
I'M INPUTTING ALL THE INFORMATION ONTO THE HARD DRIVE IN MY HEAD.
AND IF I ACCESS THE INFORMATION...
"OH, I'VE STILL GOT A LONG WAYS TO GO."
DR. TENMA WAS MODEST WHEN I COMMENTED ON HIS TALENT.
...
THE POLICE, HUH? THEY MAY BE AFTER YOU.

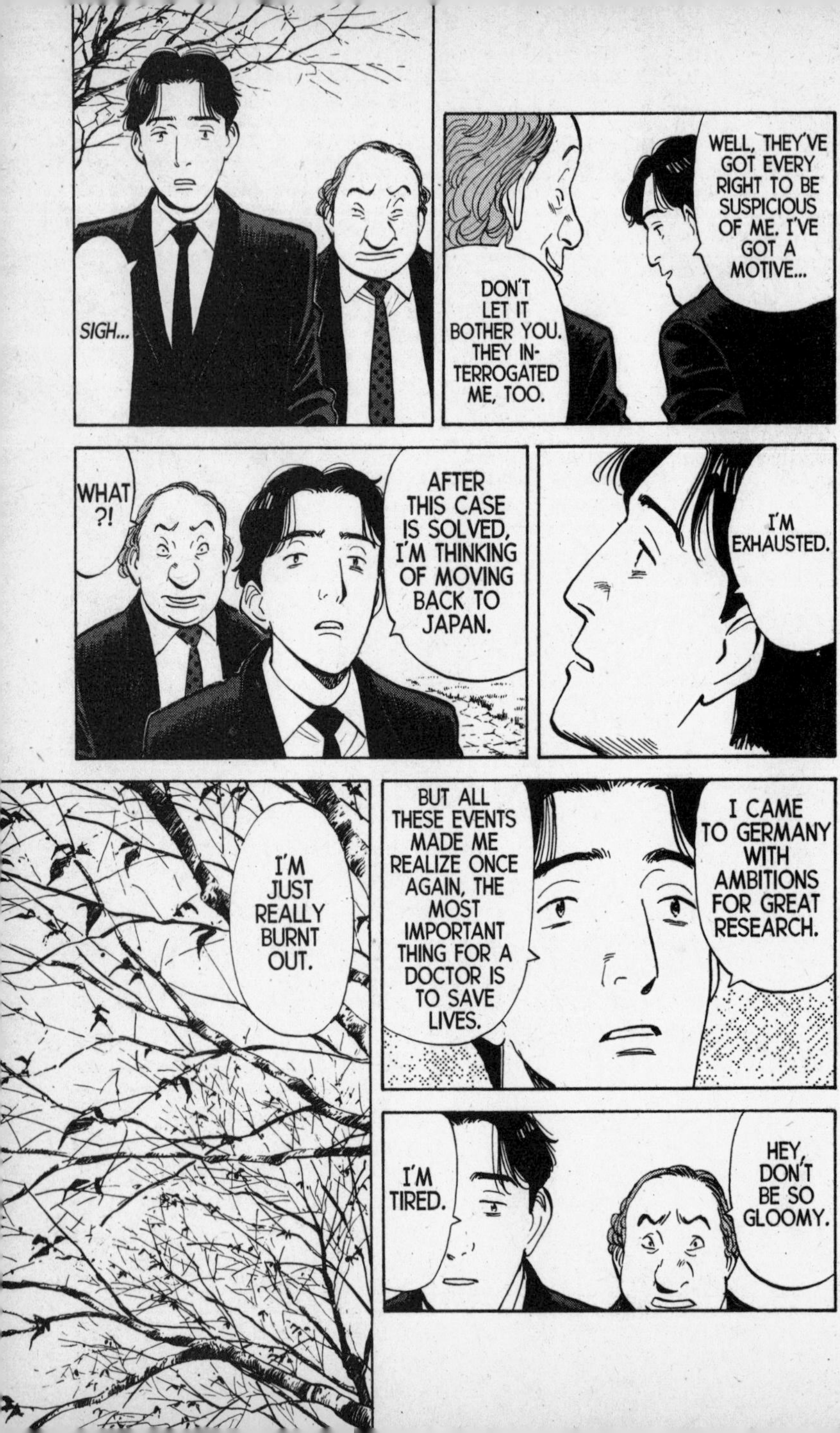
WELL, THEY'VE GOT EVERY RIGHT TO BE SUSPICIOUS OF ME. I'VE GOT A MOTIVE...
DON'T LET IT BOTHER YOU. THEY IN-TERROGATED ME, TOO.
SIGH...
I'M EXHAUSTED.
AFTER THIS CASE IS SOLVED, I'M THINKING OF MOVING BACK TO JAPAN.
WHAT?!
I CAME TO GERMANY WITH AMBITIONS FOR GREAT RESEARCH.
BUT ALL THESE EVENTS MADE ME REALIZE ONCE AGAIN, THE MOST IMPORTANT THING FOR A DOCTOR IS TO SAVE LIVES.
HEY, DON'T BE SO GLOOMY.
I'M TIRED.
I'M JUST REALLY BURNT OUT.

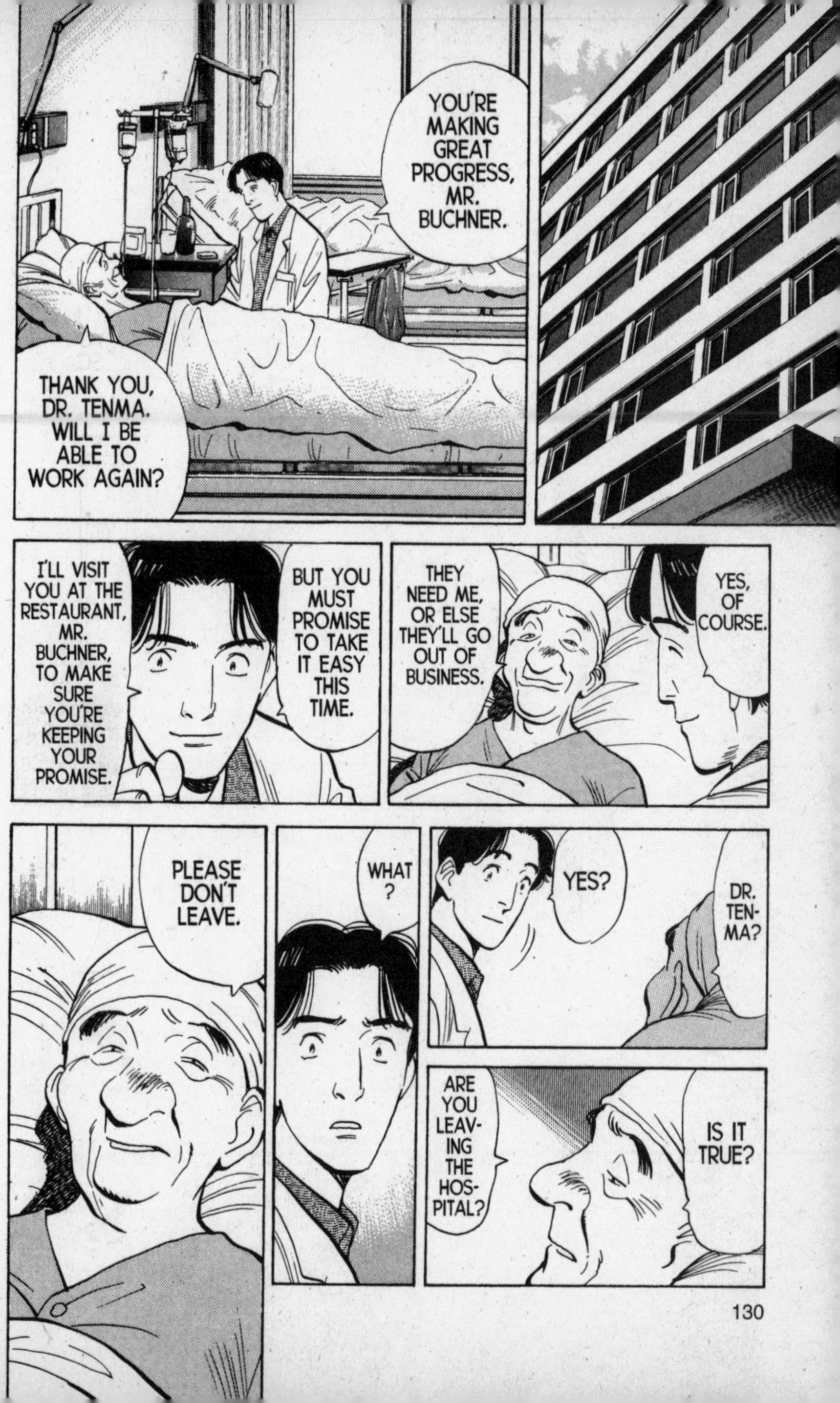
YOU'RE MAKING GREAT PROGRESS, MR. BUCHNER.
THANK YOU, DR. TENMA. WILL I BE ABLE TO WORK AGAIN?
YES, OF COURSE.
THEY NEED ME, OR ELSE THEY'LL GO OUT OF BUSINESS.
BUT YOU MUST PROMISE TO TAKE IT EASY THIS TIME.
I'LL VISIT YOU AT THE RESTAURANT, MR. BUCHNER, TO MAKE SURE YOU'RE KEEPING YOUR PROMISE.
DR. TEN-MA?
YES?
IS IT TRUE?
ARE YOU LEAVING THE HOS-PITAL?
WHAT?
PLEASE DON'T LEAVE.

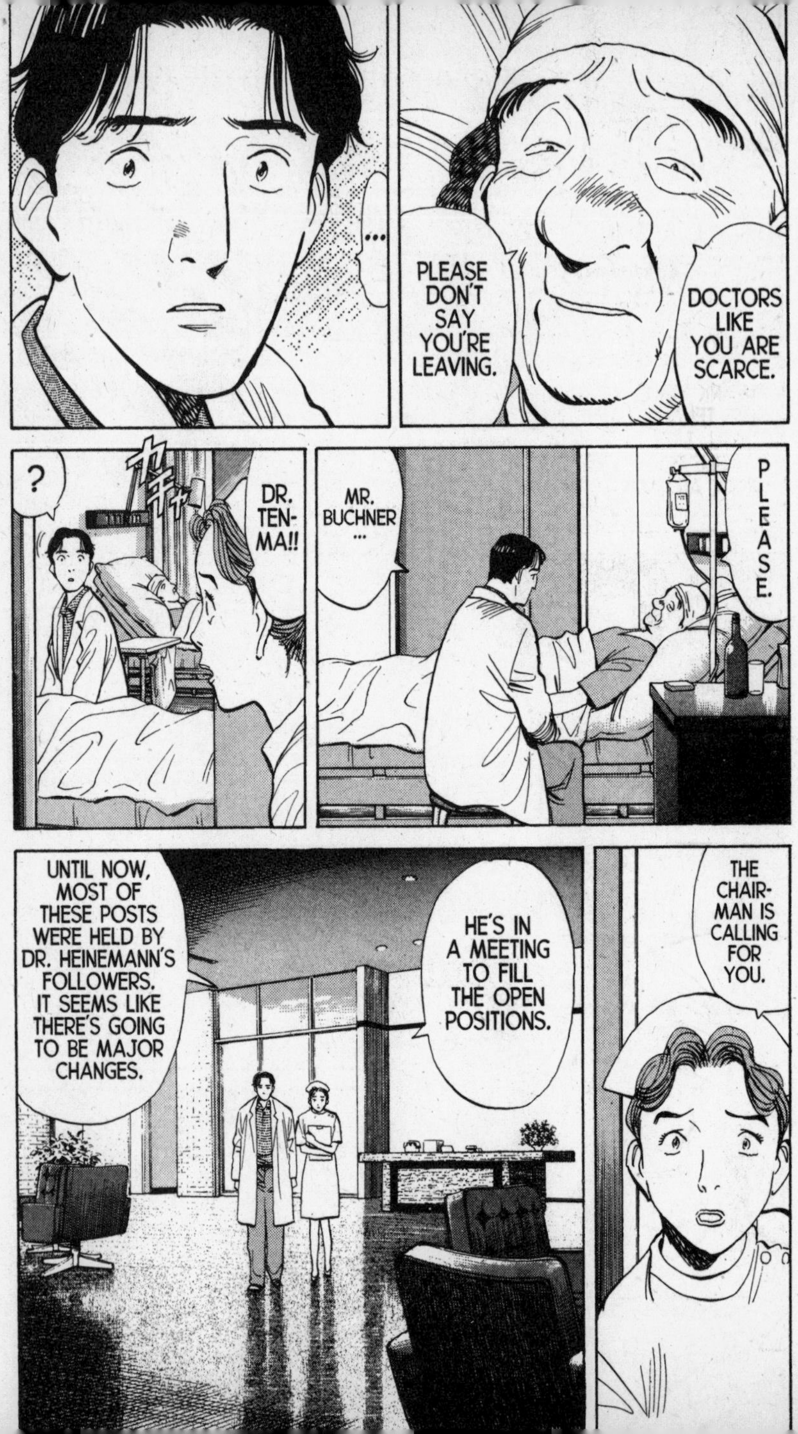
DOCTORS LIKE YOU ARE SCARCE.
PLEASE DON'T SAY YOU'RE LEAVING.
...
PLEASE.
MR. BUCHNER ...
DR. TEN-MA!!
カチャ
?
THE CHAIR-MAN IS CALLING FOR YOU.
HE'S IN A MEETING TO FILL THE OPEN POSITIONS.
UNTIL NOW, MOST OF THESE POSTS WERE HELD BY DR. HEINEMANN'S FOLLOWERS. IT SEEMS LIKE THERE'S GOING TO BE MAJOR CHANGES.

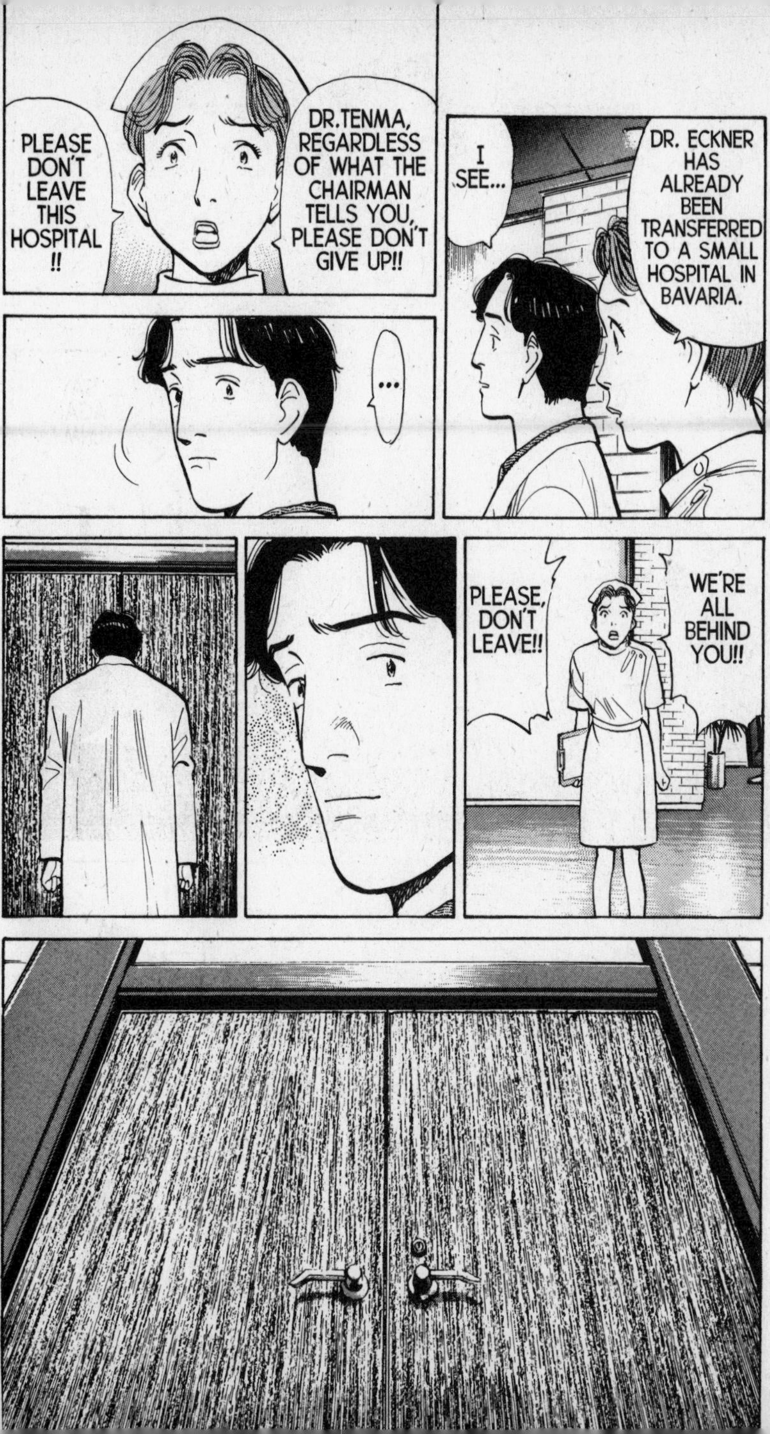
DR. ECKNER HAS ALREADY BEEN TRANSFERRED TO A SMALL HOSPITAL IN BAVARIA.
I SEE...
DR.TENMA, REGARDLESS OF WHAT THE CHAIRMAN TELLS YOU, PLEASE DON'T GIVE UP!!
PLEASE DON'T LEAVE THIS HOSPITAL !!
...
WE'RE ALL BEHIND YOU!!
PLEASE, DON'T LEAVE!!

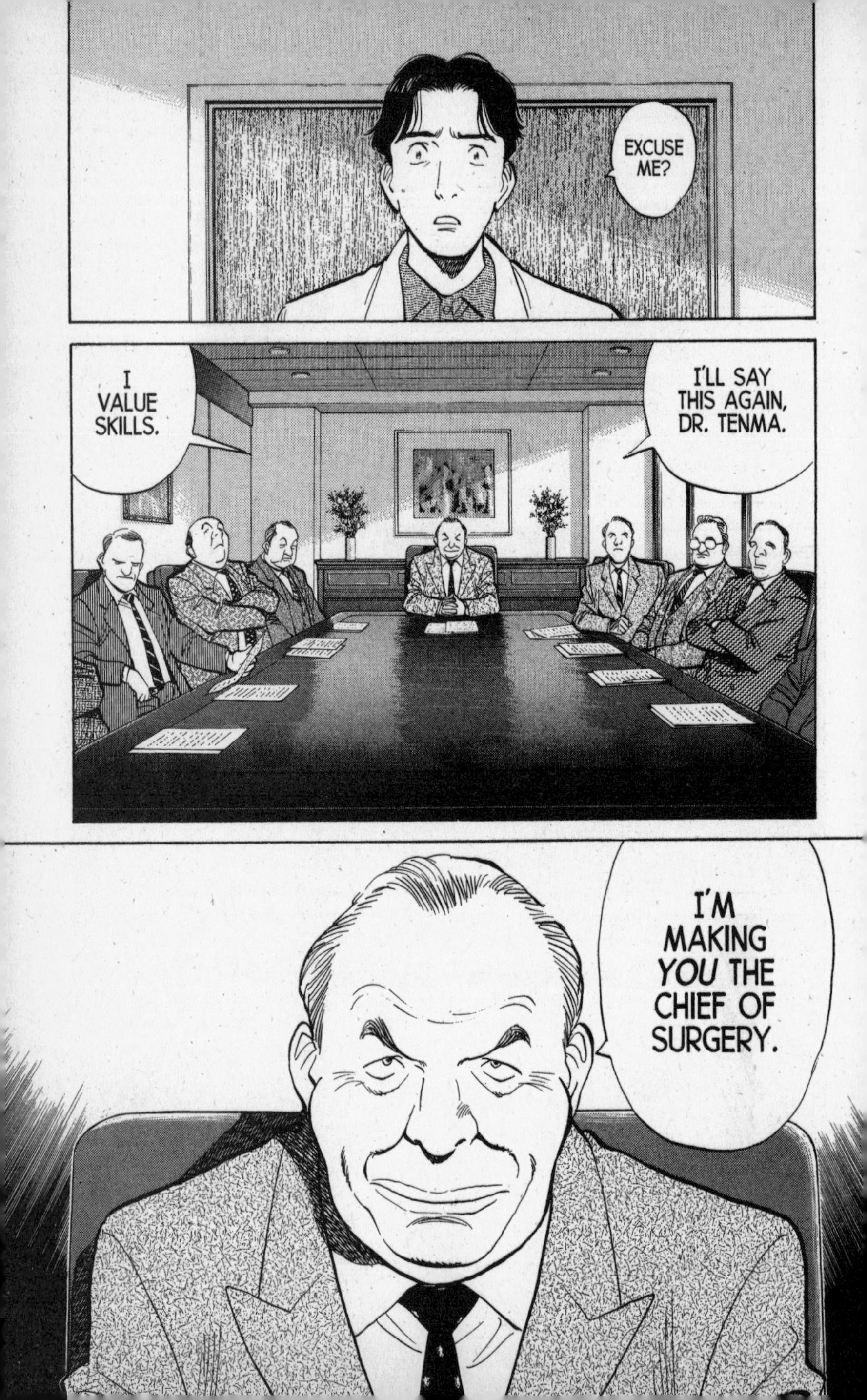
EXCUSE ME?
I'LL SAY THIS AGAIN, DR. TENMA.
I VALUE SKILLS.
I'M MAKING *YOU* THE CHIEF OF SURGERY.

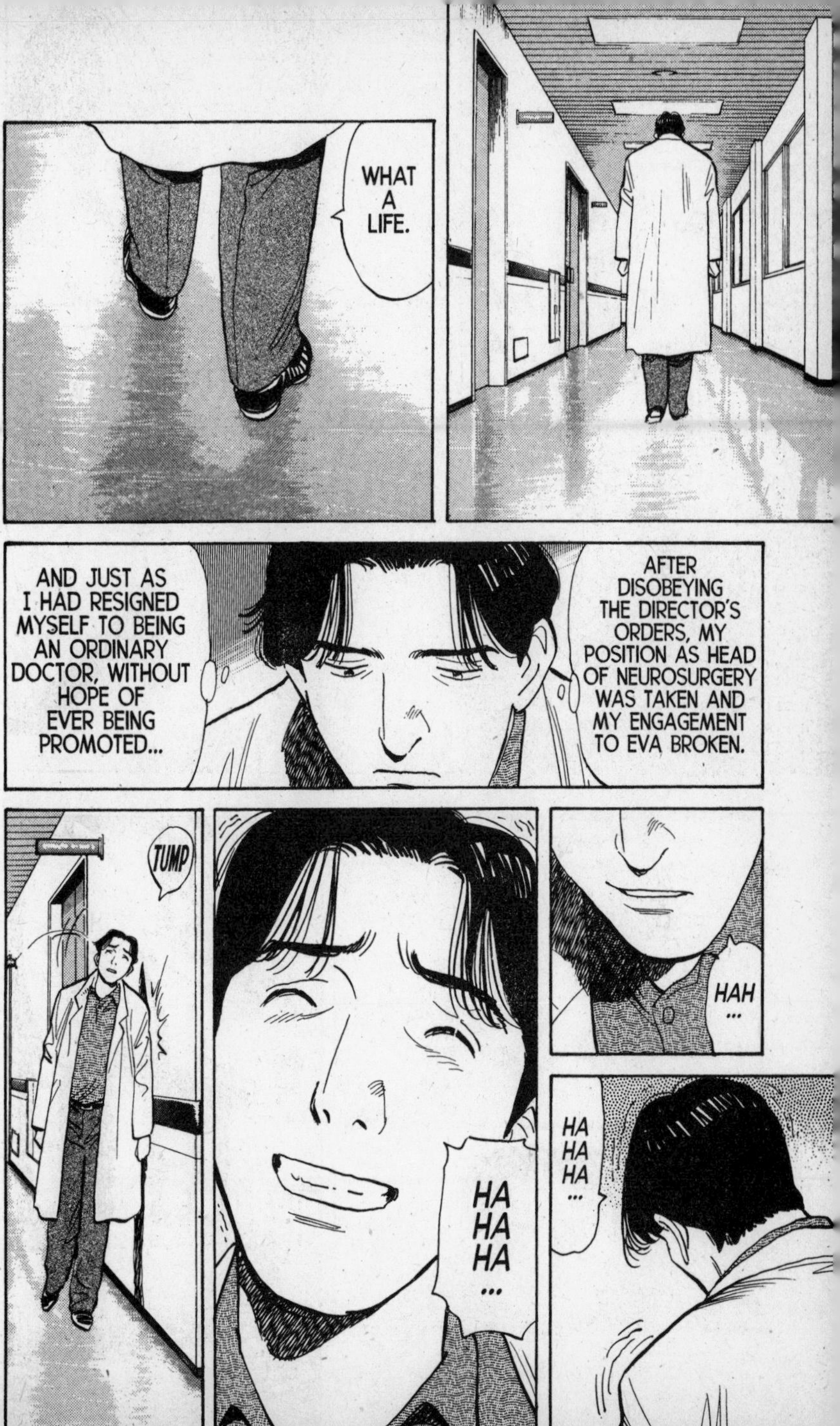
WHAT A LIFE.
AFTER DISOBEYING THE DIRECTOR'S ORDERS, MY POSITION AS HEAD OF NEUROSURGERY WAS TAKEN AND MY ENGAGEMENT TO EVA BROKEN.
AND JUST AS I HAD RESIGNED MYSELF TO BEING AN ORDINARY DOCTOR, WITHOUT HOPE OF EVER BEING PROMOTED...
HAH ...
HA HA HA ...
HA HA HA ...
TUMP

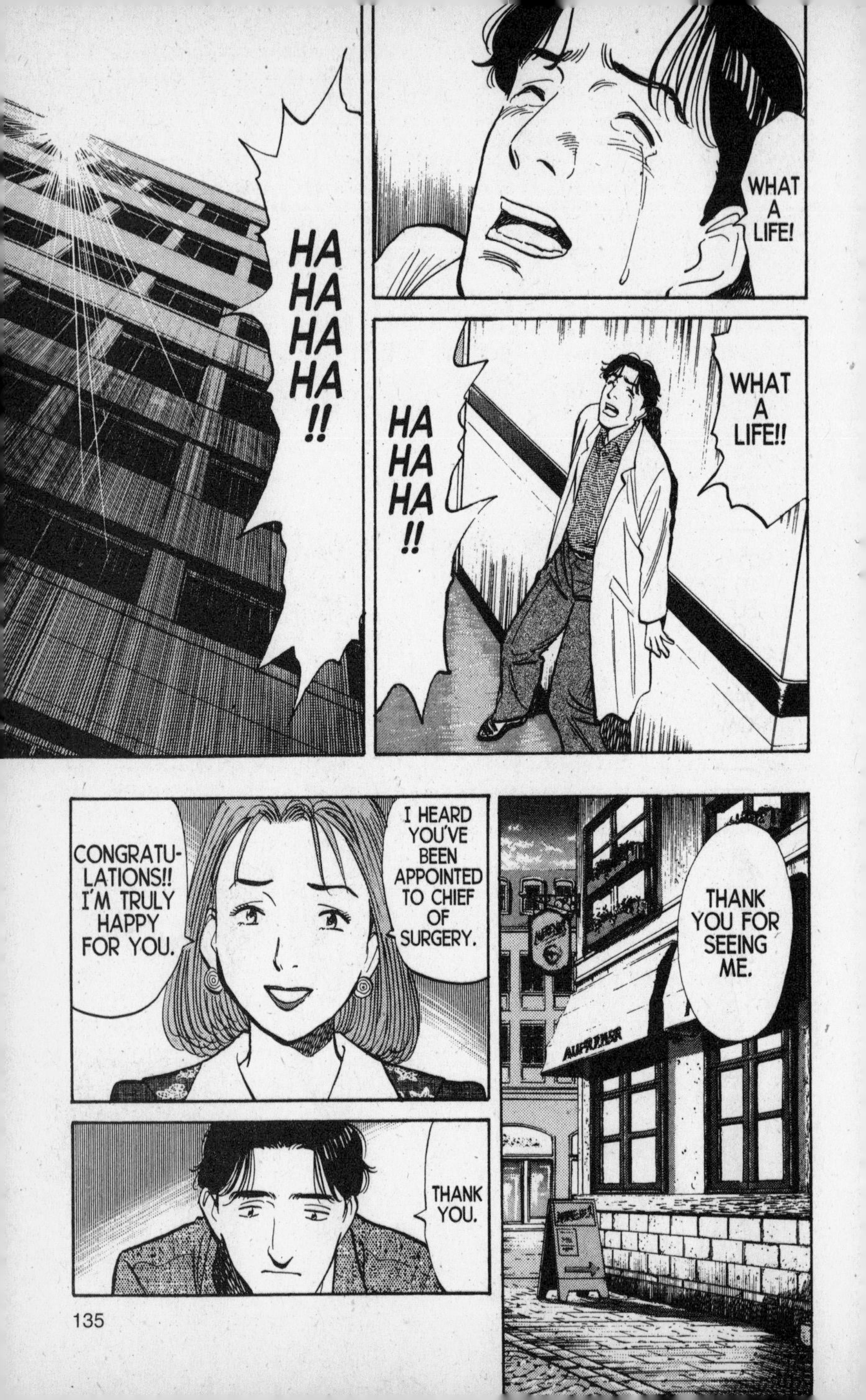
WHAT A LIFE!
WHAT A LIFE!!
HA HA HA!!
HA HA HA HA!!
THANK YOU FOR SEEING ME.
I HEARD YOU'VE BEEN APPOINTED TO CHIEF OF SURGERY.
CONGRATULATIONS!! I'M TRULY HAPPY FOR YOU.
THANK YOU.

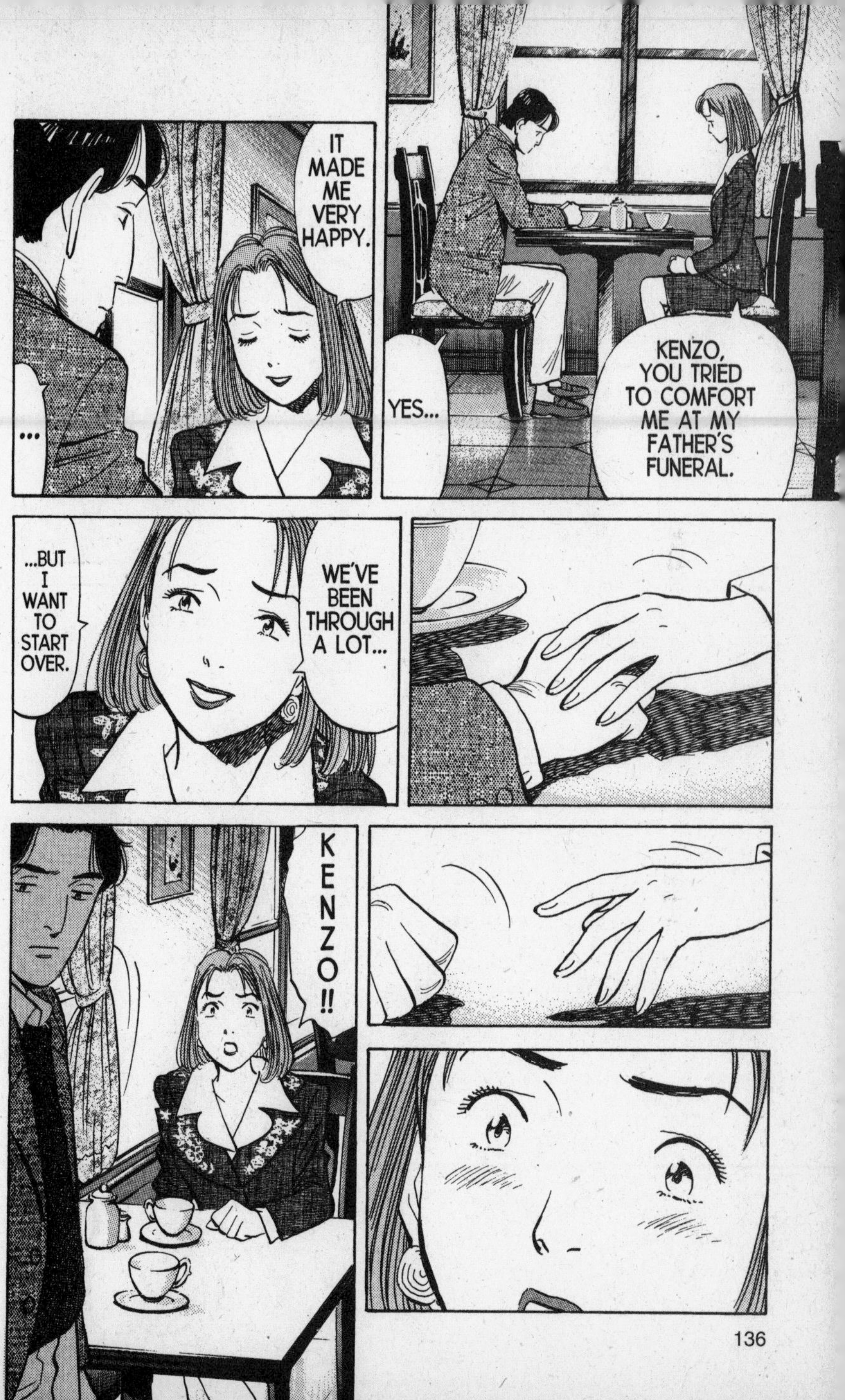

KENZO, YOU TRIED TO COMFORT ME AT MY FATHER'S FUNERAL.
YES...
IT MADE ME VERY HAPPY.
...
WE'VE BEEN THROUGH A LOT...
...BUT I WANT TO START OVER.
KENZO!!

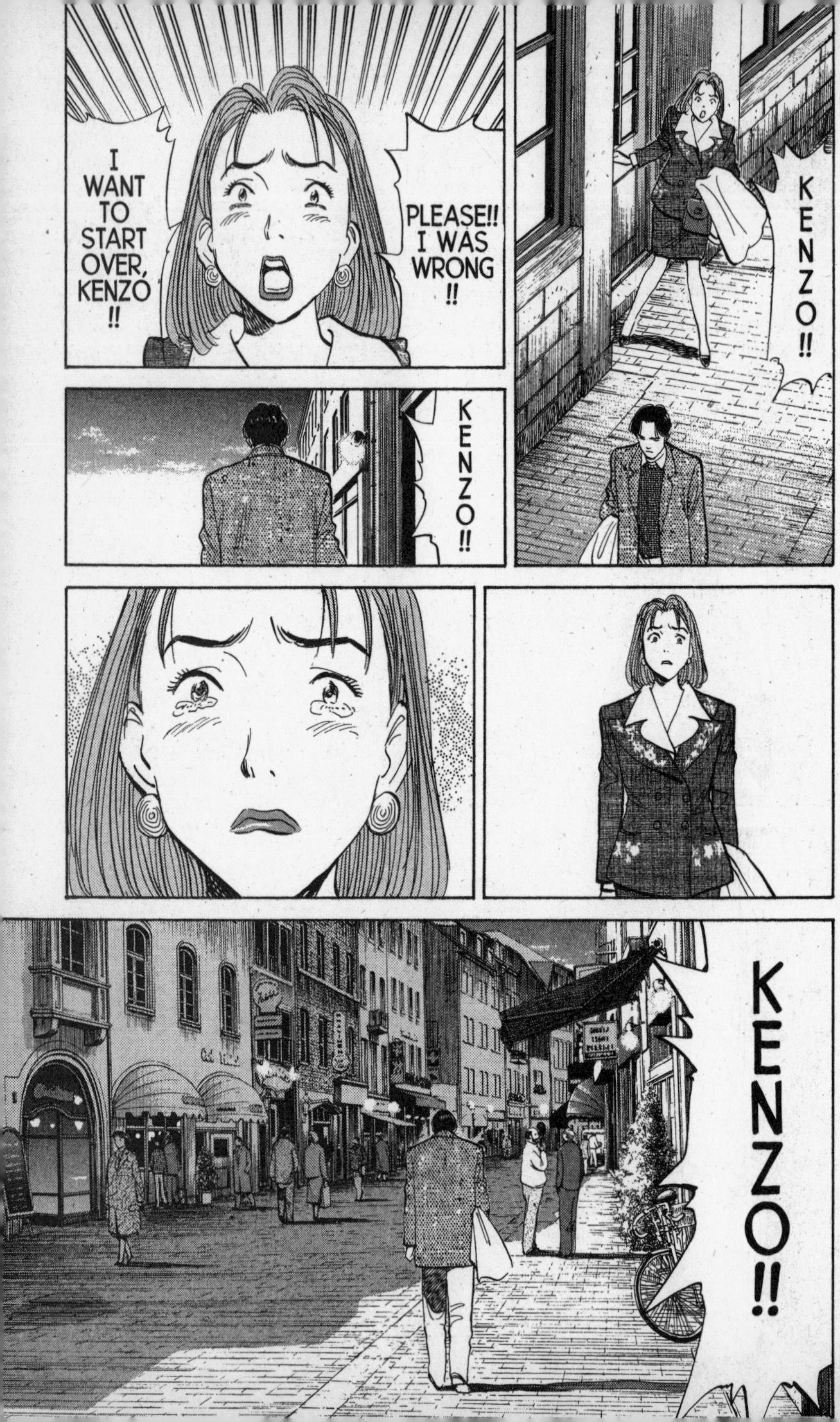
KENZO!!
PLEASE!! I WAS WRONG!!
I WANT TO START OVER, KENZO!!
KENZO!!
KENZO!!

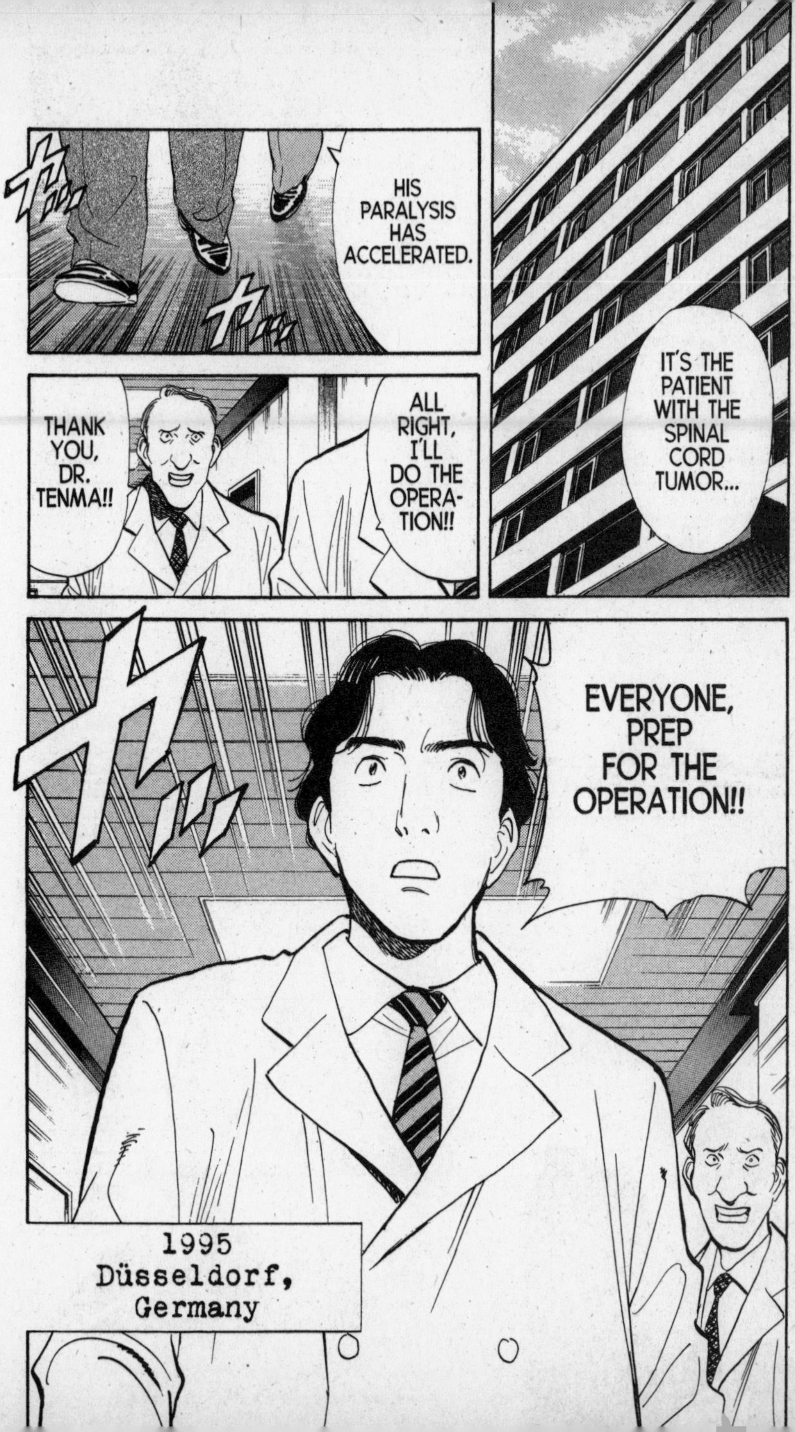
IT'S THE PATIENT WITH THE SPINAL CORD TUMOR...
HIS PARALYSIS HAS ACCELERATED.
ALL RIGHT, I'LL DO THE OPERATION!!
THANK YOU, DR. TENMA!!
EVERYONE, PREP FOR THE OPERATION!!
1995 Düsseldorf, Germany

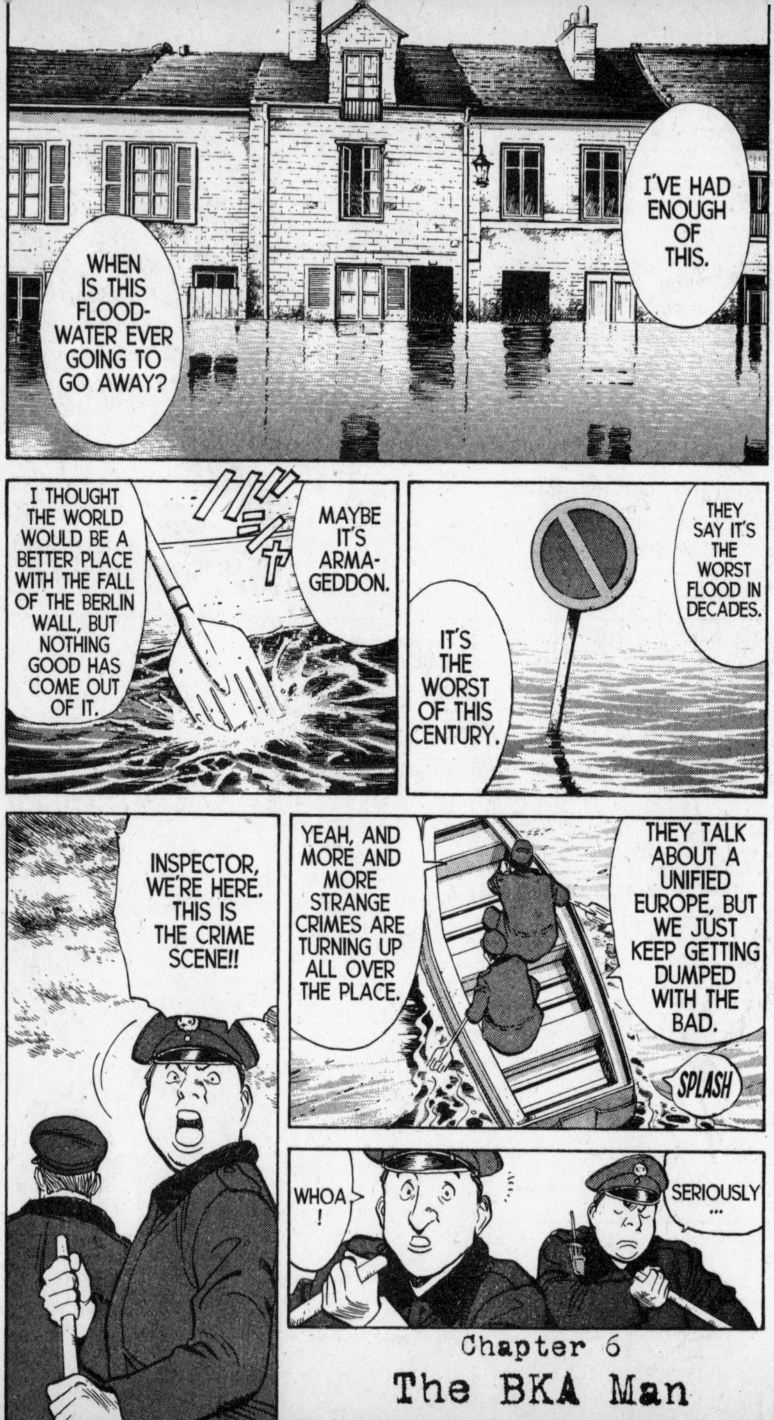
I'VE HAD ENOUGH OF THIS.
WHEN IS THIS FLOOD-WATER EVER GOING TO GO AWAY?
THEY SAY IT'S THE WORST FLOOD IN DECADES.
IT'S THE WORST OF THIS CENTURY.
MAYBE IT'S ARMA-GEDDON.
I THOUGHT THE WORLD WOULD BE A BETTER PLACE WITH THE FALL OF THE BERLIN WALL, BUT NOTHING GOOD HAS COME OUT OF IT.
THEY TALK ABOUT A UNIFIED EUROPE, BUT WE JUST KEEP GETTING DUMPED WITH THE BAD.
SPLASH
YEAH, AND MORE AND MORE STRANGE CRIMES ARE TURNING UP ALL OVER THE PLACE.
SERIOUSLY ...
WHOA !
INSPECTOR, WE'RE HERE. THIS IS THE CRIME SCENE!!

Chapter 6

The BKA Man

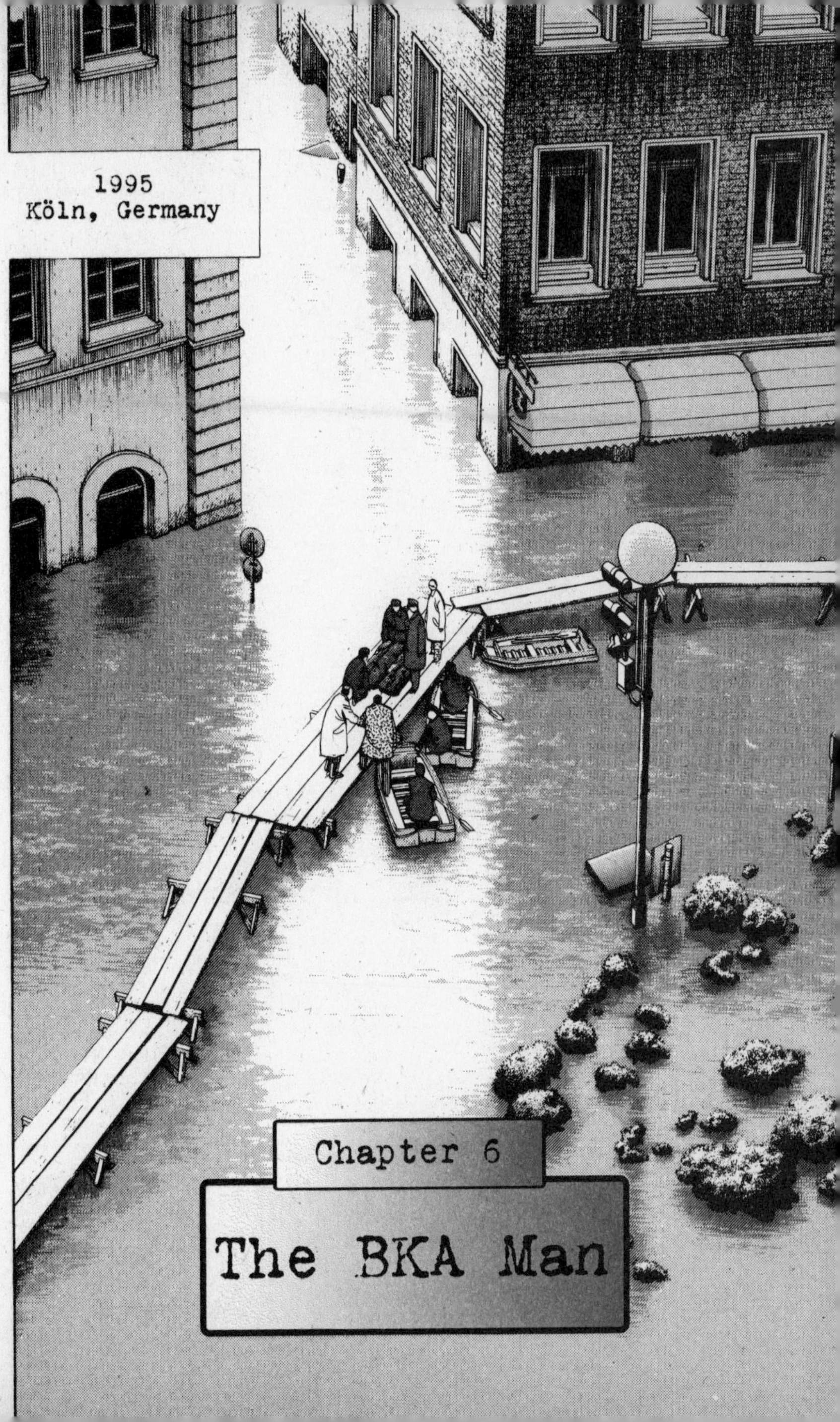
1995
Köln, Germany
Chapter 6
The BKA Man

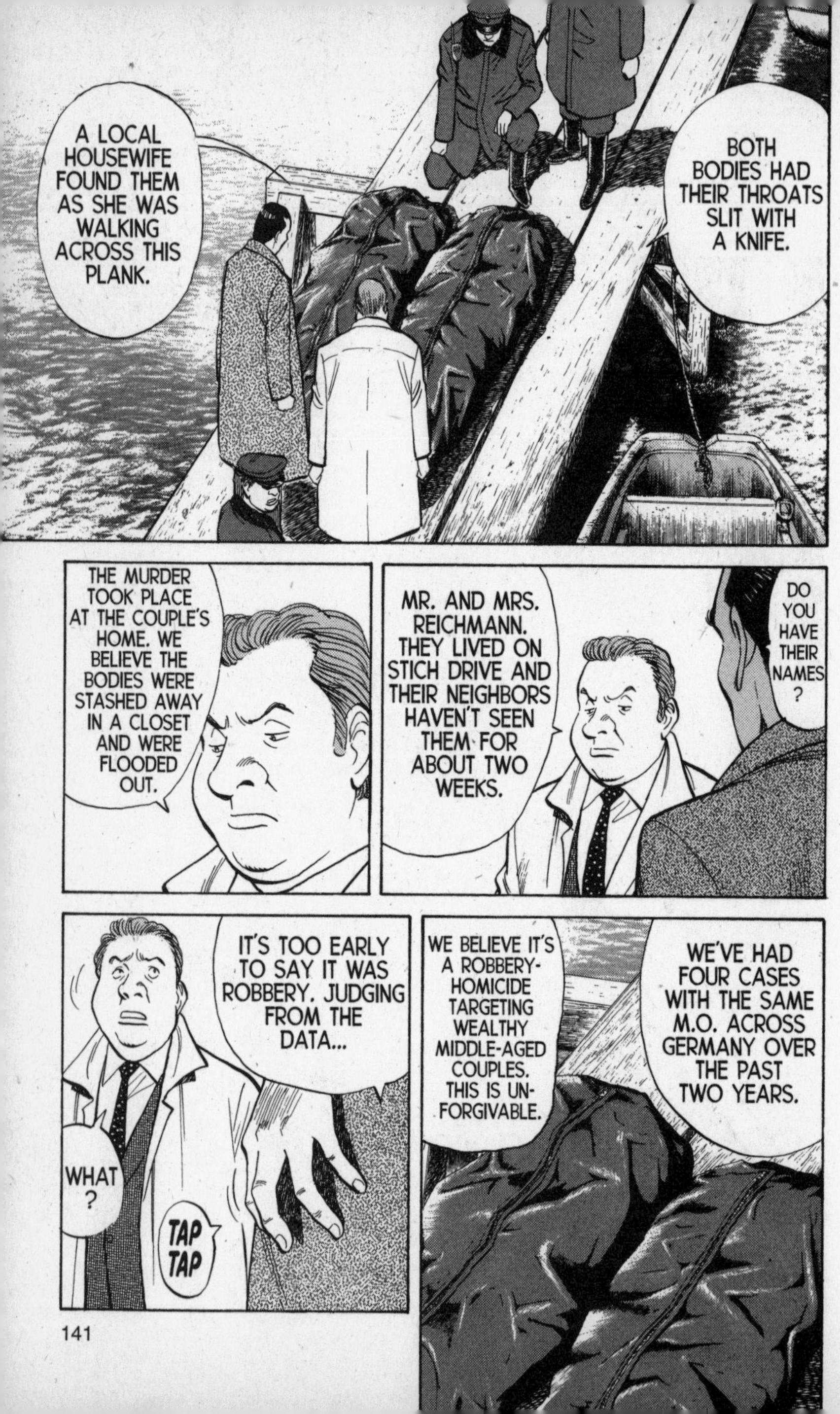
BOTH BODIES HAD THEIR THROATS SLIT WITH A KNIFE.
A LOCAL HOUSEWIFE FOUND THEM AS SHE WAS WALKING ACROSS THIS PLANK.
DO YOU HAVE THEIR NAMES?
MR. AND MRS. REICHMANN. THEY LIVED ON STICH DRIVE AND THEIR NEIGHBORS HAVEN'T SEEN THEM FOR ABOUT TWO WEEKS.
THE MURDER TOOK PLACE AT THE COUPLE'S HOME. WE BELIEVE THE BODIES WERE STASHED AWAY IN A CLOSET AND WERE FLOODED OUT.
WE'VE HAD FOUR CASES WITH THE SAME M.O. ACROSS GERMANY OVER THE PAST TWO YEARS.
WE BELIEVE IT'S A ROBBERY-HOMICIDE TARGETING WEALTHY MIDDLE-AGED COUPLES. THIS IS UN-FORGIVABLE.
IT'S TOO EARLY TO SAY IT WAS ROBBERY. JUDGING FROM THE DATA...
TAP TAP
WHAT?

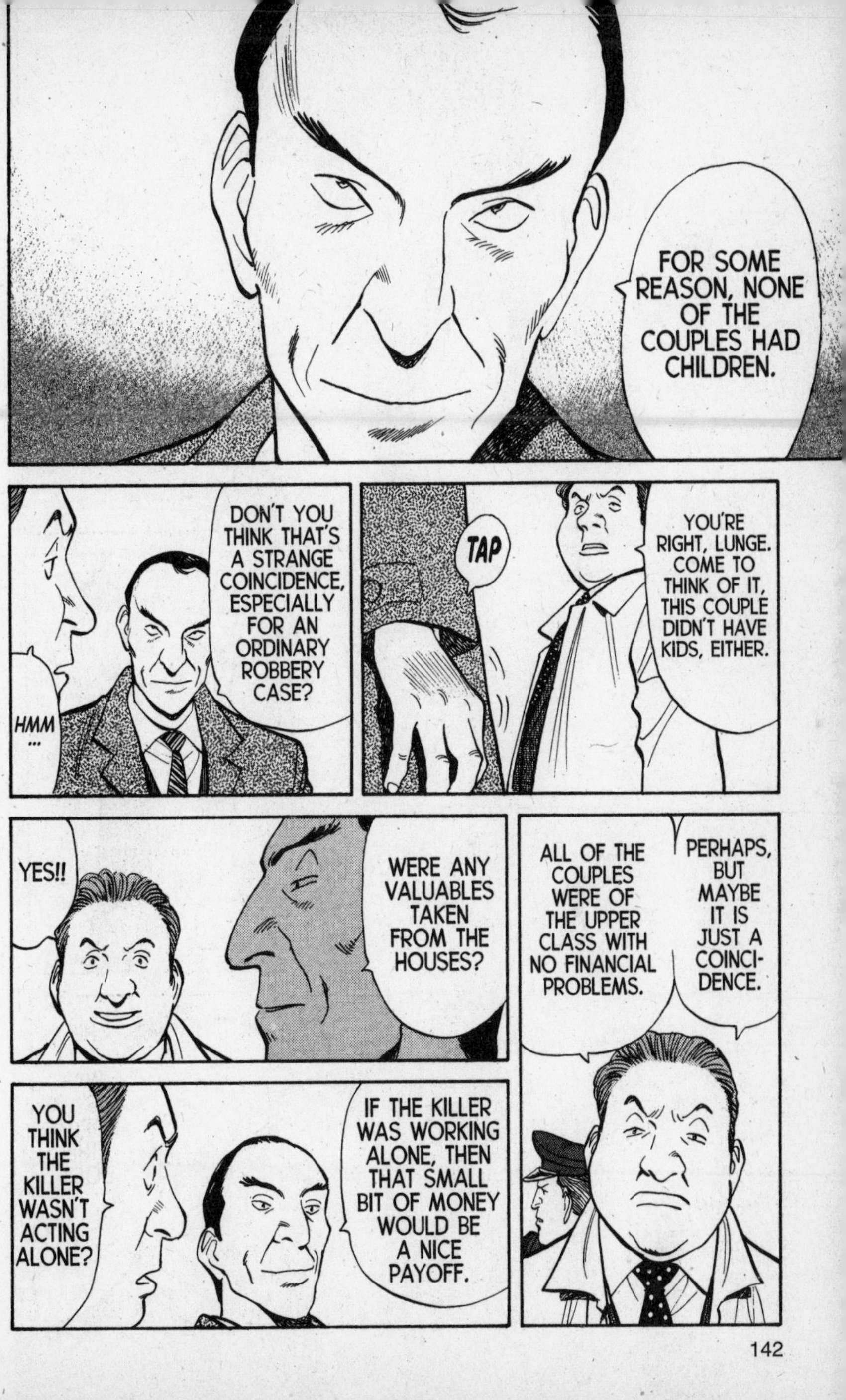
FOR SOME REASON, NONE OF THE COUPLES HAD CHILDREN.
TAP
YOU'RE RIGHT, LUNGE. COME TO THINK OF IT, THIS COUPLE DIDN'T HAVE KIDS, EITHER.
DON'T YOU THINK THAT'S A STRANGE COINCIDENCE, ESPECIALLY FOR AN ORDINARY ROBBERY CASE?
HMM ...
PERHAPS, BUT MAYBE IT IS JUST A COINCI-DENCE.
ALL OF THE COUPLES WERE OF THE UPPER CLASS WITH NO FINANCIAL PROBLEMS.
WERE ANY VALUABLES TAKEN FROM THE HOUSES?
YES!!
IF THE KILLER WAS WORKING ALONE, THEN THAT SMALL BIT OF MONEY WOULD BE A NICE PAYOFF.
YOU THINK THE KILLER WASN'T ACTING ALONE?

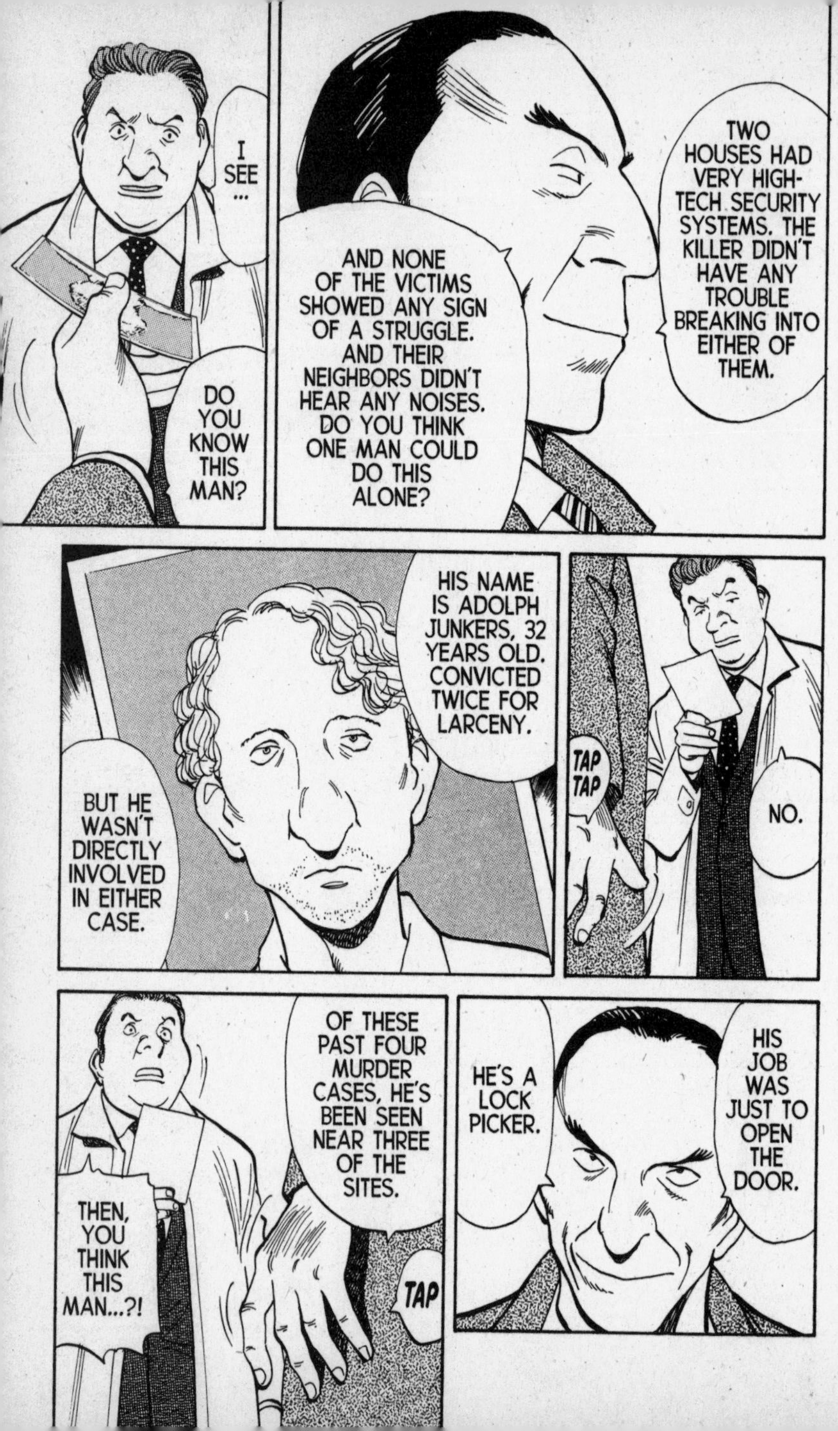
TWO HOUSES HAD VERY HIGH-TECH SECURITY SYSTEMS. THE KILLER DIDN'T HAVE ANY TROUBLE BREAKING INTO EITHER OF THEM.
AND NONE OF THE VICTIMS SHOWED ANY SIGN OF A STRUGGLE. AND THEIR NEIGHBORS DIDN'T HEAR ANY NOISES. DO YOU THINK ONE MAN COULD DO THIS ALONE?
I SEE ...
DO YOU KNOW THIS MAN?
NO.
TAP TAP
HIS NAME IS ADOLPH JUNKERS, 32 YEARS OLD. CONVICTED TWICE FOR LARCENY.
BUT HE WASN'T DIRECTLY INVOLVED IN EITHER CASE.
HIS JOB WAS JUST TO OPEN THE DOOR.
HE'S A LOCK PICKER.
OF THESE PAST FOUR MURDER CASES, HE'S BEEN SEEN NEAR THREE OF THE SITES.
TAP
THEN, YOU THINK THIS MAN...?!

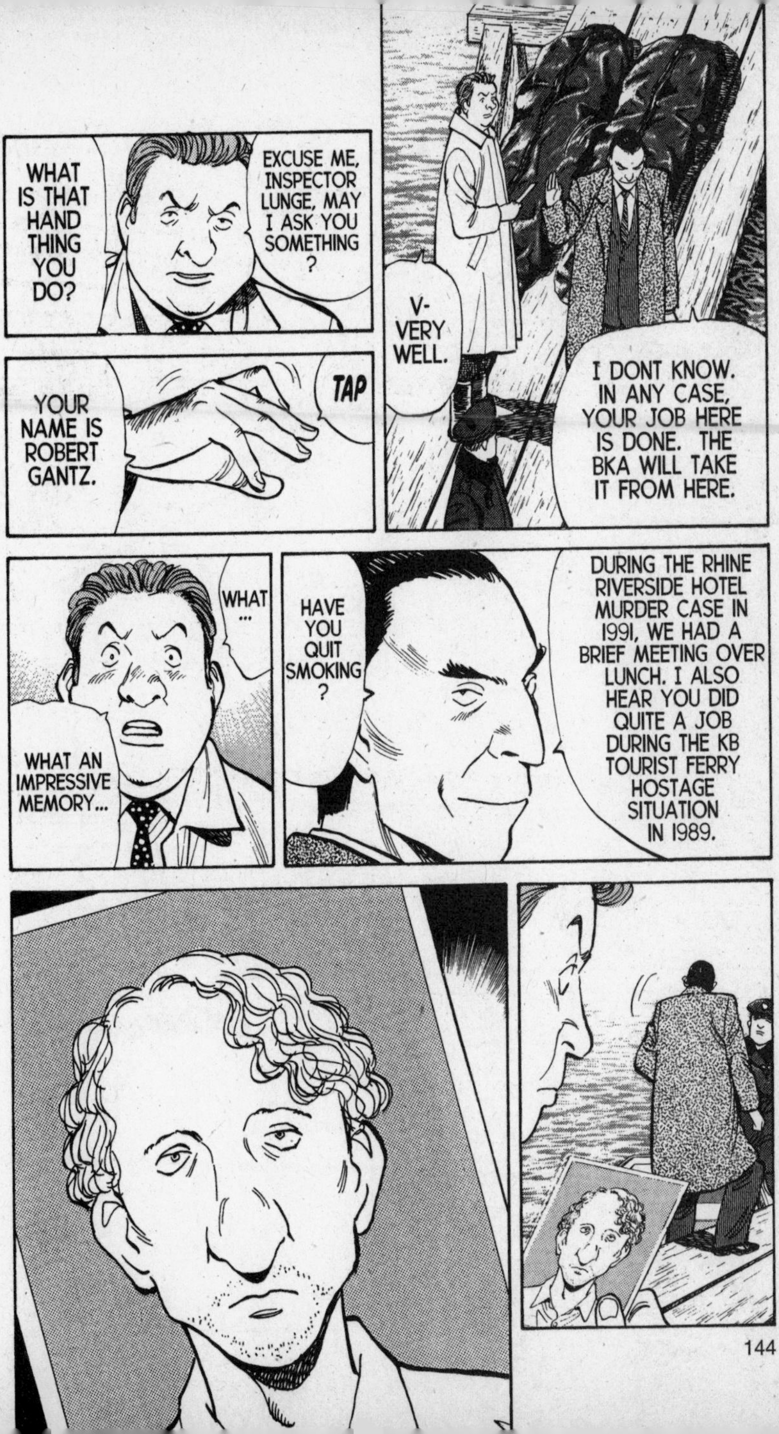
V-VERY WELL.
I DONT KNOW. IN ANY CASE, YOUR JOB HERE IS DONE. THE BKA WILL TAKE IT FROM HERE.
EXCUSE ME, INSPECTOR LUNGE, MAY I ASK YOU SOMETHING?
WHAT IS THAT HAND THING YOU DO?
TAP
YOUR NAME IS ROBERT GANTZ.
DURING THE RHINE RIVERSIDE HOTEL MURDER CASE IN 1991, WE HAD A BRIEF MEETING OVER LUNCH. I ALSO HEAR YOU DID QUITE A JOB DURING THE KB TOURIST FERRY HOSTAGE SITUATION IN 1989.
HAVE YOU QUIT SMOKING?
WHAT...
WHAT AN IMPRESSIVE MEMORY...

Eisler Memorial
Hospital
Düsseldorf, Germany

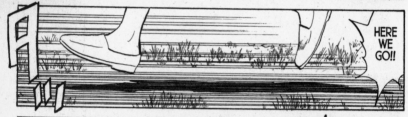

HERE WE GO!!

IT'S NO GOOD. I'VE NEVER FLOWN A KITE BEFORE.

YOU ALMOST HAD IT.

OH, NO!

PLUNK

145

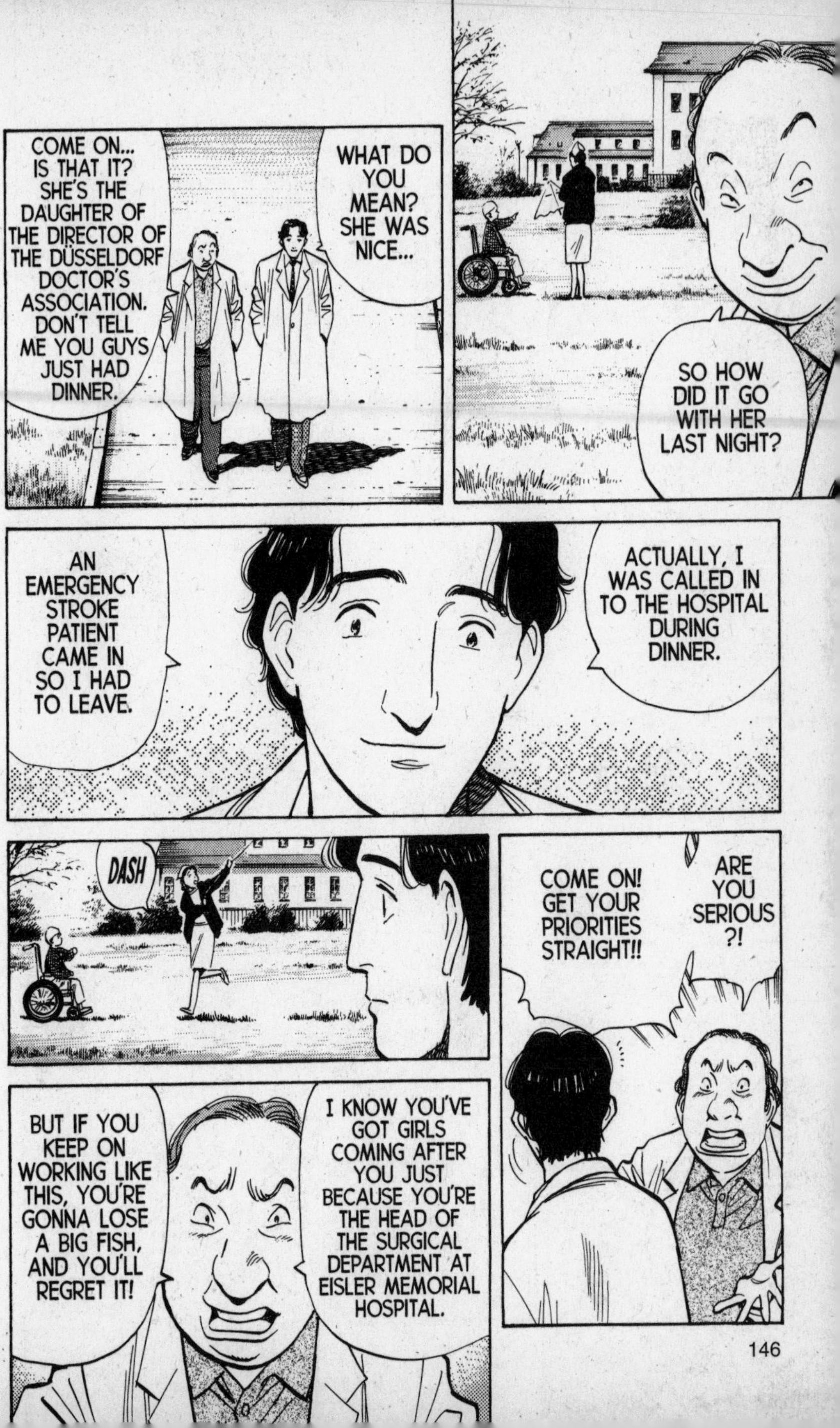
SO HOW DID IT GO WITH HER LAST NIGHT?
WHAT DO YOU MEAN? SHE WAS NICE...
COME ON... IS THAT IT? SHE'S THE DAUGHTER OF THE DIRECTOR OF THE DÜSSELDORF DOCTOR'S ASSOCIATION. DON'T TELL ME YOU GUYS JUST HAD DINNER.
ACTUALLY, I WAS CALLED IN TO THE HOSPITAL DURING DINNER.
AN EMERGENCY STROKE PATIENT CAME IN SO I HAD TO LEAVE.
ARE YOU SERIOUS?!
COME ON! GET YOUR PRIORITIES STRAIGHT!!
DASH
I KNOW YOU'VE GOT GIRLS COMING AFTER YOU JUST BECAUSE YOU'RE THE HEAD OF THE SURGICAL DEPARTMENT AT EISLER MEMORIAL HOSPITAL.
BUT IF YOU KEEP ON WORKING LIKE THIS, YOU'RE GONNA LOSE A BIG FISH, AND YOU'LL REGRET IT!

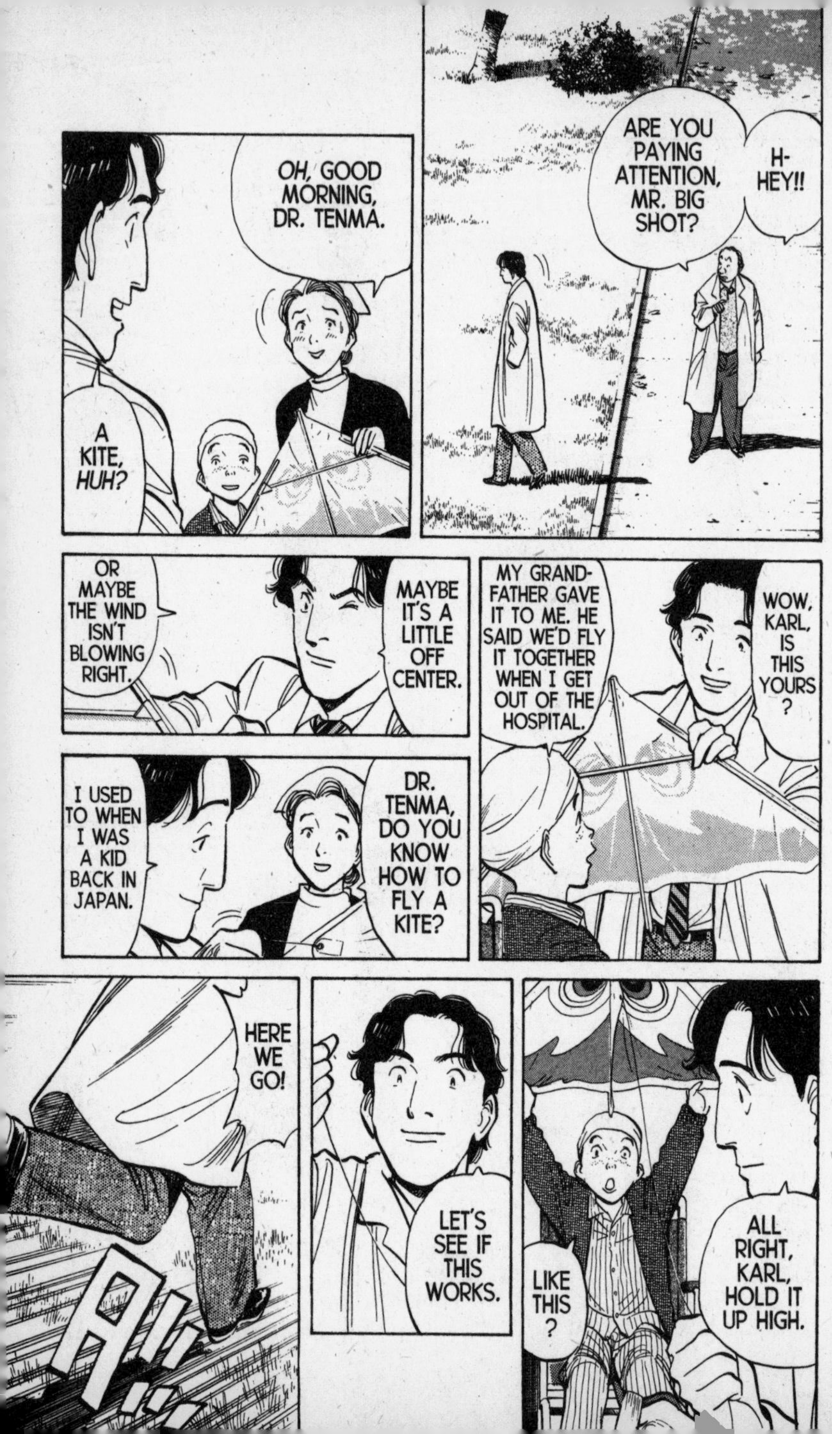
H-HEY!!
ARE YOU PAYING ATTENTION, MR. BIG SHOT?
OH, GOOD MORNING, DR. TENMA.
A KITE, *HUH?*
WOW, KARL, IS THIS YOURS?
MY GRANDFATHER GAVE IT TO ME. HE SAID WE'D FLY IT TOGETHER WHEN I GET OUT OF THE HOSPITAL.
MAYBE IT'S A LITTLE OFF CENTER.
OR MAYBE THE WIND ISN'T BLOWING RIGHT.
DR. TENMA, DO YOU KNOW HOW TO FLY A KITE?
I USED TO WHEN I WAS A KID BACK IN JAPAN.
ALL RIGHT, KARL, HOLD IT UP HIGH.
LIKE THIS?
LET'S SEE IF THIS WORKS.
HERE WE GO!

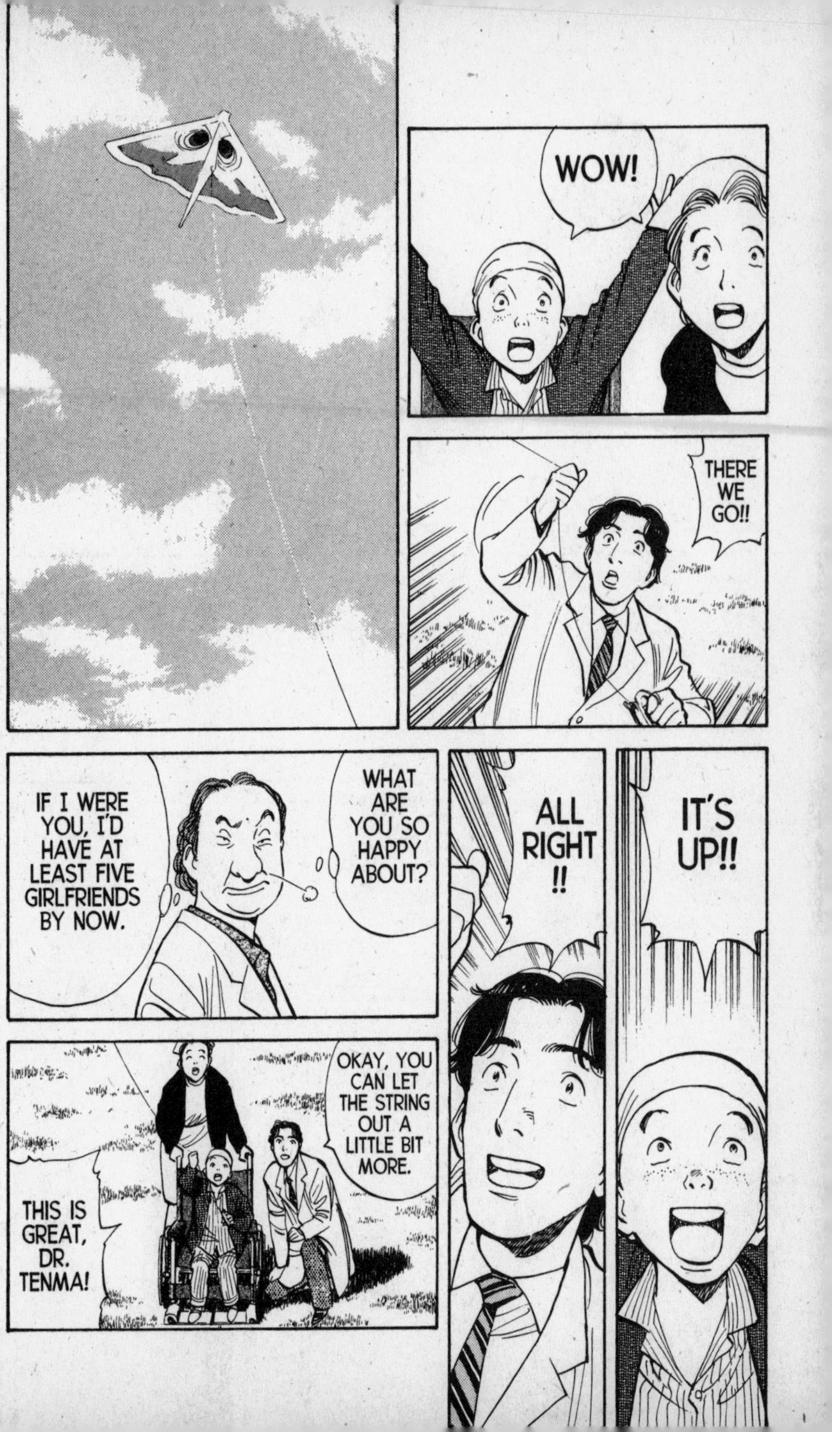
WOW!
THERE WE GO!!
IT'S UP!!
ALL RIGHT !!
WHAT ARE YOU SO HAPPY ABOUT?
IF I WERE YOU, I'D HAVE AT LEAST FIVE GIRLFRIENDS BY NOW.
OKAY, YOU CAN LET THE STRING OUT A LITTLE BIT MORE.
THIS IS GREAT, DR. TENMA!

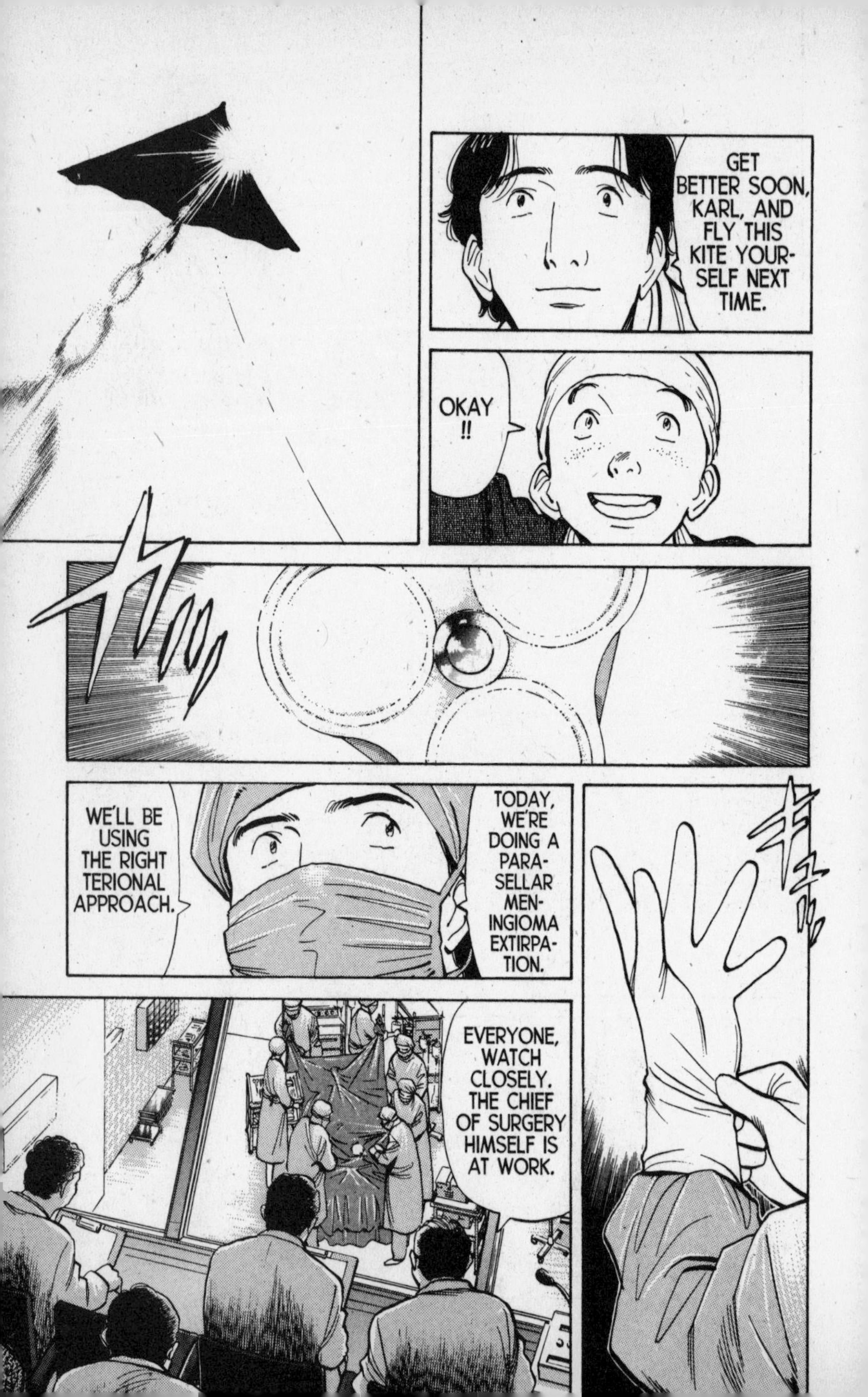
GET BETTER SOON, KARL, AND FLY THIS KITE YOURSELF NEXT TIME.
OKAY !!
TODAY, WE'RE DOING A PARASELLAR MENINGIOMA EXTIRPATION.
WE'LL BE USING THE RIGHT TERIONAL APPROACH.
EVERYONE, WATCH CLOSELY. THE CHIEF OF SURGERY HIMSELF IS AT WORK.

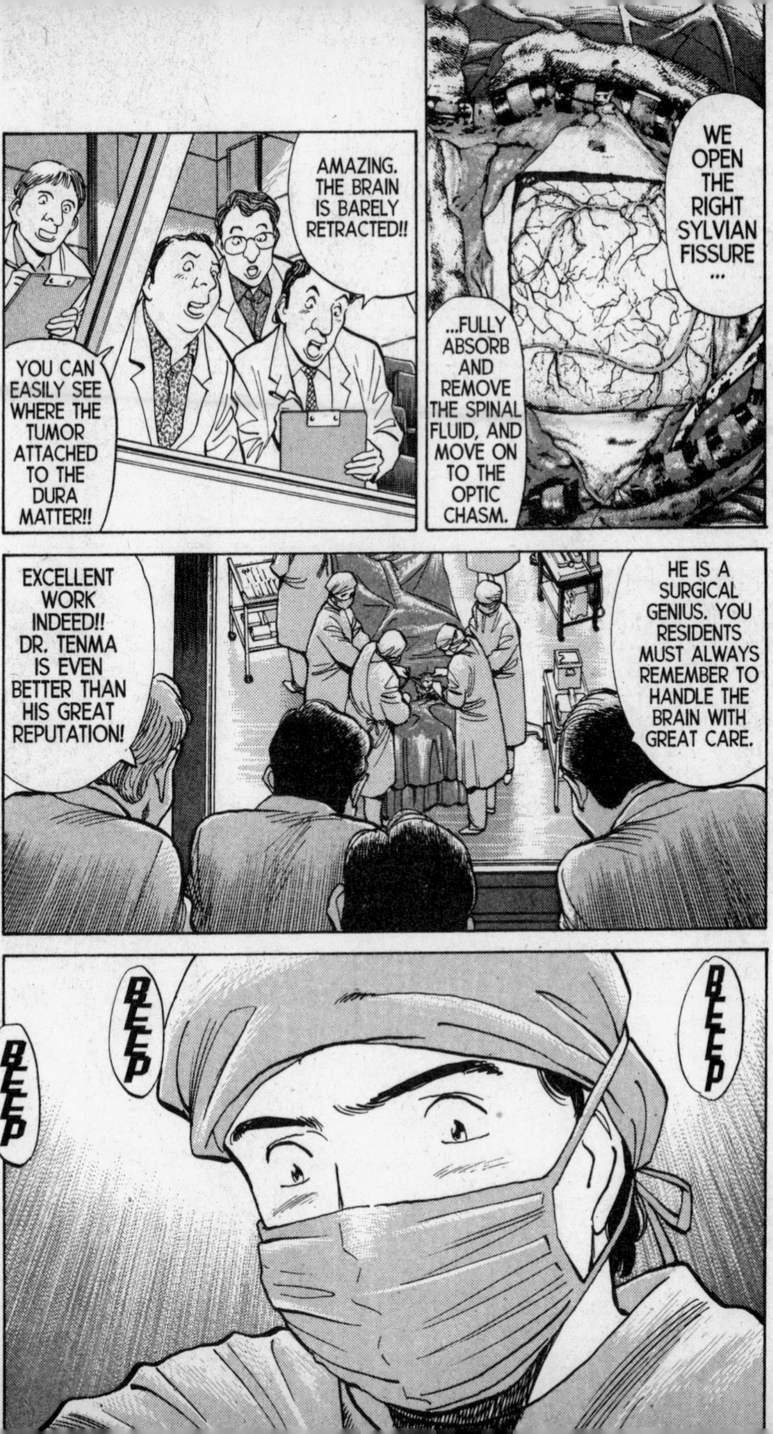
WE OPEN THE RIGHT SYLVIAN FISSURE ...
...FULLY ABSORB AND REMOVE THE SPINAL FLUID, AND MOVE ON TO THE OPTIC CHASM.
AMAZING. THE BRAIN IS BARELY RETRACTED!!
YOU CAN EASILY SEE WHERE THE TUMOR ATTACHED TO THE DURA MATTER!!
HE IS A SURGICAL GENIUS. YOU RESIDENTS MUST ALWAYS REMEMBER TO HANDLE THE BRAIN WITH GREAT CARE.
EXCELLENT WORK INDEED!! DR. TENMA IS EVEN BETTER THAN HIS GREAT REPUTATION!
BEEP
BEEP
BEEP

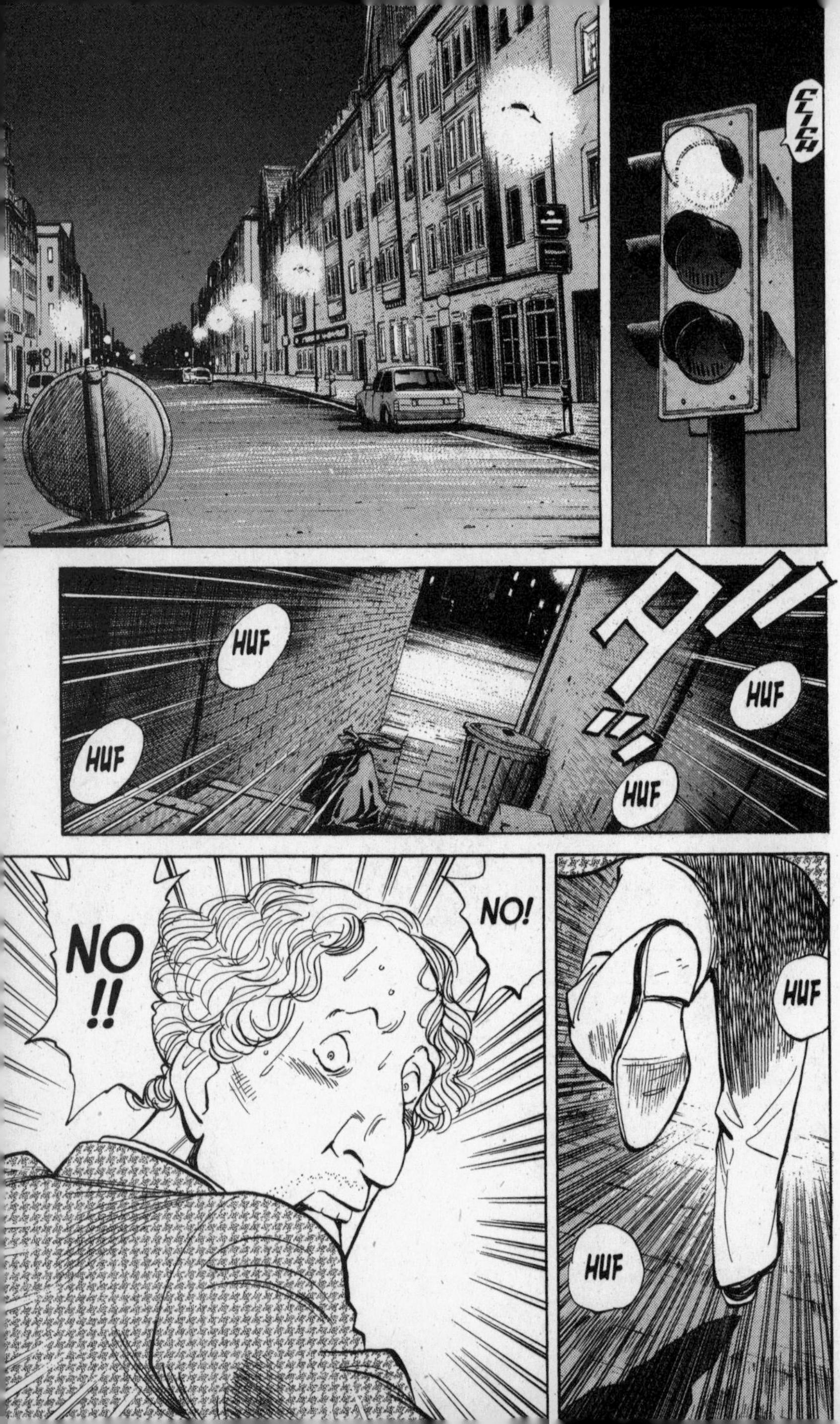
CLICK
ダッ
HUF
HUF
HUF
HUF
HUF
HUF
NO!
NO !!

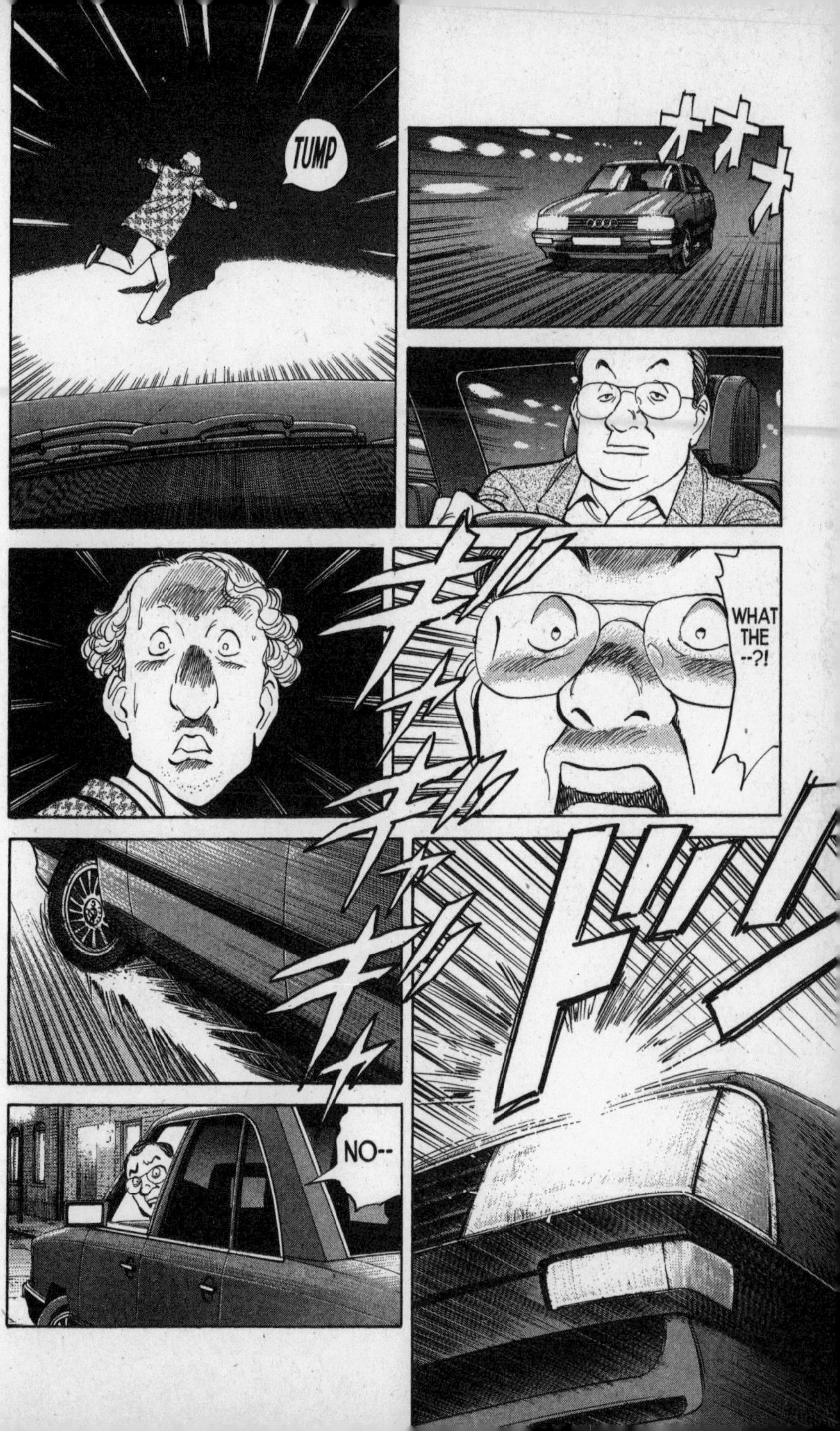
オオオ
TUMP
WHAT THE --?!
NO--

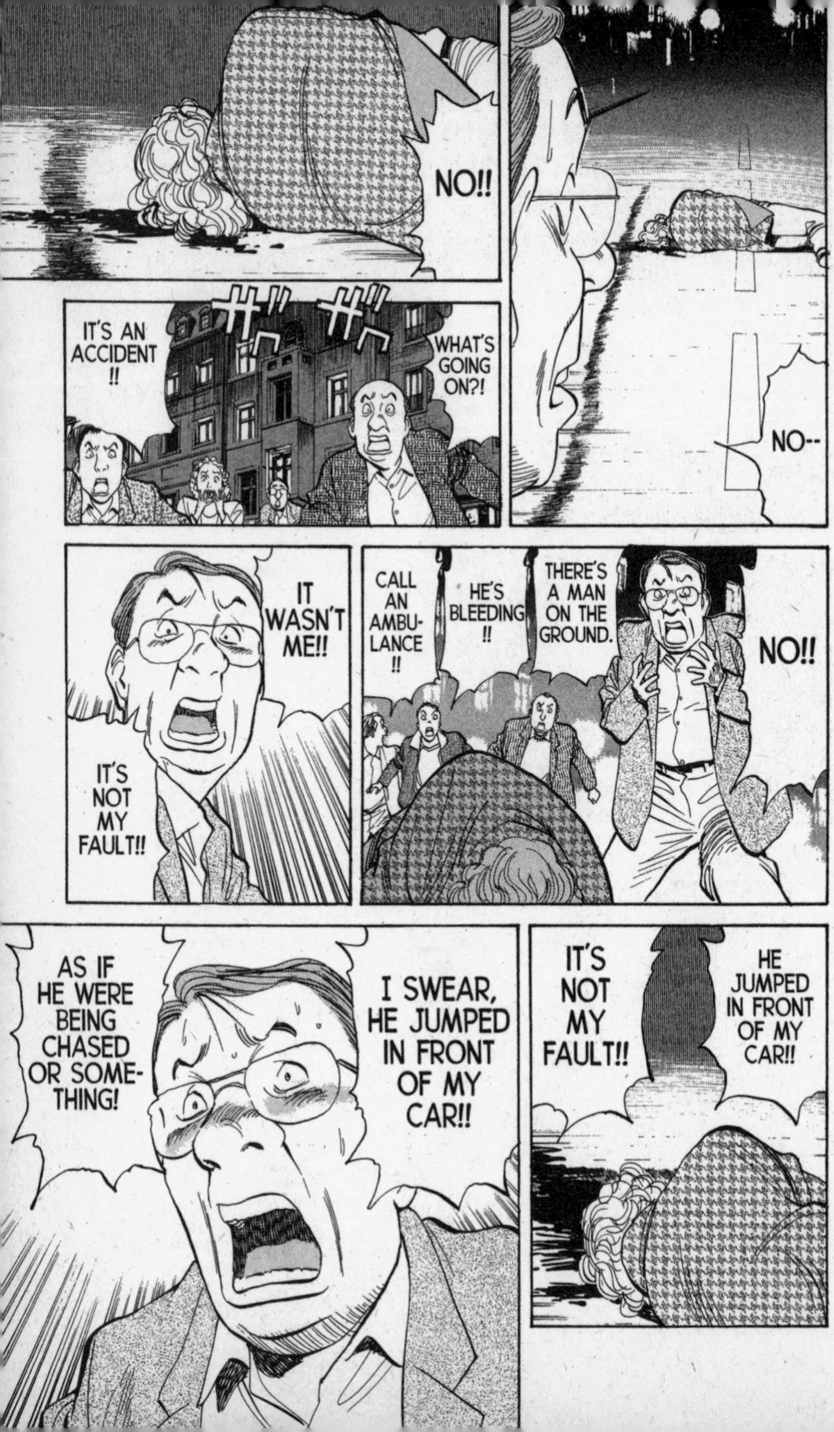

NO--
NO!!
WHAT'S GOING ON?!
ザワ ザワ
IT'S AN ACCIDENT !!
NO!!
THERE'S A MAN ON THE GROUND.
HE'S BLEEDING !!
CALL AN AMBULANCE !!
IT WASN'T ME!!
IT'S NOT MY FAULT!!
HE JUMPED IN FRONT OF MY CAR!!
IT'S NOT MY FAULT!!
I SWEAR, HE JUMPED IN FRONT OF MY CAR!!
AS IF HE WERE BEING CHASED OR SOME-THING!

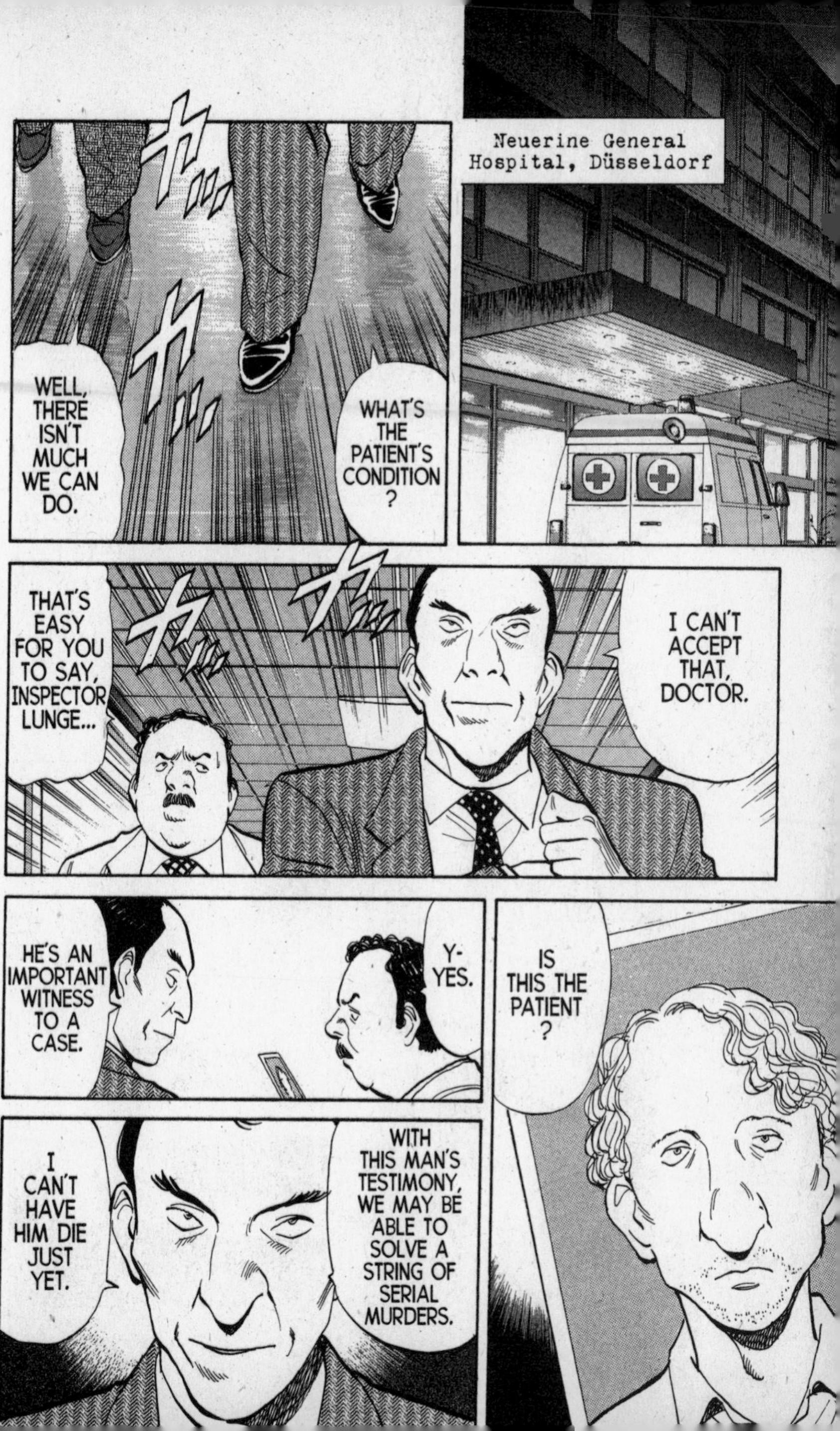
Neuerine General Hospital, Düsseldorf
WHAT'S THE PATIENT'S CONDITION?
WELL, THERE ISN'T MUCH WE CAN DO.
I CAN'T ACCEPT THAT, DOCTOR.
THAT'S EASY FOR YOU TO SAY, INSPECTOR LUNGE...
IS THIS THE PATIENT?
Y-YES.
HE'S AN IMPORTANT WITNESS TO A CASE.
WITH THIS MAN'S TESTIMONY, WE MAY BE ABLE TO SOLVE A STRING OF SERIAL MURDERS.
I CAN'T HAVE HIM DIE JUST YET.

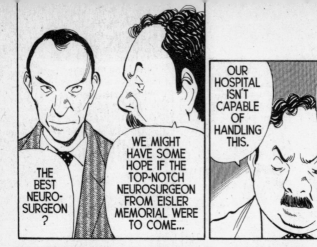

BUT THE PATIENT HAS A FRACTURED SKULL, AND FROM THE CT SCAN, WE'VE FOUND AN ACUTE EPIDURAL HEMATOMA...
...WHICH PUTS HIM IN VERY CRITICAL CONDITION.
OUR HOSPITAL ISN'T CAPABLE OF HANDLING THIS.
WE MIGHT HAVE SOME HOPE IF THE TOP-NOTCH NEUROSURGEON FROM EISLER MEMORIAL WERE TO COME...
THE BEST NEUROSURGEON?
TAP
THAT WOULD BE DR. TENMA...
THANK YOU FOR COMING OUT HERE.
PLEASE, THIS WAY.
WHAT'S THE PATIENT'S CONDITION?
WELL, DR. TENMA, HE'S IN A COMA, AND ONE OF HIS PUPILS IS DILATED.

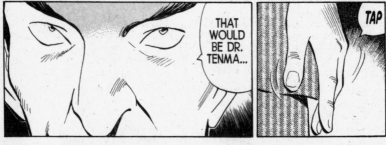

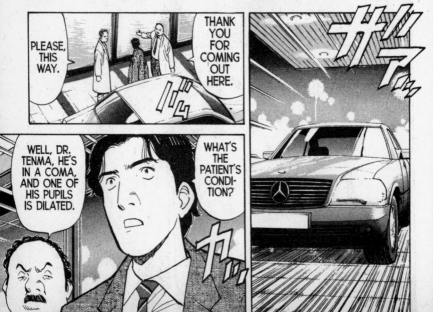

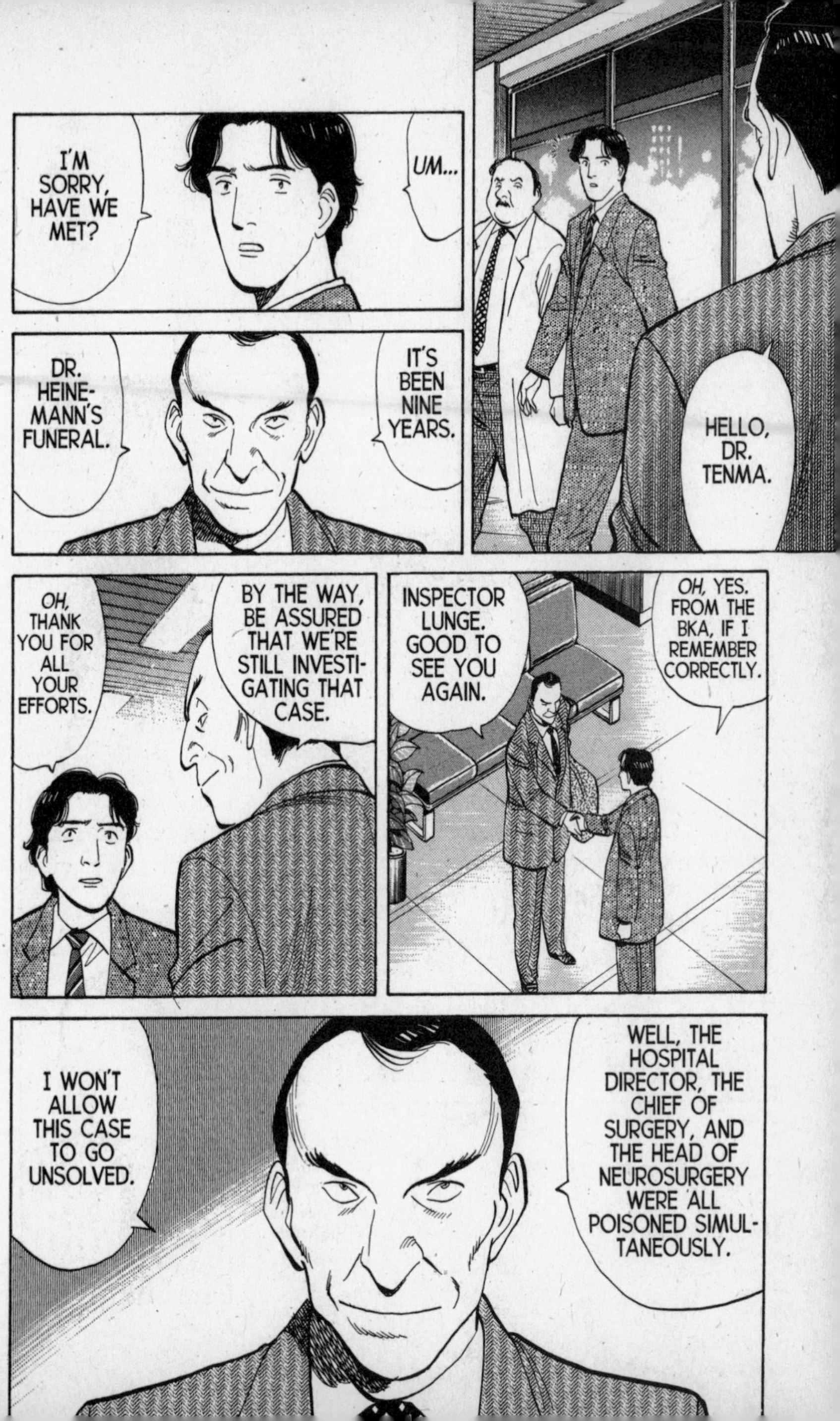
HELLO, DR. TENMA.
UM...
I'M SORRY, HAVE WE MET?
IT'S BEEN NINE YEARS.
DR. HEINEMANN'S FUNERAL.
OH, YES. FROM THE BKA, IF I REMEMBER CORRECTLY.
INSPECTOR LUNGE. GOOD TO SEE YOU AGAIN.
BY THE WAY, BE ASSURED THAT WE'RE STILL INVESTIGATING THAT CASE.
OH, THANK YOU FOR ALL YOUR EFFORTS.
WELL, THE HOSPITAL DIRECTOR, THE CHIEF OF SURGERY, AND THE HEAD OF NEUROSURGERY WERE ALL POISONED SIMULTANEOUSLY.
I WON'T ALLOW THIS CASE TO GO UNSOLVED.

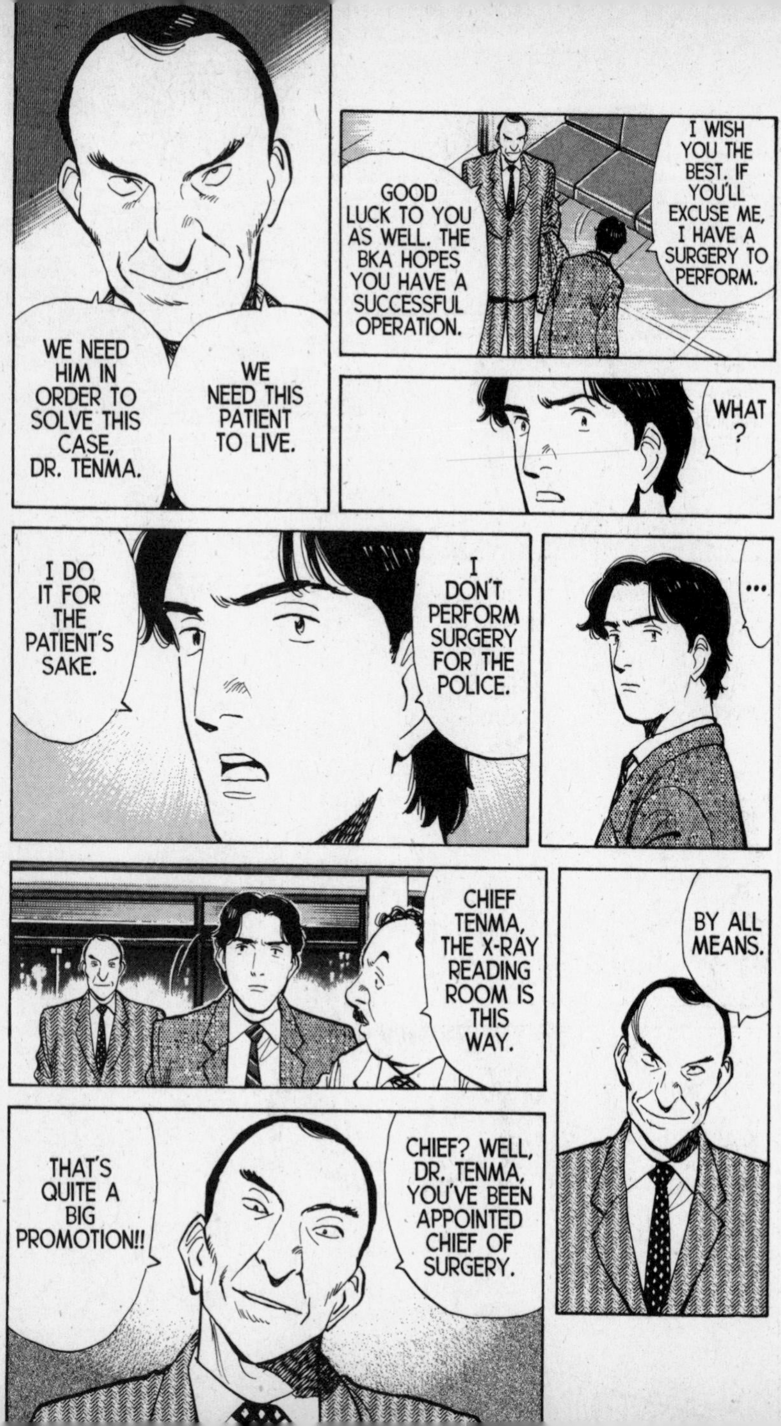
I WISH YOU THE BEST. IF YOU'LL EXCUSE ME, I HAVE A SURGERY TO PERFORM.
GOOD LUCK TO YOU AS WELL. THE BKA HOPES YOU HAVE A SUCCESSFUL OPERATION.
WHAT?
WE NEED THIS PATIENT TO LIVE.
WE NEED HIM IN ORDER TO SOLVE THIS CASE, DR. TENMA.
...
I DON'T PERFORM SURGERY FOR THE POLICE.
I DO IT FOR THE PATIENT'S SAKE.
BY ALL MEANS.
CHIEF TENMA, THE X-RAY READING ROOM IS THIS WAY.
CHIEF? WELL, DR. TENMA, YOU'VE BEEN APPOINTED CHIEF OF SURGERY.
THAT'S QUITE A BIG PROMOTION!!

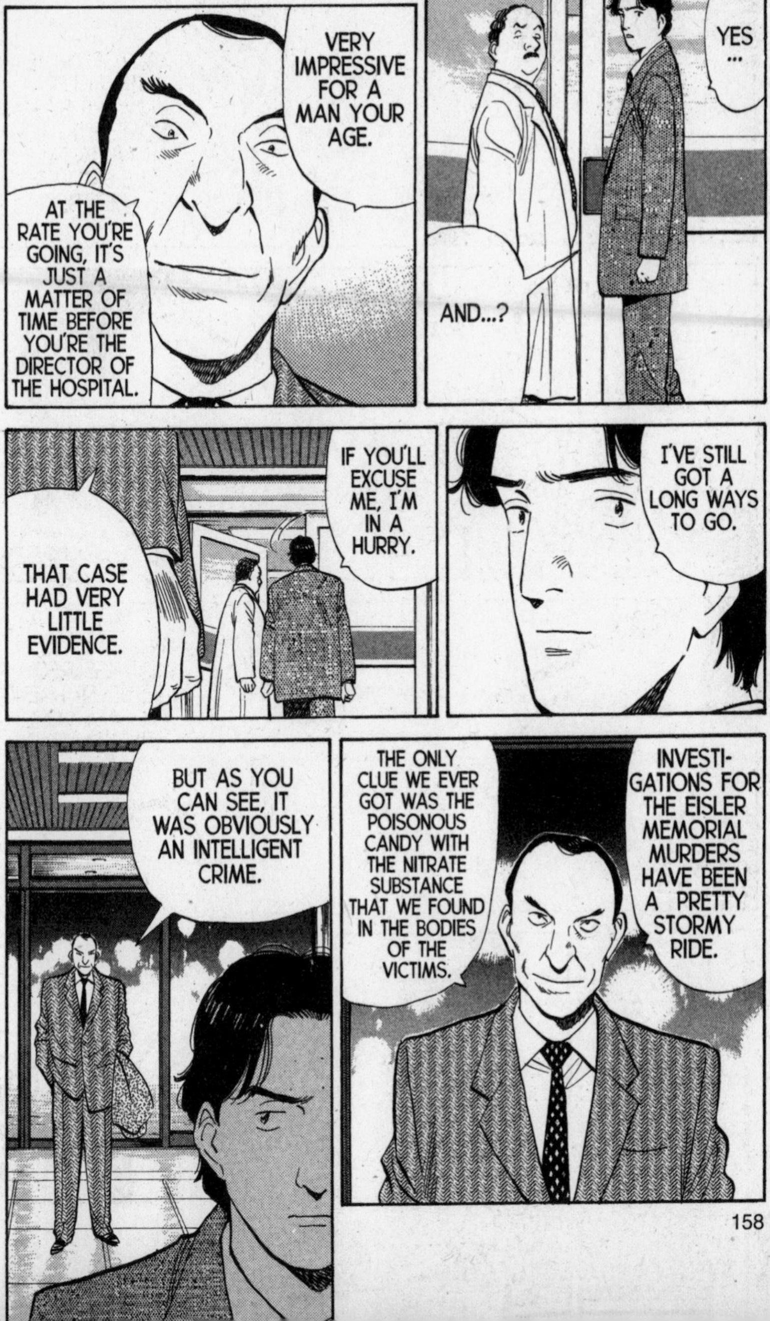
YES ...
AND...?
VERY IMPRESSIVE FOR A MAN YOUR AGE.
AT THE RATE YOU'RE GOING, IT'S JUST A MATTER OF TIME BEFORE YOU'RE THE DIRECTOR OF THE HOSPITAL.
I'VE STILL GOT A LONG WAYS TO GO.
IF YOU'LL EXCUSE ME, I'M IN A HURRY.
THAT CASE HAD VERY LITTLE EVIDENCE.
INVESTI-GATIONS FOR THE EISLER MEMORIAL MURDERS HAVE BEEN A PRETTY STORMY RIDE.
THE ONLY CLUE WE EVER GOT WAS THE POISONOUS CANDY WITH THE NITRATE SUBSTANCE THAT WE FOUND IN THE BODIES OF THE VICTIMS.
BUT AS YOU CAN SEE, IT WAS OBVIOUSLY AN INTELLIGENT CRIME.

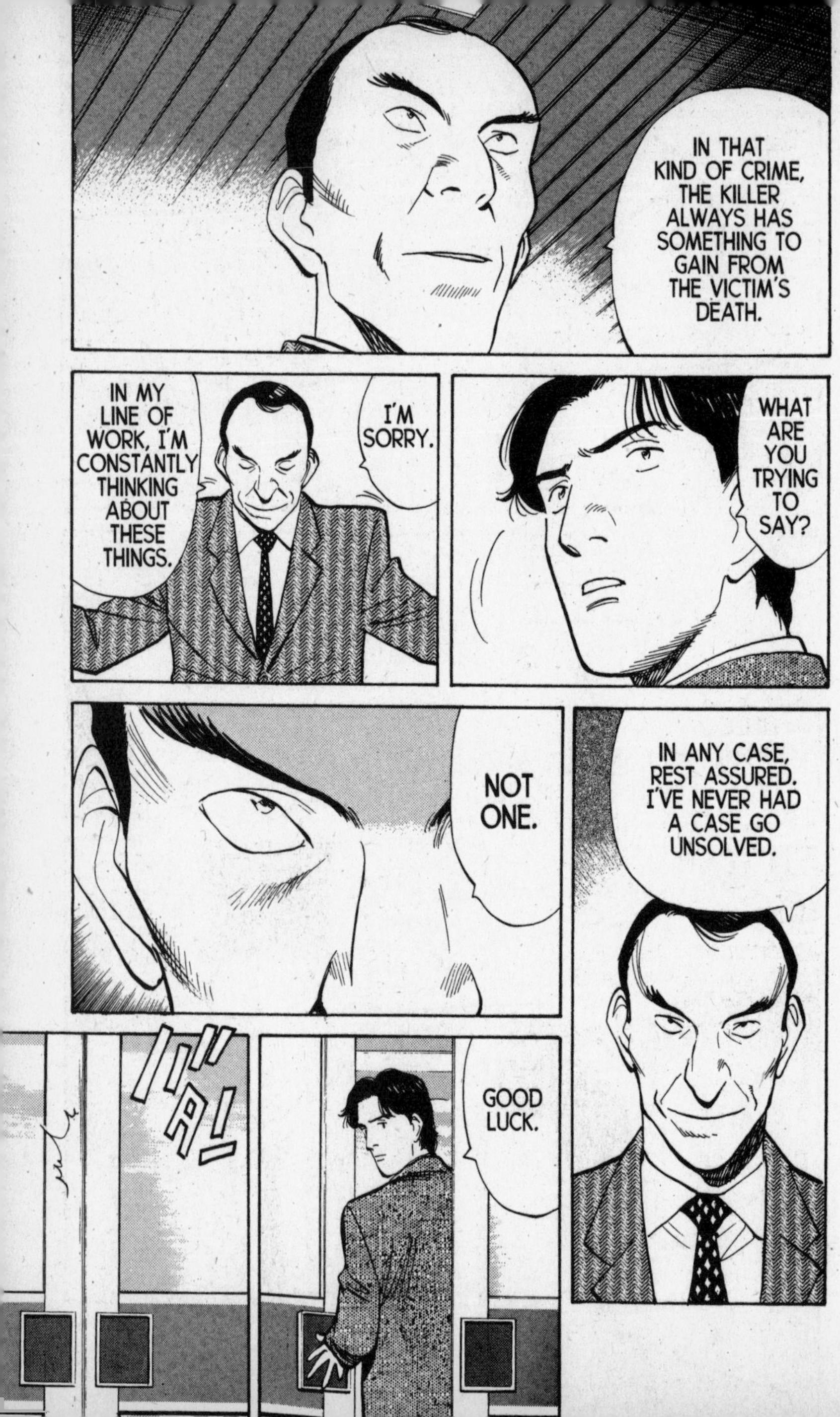
IN THAT KIND OF CRIME, THE KILLER ALWAYS HAS SOMETHING TO GAIN FROM THE VICTIM'S DEATH.
WHAT ARE YOU TRYING TO SAY?
I'M SORRY.
IN MY LINE OF WORK, I'M CONSTANTLY THINKING ABOUT THESE THINGS.
IN ANY CASE, REST ASSURED. I'VE NEVER HAD A CASE GO UNSOLVED.
NOT ONE.
GOOD LUCK.

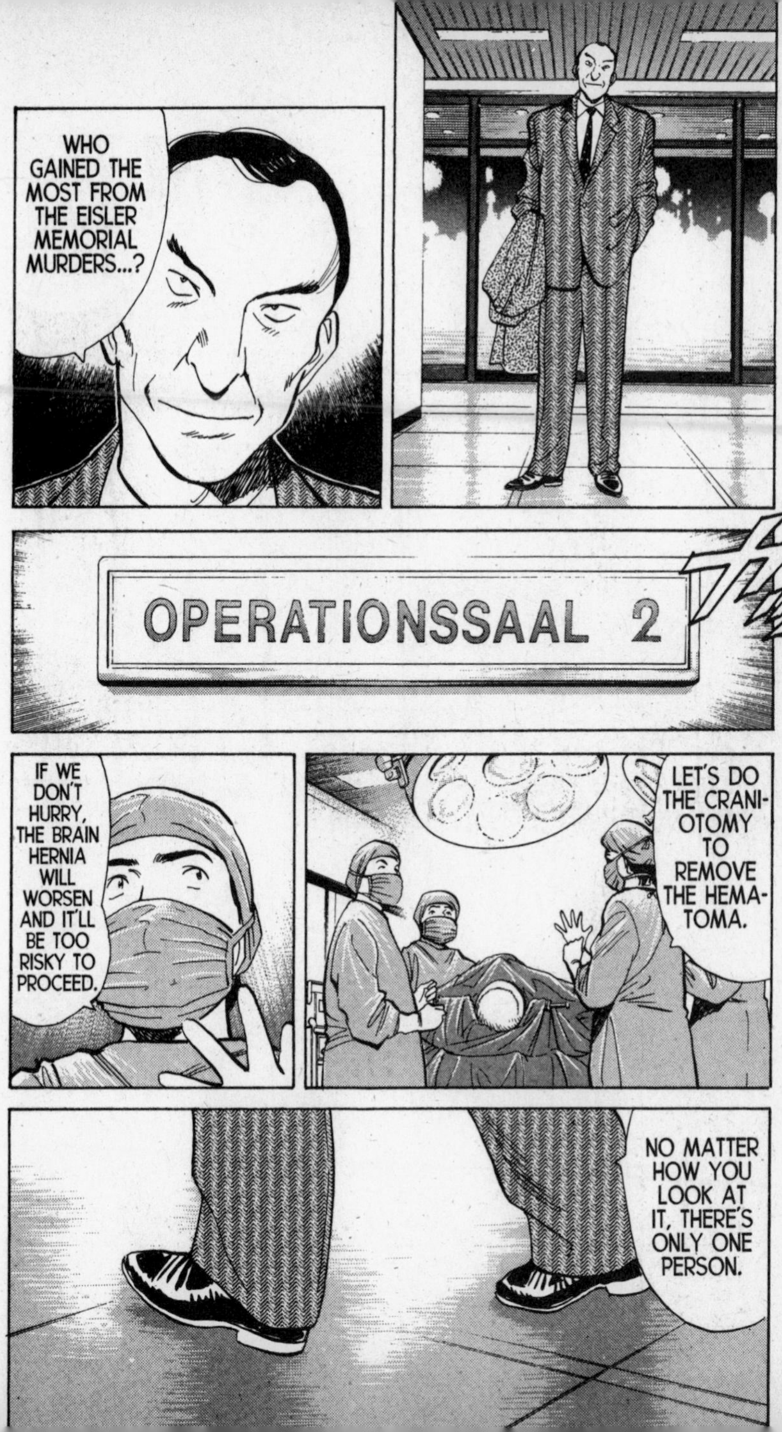
WHO GAINED THE MOST FROM THE EISLER MEMORIAL MURDERS...?
OPERATIONSSAAL 2
LET'S DO THE CRANI-OTOMY TO REMOVE THE HEMA-TOMA.
IF WE DON'T HURRY, THE BRAIN HERNIA WILL WORSEN AND IT'LL BE TOO RISKY TO PROCEED.
NO MATTER HOW YOU LOOK AT IT, THERE'S ONLY ONE PERSON.

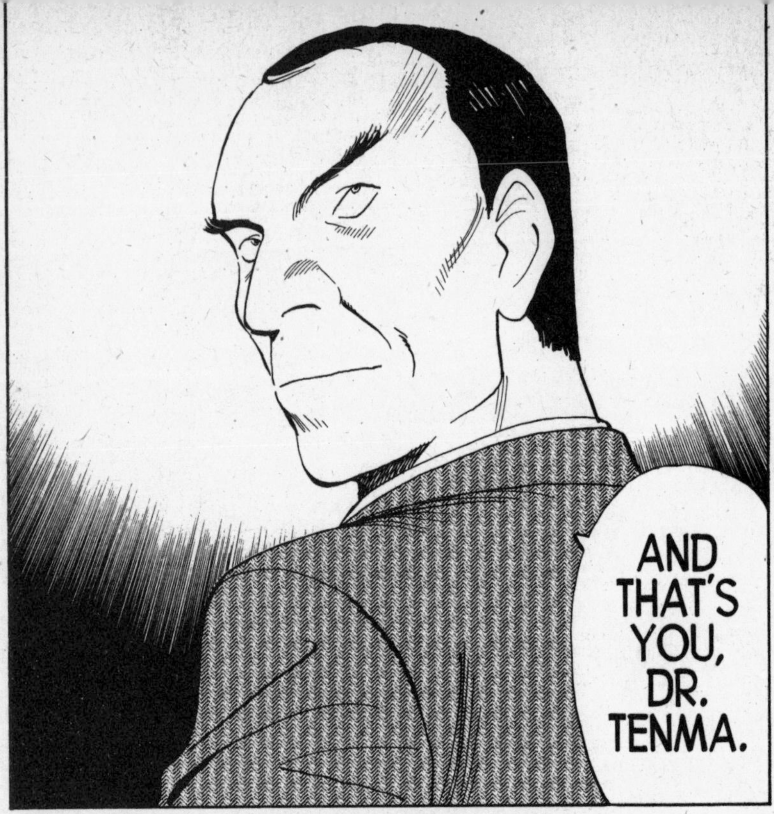
AND THAT'S YOU, DR. TENMA.
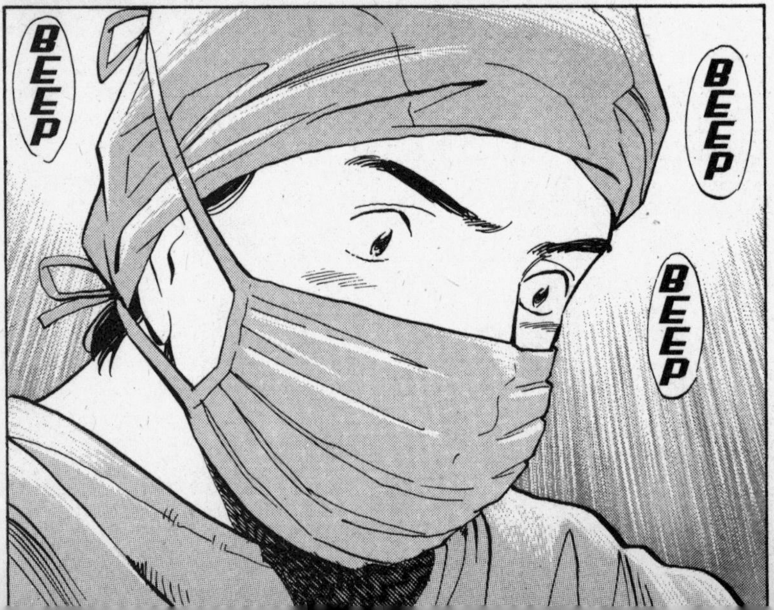
BEEP
BEEP
BEEP

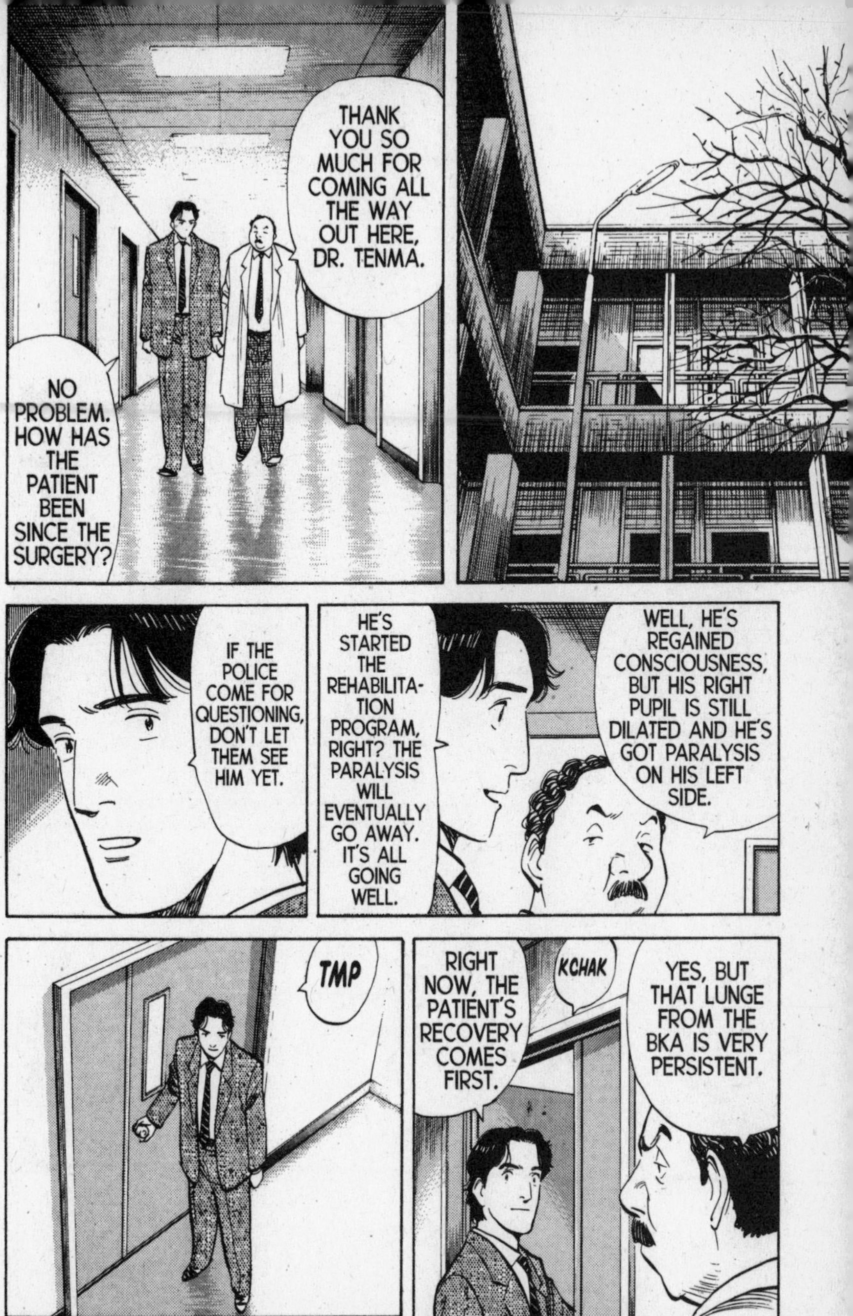
THANK YOU SO MUCH FOR COMING ALL THE WAY OUT HERE, DR. TENMA.
NO PROBLEM. HOW HAS THE PATIENT BEEN SINCE THE SURGERY?
WELL, HE'S REGAINED CONSCIOUSNESS, BUT HIS RIGHT PUPIL IS STILL DILATED AND HE'S GOT PARALYSIS ON HIS LEFT SIDE.
HE'S STARTED THE REHABILITATION PROGRAM, RIGHT? THE PARALYSIS WILL EVENTUALLY GO AWAY. IT'S ALL GOING WELL.
IF THE POLICE COME FOR QUESTIONING, DON'T LET THEM SEE HIM YET.
YES, BUT THAT LUNGE FROM THE BKA IS VERY PERSISTENT.
KCHAK
RIGHT NOW, THE PATIENT'S RECOVERY COMES FIRST.
TMP

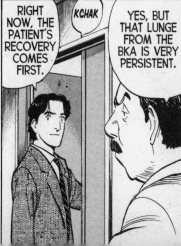

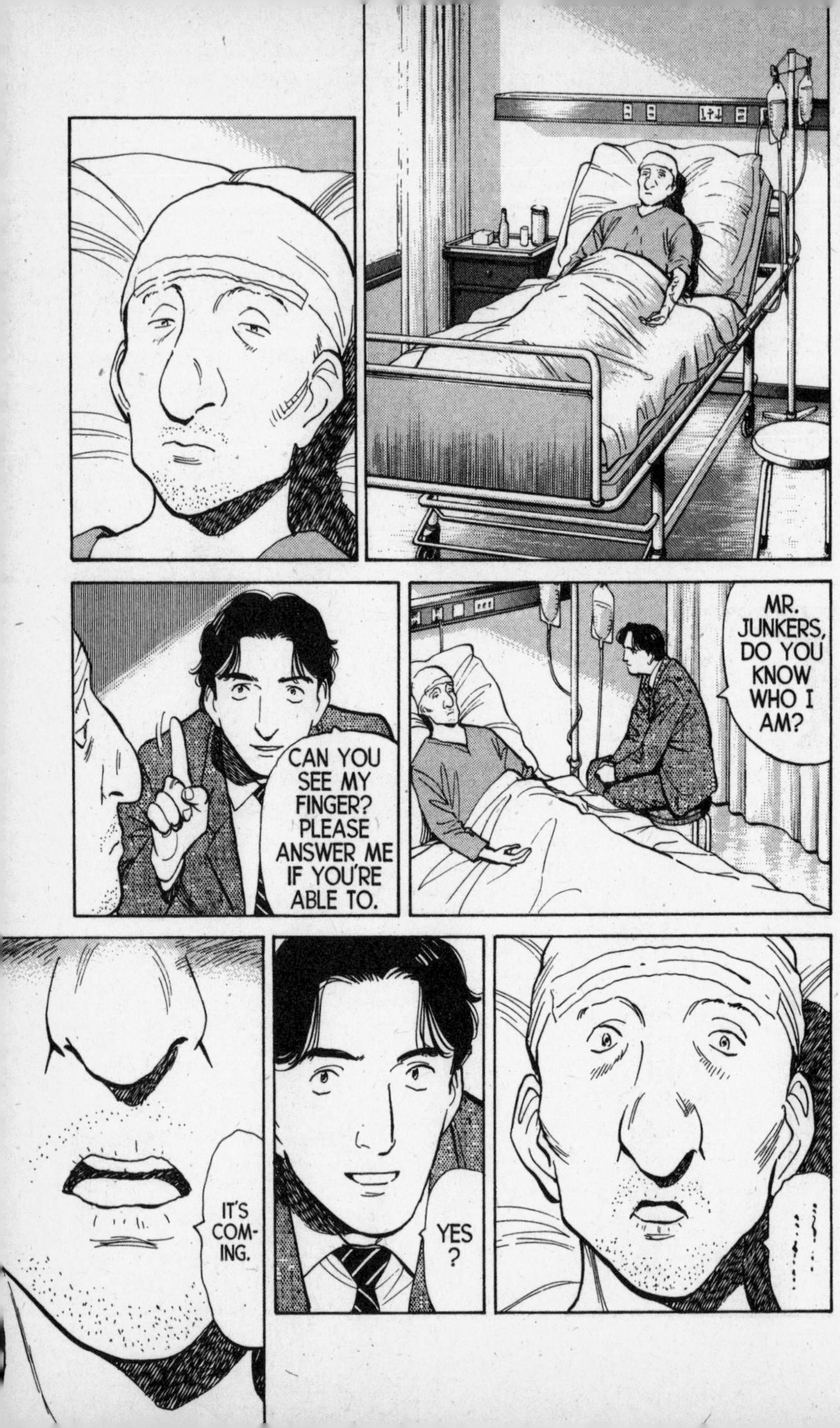
MR. JUNKERS, DO YOU KNOW WHO I AM?
CAN YOU SEE MY FINGER? PLEASE ANSWER ME IF YOU'RE ABLE TO.
YES ?
IT'S COMING.

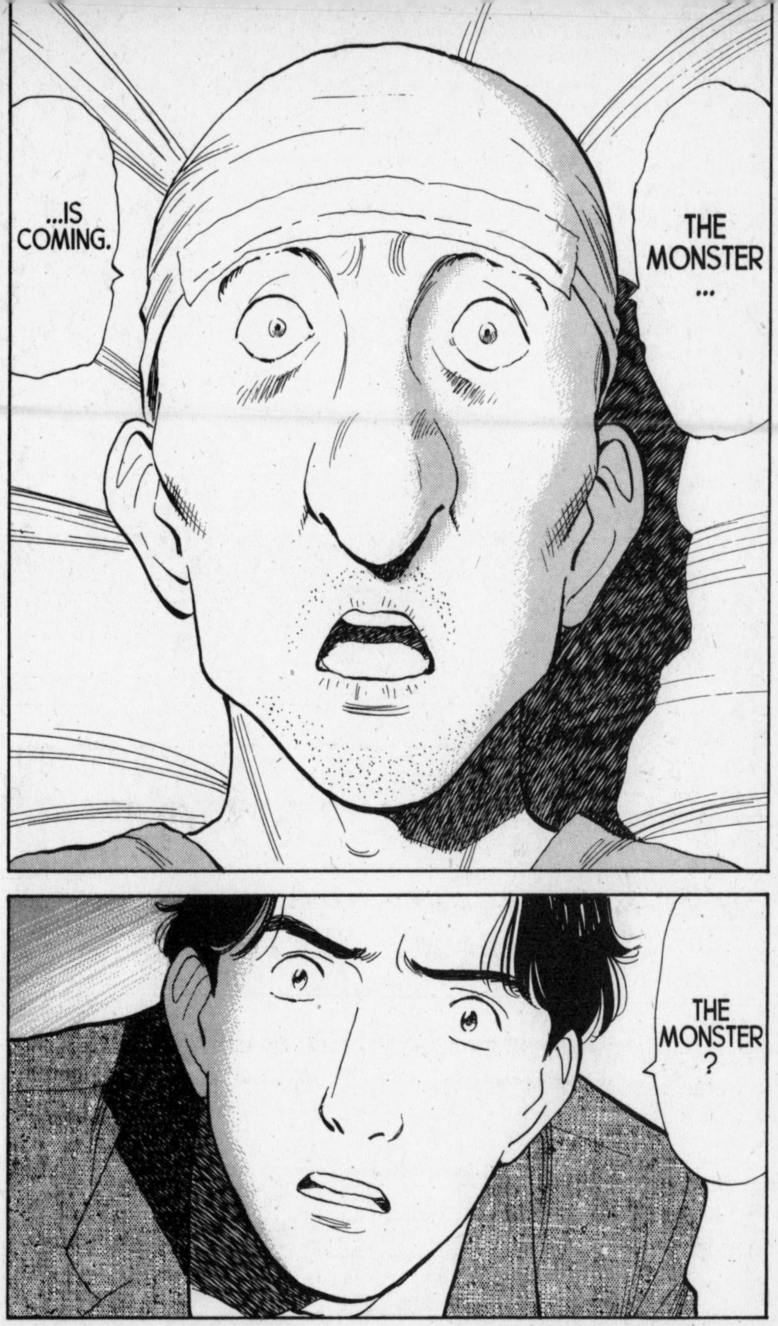
THE MONSTER ...
...IS COMING.
THE MONSTER ?

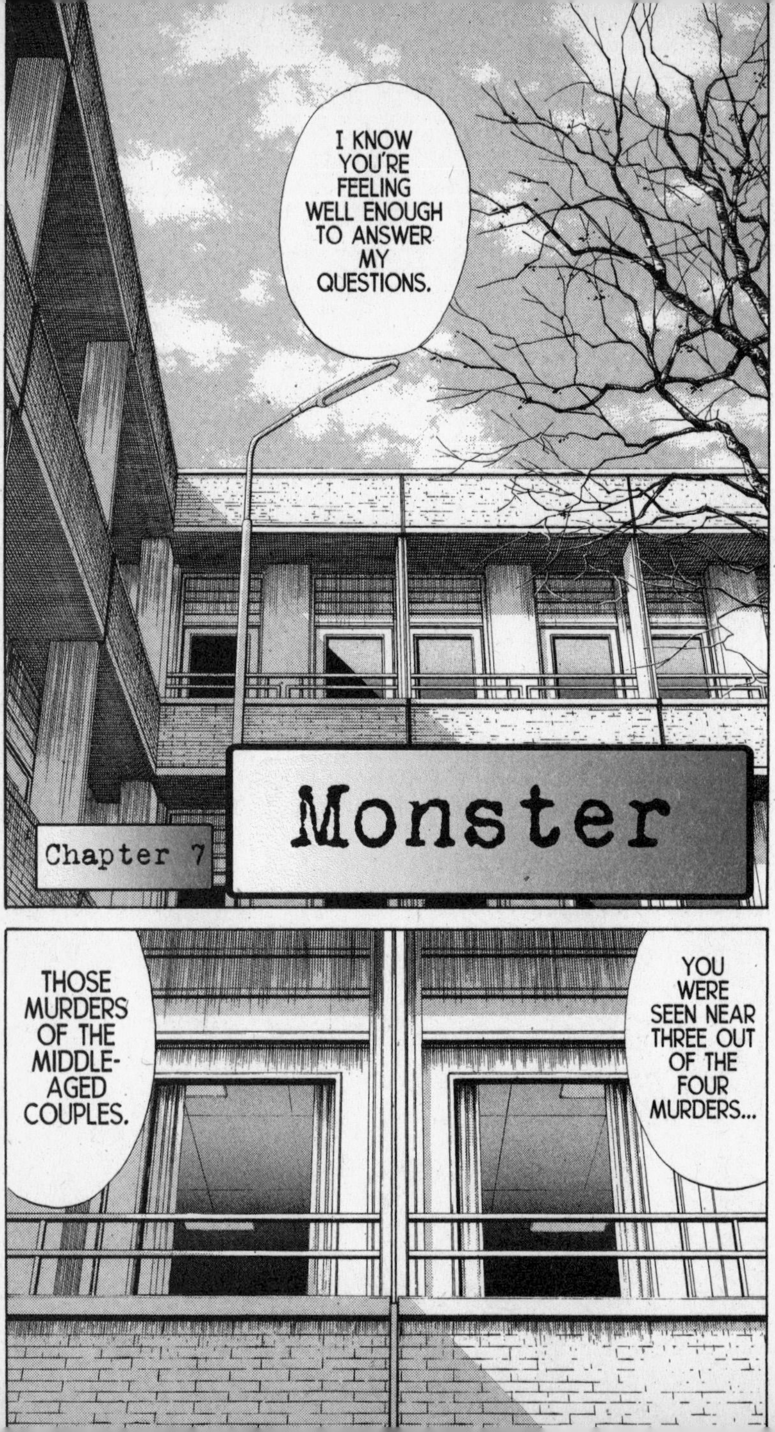
I KNOW YOU'RE FEELING WELL ENOUGH TO ANSWER MY QUESTIONS.
Monster
Chapter 7
YOU WERE SEEN NEAR THREE OUT OF THE FOUR MURDERS...
THOSE MURDERS OF THE MIDDLE-AGED COUPLES.

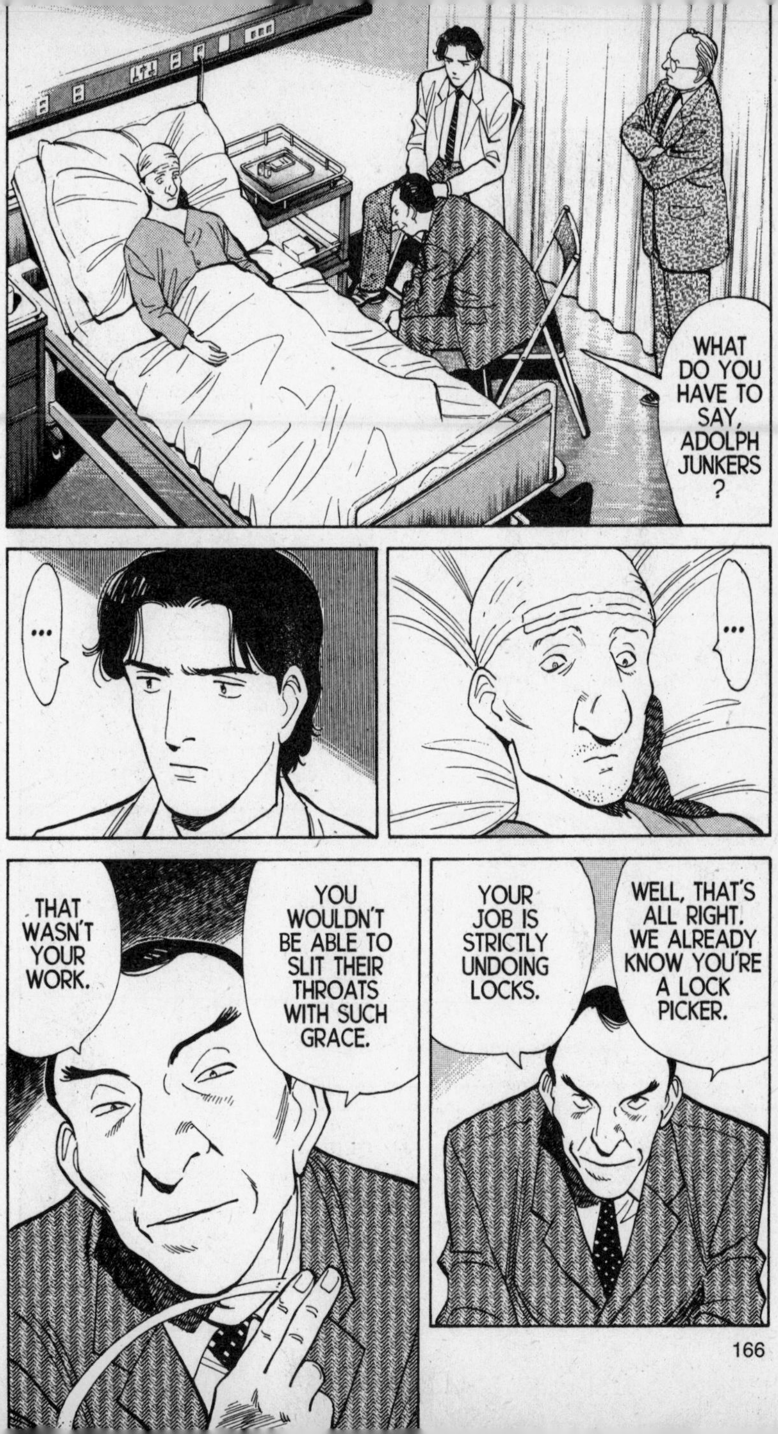
WHAT DO YOU HAVE TO SAY, ADOLPH JUNKERS?
...
...
WELL, THAT'S ALL RIGHT. WE ALREADY KNOW YOU'RE A LOCK PICKER.
YOUR JOB IS STRICTLY UNDOING LOCKS.
YOU WOULDN'T BE ABLE TO SLIT THEIR THROATS WITH SUCH GRACE.
THAT WASN'T YOUR WORK.

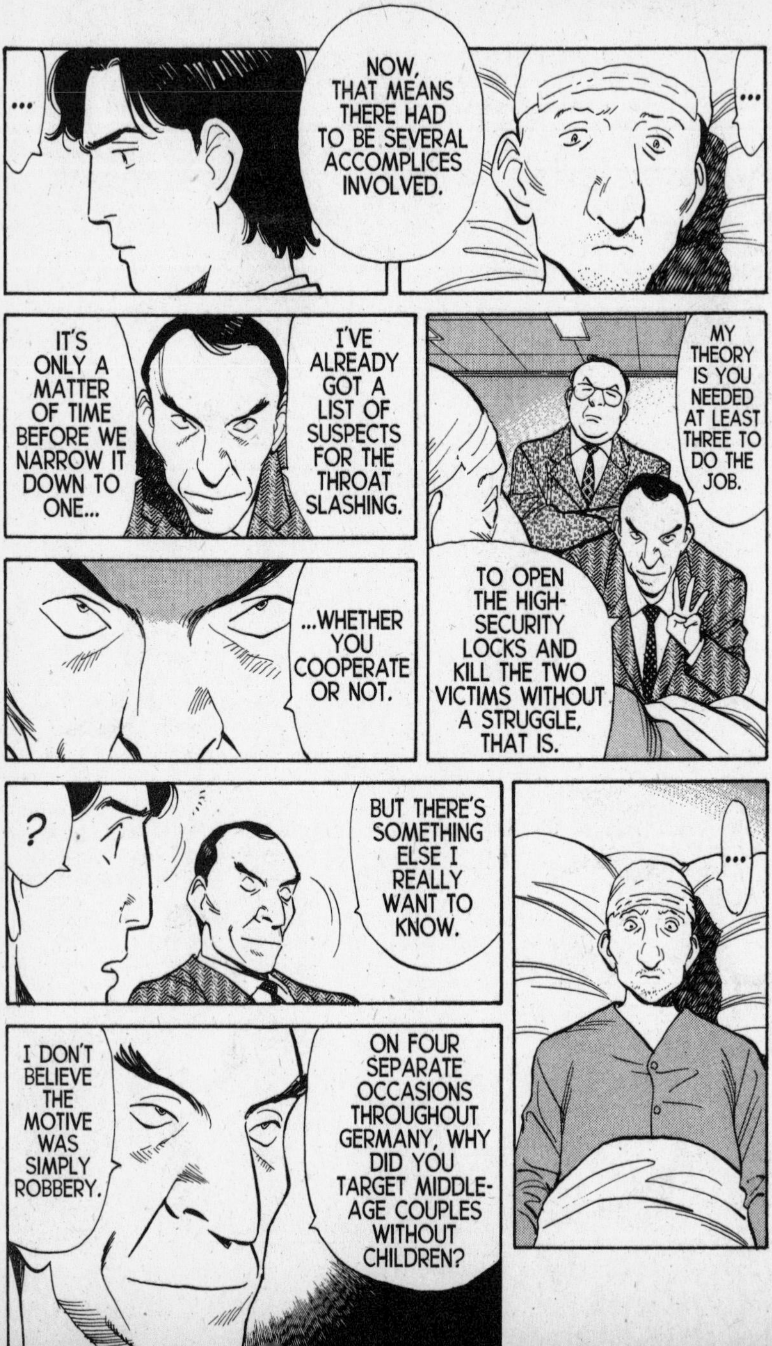
...
NOW, THAT MEANS THERE HAD TO BE SEVERAL ACCOMPLICES INVOLVED.
...
MY THEORY IS YOU NEEDED AT LEAST THREE TO DO THE JOB.
TO OPEN THE HIGH-SECURITY LOCKS AND KILL THE TWO VICTIMS WITHOUT A STRUGGLE, THAT IS.
I'VE ALREADY GOT A LIST OF SUSPECTS FOR THE THROAT SLASHING.
IT'S ONLY A MATTER OF TIME BEFORE WE NARROW IT DOWN TO ONE...
...WHETHER YOU COOPERATE OR NOT.
...
BUT THERE'S SOMETHING ELSE I REALLY WANT TO KNOW.
?
ON FOUR SEPARATE OCCASIONS THROUGHOUT GERMANY, WHY DID YOU TARGET MIDDLE-AGE COUPLES WITHOUT CHILDREN?
I DON'T BELIEVE THE MOTIVE WAS SIMPLY ROBBERY.

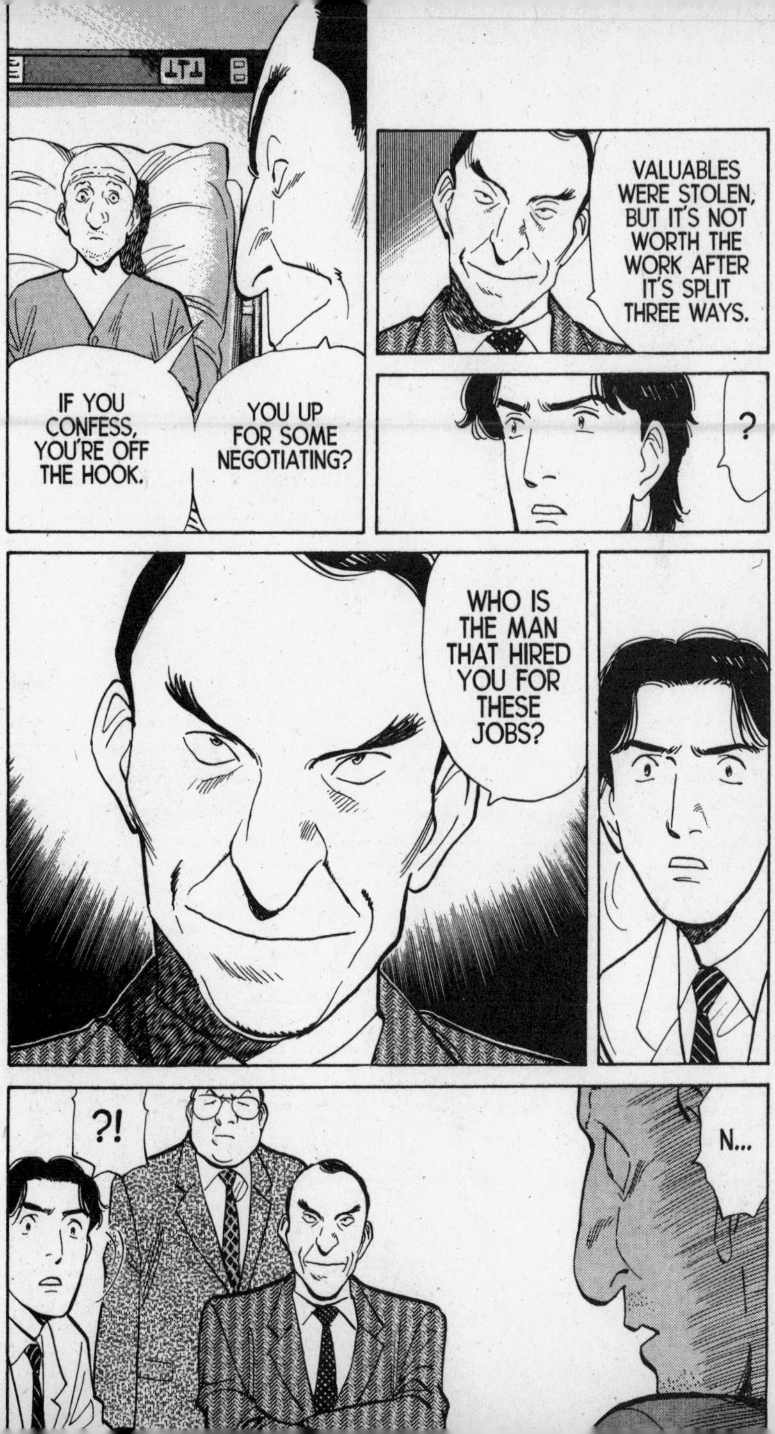
VALUABLES WERE STOLEN, BUT IT'S NOT WORTH THE WORK AFTER IT'S SPLIT THREE WAYS.
?
YOU UP FOR SOME NEGOTIATING?
IF YOU CONFESS, YOU'RE OFF THE HOOK.
WHO IS THE MAN THAT HIRED YOU FOR THESE JOBS?
N...
?!

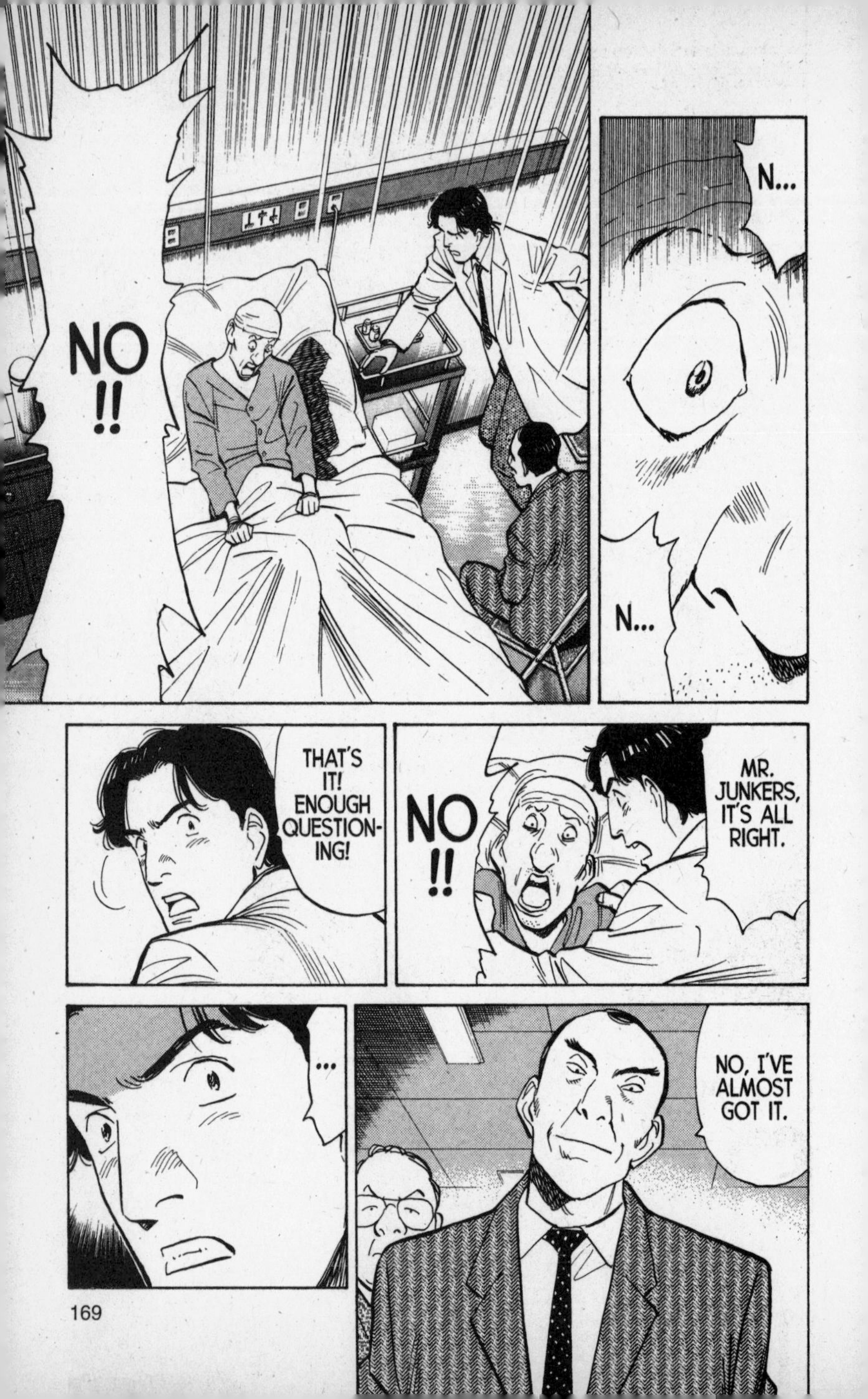
N...
N...
NO!!
MR. JUNKERS, IT'S ALL RIGHT.
NO!!
THAT'S IT! ENOUGH QUESTION-ING!
NO, I'VE ALMOST GOT IT.
...

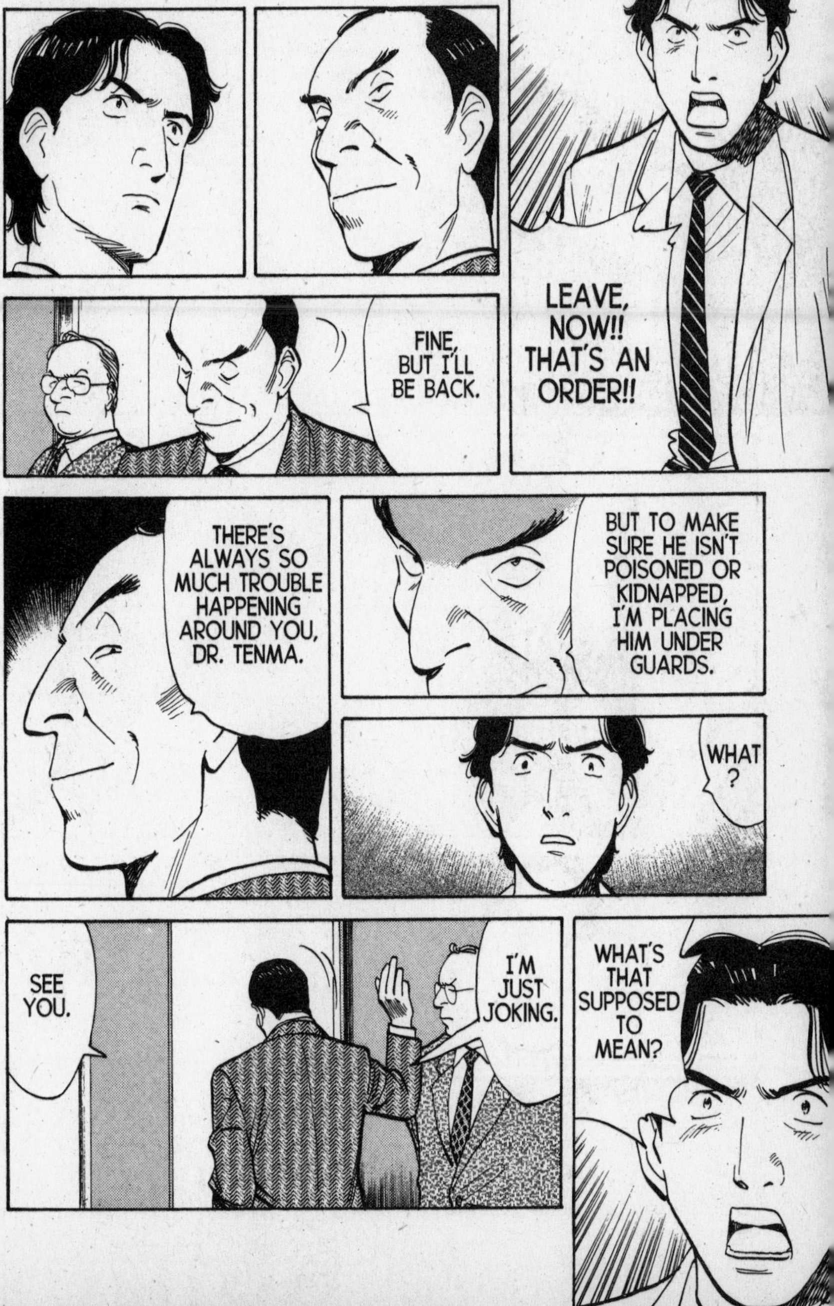
LEAVE, NOW!! THAT'S AN ORDER!!
FINE, BUT I'LL BE BACK.
BUT TO MAKE SURE HE ISN'T POISONED OR KIDNAPPED, I'M PLACING HIM UNDER GUARDS.
WHAT?
THERE'S ALWAYS SO MUCH TROUBLE HAPPENING AROUND YOU, DR. TENMA.
WHAT'S THAT SUPPOSED TO MEAN?
I'M JUST JOKING.
SEE YOU.

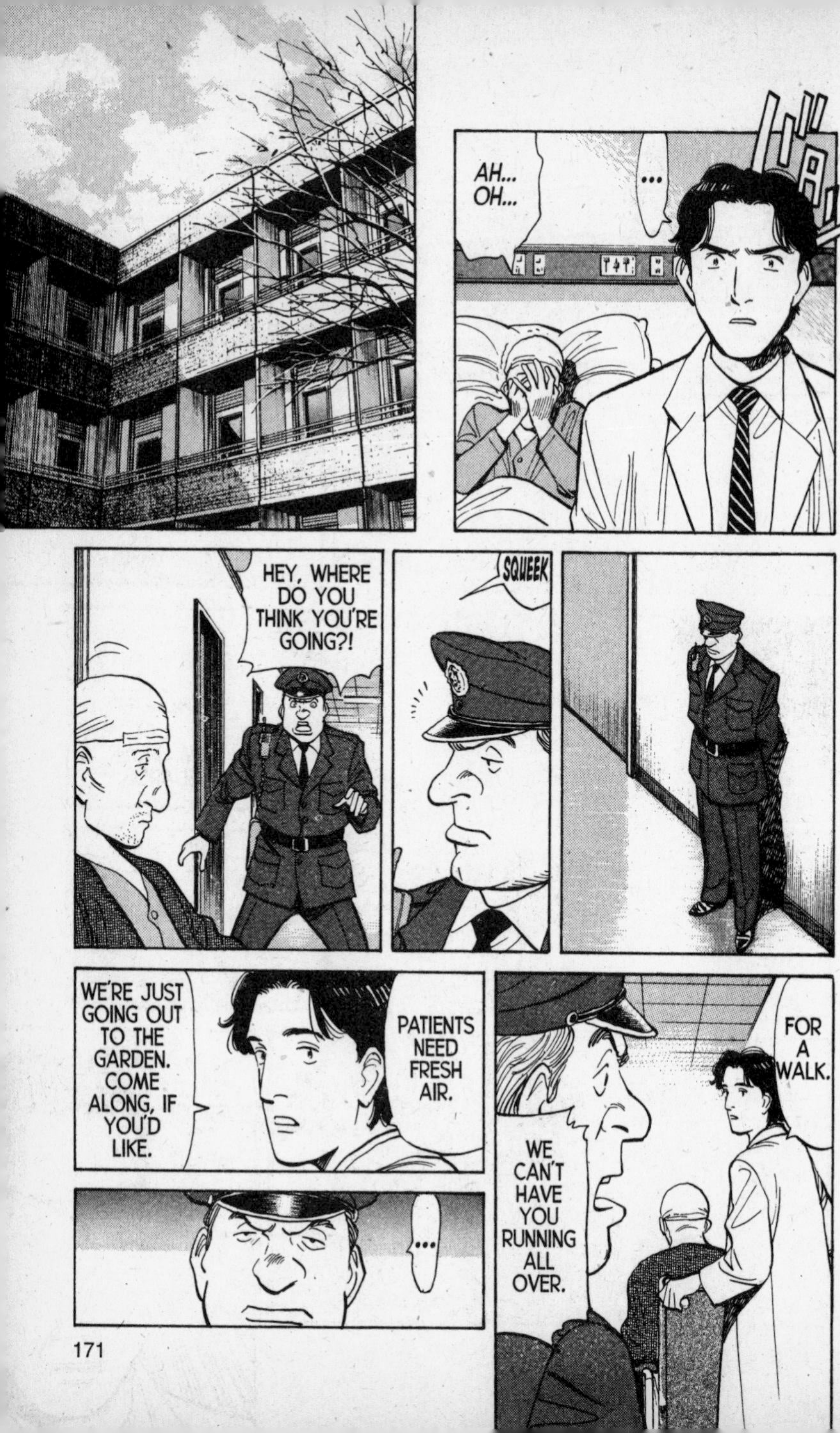
...
AH... OH...
SQUEEK
HEY, WHERE DO YOU THINK YOU'RE GOING?!
FOR A WALK.
WE CAN'T HAVE YOU RUNNING ALL OVER.
PATIENTS NEED FRESH AIR.
WE'RE JUST GOING OUT TO THE GARDEN. COME ALONG, IF YOU'D LIKE.
...

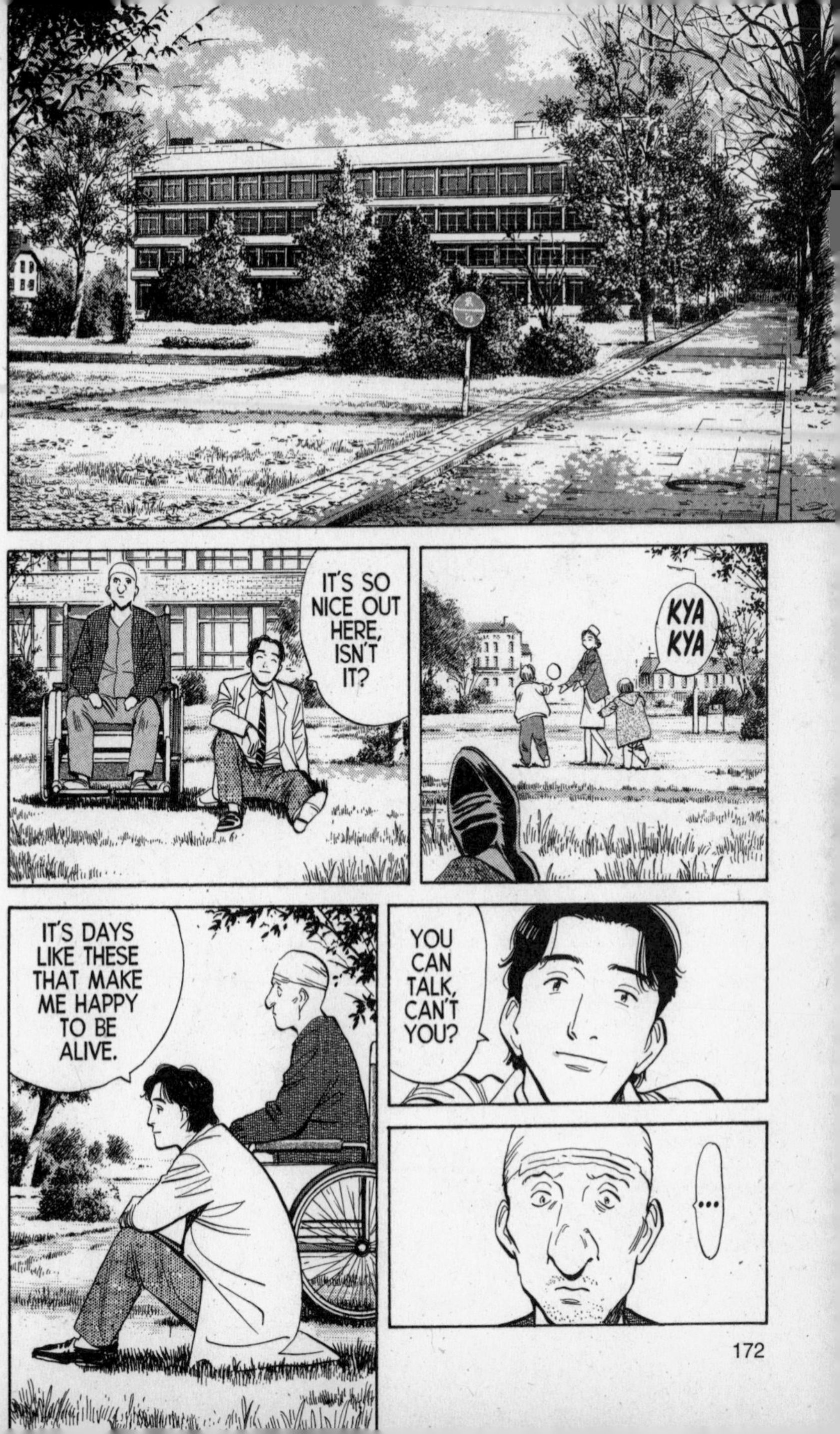
KYA KYA
IT'S SO NICE OUT HERE, ISN'T IT?
YOU CAN TALK, CAN'T YOU?
...
IT'S DAYS LIKE THESE THAT MAKE ME HAPPY TO BE ALIVE.

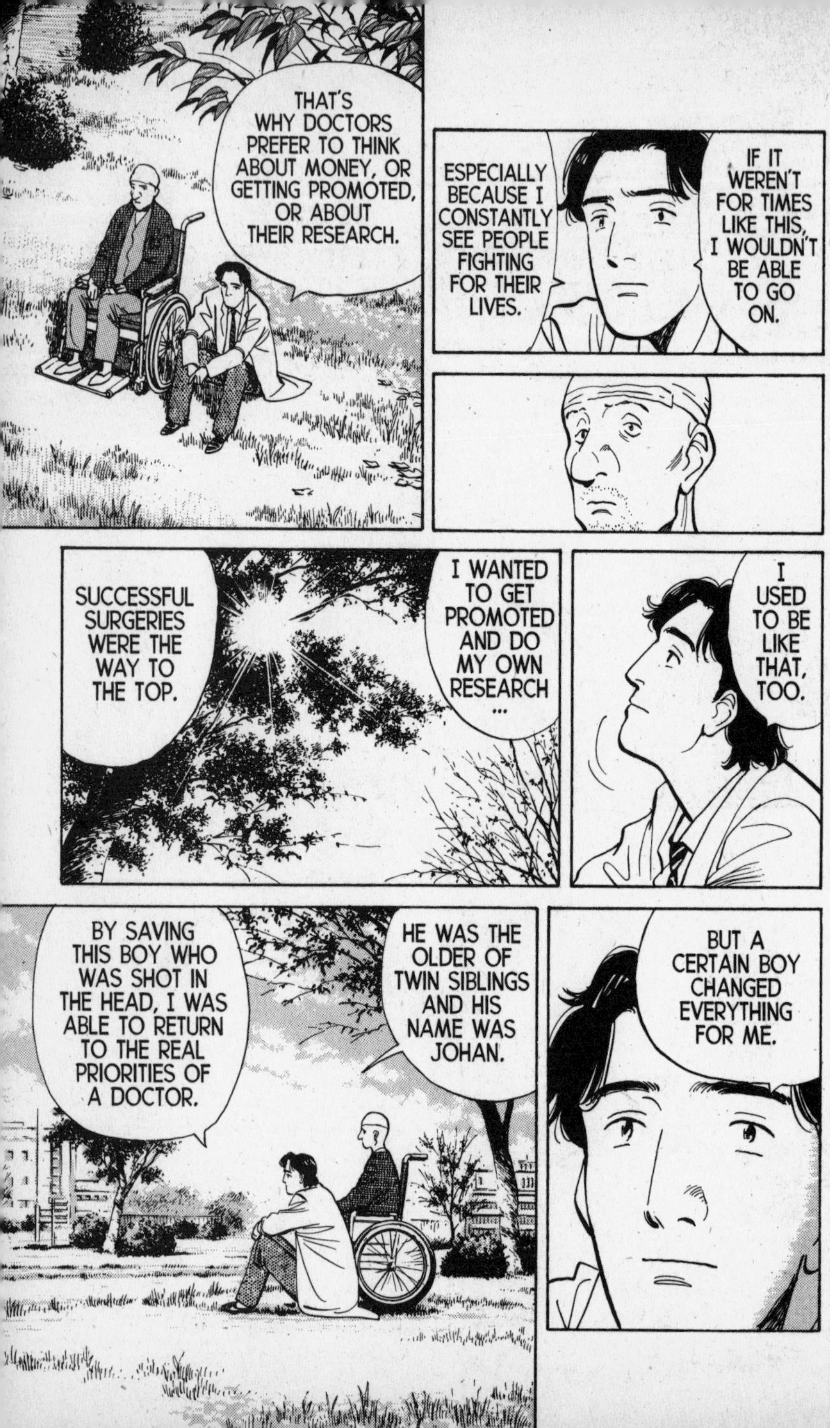
IF IT WEREN'T FOR TIMES LIKE THIS, I WOULDN'T BE ABLE TO GO ON.
ESPECIALLY BECAUSE I CONSTANTLY SEE PEOPLE FIGHTING FOR THEIR LIVES.
THAT'S WHY DOCTORS PREFER TO THINK ABOUT MONEY, OR GETTING PROMOTED, OR ABOUT THEIR RESEARCH.
I USED TO BE LIKE THAT, TOO.
I WANTED TO GET PROMOTED AND DO MY OWN RESEARCH ...
SUCCESSFUL SURGERIES WERE THE WAY TO THE TOP.
BUT A CERTAIN BOY CHANGED EVERYTHING FOR ME.
HE WAS THE OLDER OF TWIN SIBLINGS AND HIS NAME WAS JOHAN.
BY SAVING THIS BOY WHO WAS SHOT IN THE HEAD, I WAS ABLE TO RETURN TO THE REAL PRIORITIES OF A DOCTOR.

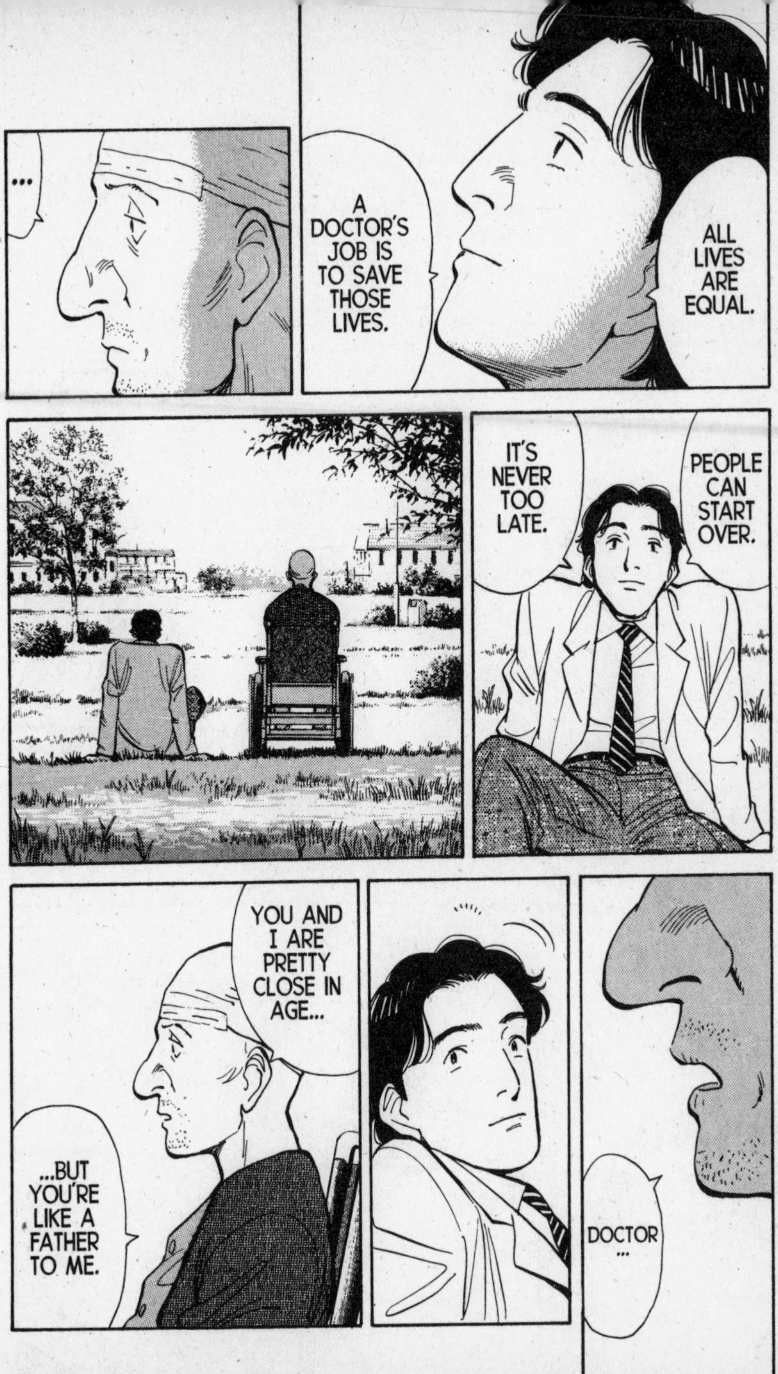
ALL LIVES ARE EQUAL.
A DOCTOR'S JOB IS TO SAVE THOSE LIVES.
...
PEOPLE CAN START OVER.
IT'S NEVER TOO LATE.
DOCTOR...
YOU AND I ARE PRETTY CLOSE IN AGE...
...BUT YOU'RE LIKE A FATHER TO ME.

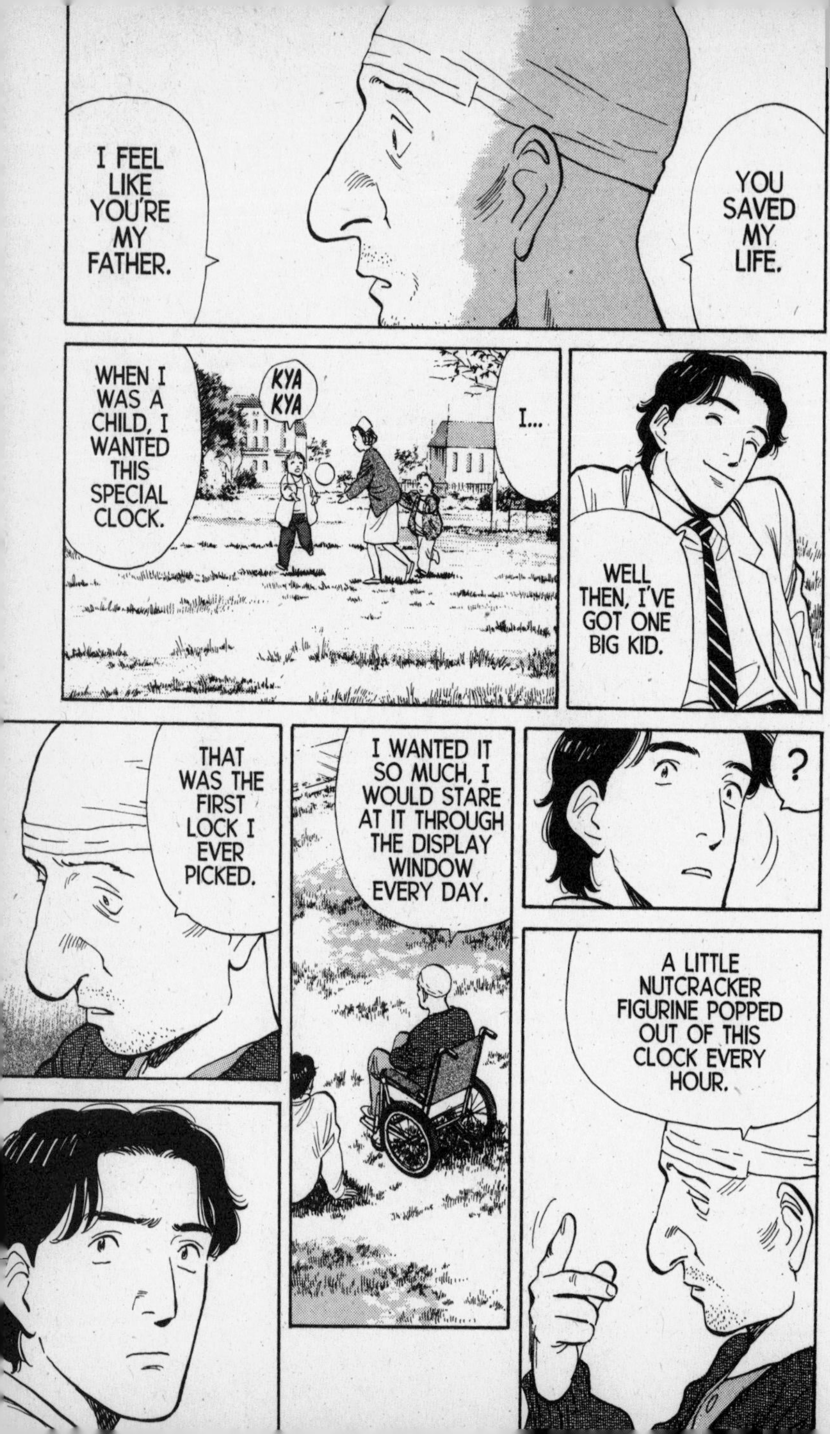
YOU SAVED MY LIFE.
I FEEL LIKE YOU'RE MY FATHER.
WELL THEN, I'VE GOT ONE BIG KID.
I...
KYA KYA
WHEN I WAS A CHILD, I WANTED THIS SPECIAL CLOCK.
?
A LITTLE NUTCRACKER FIGURINE POPPED OUT OF THIS CLOCK EVERY HOUR.
I WANTED IT SO MUCH, I WOULD STARE AT IT THROUGH THE DISPLAY WINDOW EVERY DAY.
THAT WAS THE FIRST LOCK I EVER PICKED.

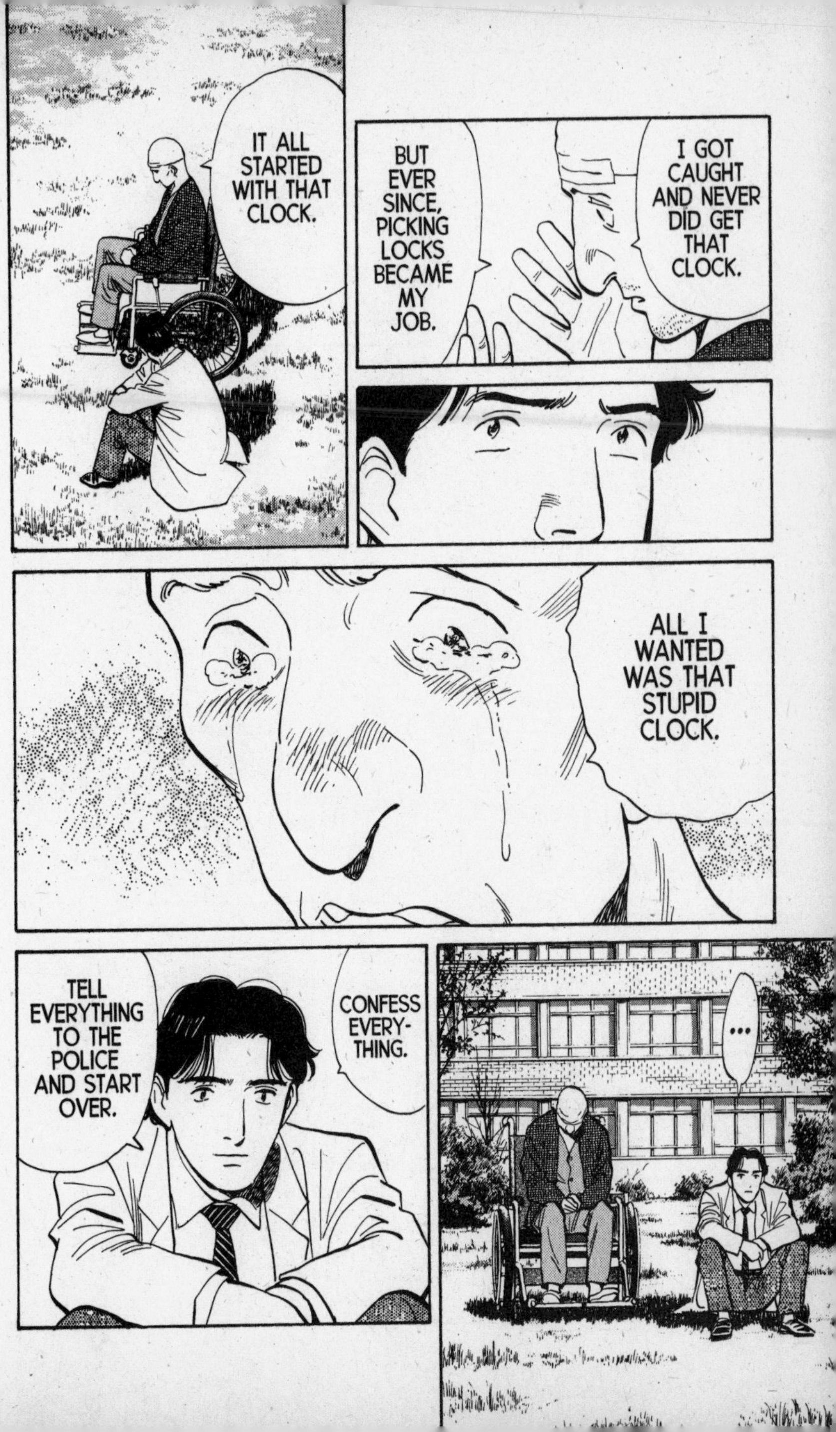
I GOT CAUGHT AND NEVER DID GET THAT CLOCK.
BUT EVER SINCE, PICKING LOCKS BECAME MY JOB.
IT ALL STARTED WITH THAT CLOCK.
ALL I WANTED WAS THAT STUPID CLOCK.
...
CONFESS EVERY-THING.
TELL EVERYTHING TO THE POLICE AND START OVER.

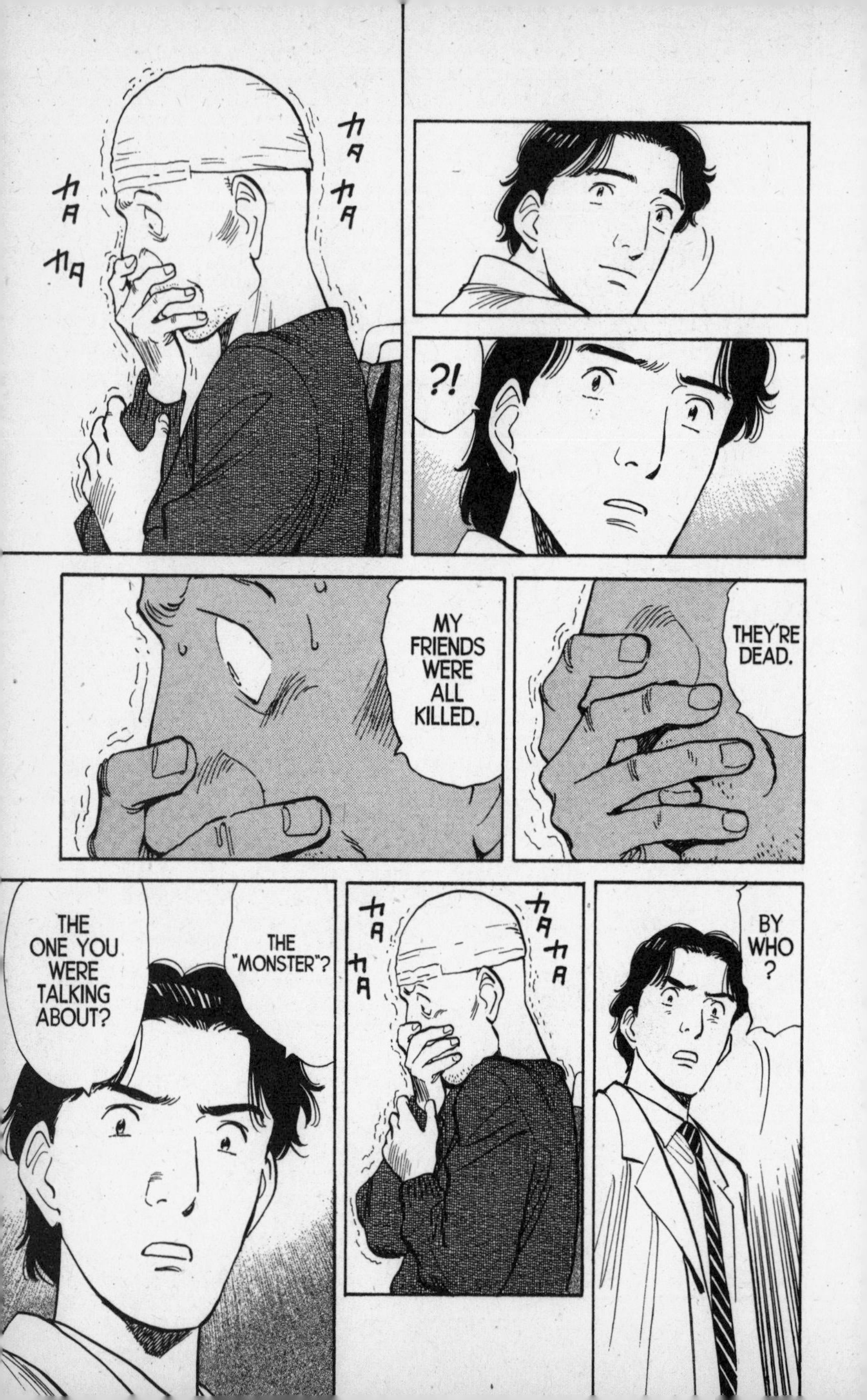
?!
カタ
カタ
カタ
カタ
THEY'RE DEAD.
MY FRIENDS WERE ALL KILLED.
BY WHO?
カタ
カタ
カタ
カタ
THE "MONSTER"?
THE ONE YOU WERE TALKING ABOUT?

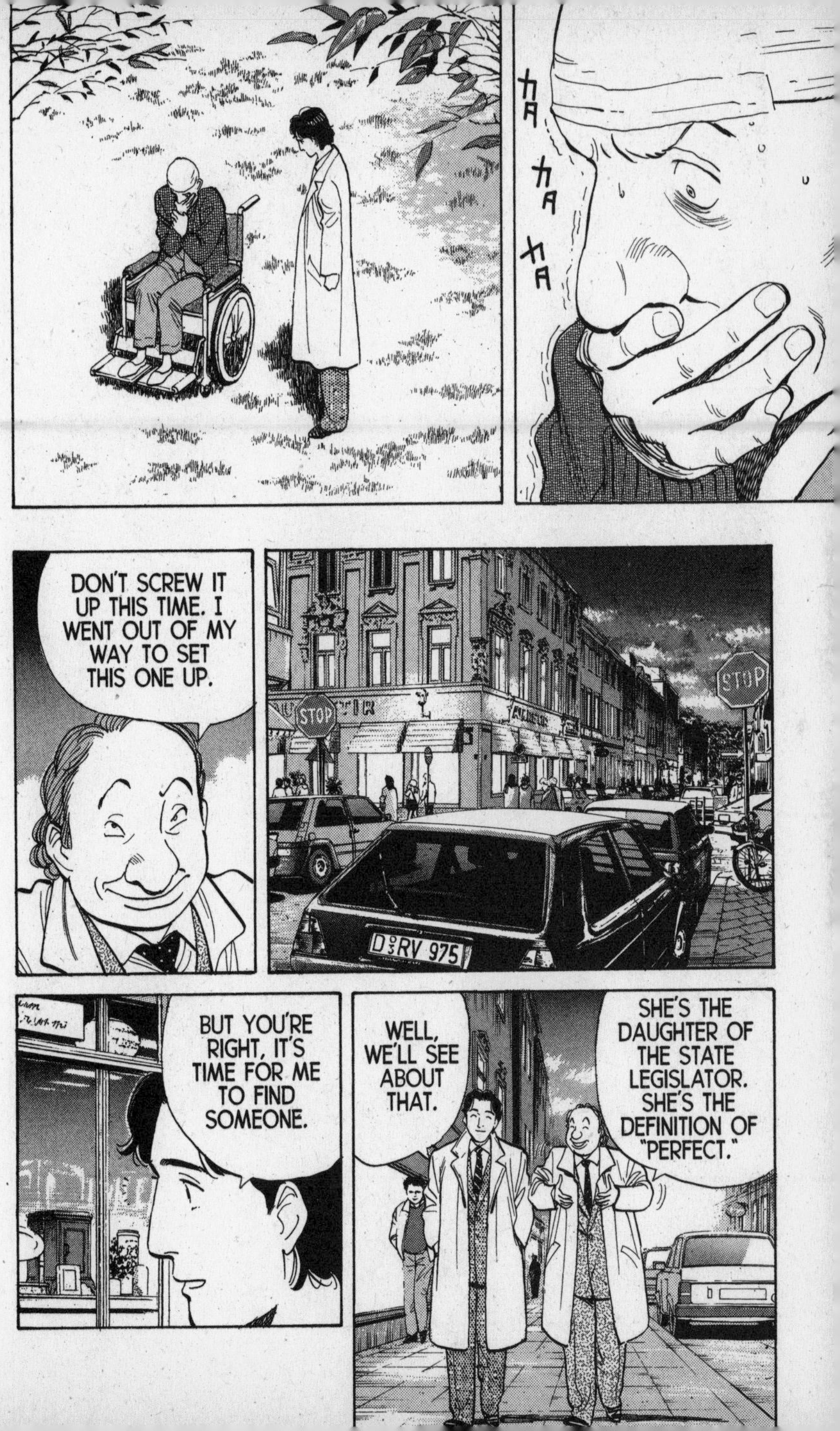
STOP
STOP
DON'T SCREW IT UP THIS TIME. I WENT OUT OF MY WAY TO SET THIS ONE UP.
SHE'S THE DAUGHTER OF THE STATE LEGISLATOR. SHE'S THE DEFINITION OF "PERFECT."
WELL, WE'LL SEE ABOUT THAT.
BUT YOU'RE RIGHT, IT'S TIME FOR ME TO FIND SOMEONE.

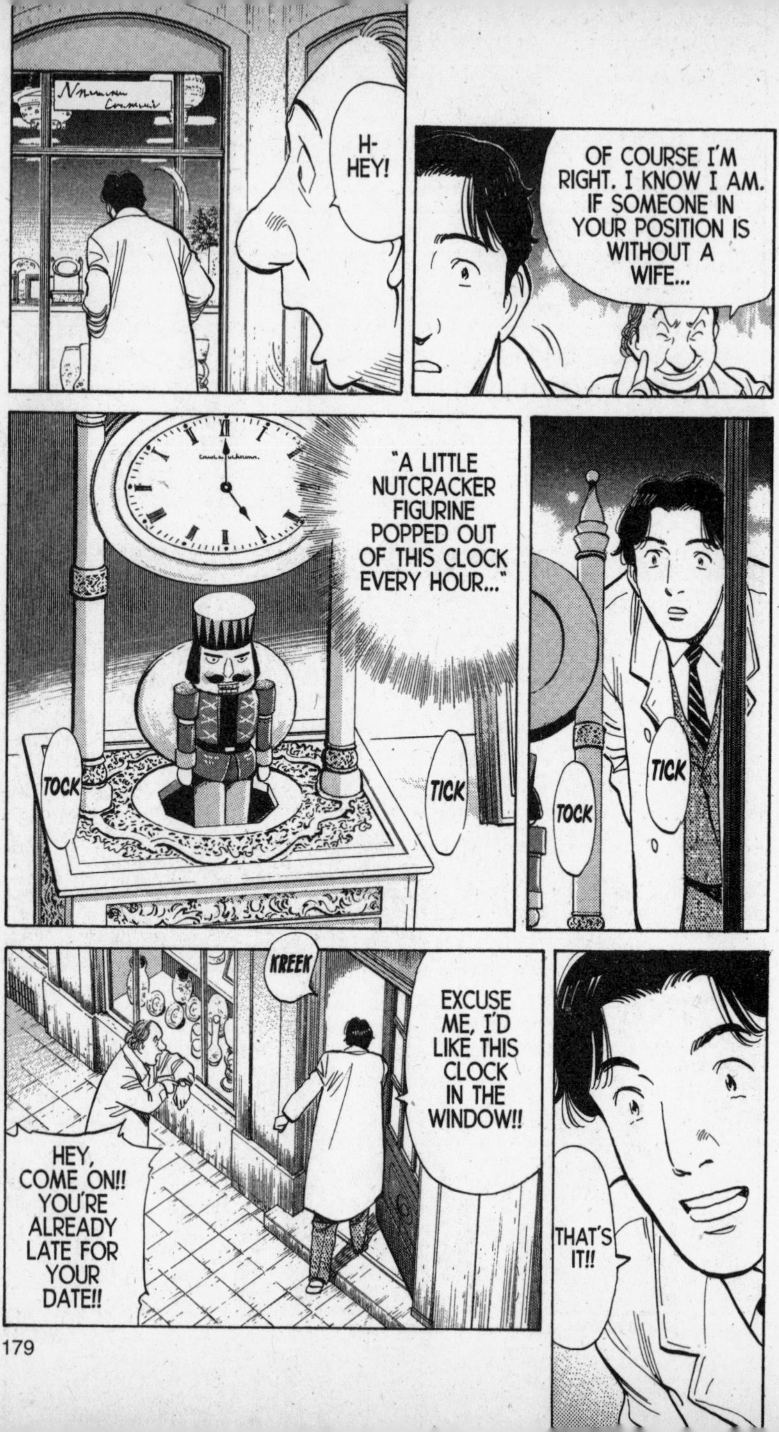

OF COURSE I'M RIGHT. I KNOW I AM. IF SOMEONE IN YOUR POSITION IS WITHOUT A WIFE...
H- HEY!
TICK
TOCK
"A LITTLE NUTCRACKER FIGURINE POPPED OUT OF THIS CLOCK EVERY HOUR..."
TICK
TOCK
THAT'S IT!!
KREEK
EXCUSE ME, I'D LIKE THIS CLOCK IN THE WINDOW!!
HEY, COME ON!! YOU'RE ALREADY LATE FOR YOUR DATE!!

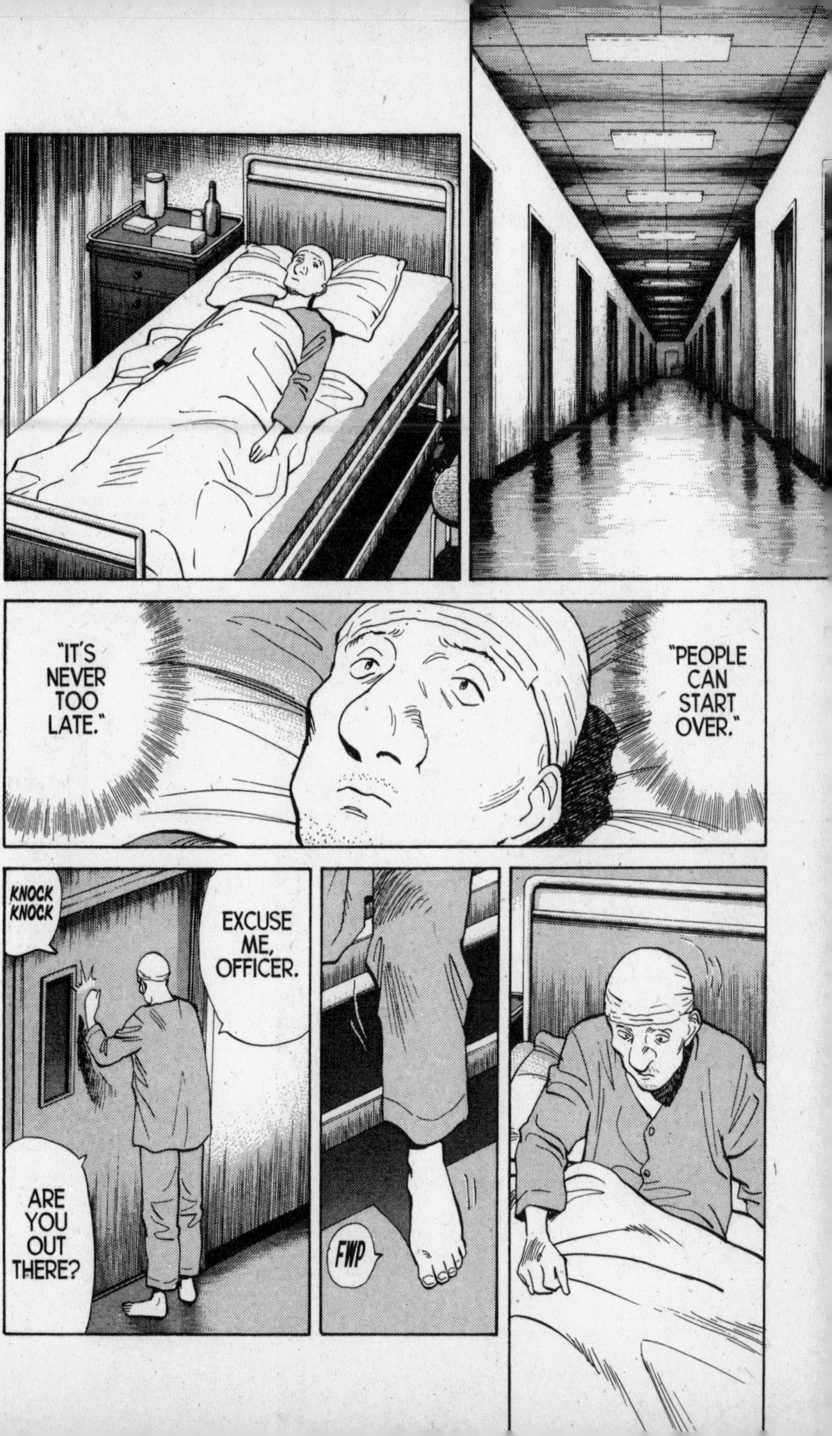
"PEOPLE CAN START OVER."
"IT'S NEVER TOO LATE."
FWP
KNOCK KNOCK
EXCUSE ME, OFFICER.
ARE YOU OUT THERE?

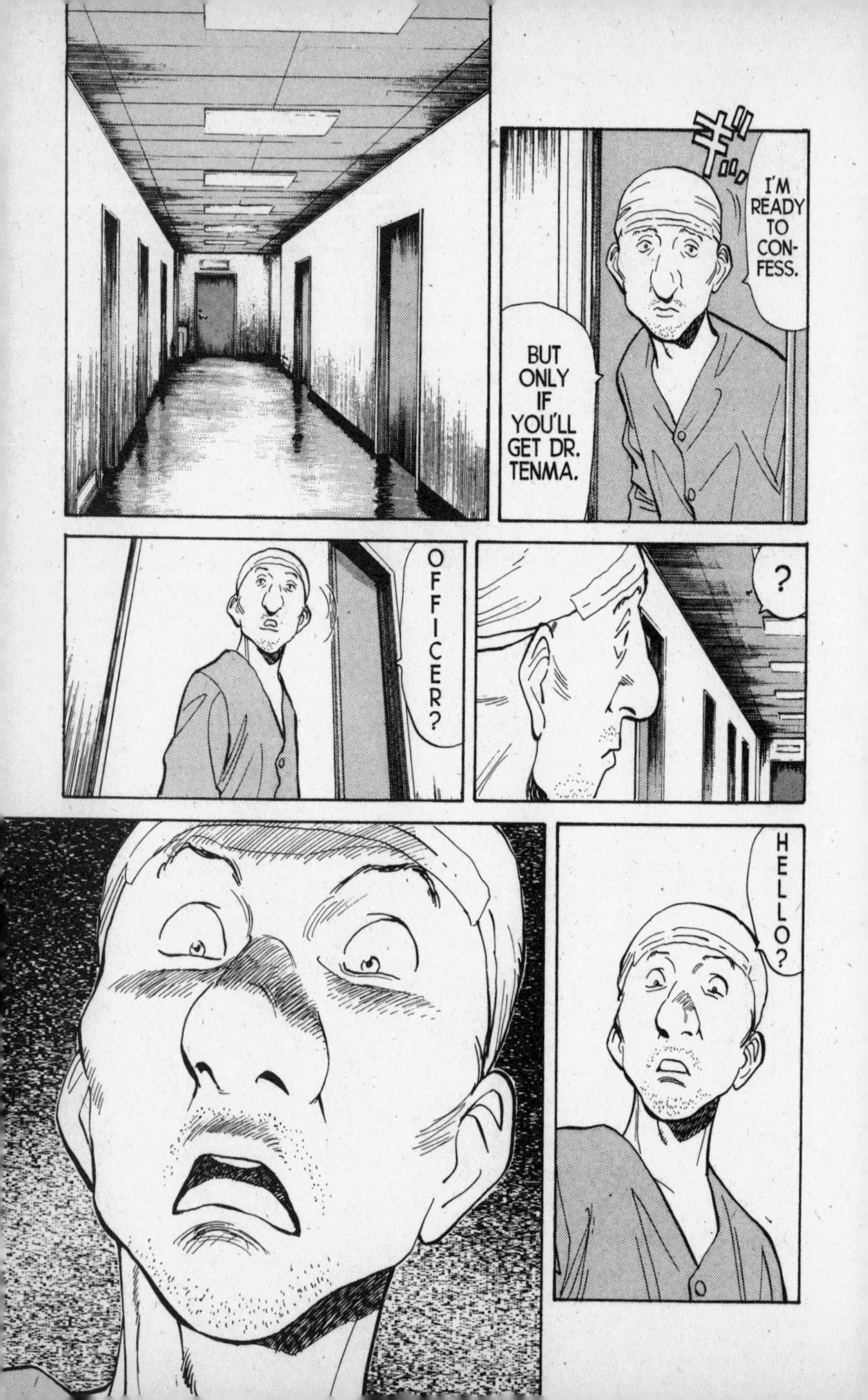
ギィ
I'M READY TO CON-FESS.
BUT ONLY IF YOU'LL GET DR. TENMA.
?
OFFICER?
HELLO?

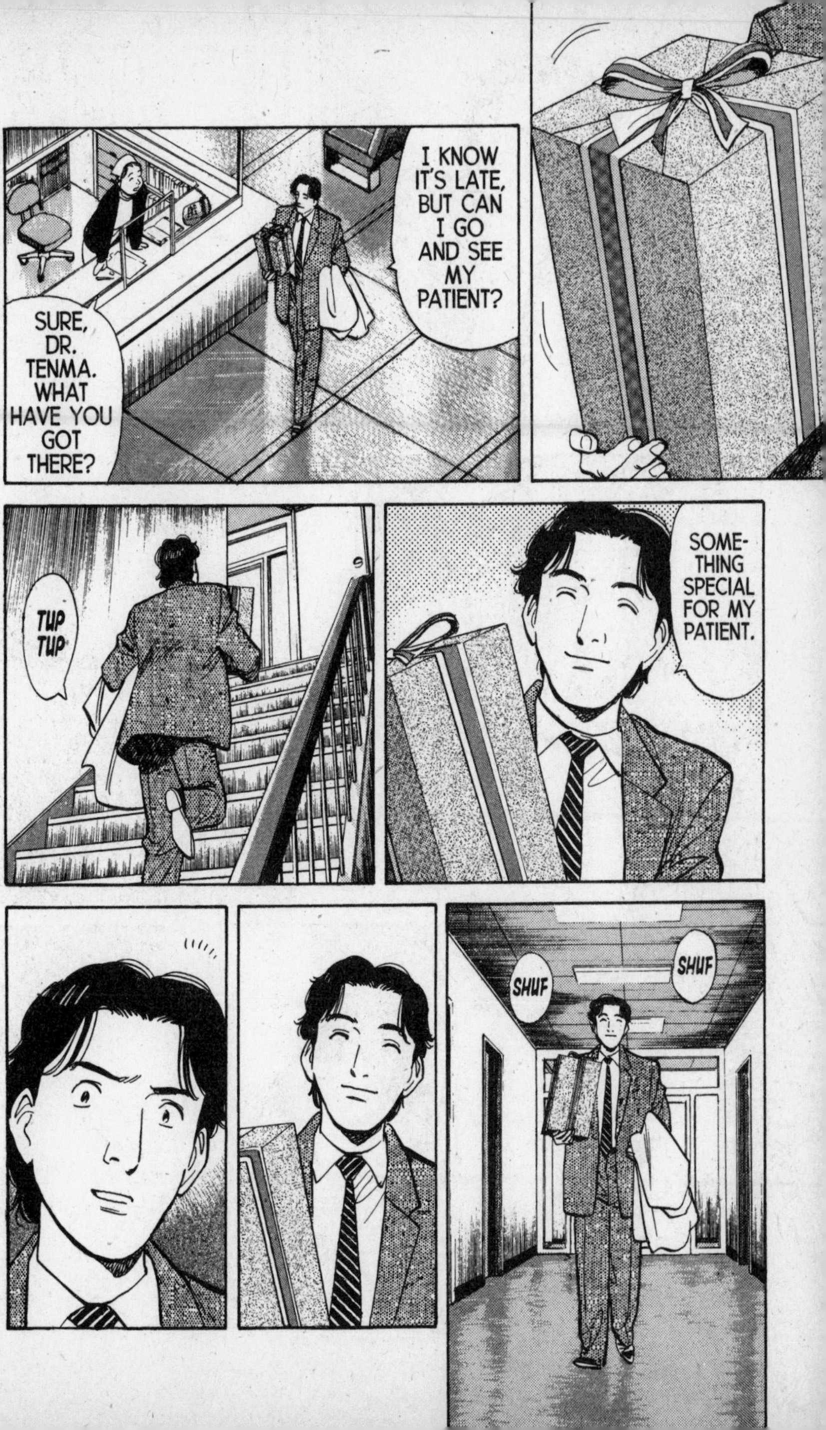
I KNOW IT'S LATE, BUT CAN I GO AND SEE MY PATIENT?
SURE, DR. TENMA. WHAT HAVE YOU GOT THERE?
SOME-THING SPECIAL FOR MY PATIENT.
TUP TUP
SHUF
SHUF

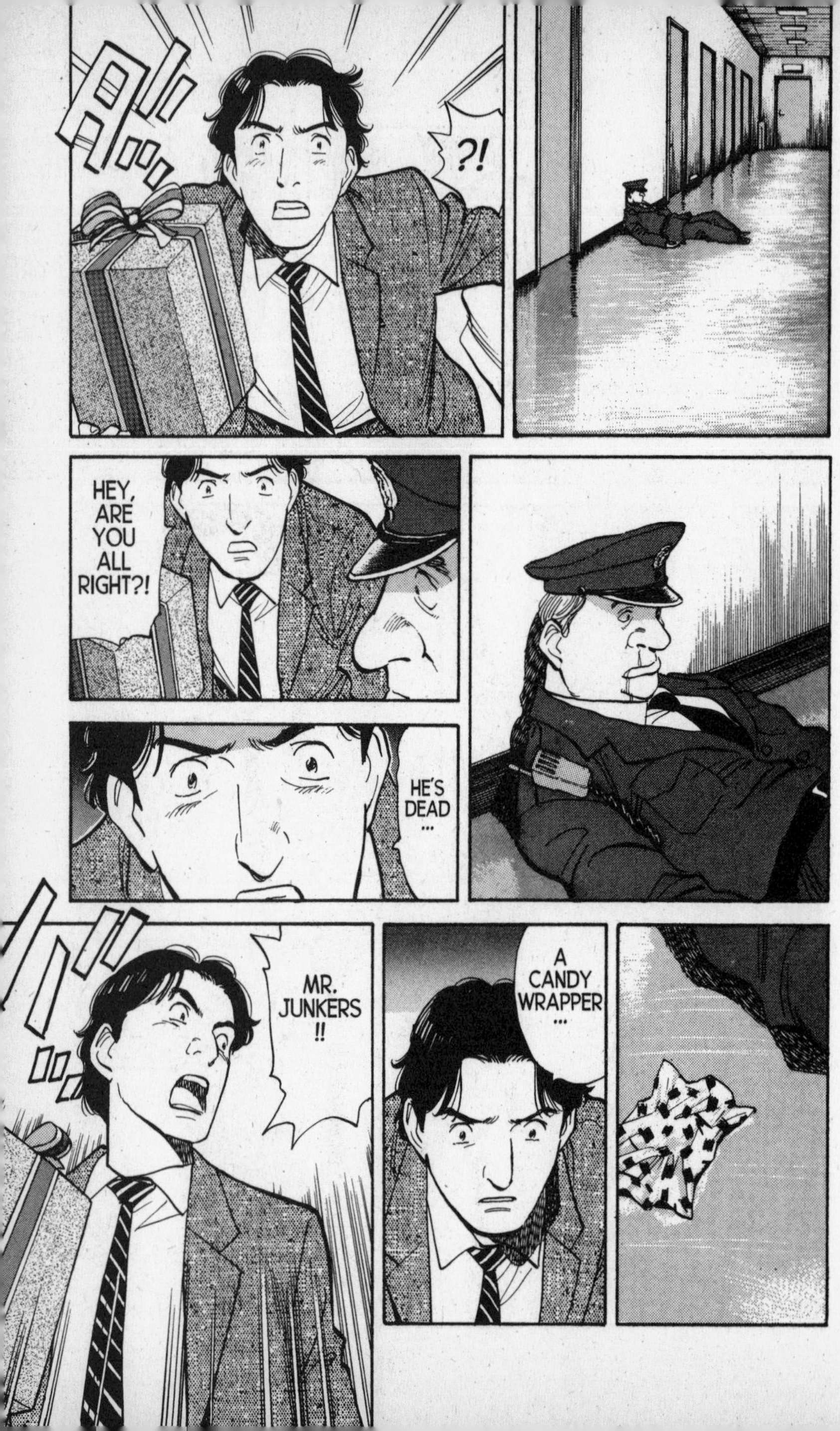
?!
HEY, ARE YOU ALL RIGHT?!
HE'S DEAD ...
A CANDY WRAPPER ...
MR. JUNKERS !!

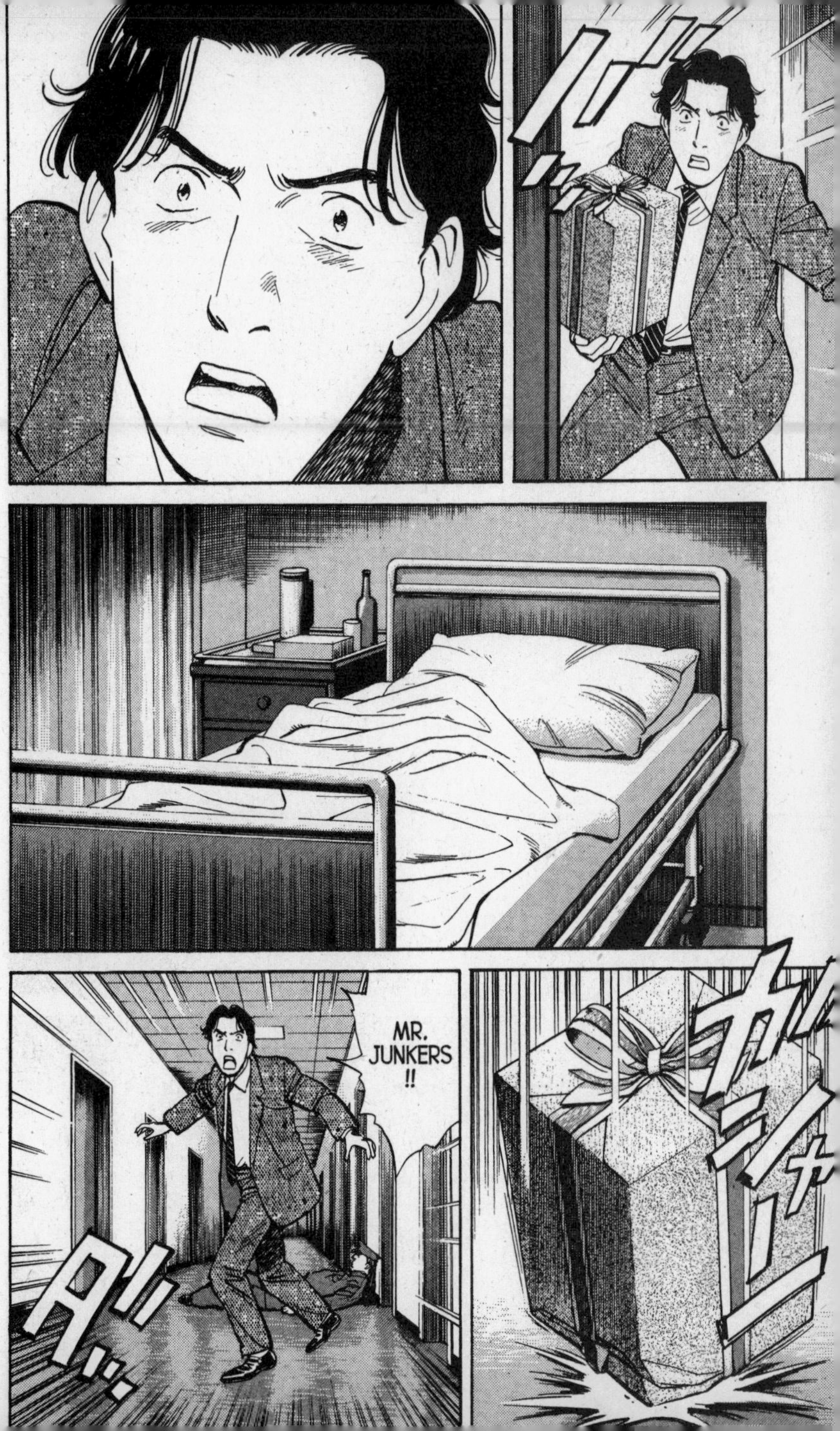
MR. JUNKERS !!

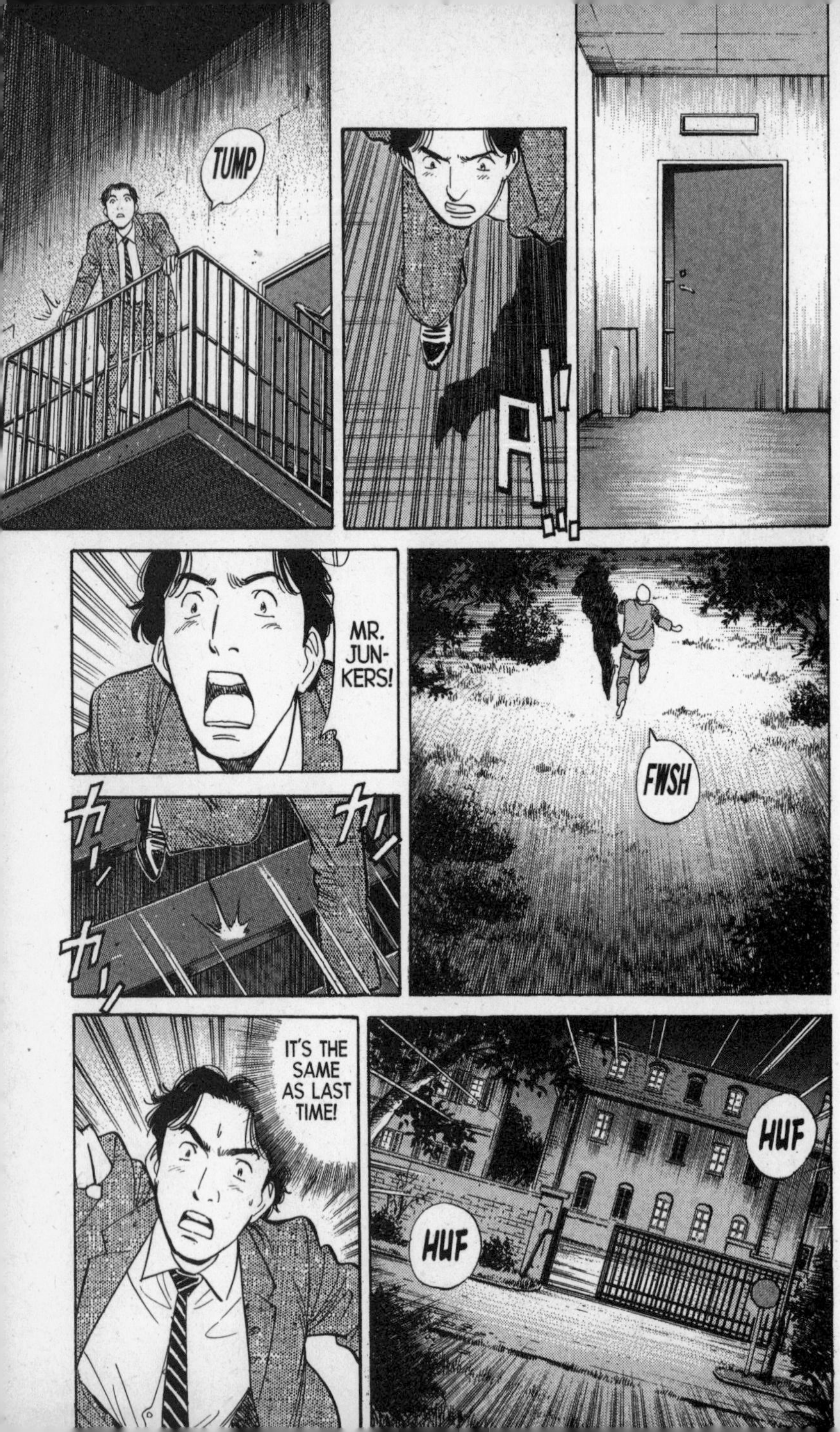
A!!
TUMP
FWSH
MR. JUNKERS!
カン
カン
カン
HUF
HUF
IT'S THE SAME AS LAST TIME!

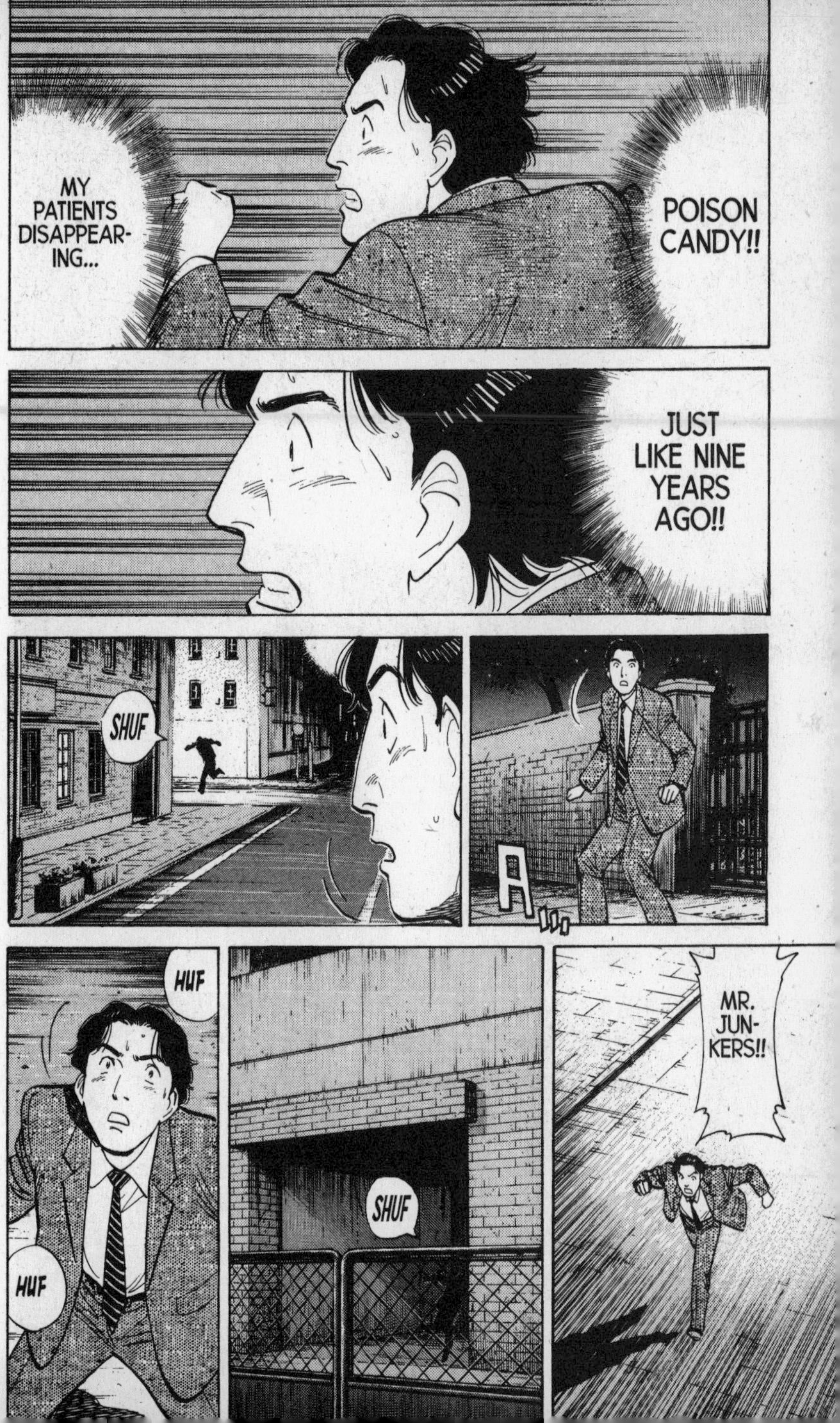
POISON CANDY!!
MY PATIENTS DISAPPEAR-ING...
JUST LIKE NINE YEARS AGO!!
A...
SHUF
MR. JUN-KERS!!
SHUF
HUF
HUF

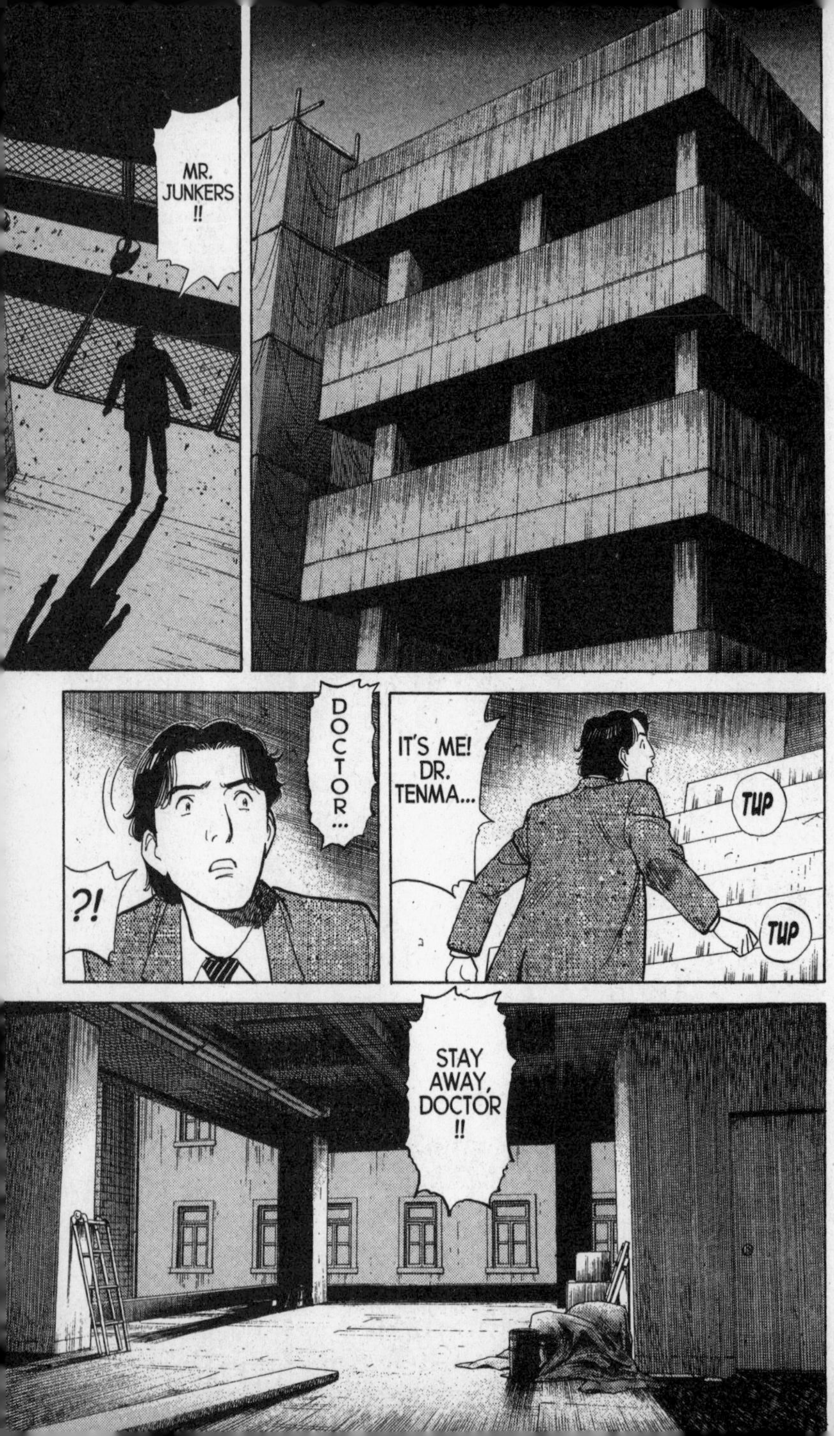
MR. JUNKERS !!
IT'S ME! DR. TENMA...
TUP
TUP
DOCTOR...
?!
STAY AWAY, DOCTOR !!

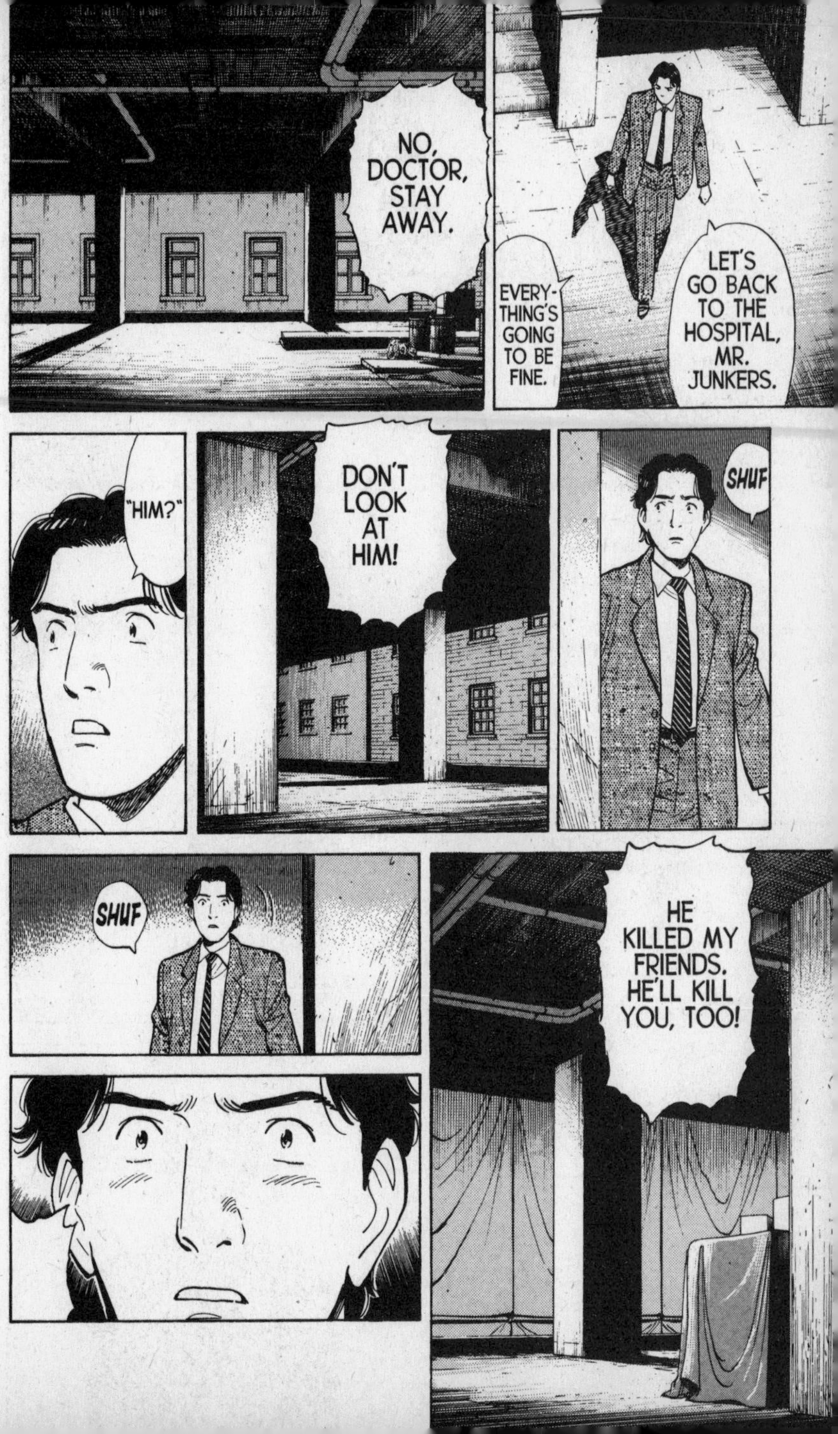
LET'S GO BACK TO THE HOSPITAL, MR. JUNKERS.
EVERY-THING'S GOING TO BE FINE.
NO, DOCTOR, STAY AWAY.
SHUF
DON'T LOOK AT HIM!
"HIM?"
HE KILLED MY FRIENDS. HE'LL KILL YOU, TOO!
SHUF

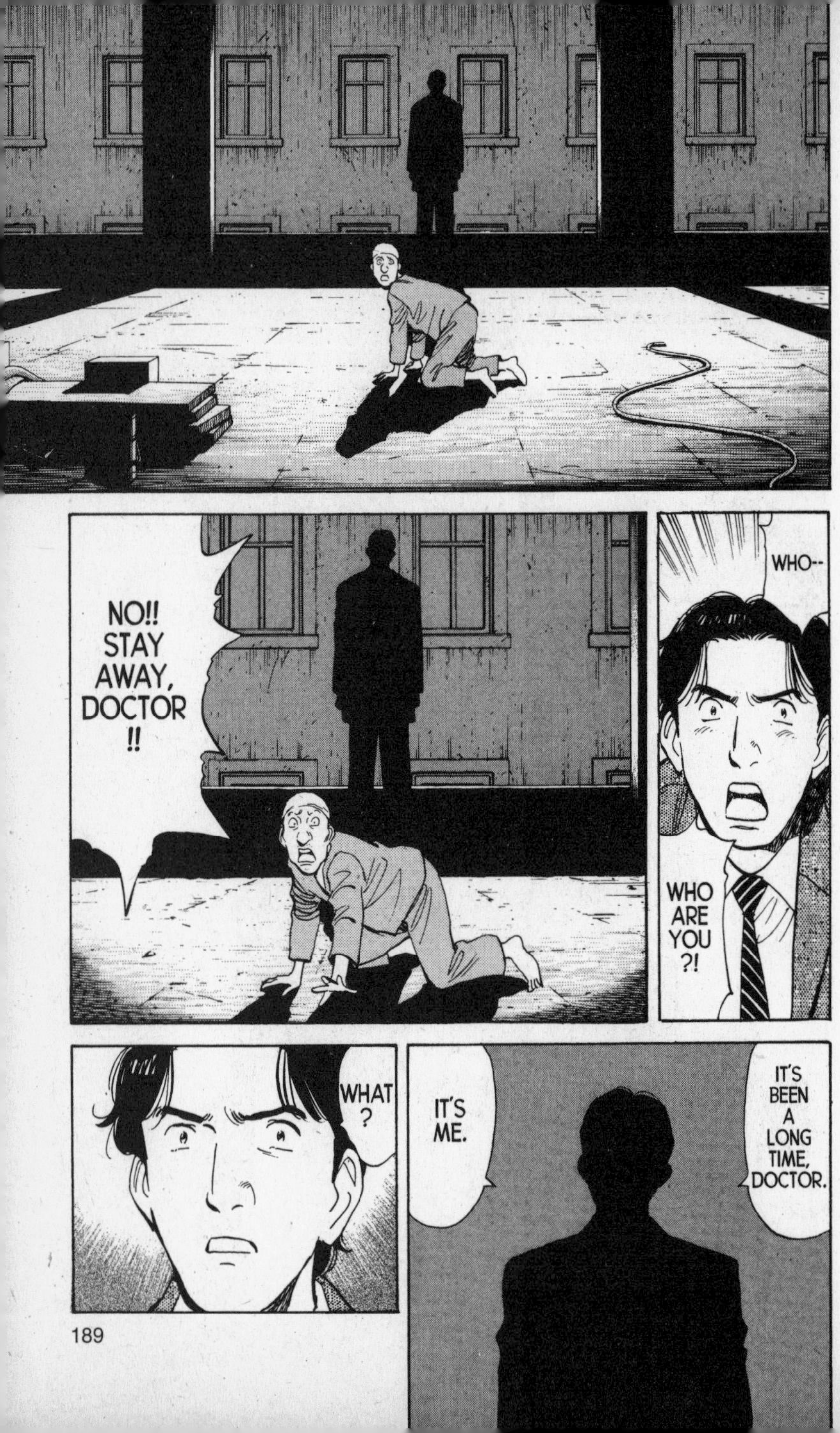
WHO--
WHO ARE YOU ?!
NO!! STAY AWAY, DOCTOR !!
IT'S BEEN A LONG TIME, DOCTOR.
IT'S ME.
WHAT ?

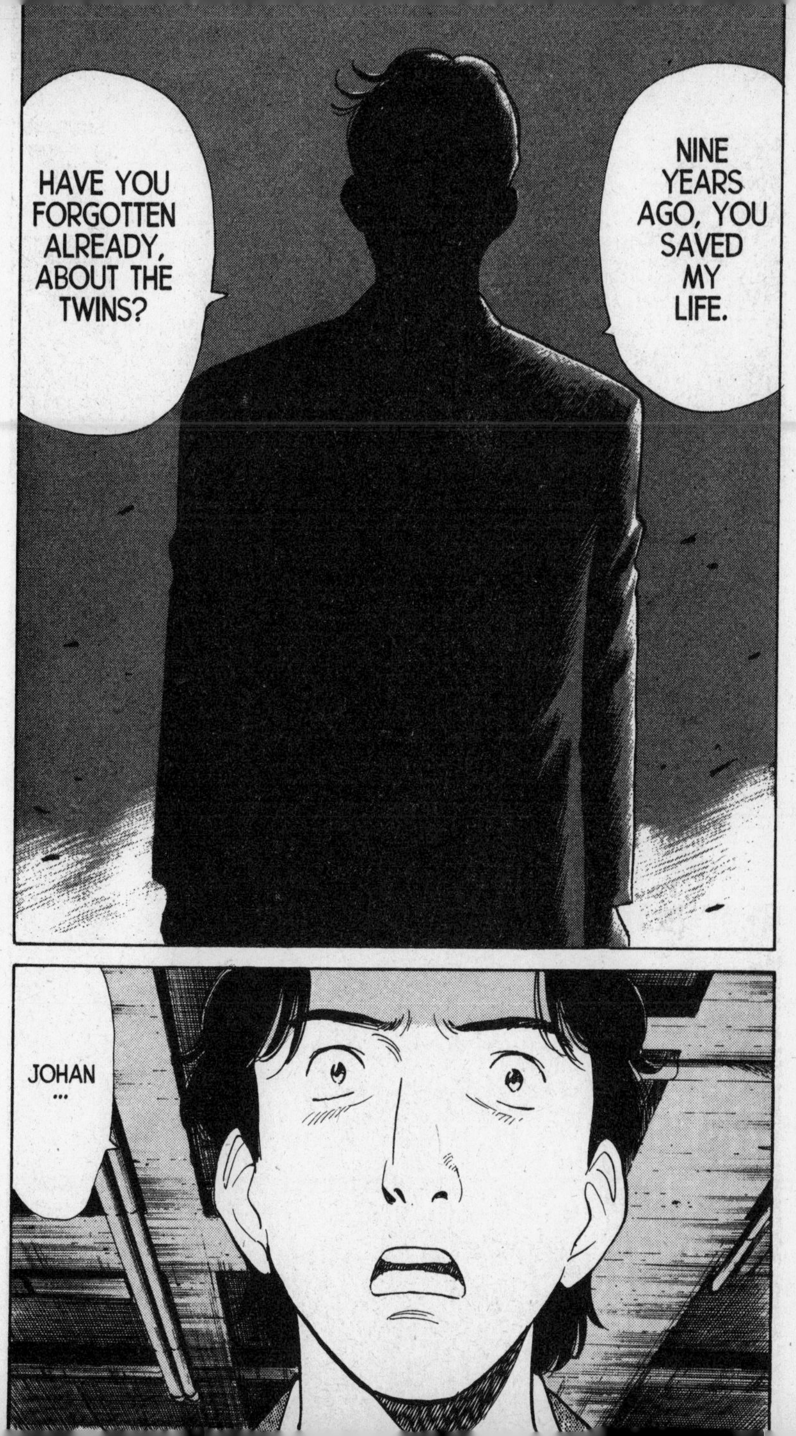
NINE YEARS AGO, YOU SAVED MY LIFE.
HAVE YOU FORGOTTEN ALREADY, ABOUT THE TWINS?
JOHAN ...

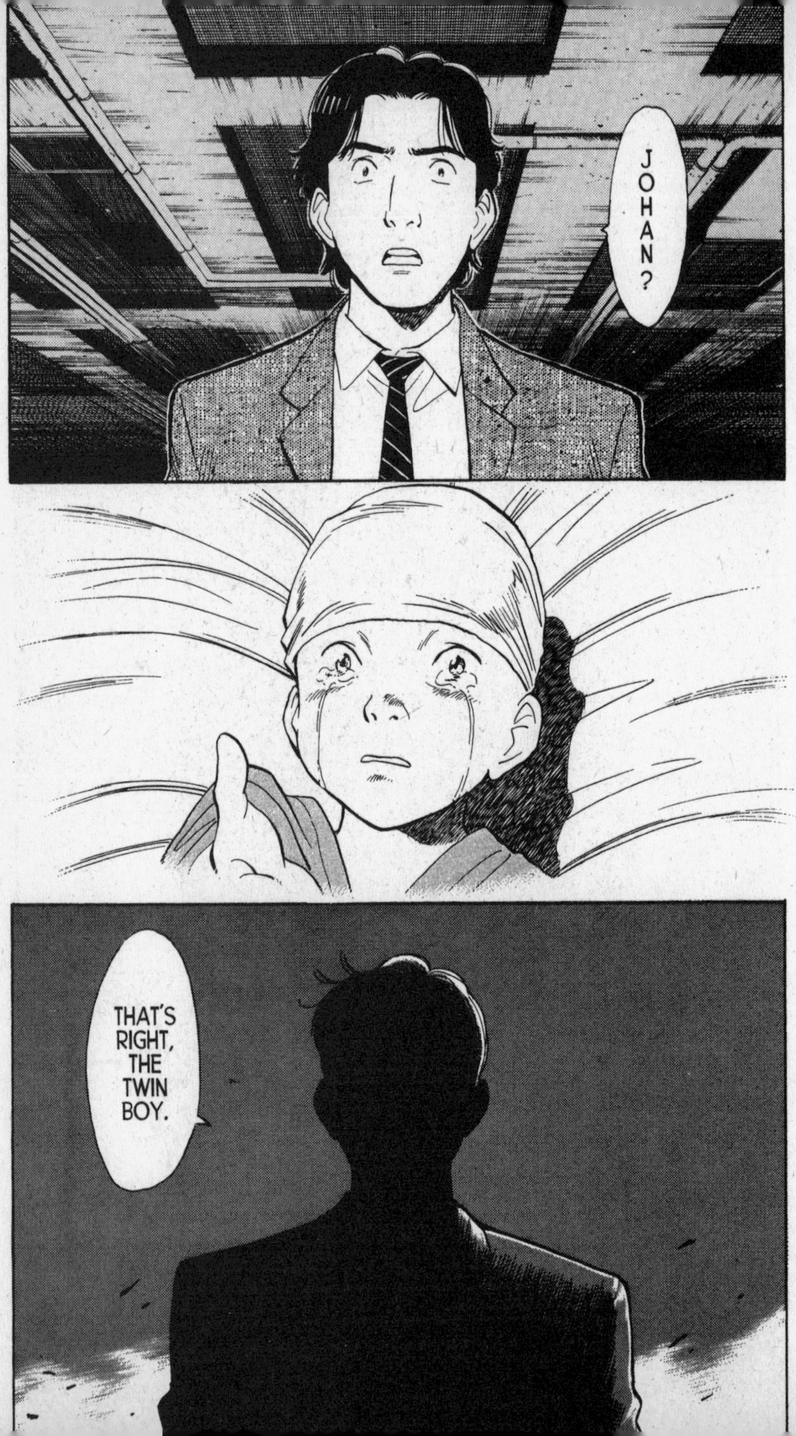
JOHAN?
THAT'S RIGHT, THE TWIN BOY.

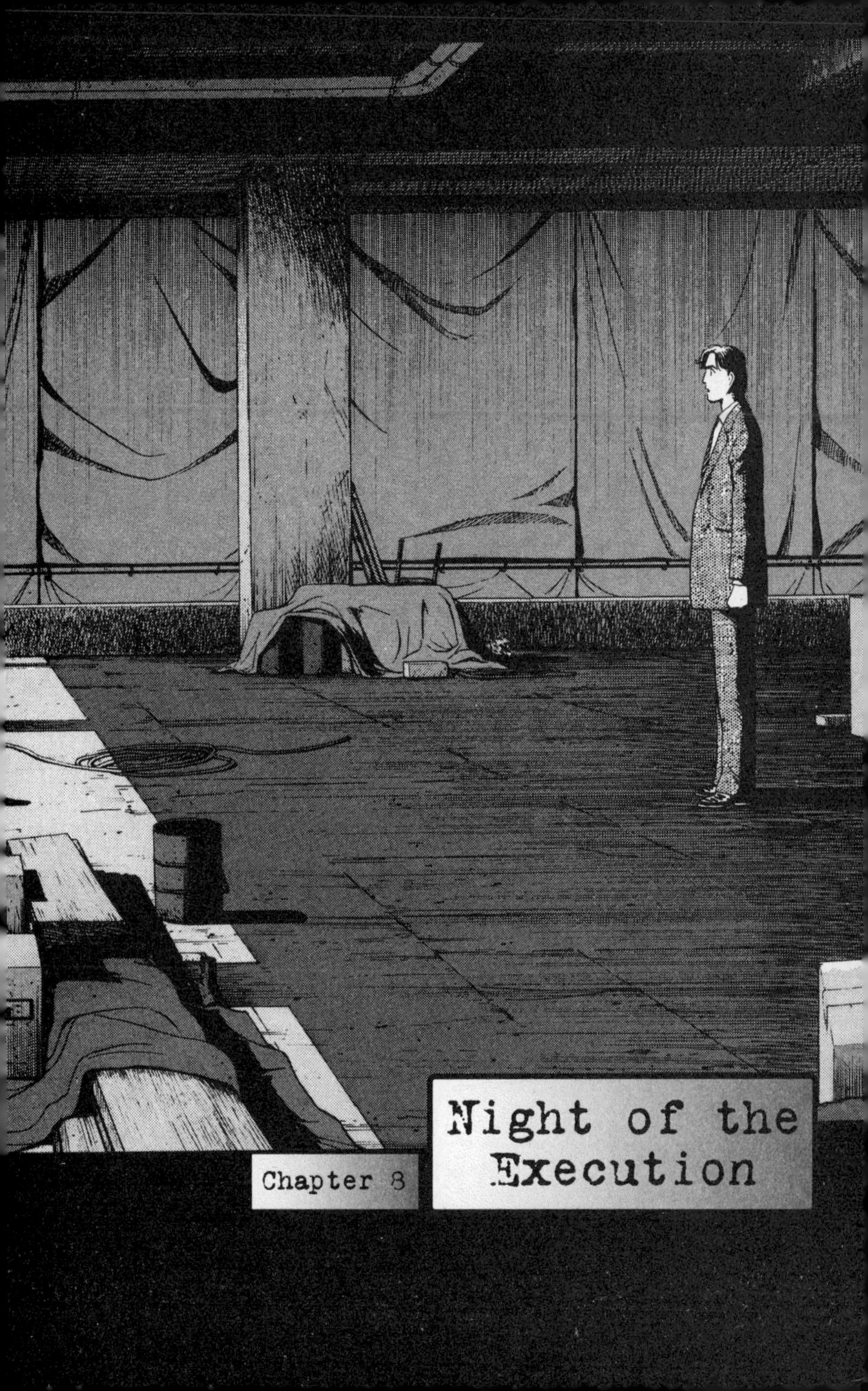
Chapter 8
Night of the Execution

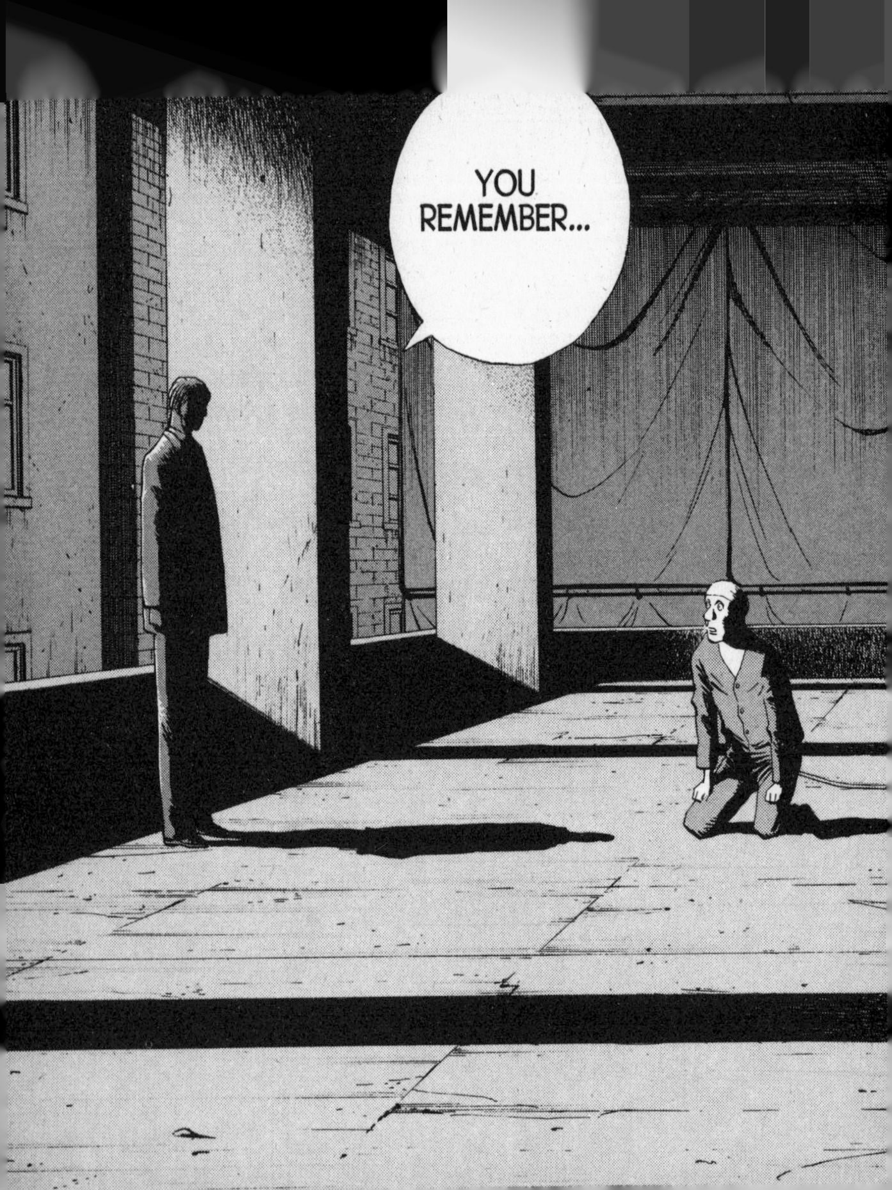
YOU REMEMBER...

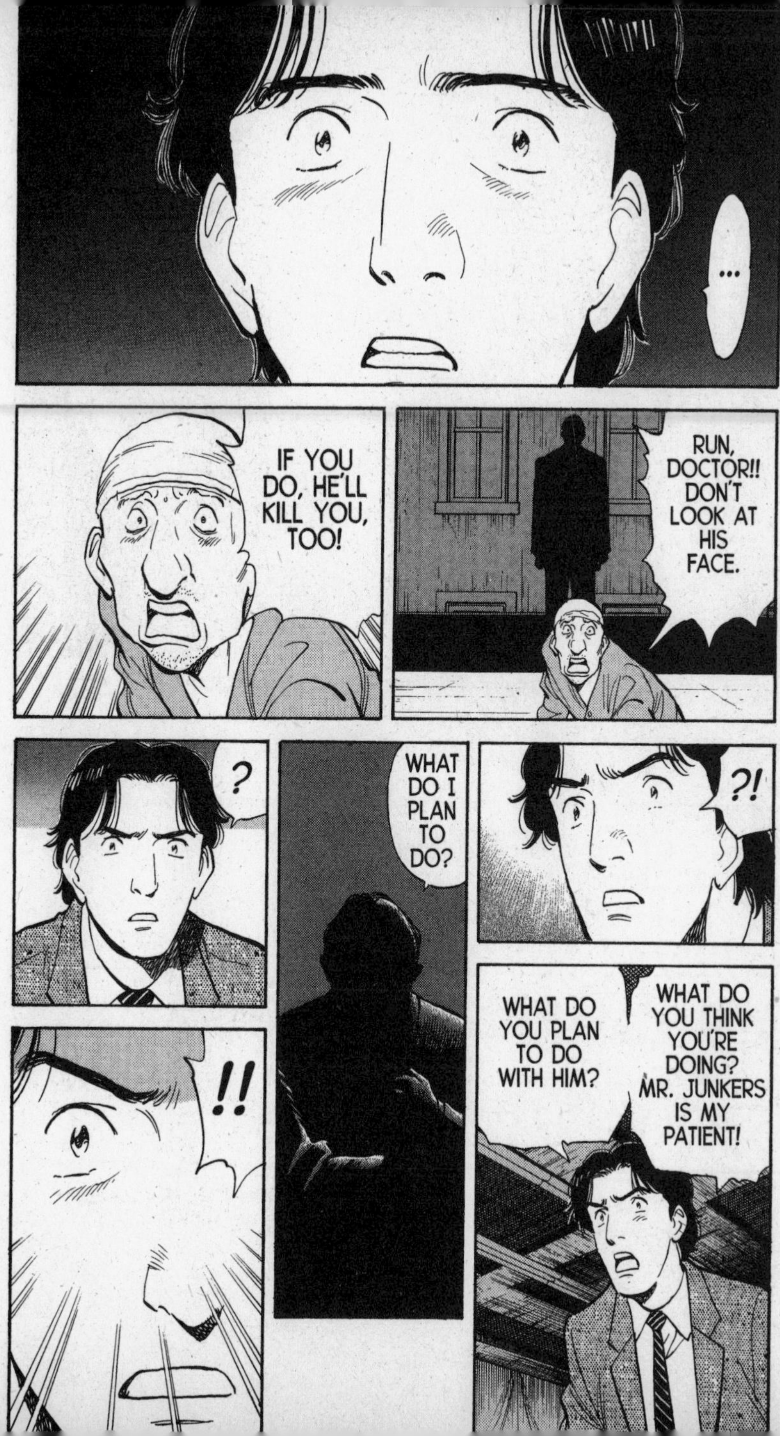
...
RUN, DOCTOR!! DON'T LOOK AT HIS FACE.
IF YOU DO, HE'LL KILL YOU, TOO!
?!
WHAT DO YOU THINK YOU'RE DOING? MR. JUNKERS IS MY PATIENT!
WHAT DO YOU PLAN TO DO WITH HIM?
WHAT DO I PLAN TO DO?
?
!!

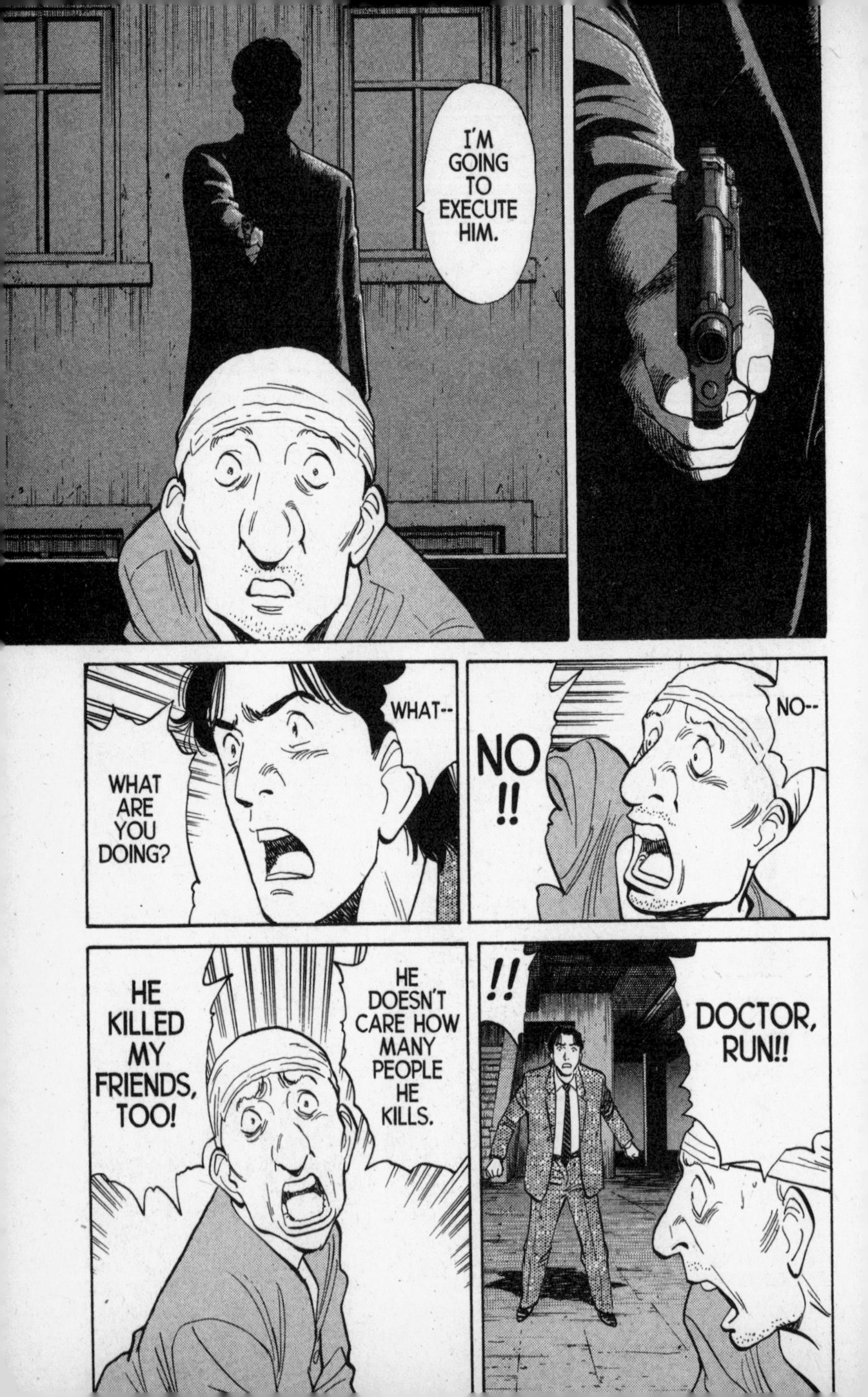
I'M GOING TO EXECUTE HIM.
NO--
NO!!
WHAT--
WHAT ARE YOU DOING?
DOCTOR, RUN!!
!!
HE DOESN'T CARE HOW MANY PEOPLE HE KILLS.
HE KILLED MY FRIENDS, TOO!

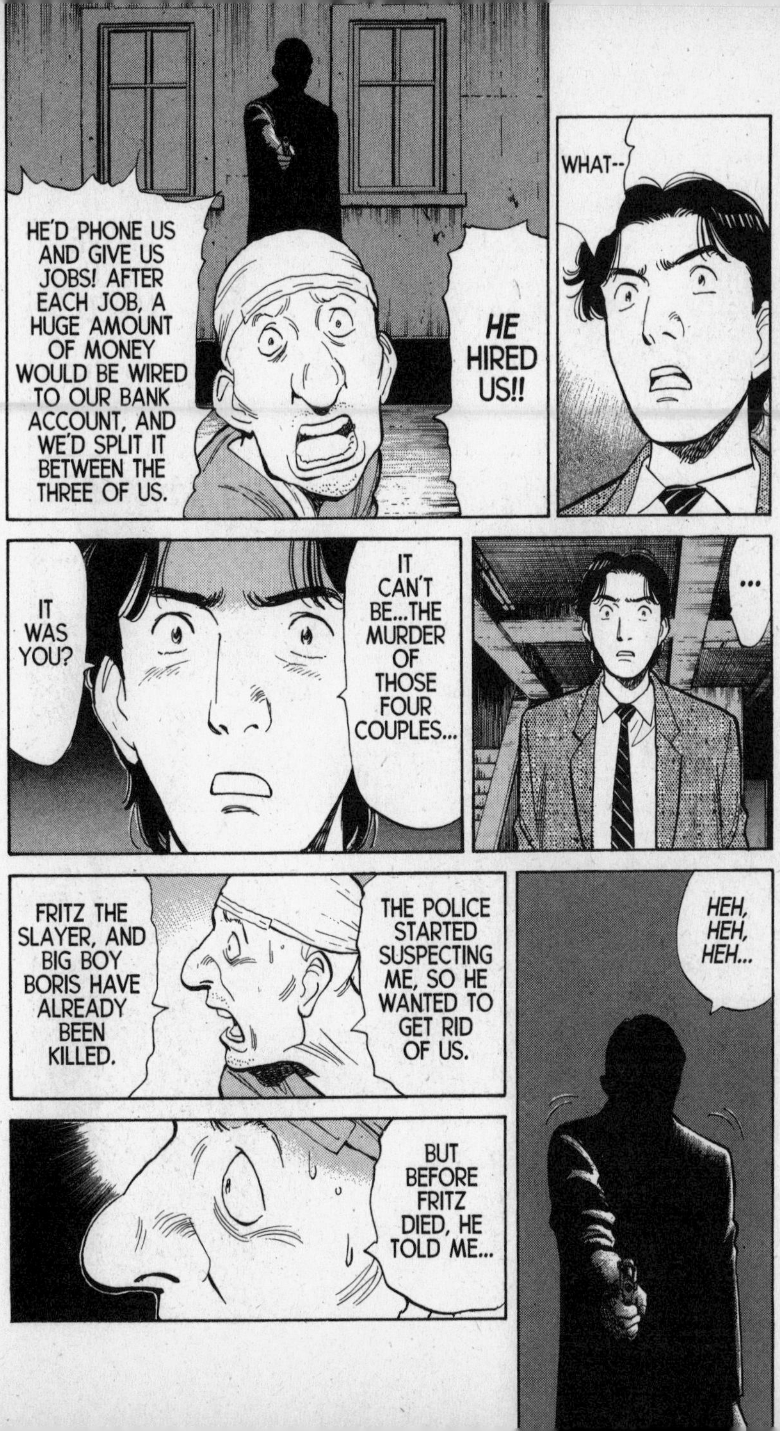
WHAT--
HE HIRED US!!
HE'D PHONE US AND GIVE US JOBS! AFTER EACH JOB, A HUGE AMOUNT OF MONEY WOULD BE WIRED TO OUR BANK ACCOUNT, AND WE'D SPLIT IT BETWEEN THE THREE OF US.
...
IT CAN'T BE...THE MURDER OF THOSE FOUR COUPLES...
IT WAS YOU?
HEH, HEH, HEH...
THE POLICE STARTED SUSPECTING ME, SO HE WANTED TO GET RID OF US.
FRITZ THE SLAYER, AND BIG BOY BORIS HAVE ALREADY BEEN KILLED.
BUT BEFORE FRITZ DIED, HE TOLD ME...

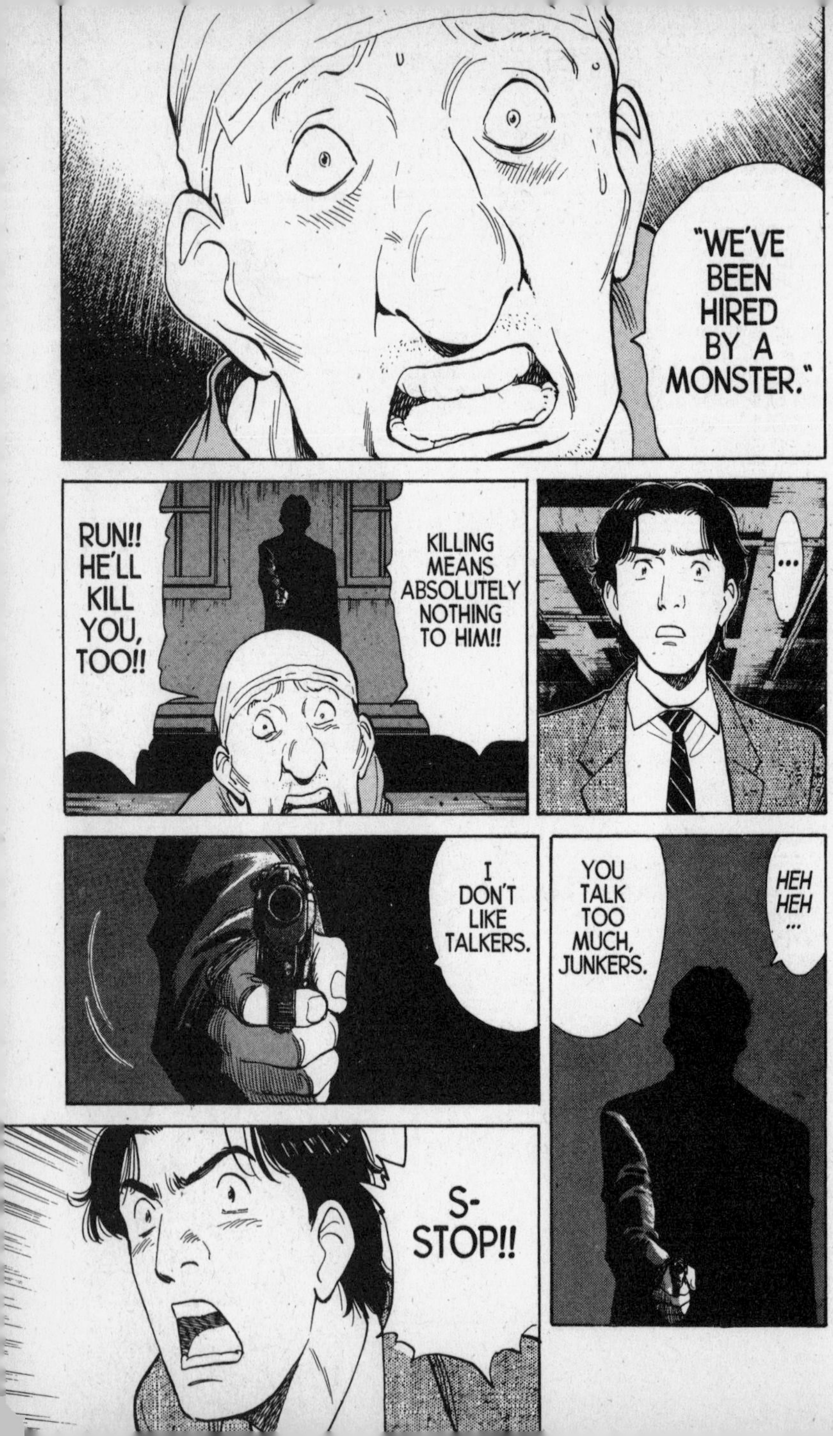
"WE'VE BEEN HIRED BY A MONSTER."
...
KILLING MEANS ABSOLUTELY NOTHING TO HIM!!
RUN!! HE'LL KILL YOU, TOO!!
HEH HEH ...
YOU TALK TOO MUCH, JUNKERS.
I DON'T LIKE TALKERS.
S-STOP!!

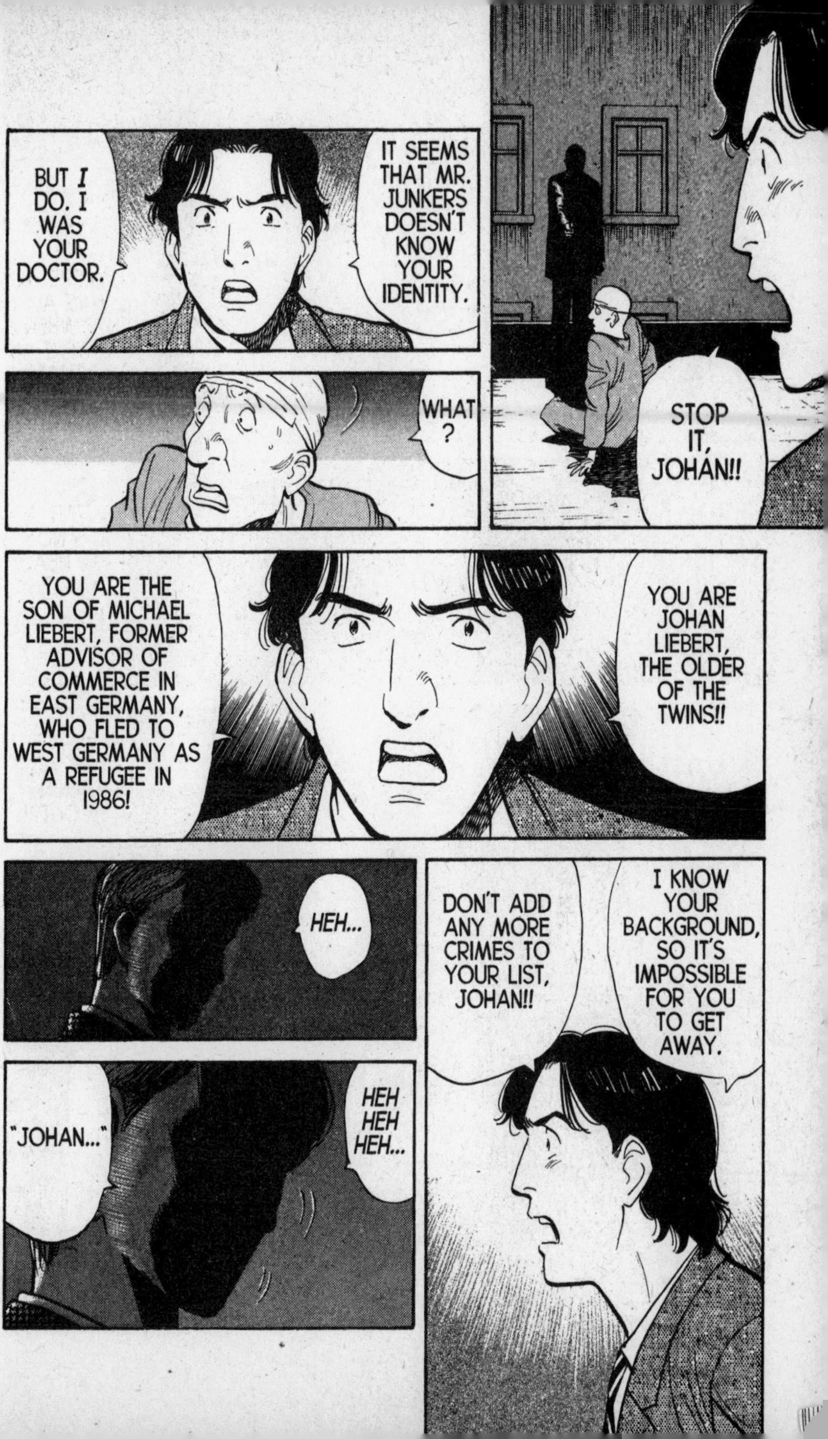
STOP IT, JOHAN!!
IT SEEMS THAT MR. JUNKERS DOESN'T KNOW YOUR IDENTITY.
BUT *I* DO. I WAS YOUR DOCTOR.
WHAT?
YOU ARE JOHAN LIEBERT, THE OLDER OF THE TWINS!!
YOU ARE THE SON OF MICHAEL LIEBERT, FORMER ADVISOR OF COMMERCE IN EAST GERMANY, WHO FLED TO WEST GERMANY AS A REFUGEE IN 1986!
I KNOW YOUR BACKGROUND, SO IT'S IMPOSSIBLE FOR YOU TO GET AWAY.
DON'T ADD ANY MORE CRIMES TO YOUR LIST, JOHAN!!
HEH...
HEH HEH HEH...
"JOHAN..."

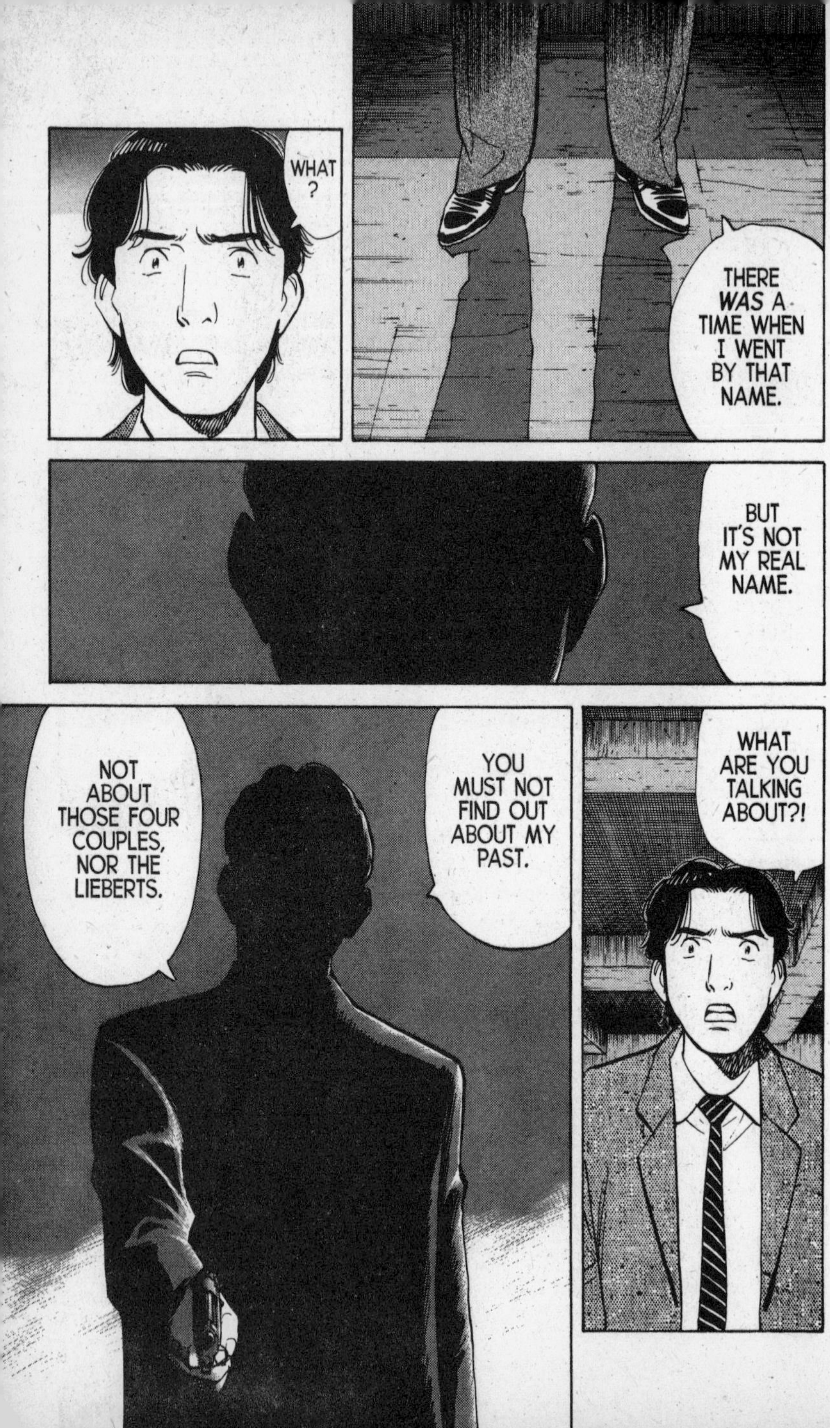
THERE *WAS* A TIME WHEN I WENT BY THAT NAME.
WHAT?
BUT IT'S NOT MY REAL NAME.
WHAT ARE YOU TALKING ABOUT?!
YOU MUST NOT FIND OUT ABOUT MY PAST.
NOT ABOUT THOSE FOUR COUPLES, NOR THE LIEBERTS.

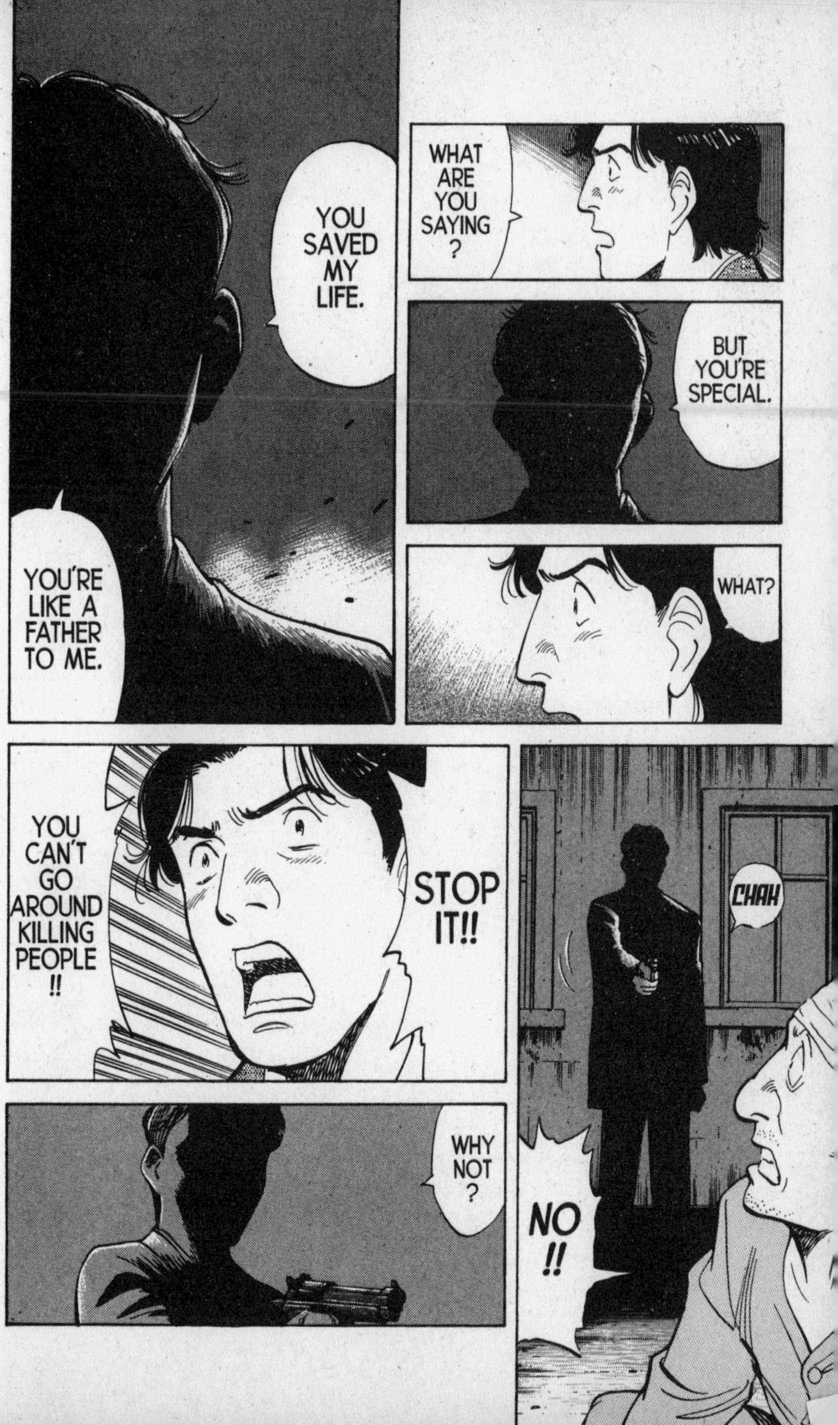
WHAT ARE YOU SAYING?
BUT YOU'RE SPECIAL.
WHAT?
YOU SAVED MY LIFE.
YOU'RE LIKE A FATHER TO ME.
CHAH
NO!!
STOP IT!!
YOU CAN'T GO AROUND KILLING PEOPLE!!
WHY NOT?

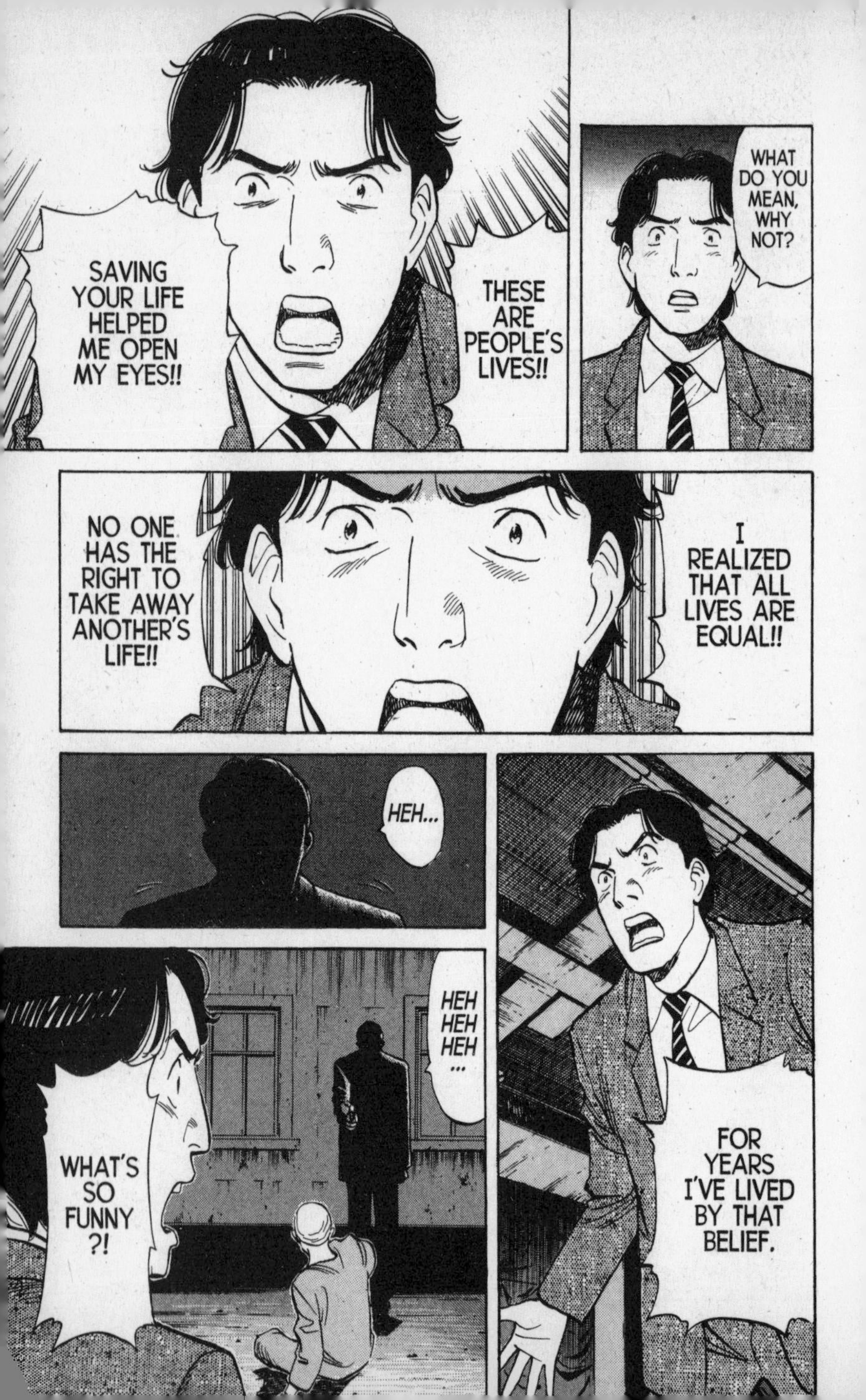
WHAT DO YOU MEAN, WHY NOT?
THESE ARE PEOPLE'S LIVES!!
SAVING YOUR LIFE HELPED ME OPEN MY EYES!!
I REALIZED THAT ALL LIVES ARE EQUAL!!
NO ONE HAS THE RIGHT TO TAKE AWAY ANOTHER'S LIFE!!
FOR YEARS I'VE LIVED BY THAT BELIEF.
HEH...
HEH HEH HEH ...
WHAT'S SO FUNNY ?!

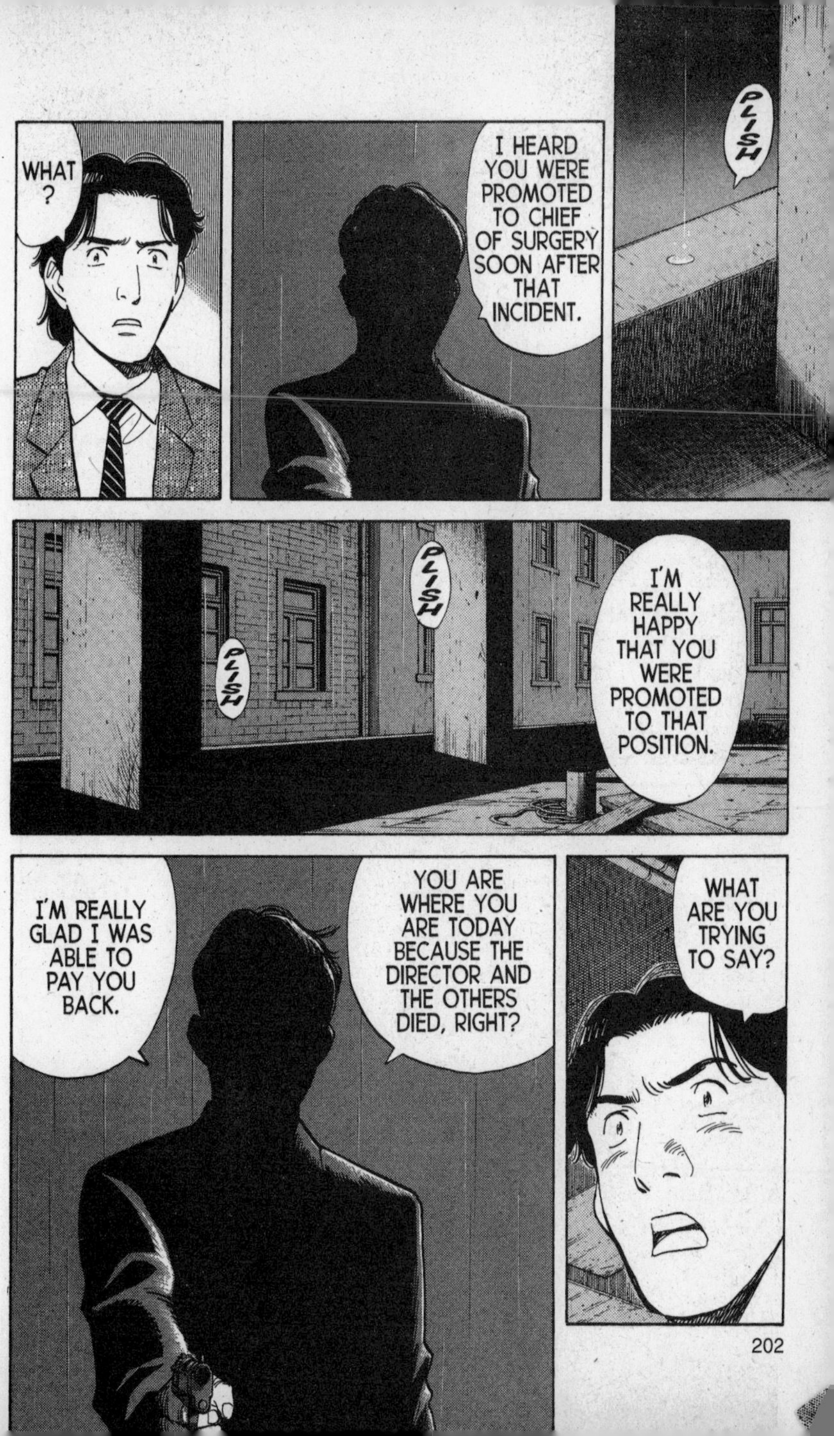
PLISH
I HEARD YOU WERE PROMOTED TO CHIEF OF SURGERY SOON AFTER THAT INCIDENT.
WHAT?
I'M REALLY HAPPY THAT YOU WERE PROMOTED TO THAT POSITION.
PLISH
PLISH
WHAT ARE YOU TRYING TO SAY?
YOU ARE WHERE YOU ARE TODAY BECAUSE THE DIRECTOR AND THE OTHERS DIED, RIGHT?
I'M REALLY GLAD I WAS ABLE TO PAY YOU BACK.

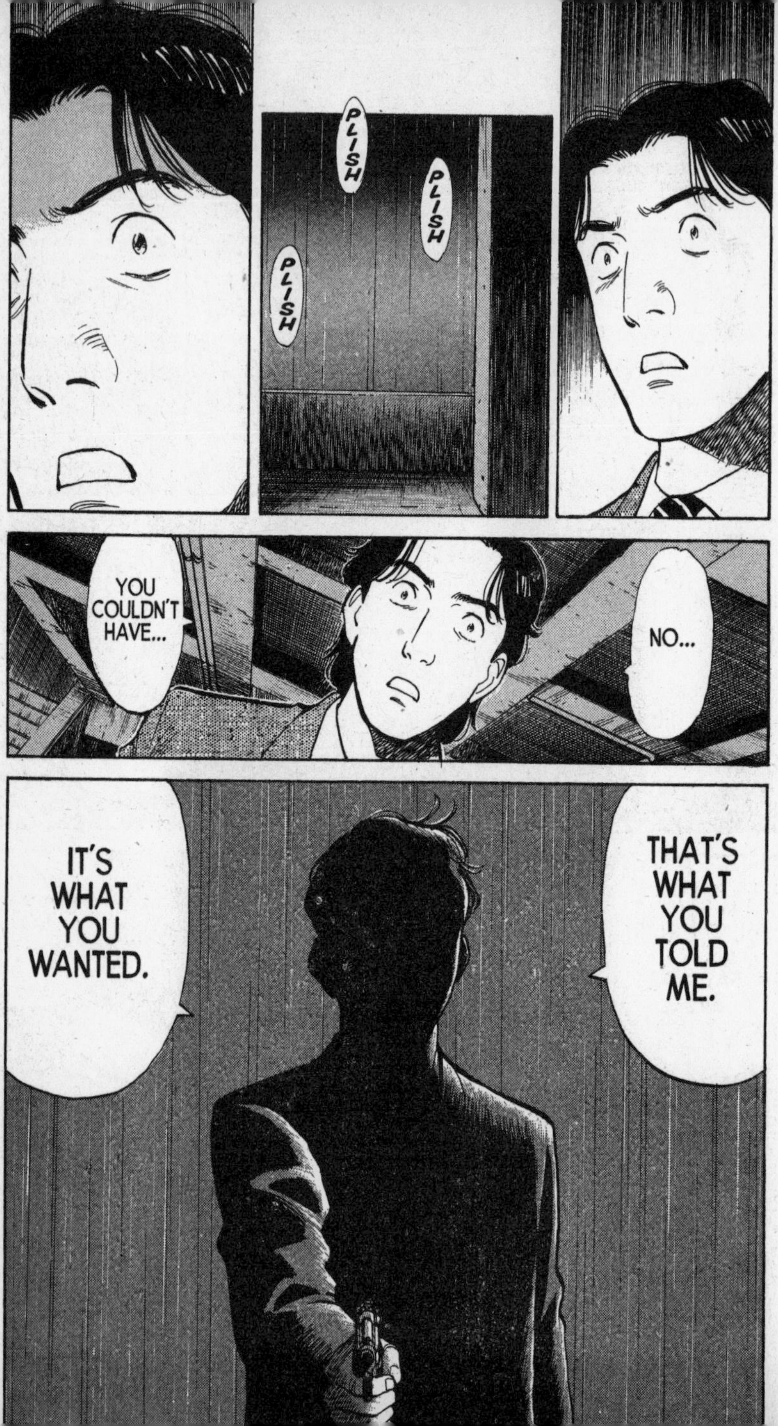
PLISH
PLISH
PLISH
NO...
YOU COULDN'T HAVE...
THAT'S WHAT YOU TOLD ME.
IT'S WHAT YOU WANTED.

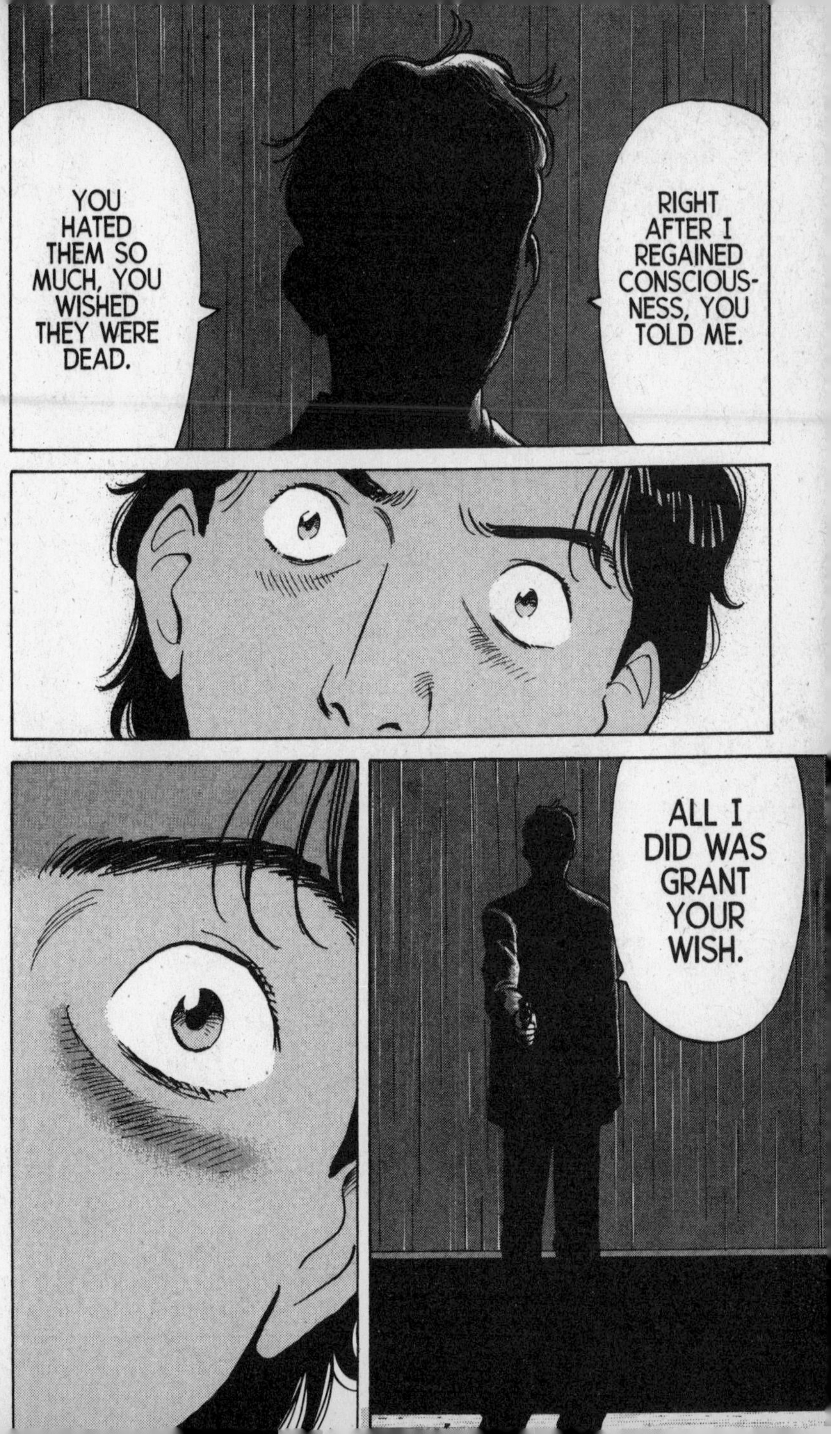
RIGHT AFTER I REGAINED CONSCIOUS-NESS, YOU TOLD ME.
YOU HATED THEM SO MUCH, YOU WISHED THEY WERE DEAD.
ALL I DID WAS GRANT YOUR WISH.

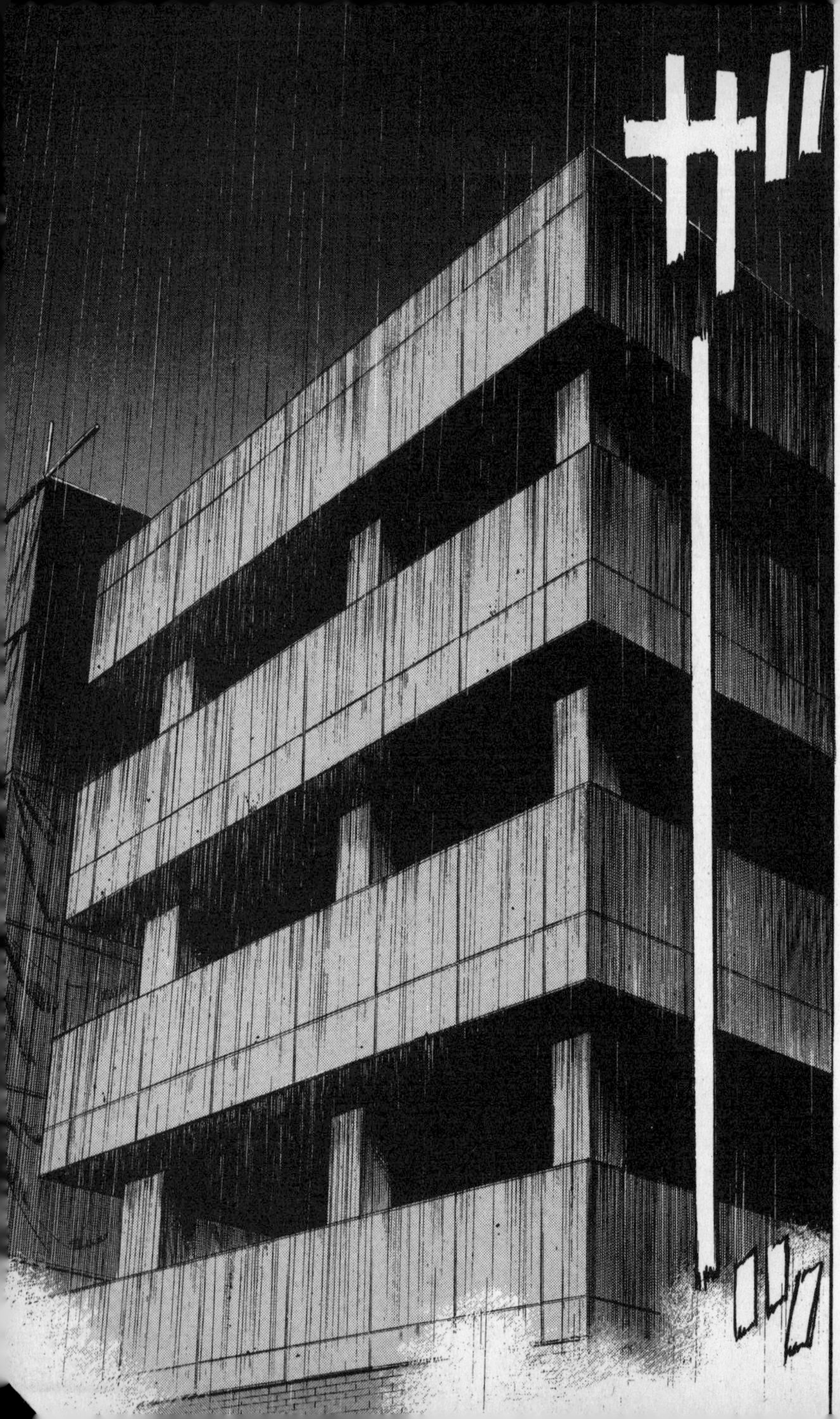
ザーッ

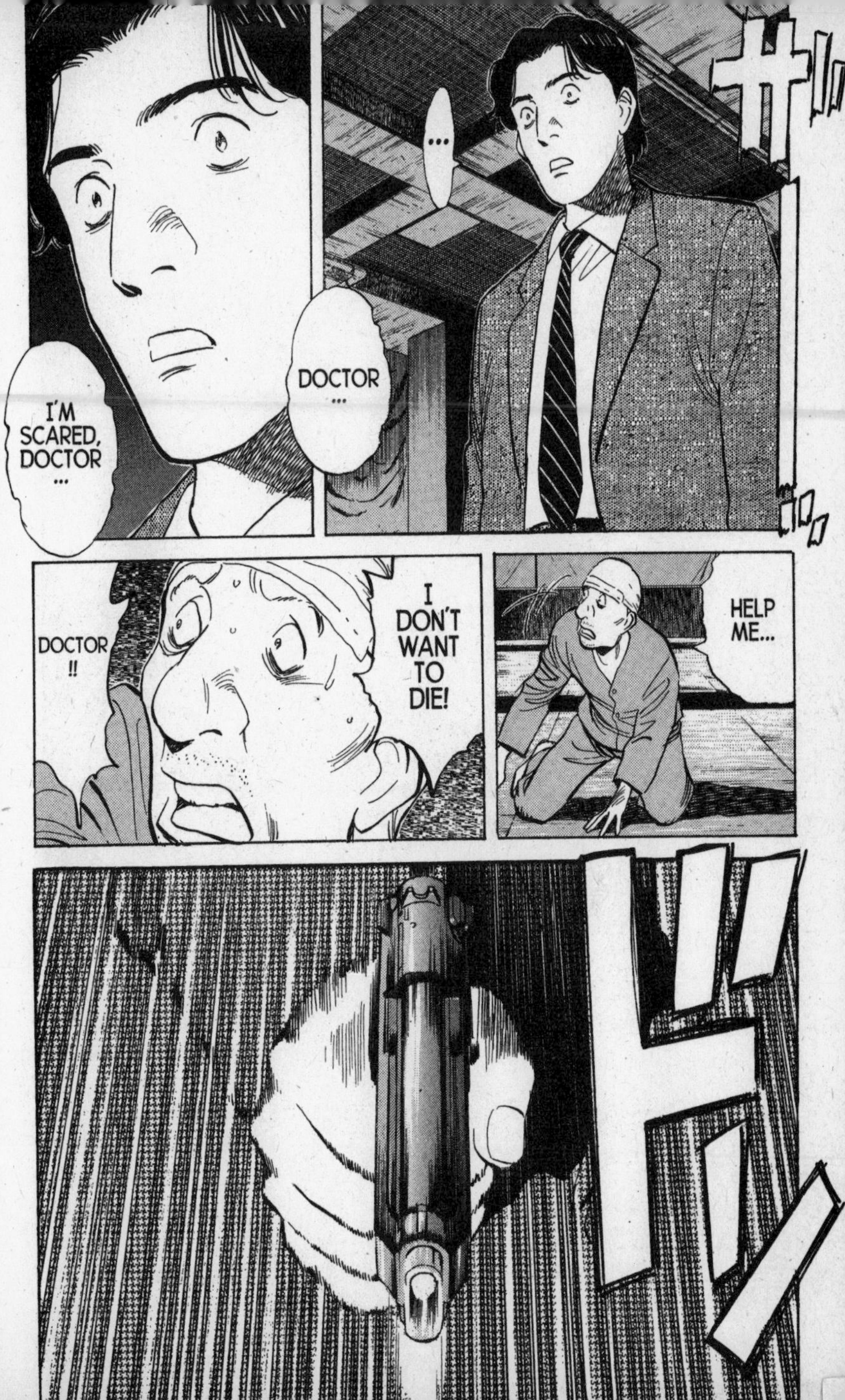
...
DOCTOR ...
I'M SCARED, DOCTOR ...
HELP ME...
I DON'T WANT TO DIE!
DOCTOR !!

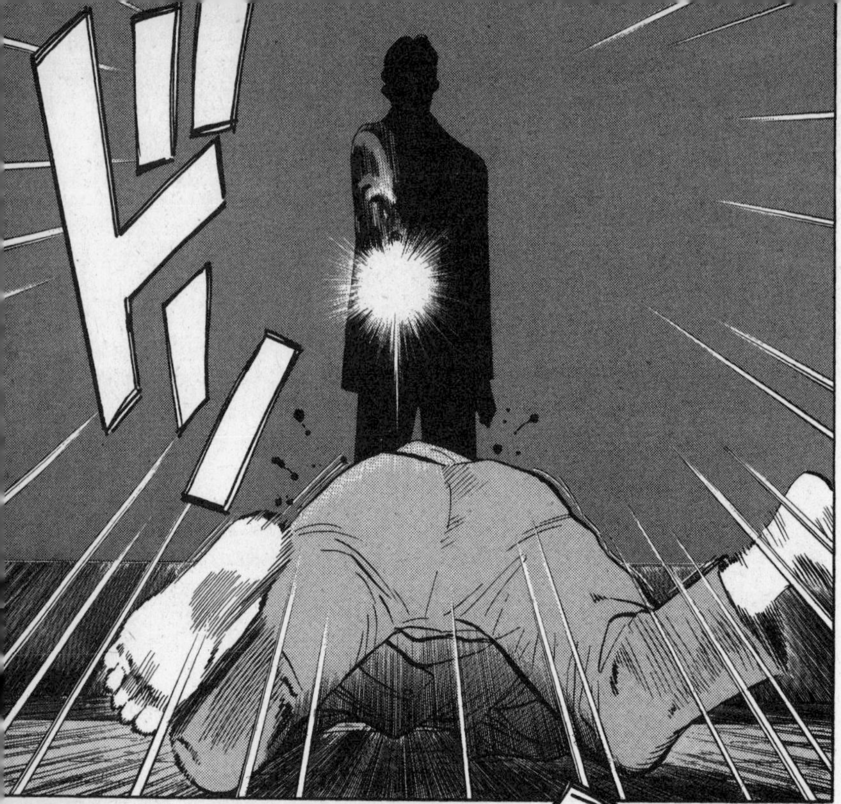

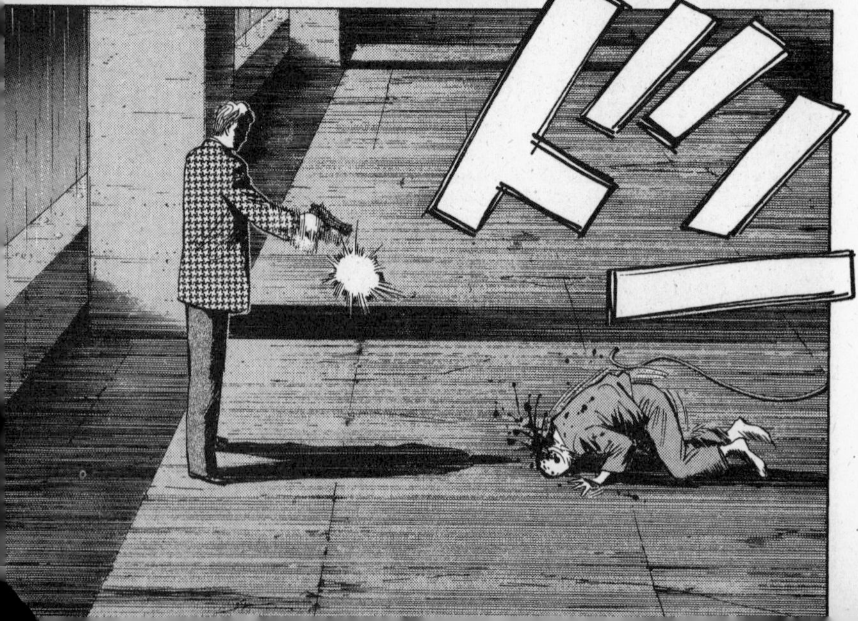

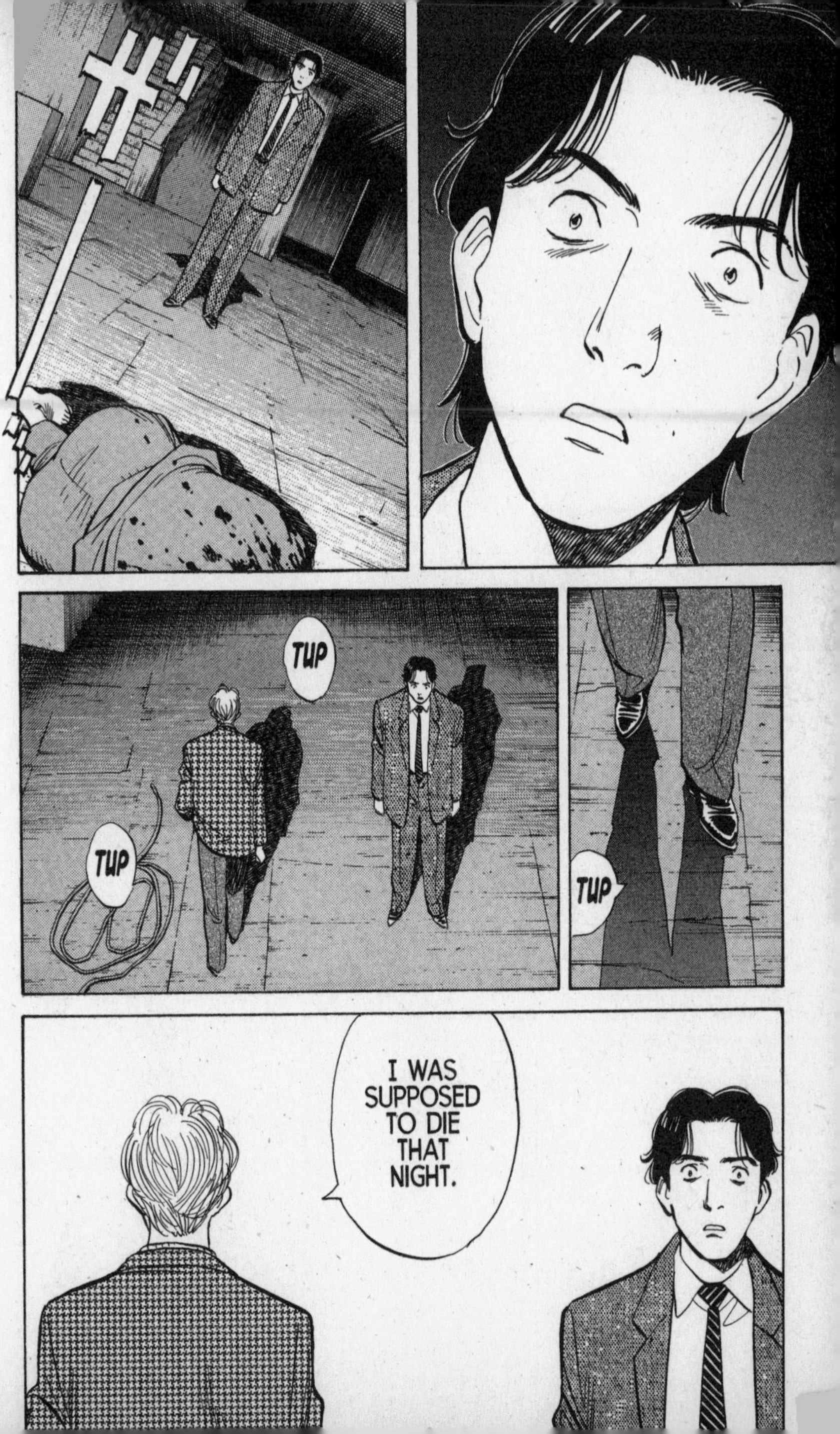
TUP
TUP
TUP
I WAS SUPPOSED TO DIE THAT NIGHT.

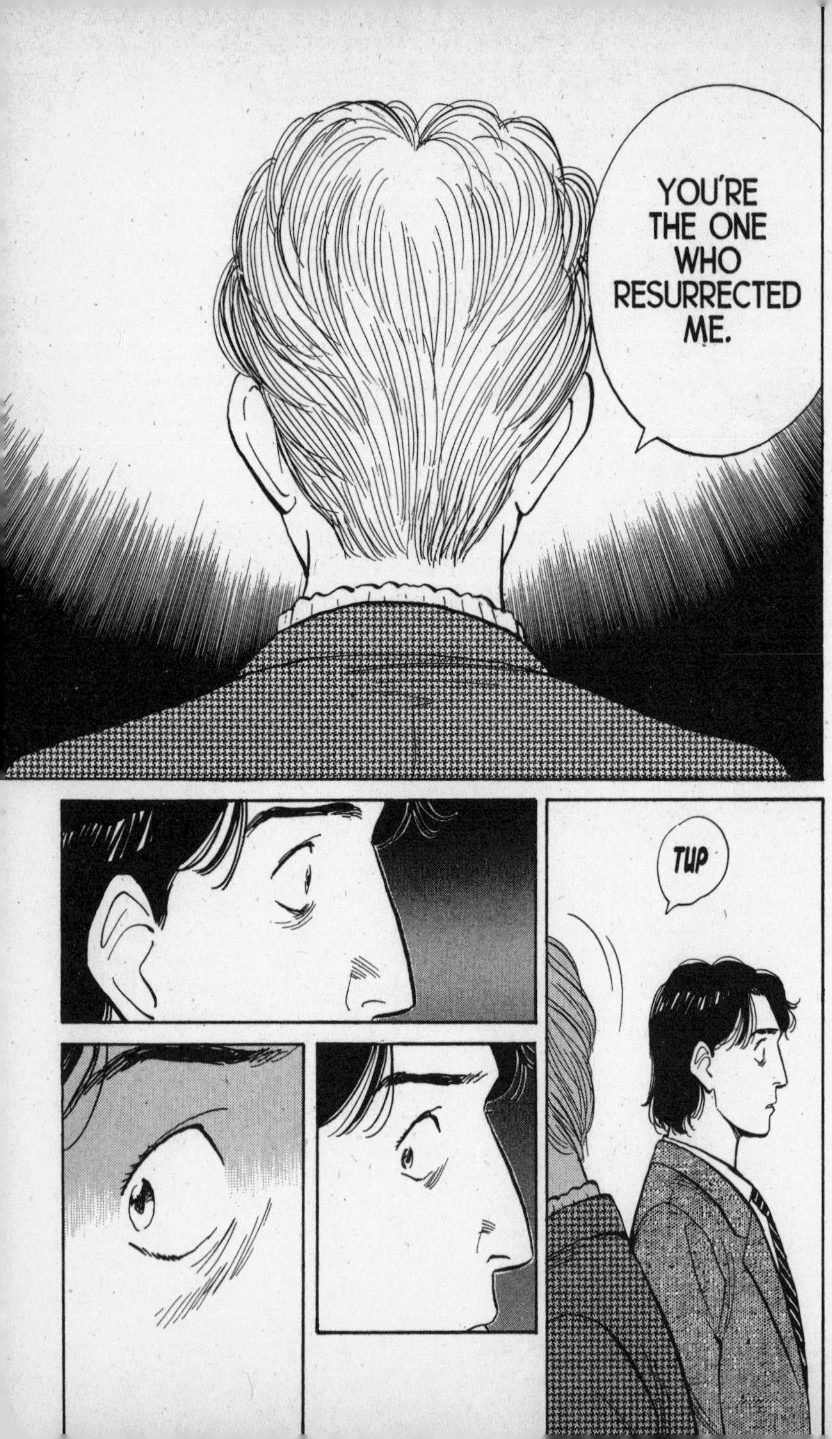
YOU'RE THE ONE WHO RESURRECTED ME.
TUP

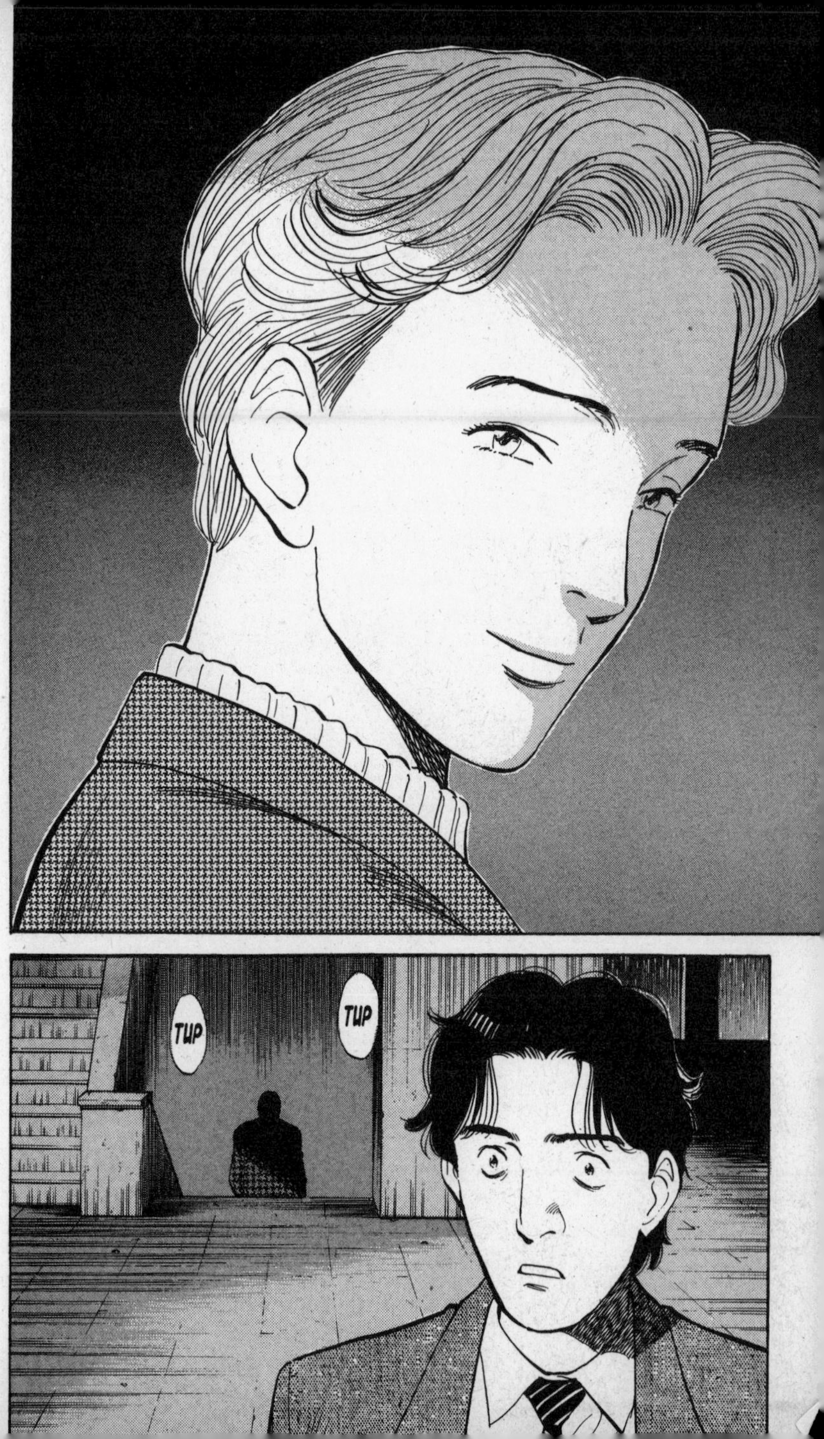
TUP
TUP

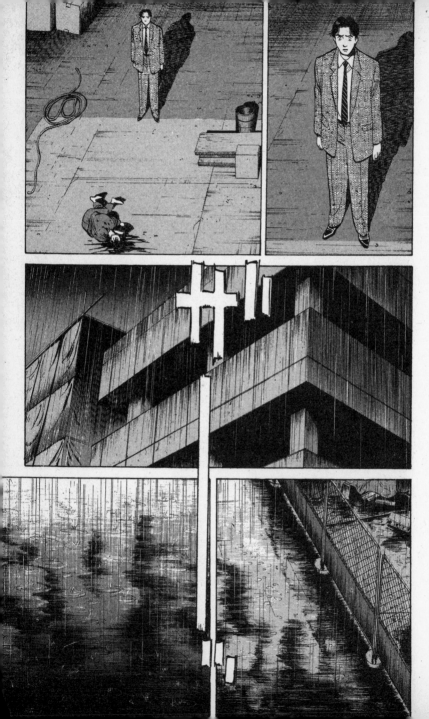

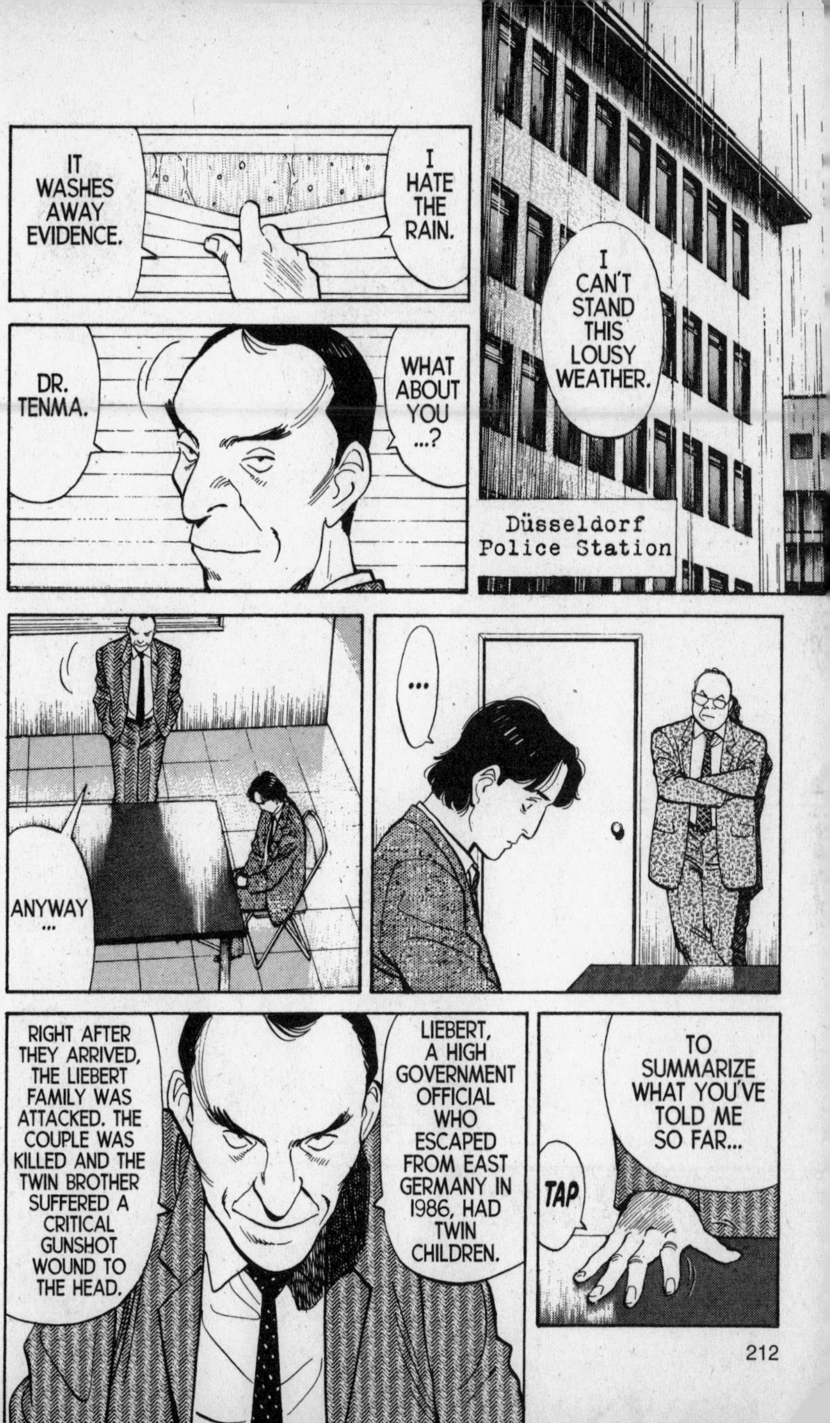
I CAN'T STAND THIS LOUSY WEATHER.
Düsseldorf Police Station
I HATE THE RAIN.
IT WASHES AWAY EVIDENCE.
WHAT ABOUT YOU ...?
DR. TENMA.
...
ANYWAY ...
TO SUMMARIZE WHAT YOU'VE TOLD ME SO FAR...
TAP
LIEBERT, A HIGH GOVERNMENT OFFICIAL WHO ESCAPED FROM EAST GERMANY IN 1986, HAD TWIN CHILDREN.
RIGHT AFTER THEY ARRIVED, THE LIEBERT FAMILY WAS ATTACKED. THE COUPLE WAS KILLED AND THE TWIN BROTHER SUFFERED A CRITICAL GUNSHOT WOUND TO THE HEAD.

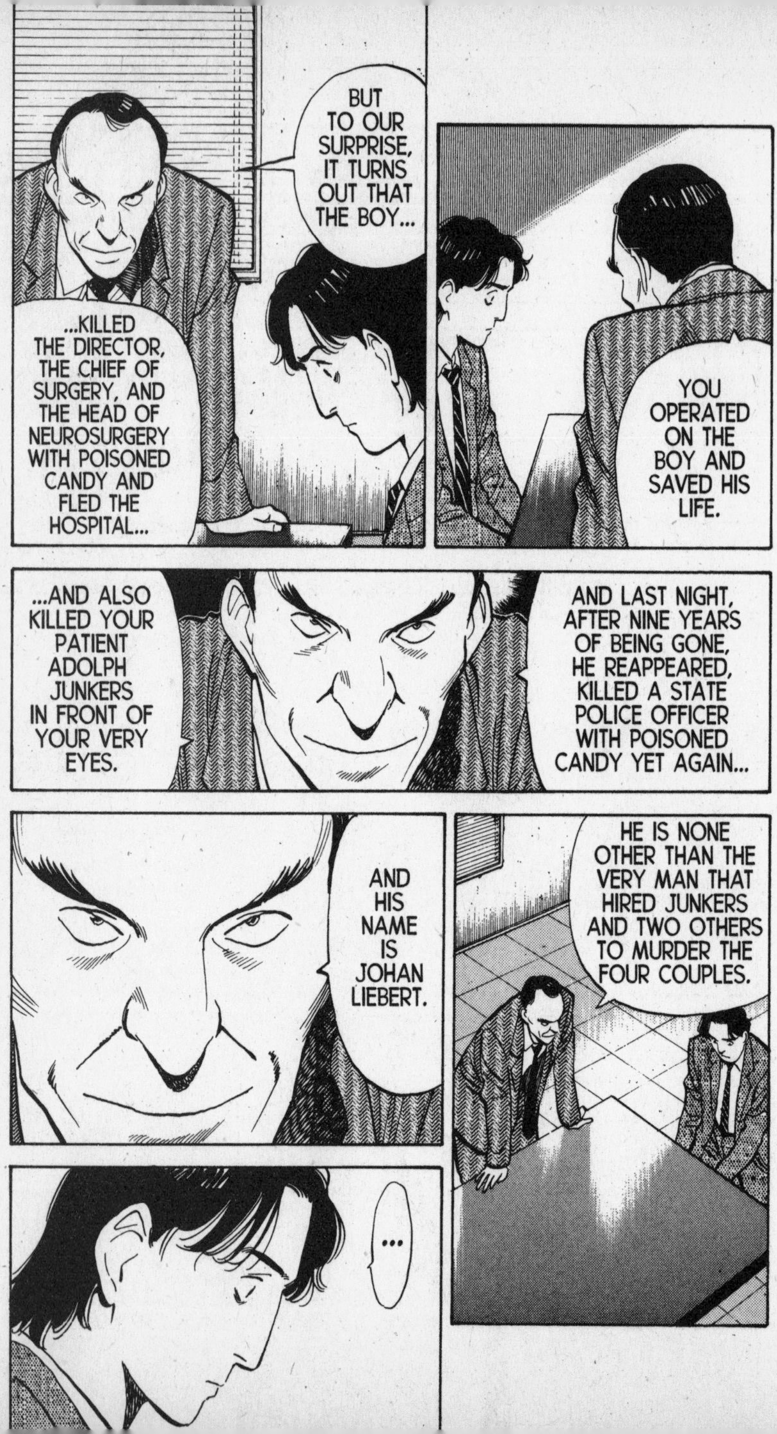
YOU OPERATED ON THE BOY AND SAVED HIS LIFE.
BUT TO OUR SURPRISE, IT TURNS OUT THAT THE BOY...
...KILLED THE DIRECTOR, THE CHIEF OF SURGERY, AND THE HEAD OF NEUROSURGERY WITH POISONED CANDY AND FLED THE HOSPITAL...
AND LAST NIGHT, AFTER NINE YEARS OF BEING GONE, HE REAPPEARED, KILLED A STATE POLICE OFFICER WITH POISONED CANDY YET AGAIN...
...AND ALSO KILLED YOUR PATIENT ADOLPH JUNKERS IN FRONT OF YOUR VERY EYES.
HE IS NONE OTHER THAN THE VERY MAN THAT HIRED JUNKERS AND TWO OTHERS TO MURDER THE FOUR COUPLES.
AND HIS NAME IS JOHAN LIEBERT.
...

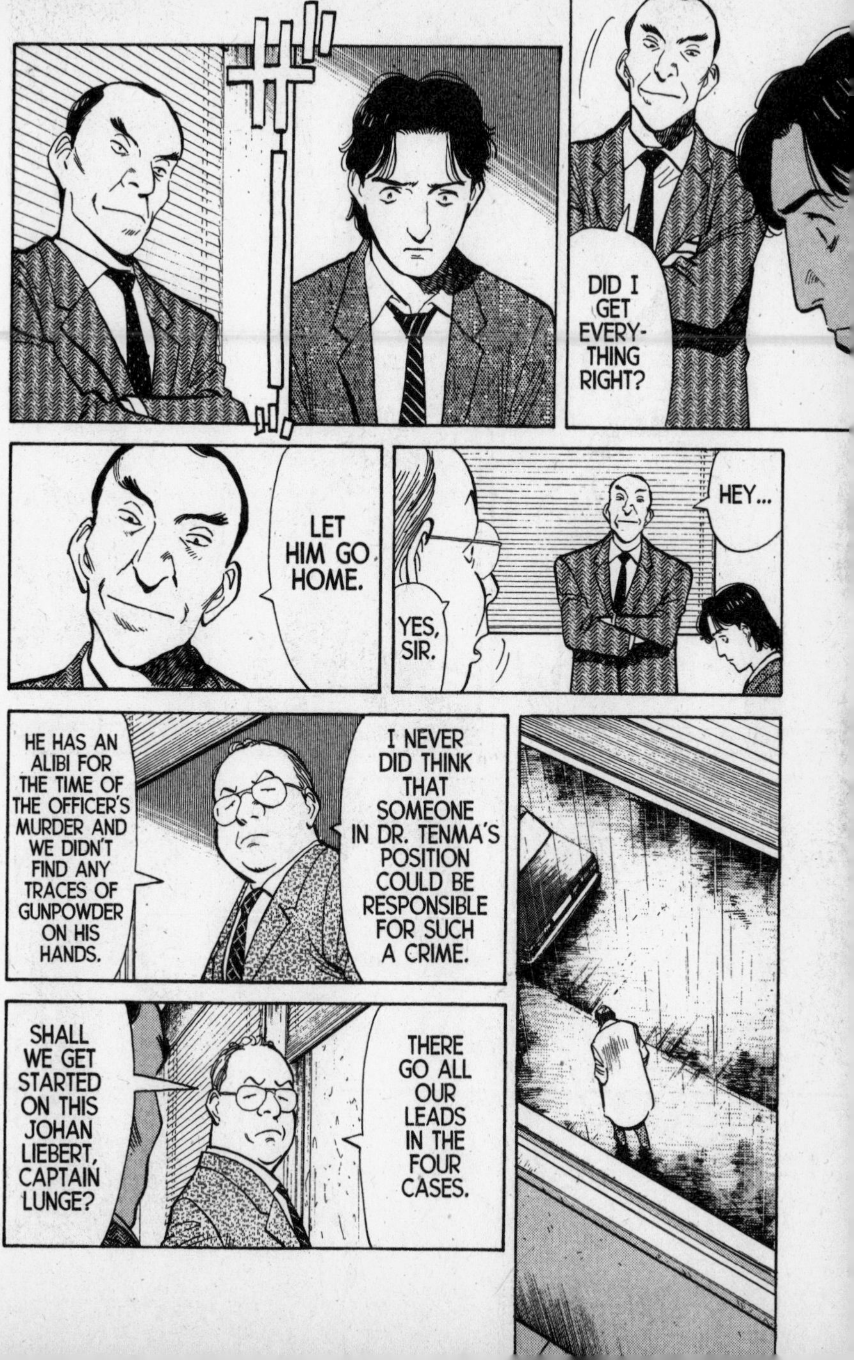
DID I GET EVERY-THING RIGHT?
HEY...
YES, SIR.
LET HIM GO HOME.
I NEVER DID THINK THAT SOMEONE IN DR. TENMA'S POSITION COULD BE RESPONSIBLE FOR SUCH A CRIME.
HE HAS AN ALIBI FOR THE TIME OF THE OFFICER'S MURDER AND WE DIDN'T FIND ANY TRACES OF GUNPOWDER ON HIS HANDS.
THERE GO ALL OUR LEADS IN THE FOUR CASES.
SHALL WE GET STARTED ON THIS JOHAN LIEBERT, CAPTAIN LUNGE?

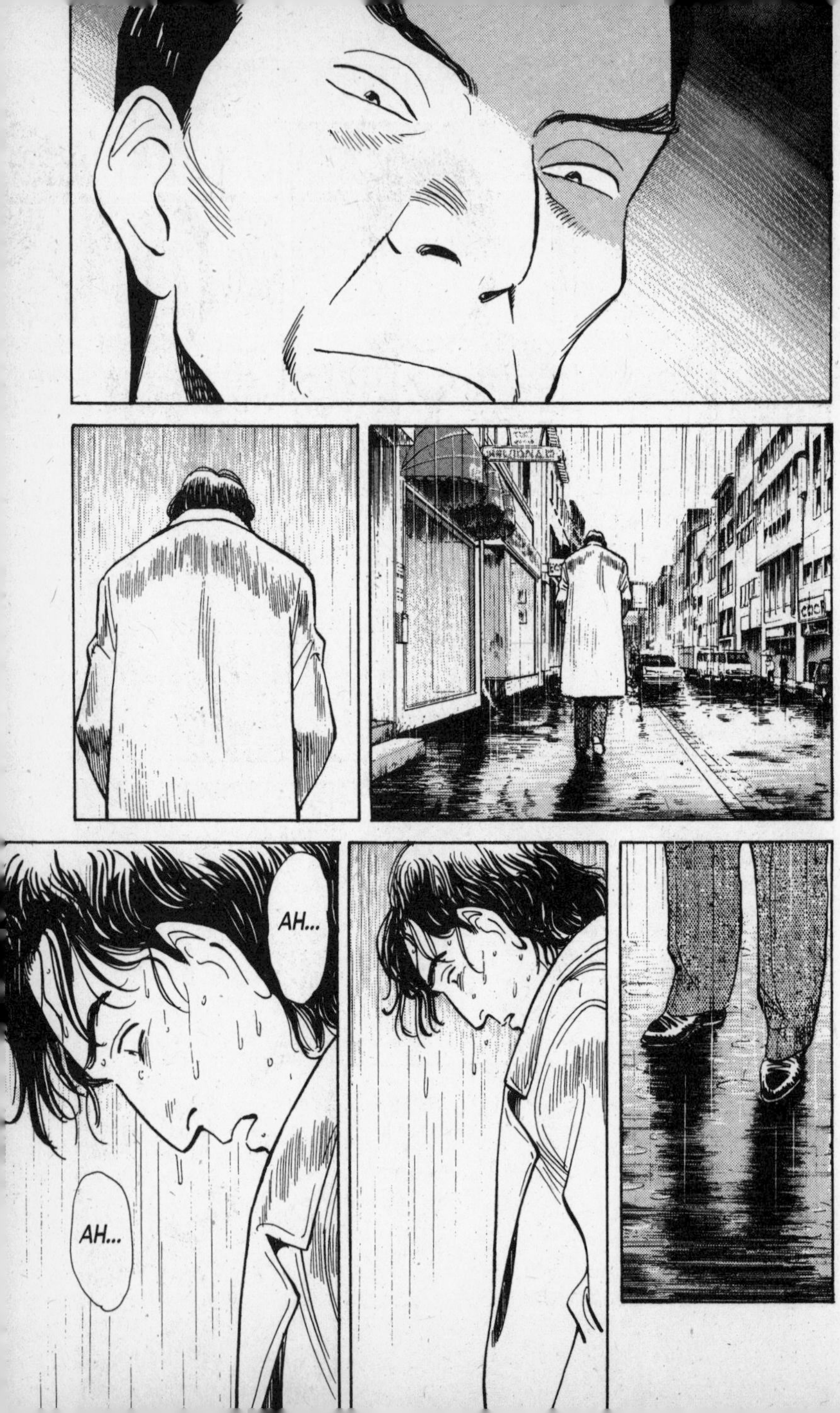
AH...
AH...

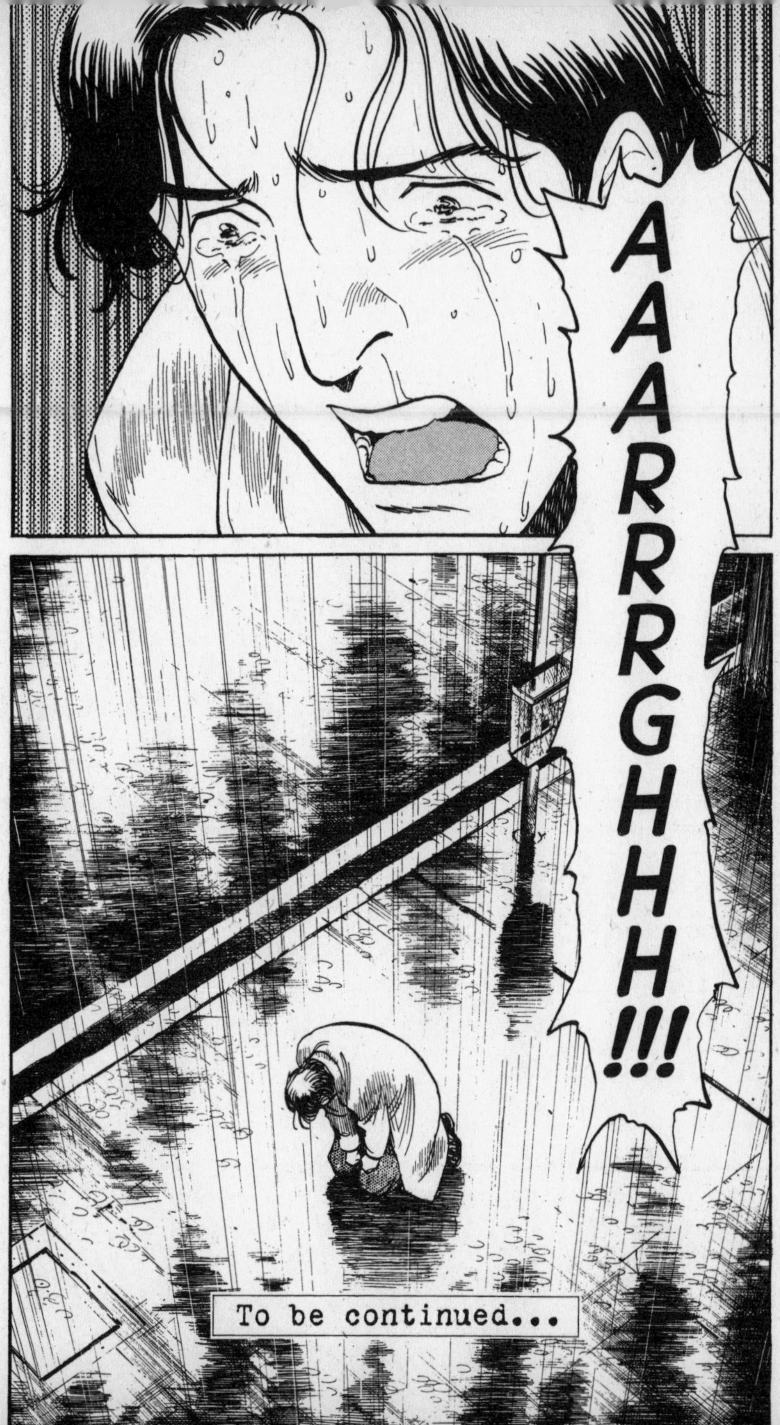
AAARRRGHHH!!!
To be continued...

NAOKI URASAWA'S

MONSTER

108.7—FX: Don gara gan
(crash boom bam)

109.5—FX: Gi (creak)

111.5—FX: Gi (creak)

Chapter 5

113.3—FX: Yoro (wobble)

113.4—FX: Gi (creak)

115.2—FX: Wai wai wai
(crowd noise)

116.1—FX: Dodo (dadum)

116.4—FX: Da (dash)

116.5—FX: Zawa zawa
(crowd noise)

117.2—FX: Ka (step)

118.3—FX: Don (shove)

119.3—FX: Da (running)

119.4—FX: Da da (running)

119.5—FX: Ba (opening door)

123.3—FX: Za (shf)

123.5—FX: Ba (swak)

125.1—FX: Za (shf)

138.2—FX: Ka ka (step step)

138.4—FX: Ka (step)

Chapter 6

139.3—FX: Basha (splash)

145.2—FX: Ta (step)

145.3—FX: Hyuun (fwoosh)

147.8—FX: Da (dash)

149.4—FX: Ka (flash)

149.5—FX: Kyu (stretch)

151.3—FX: Da (dash)

152.1—FX: Ohh (roar)

152.4—FX: Gya gya gya
(screech)

152.6—FX: Don (thud)

153.3—FX: Zawa zawa
(crowd noise)

154.2—FX: Ka ka (step step)

154.3—FX: Ka ka (step step)

155.5—FX: Zaa (vwoosh)

155.6—FX: Bamu
(door shutting)

155.7—FX: Ka (step)

159.7—FX: Batan (slam)

160.3—FX: Ka (flash)

Chapter 7

171.1 —FX: Batan (slam)

177.3 —FX: Kata kata kata
kata (shake shake)

177.7 —FX: Kata kata kata
kata (shake shake)

178.1 —FX: Kata kata kata
(shake shake)

181.1 —FX: Gii (creak)

183.2 —FX: Da (dash)

183.8 —FX: Ba (fwsh)

184.1 —FX: Ba (fwsh)

184.4 —FX: Gashan (crash)

184.5 —FX: Da (dash)

185.2 —FX: Da (dash)

185.6 —FX: Kan kan kan
(step step step)

186.3 —FX: Ta (step)

Chapter 8

205.1 —FX: Zaaa (rainfall)

206.1 —FX: Zaa (rainfall)

206.5 —FX: Don (bang)

207.1 —FX: Don (bang)

207.2 —FX: Don (bang)

208.2 —FX: Zaaa (rainfall)

211.3 —FX: Zaaa (rainfall)

214.2 —FX: Zaaa (rainfall)

glossary

Chapter 1

5.4—FX: Ka ka (step step)

5.7—FX: Ga (grab)

6.3—FX: Ka (glare)

24.3—FX: Don don (thump thump)

24.4—FX: Don don (thump thump)

24.5—FX: Don don (thump thump)

24.6—FX: Don don (thump thump)

25.1—FX: Don (thump)

29.2—FX: Zaa (rainfall)

29.3—FX: Paho paho (siren)

29.4—FX: Kii kii (screech)

30.2—FX: Zawa zawa zawa (crowd noise)

31.3—FX: Da (dash)

31.7—FX: Ba (slam)

33.1—FX: Da (fwash)

34.1—FX: Zaaa (rainfall)

Chapter 2

35.1—FX: Za (rainfall)

36.6—FX: Bamu (car door shutting)

41.7—FX: Paa (flash)

42.2—FX: Kii (screech)

42.2—FX: Goh (roar)

42.5—FX: Gan (bam)

43.2—FX: Ta (step)

43.5—FX: Ka ka (step step)

45.4—FX: Ka (step)

46.7—FX: Batamu (door closing)

48.1—FX: Zaa (water rushing down)

48.7—FX: Gii (creak)

49.3—FX: Ka (flash)

52.3—FX; Ka (step)

52.6—FX: Ka ka (step step)

54.2—FX: Don don (thump thump)

54.4—FX: Don don don (thump thump thump)

58.1—FX: Gi (creak)

58.2—FX: Bamu (slam)

58.3—FX: Ka (flash)

Chapter 3

65.7—FX: Ka (step)

67.1—FX: Ka (step)

73.3—FX: Ka (step)

75.3—FX: Pach pachi pachi (clap clap clap)

75.4—FX: Pachi pachi pachi (clap clap clap)

76.2—FX: Pachi pachi pachi (clap clap clap)

76.3—FX: Pachi pachi pachi (clap clap clap)

76.4—FX: Wai wai wai wai (crowd chatter)

76.5—FX: Ha ha ha (laughter)

78.2—FX: Waaa (cheering)

78.2—FX: Pachi pachi pachi (clap clap clap)

78.3—FX: Pachi pachi pachi (clap clap clap)

79.7—FX: Pachi pachi pachi (clap clap clap)

84.6—FX: Don (thud)

Chapter 4

100.2—FX: Ta (step)

101.1—FX: Da (dash)

103.2—FX: Ga (grab)

105.6—FX: Don (shove)

105.7—FX: Batan (slam)

107.1—FX: Ka (step)

108.2—FX: Gi (step)

about the author

Naoki Urasawa, born in Tokyo in 1960, is Japan's manga master of the suspense thriller. Critically acclaimed and immensely popular, his award-winning works include *20th Century Boys*, *Master Keaton*, *Pineapple Army*, and *Yawara*.

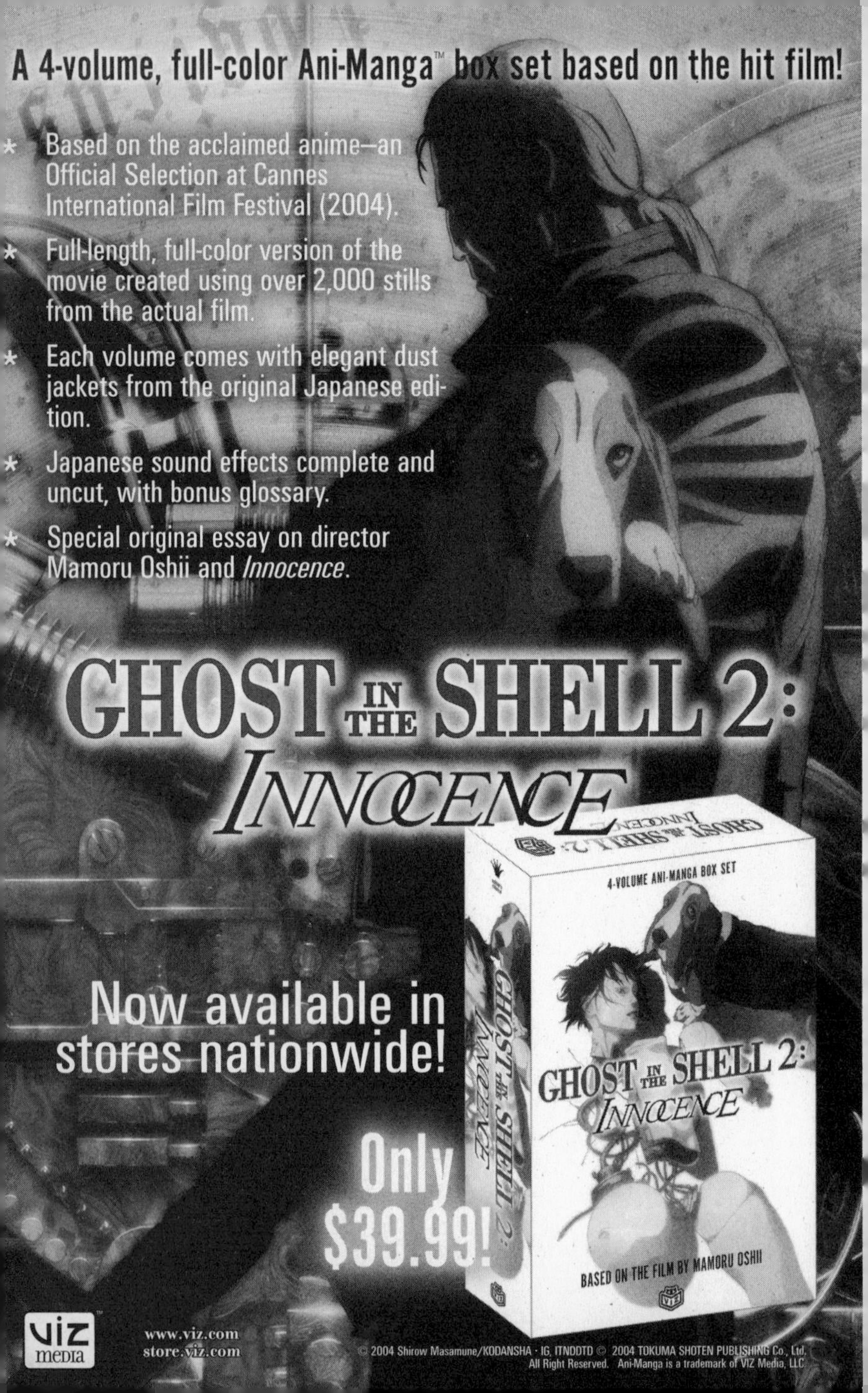

A 4-volume, full-color Ani-Manga™ box set based on the hit film!
★ Based on the acclaimed anime—an Official Selection at Cannes International Film Festival (2004).
★ Full-length, full-color version of the movie created using over 2,000 stills from the actual film.
★ Each volume comes with elegant dust jackets from the original Japanese edition.
★ Japanese sound effects complete and uncut, with bonus glossary.
★ Special original essay on director Mamoru Oshii and *Innocence*.
GHOST IN THE SHELL 2: INNOCENCE
4-VOLUME ANI-MANGA BOX SET
GHOST IN THE SHELL 2: INNOCENCE
BASED ON THE FILM BY MAMORU OSHII
Now available in stores nationwide!
Only $39.99!
VIZ media
www.viz.com
store.viz.com
© 2004 Shirow Masamune/KODANSHA · IG, ITNDDTD © 2004 TOKUMA SHOTEN PUBLISHING Co., Ltd. All Right Reserved. Ani-Manga is a trademark of VIZ Media, LLC

LOVE MANGA? LET US KNOW!

☐ Please do NOT send me information about VIZ Media products, news and events, special offers, or other information.

☐ Please do NOT send me information from VIZ Media's trusted business partners.

Name: _____

Address: _____

City: _____ State: _____ Zip: _____

E-mail: _____

☐ Male ☐ Female   Date of Birth (mm/dd/yyyy): ___ / ___ / ___   (Under 13? Parental consent required)

What race/ethnicity do you consider yourself? (check all that apply)

☐ White/Caucasian   ☐ Black/African American   ☐ Hispanic/Latino

☐ Asian/Pacific Islander   ☐ Native American/Alaskan Native   ☐ Other: _____

What VIZ Media title(s) did you purchase? (indicate title(s) purchased) _____

_____

What other VIZ Media titles do you own? _____

_____

Reason for purchase: (check all that apply)

☐ Special offer   ☐ Favorite title / author / artist / genre

☐ Gift   ☐ Recommendation   ☐ Collection

☐ Read excerpt in VIZ Media manga sampler   ☐ Other _____

Where did you make your purchase? (please check one)

☐ Comic store   ☐ Bookstore   ☐ Grocery Store

☐ Convention   ☐ Newsstand   ☐ Video Game Store

☐ Online (site:_____)   ☐ Other _____

How many manga titles have you purchased in the last year? How many were VIZ Media titles?
(please check one from each column)

MANGA	VIZ Media
☐ None	☐ None
☐ 1 – 4	☐ 1 – 4
☐ 5 – 10	☐ 5 – 10
☐ 11+	☐ 11+

How much influence do special promotions and gifts-with-purchase have on the titles you buy?
(please circle, with 5 being great influence and 1 being none)

1 2 3 4 5

Do you purchase every volume of your favorite series?

☐ Yes! Gotta have 'em as my own ☐ No. Please explain: ________________

What kind of manga storylines do you most enjoy? **(check all that apply)**

☐ Action / Adventure	☐ Science Fiction	☐ Horror
☐ Comedy	☐ Romance (shojo)	☐ Fantasy (shojo)
☐ Fighting	☐ Sports	☐ Historical
☐ Artistic / Alternative	☐ Other ________________	

If you watch the anime or play a video or TCG game from a series, how likely are you to buy the manga? **(please circle, with 5 being very likely and 1 being unlikely)**

1 2 3 4 5

If unlikely, please explain: ________________

Who are your favorite authors / artists? ________________

What titles would like you translated and sold in English? ________________

THANK YOU! Please send the completed form to:

NJW Research
42 Catharine Street
Poughkeepsie, NY 12601

Your privacy is very important to us. All information provided will be used for internal purposes only and will not be sold or otherwise divulged.